Nelson
Comprehension

Teacher's Book 2

for Books 3, 4, 5 & 6

CONTENTS

How Nelson Comprehension Works

YEAR	PUPIL BOOK	RESOURCES & ASSESSMENT	REVISION BOOK	TEACHING SUPPORT
YEAR 1 / P2	Nelson Comprehension Pupil Book 1	Nelson Comprehension Resources and Assessment Book For Books 1 & 2		Nelson Comprehension Teacher's Book 1 For Books 1 & 2
YEAR 2 / P3	Nelson Comprehension Pupil Book 2			
YEAR 3 / P4	Nelson Comprehension Pupil Book 3	Nelson Comprehension Resources and Assessment Book For Books 3 & 4		Nelson Comprehension Teacher's Book 2 For Books 3 & 4
YEAR 4 / P5	Nelson Comprehension Pupil Book 4			
YEAR 5 / P6	Nelson Comprehension Pupil Book 5	Nelson Comprehension Resources and Assessment Book For Books 5 & 6		
YEAR 6 / P7	Nelson Comprehension Pupil Book 6		Nelson Comprehension Revision Book	

Nelson Comprehension is an easy-to-use, rigorous programme for the teaching and practising of comprehension skills for children aged 5 – 11. It covers all types of comprehension — from literal understanding to higher-order skills such as inference, deduction and using prior knowledge or personal experience to help understand a text.

Each **Pupil Book** contains ten units. At key stage 1, each unit comprises two sets of texts and questions; at key stage 2, each unit comprises three sets of texts and questions. The texts and questions in each unit share the same genre and learning focus: for example, fiction extracts that focus on characters' feelings.

Questions are differentiated through their colour-coding, so you can choose which sets of questions you want the children to tackle, depending on which skills they need to practise.

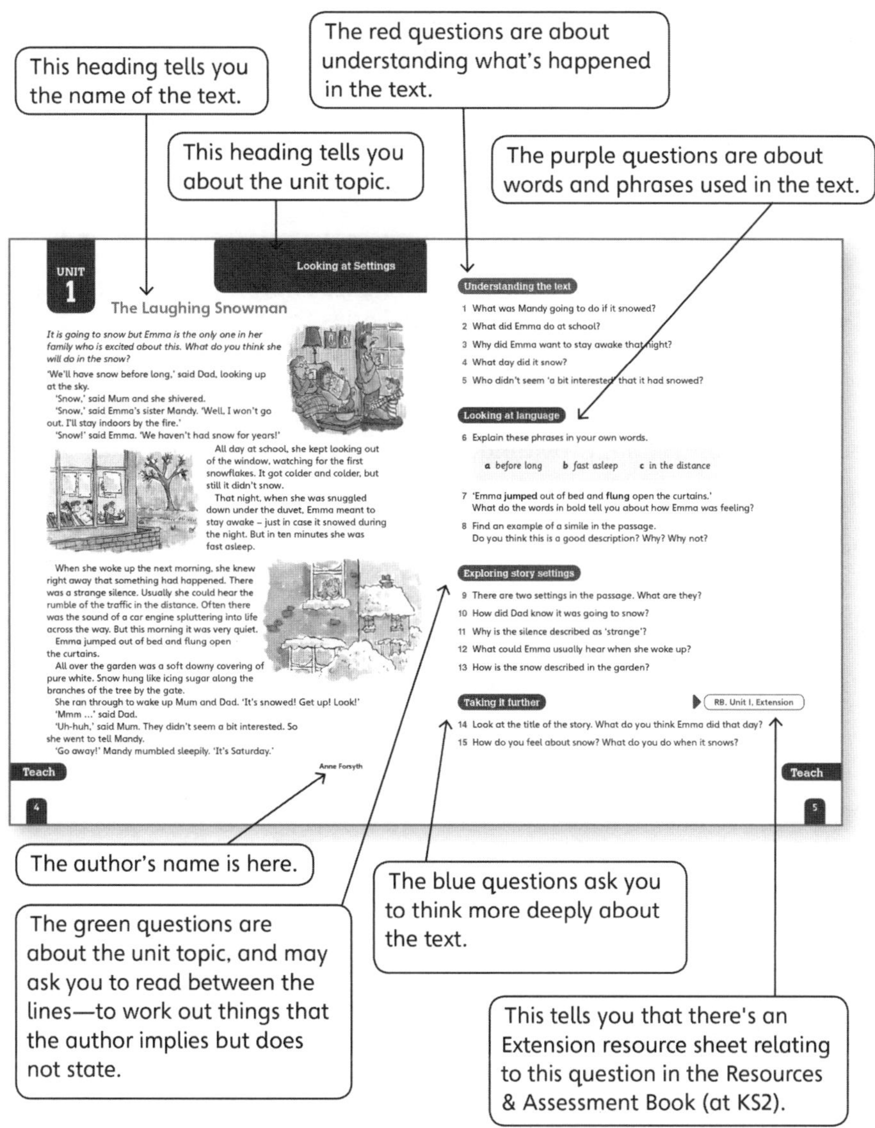

Using a dictionary
Purple vocabulary questions will often ask children to look up the meaning of words in a dictionary. At key stage 2, children may not find these words in a junior dictionary and may need to consult an accessible full dictionary, such as www.oxforddictionaries.com.

There are three **Resources and Assessment Books**: one for Pupil Books 1 & 2, one for Pupil Books 3 & 4 and one for Pupil Books 5 & 6. Two differentiated, photocopiable resource sheets are given for every text in the Pupil Books, offering further practice of comprehension skills.

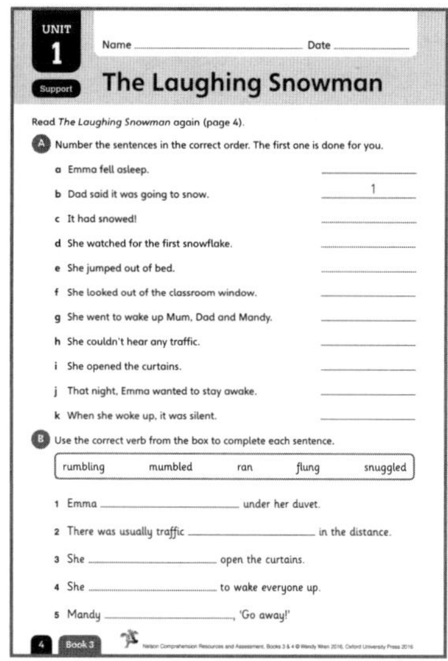

UNIT 1 Name ______ Date ______

Support **The Laughing Snowman**

Read *The Laughing Snowman* again (page 4).

A Number the sentences in the correct order. The first one is done for you.

a Emma fell asleep. ______
b Dad said it was going to snow. 1
c It had snowed! ______
d She watched for the first snowflake. ______
e She jumped out of bed. ______
f She looked out of the classroom window. ______
g She went to wake up Mum, Dad and Mandy. ______
h She couldn't hear any traffic. ______
i She opened the curtains. ______
j That night, Emma wanted to stay awake. ______
k When she woke up, it was silent. ______

B Use the correct verb from the box to complete each sentence.

rumbling mumbled ran flung snuggled

1 Emma ______ under her duvet.
2 There was usually traffic ______ in the distance.
3 She ______ open the curtains.
4 She ______ to wake everyone up.
5 Mandy ______, 'Go away!'

4 Book 3

The **Support** sheet offers more practice of literal comprehension skills.

UNIT 1 Name ______ Date ______

Extension **The Laughing Snowman**

A Think about what Emma did that day and what you do when it snows.

1 What is the title of the story? ______
2 Look at the picture. Write a sentence to say what you think Emma did the day it snowed.
3 When it snows, are you like:
• Mum and Mandy? Do you 'shiver'? Do you stay indoors?
• Emma? Do you watch 'for the first snowflakes'? Do you try staying awake to see the snow? Do you Feel excited when you woke up to snow?

Write about how you feel when it snows.

4 Look at the pictures. Write what the children are doing.
5 What do you do when it snows?

Book 3 5

The **Extension** sheet provides questions and activities for those ready to be challenged further. At key stage 2, some of the final Extension resource sheets in a unit will ask children to think about all three texts in the unit.

The **Teacher's Book** guides you through each unit, providing:

- a quick-reference spread from the Pupil Book.
- suggestions for discussion.
- answers to the
  - Pupil Book questions.
  - Support resource sheets from the Resources and Assessment Books.
  - Example test papers for Years 2 and 4 (P3 and 5) from the Resources and Assessment Books.
  - Example test papers for Year 6 from the Revision Book.
- answers have not been provided for the Extension resource sheets as these require individual responses from the children.

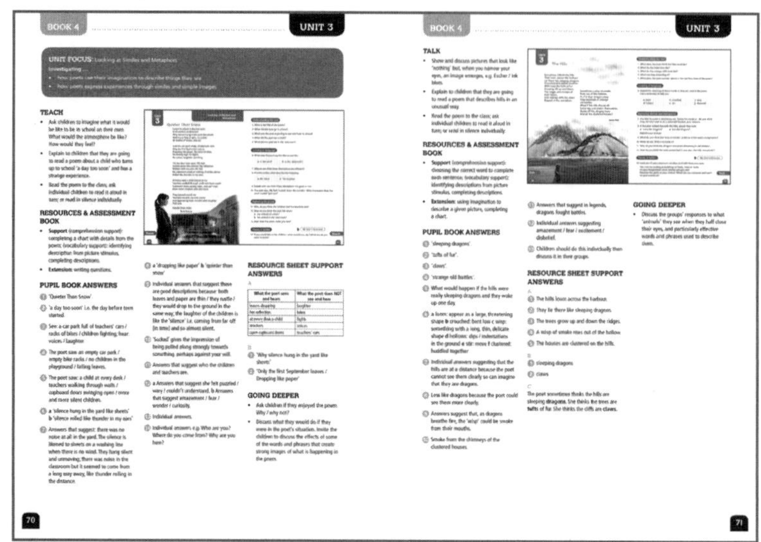

The **Revision Book** contains three end-of-key stage 2 example test papers.

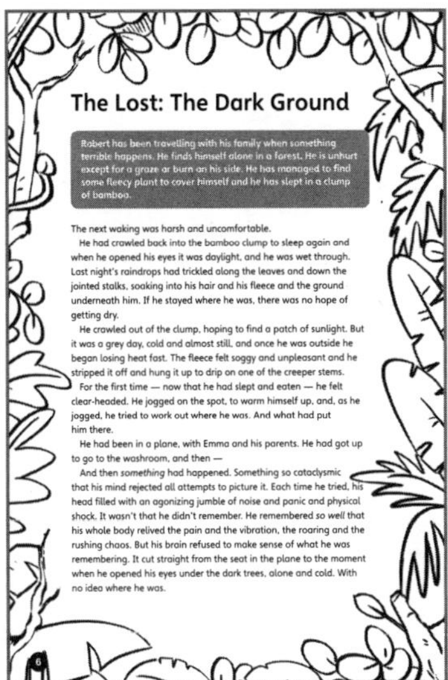

The Lost: The Dark Ground

Robert has been travelling with his family when something terrible happens. He finds himself alone in a forest. He is unhurt except for a graze or burn on his side. He has managed to find some fleecy plant to cover himself and he has slept in a clump of bamboo.

The next waking was harsh and uncomfortable.

He had crawled back into the bamboo clump to sleep again and when he opened his eyes it was daylight, and he was wet through. Last night's raindrops had trickled along the leaves and down the jointed stalks, soaking into his hair and his fleece and the ground underneath him. If he stayed where he was, there was no hope of getting dry.

He crawled out of the clump, hoping to find a patch of sunlight. But it was a grey day, cold and almost still, and once he was outside he began losing heat fast. The fleece felt soggy and unpleasant and he stripped it off and hung it up to drip on one of the creeper stems.

For the first time — now that he had slept and eaten — he felt clear-headed. He jogged on the spot, to warm himself up, and, as he jogged, he tried to work out where he was. And what had put him there.

He had been in a plane, with Emma and his parents. He had got up to go to the washroom, and then —

And then *something* had happened. Something so cataclysmic that his mind rejected all attempts to picture it. Each time he tried, his head filled with an agonizing jumble of noise and panic and physical shock. It wasn't that he didn't remember. He remembered *so well* that his whole body relived the pain and the vibration, the roaring and the rushing chaos. But his brain refused to make sense of what he was remembering. It cut straight from the seat in the plane to the moment when he opened his eyes under the dark trees, alone and cold. With no idea where he was.

6

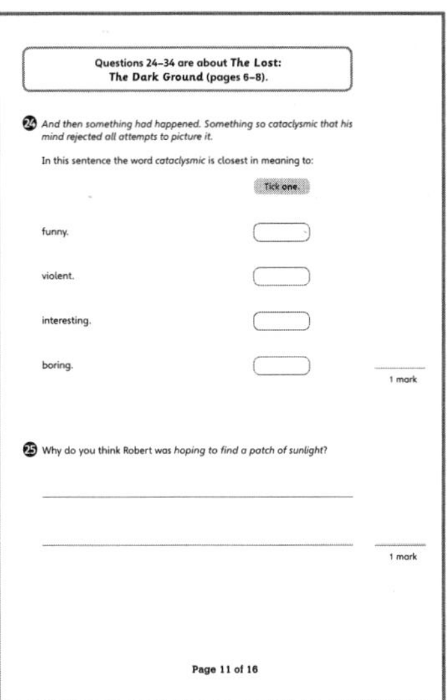

Questions 24–34 are about The Lost: The Dark Ground (pages 6–8).

24 *And then something had happened. Something so cataclysmic that his mind rejected all attempts to picture it.*

In this sentence the word *cataclysmic* is closest in meaning to:

Tick one.

funny. ☐

violent. ☐

interesting. ☐

boring. ☐

1 mark

25 Why do you think Robert was *hoping to find a patch of sunlight*?

____

____

1 mark

Page 11 of 16

Assessment

Resources and Assessment Book for Books 1 & 2 contains two photocopiable end of key stage 1 example reading test papers, so that you can prepare children for their Year 2 reading test.

Paper 1 consists of a combined reading prompt and answer booklet. You will need to spend at least five minutes introducing the paper, reading the practice text, and modelling the practice questions with the whole class. Children will then have 30 minutes (not strictly timed) to read the text and answer the questions in the paper.

Paper 2 consists of a reading booklet containing one fiction and one non-fiction text, and a question booklet. Children have 40 minutes to read the texts and answer the questions in this paper.

More information on how to administer these tests can be found in the *Resources and Assessment Book for Books 1 & 2.*

At key stage 2 *Resources and Assessment Book for Books 3 & 4* contains two example reading test papers for Year 4 children, enabling you to monitor children's progress and help avoid a plateauing in their progression. The two Year 4 papers each consist of a reading booklet, containing one fiction and one non-fiction text, and a question booklet. Children should be given one hour (not strictly timed) to read the texts in the booklet and answer the questions.

The *Revision Book* contains three end of key stage 2 example test papers, enabling you to prepare your Year 6 children for their reading test, and give them confidence as they enter the test. Each test comprises a reading booklet, containing one fiction text, one non-fiction text and one poem; and a question and answer booklet. Children should be given one hour to read the three texts in the reading booklet and complete the questions at their own pace. They should be encouraged to read one text at a time and then answer the questions on that text, before moving on to the next text.

Teaching approaches

Flexible teaching

Nelson Comprehension has been written so that any set of text and questions in the Pupil Books can be used for whole-class teaching, group work, or individual written work.

Teach Talk Write

If you choose, you can follow the *Teach Talk Write* approach for *Nelson Comprehension*, which enables you to work through each unit first as a class or in groups and then individually.

At Key Stage 1

The first text and questions in each unit is **Teach / Talk**: you can read the extract to the children and then answer the questions as a whole class or in groups, discussing the text, modelling key comprehension skills and demonstrating to children how they can find answers to the questions.

The second text and questions in each unit is **Write**: children can try reading the text and answering the questions on their own.

At Key Stage 2

The first text and questions in each unit is **Teach**: you can read the text to the class, and then work through the questions together, modelling comprehension skills and showing children how to find answers to the questions.

The second text and questions in each unit is **Talk**: children can read the text in turn and then attempt the questions in groups.

The third text and questions in each unit is **Write**: children read the text and answer the text individually.

The National Curriculum in England

Nelson Comprehension provides a carefully structured course for teaching comprehension skills to children in Years 1 – 6. The course is designed to build children's competence and confidence in reading comprehension, while providing lively, engaging extracts which they will enjoy. The chart below matches units in the Pupil Books to the National Curriculum in England. The Scope and Sequence charts for each book give a detailed breakdown of the comprehension skills covered in the Resources and Assessment Books as well as the Pupil Books.

Programme of Study	Book 1	Book 2	Book 3	Book 4	Book 5	Book 6
YEAR 1						
Pupils should be taught to:						
develop pleasure in reading, motivation to read, vocabulary and understanding by:						
listening to and discussing a wide range of poems, stories and non-fiction at a level beyond that at which they can read independently	Units 2 3, 4, 5, 6, 7, 8, 9	Units 1, 6	Unit 7	Units 2, 4, 10	Units 3, 5, 10	Units 8, 9, 10
being encouraged to link what they read or hear to their own experiences	Units 1, 5, 7, 9, 10	Units 1, 2, 9, 10	Units 1, 6, 8	Units 3, 4	Unit 4	Units 3, 4, 9
becoming very familiar with key stories, fairy stories and traditional tales, retelling them and considering their particular characteristics	Units 3, 6	Unit 3	Unit 5	Unit 8	Units 1, 9, 10	Units 2, 8
recognising and joining in with predictable phrases	Units 3, 5, 10	Units 5, 10				
learning to appreciate rhymes and poems, and to recite some by heart	Units 5, 10	Units 5, 10	Unit 3	Unit 3	Unit 6	Units 4, 9
discussing word meanings, linking new meanings to those already known	Units 3, 5, 6, 7, 8, 9	Units 1, 3, 4, 6, 7	All units	All units	All units	All units
understand both the books they can already read accurately and fluently and those they listen to by:						
drawing on what they already know or on background information and vocabulary provided by the teacher	Units 1, 2, 4, 5, 6, 8, 9	Units 1, 2, 9, 10	All units	All units	All units	All units
checking that the text makes sense to them as they read, and correcting inaccurate reading	All units	All units	All units	All units	All units	All units
discussing the significance of the title and events	Units 1, 5	Unit 2	Units 1, 2, 9	Units 3, 4, 7	Unit 8	
making inferences on the basis of what is being said and done	Units 1, 2, 3, 4, 5, 6, 7, 10	Units 1, 3, 7, 9, 10	Units 1, 3, 5, 7, 8, 10	Units 1, 2, 3, 5, 7, 8, 9, 10	Units 1, 2, 3, 6, 7, 8, 9, 10	Units 1, 2, 4, 5, 6, 7, 8, 9
predicting what might happen on the basis of what has been read so far	Units 1, 3, 6, 8	Units 1, 3	Units 1, 5, 7, 10	Units 1, 8, 9, 10	Units 1, 7, 9, 10	Units 2, 6
participate in discussion about what is read to them, taking turns and listening to what others say	All units	All units	All units	All units	All units	All units
explain clearly their understanding of what is read to them	All units	All units	All units	All units	All units	All units
YEAR 2						
Pupils should be taught to:						
develop pleasure in reading, motivation to read, vocabulary and understanding by:						
listening to, discussing and expressing views about a wide range of contemporary and classic poetry, stories and non-fiction at a level beyond that at which they can read independently	Units 2, 3, 4, 5, 6, 7, 8, 9	Units 1, 6	Unit 7	Units 2, 4, 10	Units 3, 5, 10	Units 8, 9, 10

The National Curriculum in England (cont.)

Programme of Study	Book 1	Book 2	Book 3	Book 4	Book 5	Book 6
discussing the sequence of events in books and how items of information are related	Units 1, 4, 7, 9	Unit 2				Units 1, 5
becoming increasingly familiar with and retelling a wider range of stories, fairy stories and traditional tales	Units 3, 6, 8	Unit 3	Unit 5	Units 1, 5, 7, 10	Units 1, 9, 10	Units 2, 8
being introduced to non-fiction books that are structured in different ways	Units 2, 4, 9	Units 2, 4, 7, 9	Units 2, 4, 6, 8, 9	Units 2, 4, 6	Units 2, 4, 5, 8	Units 1, 3, 5, 7, 10
recognising simple recurring literary language in stories and poetry	Units 3, 5, 10	Units 5, 10				
discussing and clarifying the meanings of words, linking new meanings to known vocabulary	Units 3, 5, 6, 7, 8, 9	Units 1, 3, 4, 6, 7	All units	All units	All units	All units
discussing their favourite words and phrases		Unit 10				
continuing to build up a repertoire of poems learnt by heart, appreciating these and reciting some, with appropriate intonation to make the meaning clear			Unit 3			Units 4, 9
understand both the books that they can already read accurately and fluently and those that they listen to by:						
drawing on what they already know or on background information and vocabulary provided by the teacher	Units 1, 6, 7, 8, 9	Units 1, 2, 9, 10	All units	All units	All units	All units
checking that the text makes sense to them as they read, and correcting inaccurate reading	All units	All units	All units	All units	All units	All units
making inferences on the basis of what is being said and done	Units 1, 2, 3, 4, 5, 6, 7, 10	Units 1, 3, 7, 9, 10	Units 1, 3, 5, 7, 8, 10	Units 1, 2, 3, 5, 7, 8, 9, 10	Units 1, 2, 3, 6, 7, 8, 9, 10	Units 1, 2, 4, 5, 6, 7, 8, 9
answering and asking questions	All units	All units	All units	All units	All units	All units
predicting what might happen on the basis of what has been read so far	Units 1, 3, 6, 8	Units 1, 3	Units 1, 5, 7, 10	Units 1, 8, 9, 10	Units 1, 7, 9, 10	Units 2, 6
participate in discussion about books, poems and other works that are read to them and those that they can read for themselves, taking turns and listening to what others say	All units	All units	All units	All units	All units	All units
explain and discuss their understanding of books, poems and other material, both those that they listen to and those that they read for themselves	All units	All units	All units	All units	All units	All units
YEAR 3 AND YEAR 4						
Pupils should be taught to:						
develop positive attitudes to reading, and an understanding of what they read, by:						
listening to and discussing a wide range of fiction, poetry, plays, non-fiction and reference books or textbooks	All units	All units	All units	All units	All units	All units
reading books that are structured in different ways and reading for a range of purposes	All units	All units	All units	All units	All units	All units

The National Curriculum in England (cont.)

Programme of Study	Book 1	Book 2	Book 3	Book 4	Book 5	Book 6
using dictionaries to check the meaning of words that they have read		Unit 7	Units 2, 3, 4, 5, 6, 7, 8, 9, 10	All units	All units	All units
increasing their familiarity with a wide range of books, including fairy stories, myths and legends, and retelling some of these orally	Units 3, 6, 8	Unit 3	Units 1, 5	Unit 8	Units 1, 9, 10	Units 2, 6, 8
identifying themes and conventions in a wide range of books	All units	All units	All units	All units	All units	All units
preparing poems and play scripts to read aloud and to perform, showing understanding through intonation, tone, volume and action			Units 3, 7	Unit 9	Units 1, 6, 9	Units 4, 8, 9
discussing words and phrases that capture the reader's interest and imagination		Units 1, 3, 4, 5, 6, 7, 10	Units 1, 5, 7, 10	Units 1, 3, 5, 7, 8, 10	Units 2, 3, 5, 6, 7, 9, 10	Units 2, 4, 8, 9
recognising some different forms of poetry [for example, free verse, narrative poetry]			Unit 3	Unit 3	Unit 6	Units 4, 9
understand what they read, in books they can read independently, by:						
checking that the text makes sense to them, discussing their understanding, and explaining the meaning of words in context	All units	All units	All units	All units	All units	All units
asking questions to improve their understanding of a text			Units 2, 4, 9, 10	Units 1, 2, 4, 6	Units 2, 3, 5, 7	Unit 7
drawing inferences such as inferring characters' feelings, thoughts and motives from their actions, and justifying inferences with evidence	Units 1, 2, 3, 4, 5, 6, 7, 10	Units 1, 3, 7, 9, 10	Units 1, 3, 5, 7, 8, 10	Units 1, 2, 3, 5, 7, 8, 9, 10	Units 1, 2, 3, 6, 7, 8, 9, 10	Units 1, 2, 4, 5, 6, 7, 8, 9
predicting what might happen from details stated and implied	Units 1, 3, 6, 8	Units 1, 3	Units 1, 5, 7, 10	Units 1, 8, 9, 10	Units 1, 7, 9, 10	Units 2, 6
identifying main ideas drawn from more than 1 paragraph and summarising these			Units 5, 8, 9	Unit 2	Units 5, 8	Units 1, 5
identifying how language, structure, and presentation contribute to meaning			All units	All units	All units	All units
retrieve and record information from non-fiction	Units 2, 4, 9	Units 2, 4, 7, 9	Units 2, 4, 6, 8, 9	Units 2, 4, 6	Units 2, 4, 5, 8	Units 1, 3, 5, 7, 10
participate in discussion about both books that are read to them and those they can read for themselves, taking turns and listening to what others say	All units	All units	All units	All units	All units	All units
YEAR 5 AND YEAR 6						
Pupils should be taught to:						
maintain positive attitudes to reading and an understanding of what they read by:						
continuing to read and discuss an increasingly wide range of fiction, poetry, plays, non-fiction and reference books or textbooks	All units	All units	All units	All units	All units	All units
reading books that are structured in different ways and reading for a range of purposes	All units	All units	All units	All units	All units	All units
increasing their familiarity with a wide range of books, including myths, legends and traditional stories, modern fiction, fiction from our literary heritage, and books from other cultures and traditions	Units 3, 6, 8	Units 1, 3, 6	Units 1, 5, 7, 10	Units 1, 5, 8, 10	Units 1, 3, 7, 9, 10	Units 2, 6, 8
recommending books that they have read to their peers, giving reasons for their choices	Unit 6	Units 3, 5, 6, 10	Unit 8			Units 8, 9

The National Curriculum in England (cont.)

Programme of Study	Book 1	Book 2	Book 3	Book 4	Book 5	Book 6
identifying and discussing themes and conventions in and across a wide range of writing	All units	All units	All units	All units	All units	All units
making comparisons within and across books	Units 6, 10	Units 3, 5, 6	Unit 8		Units 1, 8	Units 6, 8, 9
learning a wider range of poetry by heart						Units 4, 9
preparing poems and plays to read aloud and to perform, showing understanding through intonation, tone and volume so that the meaning is clear to an audience			Units 3, 7	Unit 9	Units 1, 6, 9	Units 4, 8, 9
understand what they read by:						
checking that the book makes sense to them, discussing their understanding and exploring the meaning of words in context	All units	All units	All units	All units	All units	All units
asking questions to improve their understanding			Units 2, 4, 9, 10	Units 1, 2, 4, 6	Units 2, 3, 5, 7	Unit 7
drawing inferences such as inferring characters' feelings, thoughts and motives from their actions, and justifying inferences with evidence	Units 1, 2, 3, 4, 5, 6, 7, 10	Units 1, 3, 7, 9, 10	Units 1, 3, 5, 7, 8, 10	Units 1, 2, 3, 5, 7, 8, 9, 10	Units 1, 2, 3, 6, 7, 8, 9, 10	Units 1, 2, 4, 5, 6, 7, 8, 9
predicting what might happen from details stated and implied	Units 1, 3, 6, 8	Units 1, 3	Units 1, 5, 7, 10	Units 1, 8, 9, 10	Units 1, 7, 9, 10	Units 2, 6
summarising the main ideas drawn from more than 1 paragraph, identifying key details that support the main ideas			Units 5, 8, 9	Unit 2	Units 5, 8	Units 1, 5
identifying how language, structure and presentation contribute to meaning			All units	All units	All units	All units
discuss and evaluate how authors use language, including figurative language, considering the impact on the reader			Units 1, 5, 7, 10	Units 1, 3, 5, 7, 8, 10	Units 2, 3, 5, 6, 7, 9, 10	Units 2, 4, 8, 9
distinguish between statements of fact and opinion				Unit 2	Unit 8	Units 7,10
retrieve, record and present information from non-fiction	Units 2, 4, 9	Units 2, 4, 7, 9	Units 2, 4, 6, 8, 9	Units 2, 4, 6	Units 2, 4, 5, 8	Units 1, 3, 5, 7, 10
participate in discussions about books that are read to them and those they can read for themselves, building on their own and others' ideas and challenging views courteously	All units	All units	All units	All units	All units	All units
explain and discuss their understanding of what they have read, including through formal presentations and debates, maintaining a focus on the topic and using notes where necessary					Units 2, 3, 5	Unit 4
provide reasoned justifications for their views	Units 1, 2, 4, 6, 7, 9	Units 3, 5, 6, 7, 9, 10		Units 1, 2, 3, 4, 6, 7, 8, 9, 10	All units	Units 3, 4, 5, 6, 7, 8, 9, 10

Scotland Curriculum for Excellence: literacy experiences and outcomes

	Book 1	Book 2	Book 3	Book 4	Book 5	Book 6
YEAR 1						
I regularly select and read, listen to or watch texts which I enjoy and find interesting, and I can explain why I prefer certain texts and authors. (LIT 1-11a / LIT 2-11a)	Units 2, 3, 4, 5, 6, 7, 8, 9, 10	Units 1, 3, 5, 6, 10	Units 3, 5, 7	Units 2, 3, 4, 8, 10	Units 1, 3, 5, 6, 9, 10	Units 2, 4, 8, 9, 10
I can use my knowledge of sight vocabulary, phonics, context clues, punctuation and grammar to read with understanding and expression. (ENG 1-12a)	All units	All units	All units	All units	All units	All units
I am learning to select and use strategies and resources before I read, and as I read, to help make the meaning of texts clear. (LIT 1-13a)	All units	All units	All units	All units	All units	All units
Using what I know about the features of different types of texts, I can find, select, sort and use information for a specific purpose. (LIT 1-14a)	Units 1, 2, 4, 5, 6, 8, 9	Units 1, 2, 9, 10	All units	All units	All units	All units
I am learning to make notes under given headings and use them to understand information, explore ideas and problems and create new texts. (LIT 1-15a)						
To show my understanding across different areas of learning, I can identify and consider the purpose and main ideas of a text. (LIT 1-16a)		Units 1, 5	Unit 2	Units 1, 2, 9	Units 3, 4, 7	Unit 8
To show my understanding, I can respond to different kinds of questions and other close reading tasks and I am learning to create some questions of my own. (ENG 1-17a)	All units	All units	All units	All units	All units	All units
To help me develop an informed view, I can recognize the difference between fact and opinion. (LIT 1-18a)				Unit 2	Unit 8	Units 7, 10
I can share my thoughts about structure, characters and/or setting, recognize the writer's message and relate it to my own experiences, and comment on the effective choice of words and other features. (ENG 1-19a)	All units	All units	All units	All units	All units	All units
YEAR 2						
I regularly select and read, listen to or watch texts which I enjoy and find interesting, and I can explain why I prefer certain texts and authors. (LIT 1-11a / LIT 2-11a)	Units 2, 3, 4, 5, 6, 7, 8, 9	Units 1, 6	Unit 7	Units 2, 4, 10	Units 3, 5, 10	Units 8, 9, 10
I can use my knowledge of sight vocabulary, phonics, context clues, punctuation and grammar to read with understanding and expression. (ENG 1-12a)	All units	All units	All units	All units	All units	All units
I am learning to select and use strategies and resources before I read, and as I read, to help make the meaning of texts clear. (LIT 1-13a)	Units 1, 3, 5, 6, 7, 8, 9	Units 1, 2, 3, 4, 6, 7, 9, 10	All units	All units	All units	All units
Using what I know about the features of different types of texts, I can find, select, sort and use information for a specific purpose. (LIT 1-14a)	Units 2, 4, 9	Units 2, 4, 7, 9	Units 2, 4, 6, 8, 9	Units 2, 4, 6	Units 2, 4, 5, 8	Units 1, 3, 5, 7, 10
I am learning to make notes under given headings and use them to understand information, explore ideas and problems and create new texts. (LIT 1-15a)						
To show my understanding across different areas of learning, I can identify and consider the purpose and main ideas of a text. (LIT 1-16a)	All units	All units	All units	All units	All units	All units

Scotland Curriculum (cont.)

	Book 1	Book 2	Book 3	Book 4	Book 5	Book 6
To show my understanding, I can respond to different kinds of questions and other close reading tasks and I am learning to create some questions of my own. (ENG 1-17a)	All units	All units	All units	All units	All units	All units
To help me develop an informed view, I can recognize the difference between fact and opinion. (LIT 1-18a)				Unit 2	Unit 8	Units 7, 10
I can share my thoughts about structure, characters and/or setting, recognize the writer's message and relate it to my own experiences, and comment on the effective choice of words and other features. (ENG 1-19a)	All units	All units	All units	All units	All units	All units
YEAR 3						
I regularly select and read, listen to or watch texts which I enjoy and find interesting, and I can explain why I prefer certain texts and authors. (LIT 1-11a / LIT 2-11a)	All units	All units	All units	All units	All units	All units
I can use my knowledge of sight vocabulary, phonics, context clues, punctuation and grammar to read with understanding and expression. (ENG 1-12a)	All units	All units	All units	All units	All units	All units
I am learning to select and use strategies and resources before I read, and as I read, to help make the meaning of texts clear. (LIT 1-13a)		Unit 7	Units 2, 3, 4, 5, 6, 7, 8, 9, 10	All units	All units	All units
Using what I know about the features of different types of texts, I can find, select, sort and use information for a specific purpose. (LIT 1-14a)	All units	All units	All units	All units	All units	All units
I am learning to make notes under given headings and use them to understand information, explore ideas and problems and create new texts. (LIT 1-15a)	Units 2, 4, 9	Units 2, 4, 7, 9	Units 2, 4, 5, 6, 8, 9	Units 2, 4, 6	Units 2, 4, 5, 8	Units 1, 3, 5, 7, 10
To show my understanding across different areas of learning, I can identify and consider the purpose and main ideas of a text. (LIT 1-16a)	All units	All units	All units	All units	All units	All units
To show my understanding, I can respond to different kinds of questions and other close reading tasks and I am learning to create some questions of my own. (ENG 1-17a)	All units	All units	All units	All units	All units	All units
To help me develop an informed view, I can recognize the difference between fact and opinion (LIT 1-18a)				Unit 2	Unit 8	Units 7, 10
I can share my thoughts about structure, characters and/or setting, recognize the writer's message and relate it to my own experiences, and comment on the effective choice of words and other features. (ENG 1-19a)	Units 1, 2, 3, 4, 5, 6, 7, 8, 10	Units 1, 3, 4, 5, 6, 7, 9, 10	All units	All units	All units	All units
YEAR 4						
I regularly select and read, listen to or watch texts which I enjoy and find interesting, and I can explain why I prefer certain texts and authors. (LIT 1-11a / LIT 2-11a)	All units	All units	All units	All units	All units	All units
Through developing my knowledge of context clues, punctuation, grammar and layout, I can read unfamiliar texts with increasing fluency, understanding and expression. (ENG 2-12a / ENG 3-12a / ENG 4-12a)	All units	All units	All units	All units	All units	All units
I can select and use a range of strategies and resources before I read, and as I read, to make meaning clear and give reasons for my selection. (LIT 2-13a)		Unit 7	Units 2, 3, 4, 5, 6, 7, 8, 9, 10	All units	All units	All units

Scotland Curriculum (cont.)

	Book 1	Book 2	Book 3	Book 4	Book 5	Book 6
Using what I know about the features of different types of texts, I can find, select and sort information from a variety of sources and use this for different purposes. (LIT 2-14a)	All units	All units	All units	All units	All units	All units
I can make notes, organize them under suitable headings and use them to understand information, develop my thinking, explore problems and create new texts, using my own words as appropriate. (LIT 2-15a)	Units 2, 4, 9	Units 2, 4, 7, 9	Units 2, 4, 5, 6, 8, 9	Units 2, 4, 6	Units 2, 4, 5, 8	Units 1, 3, 5, 7, 10
To show my understanding across different areas of learning, I can identify and consider the purpose and main ideas of a text and use supporting detail. (LIT 2-16a)	All units	All units	All units	All units	All units	All units
To show my understanding, I can respond to literal, inferential and evaluative questions and other close reading tasks and can create different kinds of questions of my own. (ENG 2-17a)	All units	All units	All units	All units	All units	All units
To help me develop an informed view, I can identify and explain the difference between fact and opinion, recognize when I am being influenced, and have assessed how useful and believable my sources are. (LIT 2-18a)				Unit 2	Unit 8	Units 7, 10
I can: • recognize the relevance of the writer's theme and how this relates to my own and others' experiences • discuss the writer's style and other features appropriate to genre. (ENG 2-19a)	All units	All units	All units	All units	All units	All units
YEAR 5						
I regularly select and read, listen to or watch texts which I enjoy and find interesting, and I can explain why I prefer certain texts and authors. (LIT 1-11a / LIT 2-11a)	All units	All units	All units	All units	All units	All units
Through developing my knowledge of context clues, punctuation, grammar and layout, I can read unfamiliar texts with increasing fluency, understanding and expression. (ENG 2-12a / ENG 3-12a / ENG 4-12a)	All units	All units	All units	All units	All units	All units
I can select and use a range of strategies and resources before I read, and as I read, to make meaning clear and give reasons for my selection. (LIT 2-13a)	All units	All units	All units	All units	All units	All units
Using what I know about the features of different types of texts, I can find, select and sort information from a variety of sources and use this for different purposes. (LIT 2-14a)	All units	All units	All units	All units	All units	All units
I can make notes, organize them under suitable headings and use them to understand information, develop my thinking, explore problems and create new texts, using my own words as appropriate. (LIT 2-15a)	Units 2, 4, 9	Units 2, 4, 7, 9	Units 2, 4, 5, 6, 8, 9	Units 2, 4, 6	Units 2, 3, 4, 5, 8	Units 1, 3, 4, 5, 7, 10
To show my understanding across different areas of learning, I can identify and consider the purpose and main ideas of a text and use supporting detail. (LIT 2-16a)	All units	All units	All units	All units	All units	All units

Scotland Curriculum (cont.)

	Book 1	Book 2	Book 3	Book 4	Book 5	Book 6
To show my understanding, I can respond to literal, inferential and evaluative questions and other close reading tasks and can create different kinds of questions of my own. (ENG 2-17a)	Units 1, 2, 3, 4, 5, 6, 7, 8, 10	Units 1, 3, 7, 9, 10	Units 1, 2, 3, 4, 5, 7, 8, 9, 10	Units 1, 2, 3, 4, 5, 6, 7, 8, 9, 10	Units 1, 2, 3, 5, 6, 7, 8, 9, 10	Units 1, 2, 4, 5, 6, 7, 8, 9
To help me develop an informed view, I can identify and explain the difference between fact and opinion, recognize when I am being influenced, and have assessed how useful and believable my sources are. (LIT 2-18a)	All units	All units	All units	All units	All units	All units
I can: • recognize the relevance of the writer's theme and how this relates to my own and others' experiences • discuss the writer's style and other features appropriate to genre. (ENG 2-19a)	All units	All units	All units	All units	All units	All units
YEAR 6						
I regularly select and read, listen to or watch texts which I enjoy and find interesting, and I can explain why I prefer certain texts and authors. (LIT 1-11a / LIT 2-11a)	All units	All units	All units	All units	All units	All units
Through developing my knowledge of context clues, punctuation, grammar and layout, I can read unfamiliar texts with increasing fluency, understanding and expression. (ENG 2-12a / ENG 3-12a / ENG 4-12a)	All units	All units	All units	All units	All units	All units
I can select and use a range of strategies and resources before I read, and as I read, to make meaning clear and give reasons for my selection. (LIT 2-13a)	All units	All units	All units	All units	All units	All units
Using what I know about the features of different types of texts, I can find, select and sort information from a variety of sources and use this for different purposes. (LIT 2-14a)	All units	All units	All units	All units	All units	All units
I can make notes, organize them under suitable headings and use them to understand information, develop my thinking, explore problems and create new texts, using my own words as appropriate. (LIT 2-15a)	Units 2, 4, 9	Units 2, 4, 7, 9	Units 2, 4, 5, 6, 8, 9	Units 2, 4, 6	Units 2, 3, 4, 5, 8	Units 1, 3, 4, 5, 7, 10
To show my understanding across different areas of learning, I can identify and consider the purpose and main ideas of a text and use supporting detail. (LIT 2-16a)	All units	All units	All units	All units	All units	All units
To show my understanding, I can respond to literal, inferential and evaluative questions and other close reading tasks and can create different kinds of questions of my own. (ENG 2-17a)	Units 1, 2, 3, 4, 5, 6, 7, 8, 10	Units 1, 3, 7, 9, 10	Units 1, 2, 3, 4, 5, 7, 8, 9, 10	All units	Units 1, 2, 3, 5, 6, 7, 8, 9, 10	Units 1, 2, 4, 5, 6, 7, 8, 9
To help me develop an informed view, I can identify and explain the difference between fact and opinion, recognize when I am being influenced, and have assessed how useful and believable my sources are. (LIT 2-18a)	All units	All units	All units	All units	All units	All units
I can: • recognize the relevance of the writer's theme and how this relates to my own and others' experiences • discuss the writer's style and other features appropriate to genre. (ENG 2-19a)	All units	All units	All units	All units	All units	All units

Curriculum for Wales

Programme of Study for English: Reading

	Book 1	Book 2	Book 3	Book 4	Book 5	Book 6
YEAR 1						
Reading: Strategies						
choose reading materials and explain what the text is about and why they like it (Y1_ReadStrat.1)	Units 5, 10	Units 5, 10	Unit 3	Unit 3	Unit 6	Units 4, 9
talk about features of books such as contents page and titles (Y1_ReadStrat.2)	All units	All units	All units	All units	All units	All units
link and identify spoken sounds to blends of letters and letter names (Y1_ReadStrat.3)						
recognize and use an increasing number of phonemes and their corresponding graphemes when blending and segmenting words of up to two syllables (Y1_ReadStrat.4)						
apply the following reading strategies with increasing independence – phonic strategies to decode words (Y1_ReadStrat.5i)						
– recognition of high-frequency words (Y1_ReadStrat.5ii)						
– context clues, e.g. prior knowledge (Y1_ReadStrat.5iii)	Units 1, 2, 4, 5, 6, 8, 9	Units 1, 2, 9, 10	All units	All units	All units	All units
– graphic and syntactic clues (Y1_ReadStrat.5iv)						
– self-correction, including re-reading and reading ahead (Y1_ReadStrat.5v)	All units	All units	All units	All units	All units	All units
track print with eyes, finger pointing only at points of difficulty (Y1_ReadStrat.6)						
decode unknown words containing blended consonants and vowels by using strategies, e.g. segmenting phonemes, onset and rime (Y1_ReadStrat.7)						
read suitable texts with accuracy and fluency (Y1_ReadStrat.8)	All units	All units	All units	All units	All units	All units
read aloud with attention to full stops and question marks (Y1_ReadStrat.9)	All units	All units	All units	All units	All units	All units
read aloud with expression, showing awareness of exclamation and speech marks (Y1_ReadStrat.10)	All units	All units	All units	All units	All units	All units
identify simple text features such as titles and pictures to indicate what the text is about (Y1_ReadStrat.11)	Units 1, 5	Unit 2	Units 1, 2, 9	Units 3, 4, 7	Unit 8	
look for clues in the text to understand information (Y1_ReadStrat.12)	Units 1, 2, 3, 4, 5, 6, 7, 8, 10	Units 1, 3, 7, 9, 10	Units 1, 3, 5, 7, 8, 10	Units 1, 2, 3, 5, 7, 8, 9, 10	Units 1, 2, 3, 6, 7, 8, 9, 10	Units 1, 2, 4, 5, 6, 7, 8, 9
understand the meaning of visual features and link to written text, e.g. illustrations, photographs, diagrams and charts (Y1_ReadStrat.13)	Units 2, 4, 9	Units 2, 4, 7, 9	Units 2, 4, 6, 8, 9	Units 2, 4, 6	Units 2, 4, 5, 8	Units 1, 3, 5, 7, 10
identify words and pictures on-screen which are related to a topic (Y1_ReadStrat.14)						
Reading: Comprehension						
retell events from a narrative in the right order (Y1_ReadComp.1)	Units 3, 6	Unit 3	Unit 5	Unit 8	Units 1, 9, 10	Units 2, 8

Curriculum for Wales (cont.)

	Book 1	Book 2	Book 3	Book 4	Book 5	Book 6
identify information related to the subject of a text (Y1_ReadComp.2)	All units	All units	All units	All units	All units	All units
recall details from information texts (Y1_ReadComp.3)	All units	All units	All units	All units	All units	All units
use personal experience to support understanding of texts (Y1_ReadComp.4)	Units 1, 5, 7, 9, 10	Units 1, 2, 9, 10	Units 1, 6, 8	Units 3, 4	Unit 4	Units 3, 4, 9
use prediction in stories, adding more detail (Y1_ReadComp.5)	Units 1, 3, 6, 8	Units 1,3	Units 1, 5, 7, 10	Units 1, 8, 9, 10	Units 1, 7, 9, 10	Units 2, 6
Reading: Response and Analysis						
express a view about the information in a text (Y1_ReadResp.1)	All units	All units	All units	All units	All units	All units
explore language, information and events in texts (Y1_ReadResp.2)	All units	All units	All units	All units	All units	All units
make links between texts read and other information about the topic (Y1_ReadResp.3)	Units 1, 2, 4, 5, 6, 8, 9	Units 1, 2, 9, 10	All units	All units	All units	All units
YEAR 2						
Reading: Strategies						
choose reading materials independently, giving reasons for their choices (Y2_ReadStrat.1)	Units 2, 3, 4, 5, 6, 7, 8, 9	Units 1, 6	Unit 7	Units 2, 4, 10	Units 3, 5, 10	Units 8, 9, 10
use contents page and glossary within a range of texts (Y2_ReadStrat.2)			Unit 2			
confidently use all phonemes and their corresponding graphemes when blending and segmenting polysyllabic words (Y2_ReadStrat.3)						
apply the following reading strategies with increasing independence to a range of familiar and unfamiliar texts: – phonic strategies (Y2_ReadStrat.4i)						
– recognition of high-frequency words (Y2_ReadStrat.4ii)						
– context clues, e.g. prior knowledge (Y2_ReadStrat.4iii)						
– graphic and syntactic clues (Y2_ReadStrat.4 iv)						
self-correction (Y2_ReadStrat.4v)						
track a page of print with eyes without difficulty (Y2_ReadStrat.5)	All units	All units	All units	All units	All units	All units
decode text with unfamiliar content or vocabulary sustaining comprehension throughout (Y2_ReadStrat.6)	All units	All units	All units	All units	All units	All units
read a range of suitable texts with increasing accuracy and fluency (Y2_ReadStrat.7)	Units 2, 3, 4, 5, 6, 7, 8, 9	Units 1, 6	Unit 7	Units 2, 4, 10	Units 3, 5, 10	Units 8, 9, 10
read aloud with attention to punctuation, including full stops, question, exclamation and speech marks, varying intonation and pace (Y2_ReadStrat.4)	All units	All units	All units	All units	All units	All units
identify and use text features, e.g. Titles, headings and pictures, to locate and understand specific information (Y2_ReadStrat.5)	Units 2, 4, 9	Units 2, 4, 7, 9	Units 2, 4, 6, 8, 9	Units 2, 4, 6	Units 2, 4, 5, 8	Units 1, 3, 5, 7, 10

Curriculum for Wales (cont.)

	Book 1	Book 2	Book 3	Book 4	Book 5	Book 6
look for key words to find out what the text is about (Y2_ReadStrat.6)	All units	All units	All units	All units	All units	All units
use the different features of texts to make meaning, e.g. pictures, charts, and layout (Y2_ReadStrat.7)	Units 2, 4, 9	Units 2, 4, 7, 9	Units 2, 4, 6, 8, 9	Units 2, 4, 6	Units 2, 4, 5, 8	Units 1, 3, 5, 7, 10
identify key words to search for information on-screen, and modify search words as necessary (Y2_ReadStrat.8)						
Reading: Comprehension						
recall and retell narratives and information from texts with some details (Y2_ReadComp.1)	Units 3, 6, 8	Unit 3	Unit 5	Units 1, 5, 7, 10	Units 1, 9, 10	Units 2, 8
identify information from a text accurately and sort into categories or headings (Y2_ReadComp.2)						
explain relevant details from texts (Y2_ReadComp.3)	Units 2, 4, 9	Units 2, 4, 7, 9	Units 2, 4, 6, 8, 9	Units 2, 4, 6	Units 2, 4, 5, 8	Units 1, 3, 5, 7, 10
draw upon relevant personal experience and prior knowledge to support understanding of texts (Y2_ReadComp.4)	Units 1, 3, 5, 6, 7, 8, 9	Units 1, 2, 3, 4, 6, 7, 9, 10	All units	All units	All units	All units
refine and revise predictions in fiction and non-fiction texts (Y2_ReadComp.5)	Units 1, 3, 6, 8	Units 1,3	Units 1, 5, 7, 10	Units 1, 8, 9, 10	Units 1, 7, 9, 10	Units 2, 6
Reading: Response and Analysis						
express views about information and details in a text, considering content, ideas, presentation, organization and the language used (Y2_ReadResp.1)	Units 1, 2, 3, 4, 5, 6, 7, 8, 9, 10	Units 1, 3, 6, 7, 9, 10	Units 1, 3, 5, 7, 8, 10	Units 1, 2, 3, 4, 5, 7, 8, 9, 10	Units 1, 2, 3, 5, 6, 7, 8, 9, 10	Units 1, 2, 4, 5, 6, 7, 8, 9, 10
show understanding and express opinions about language, information and events in texts (Y2_ReadResp.2)	Units 1, 3, 4, 5, 7, 9, 10	Units 2, 5, 10				Units 1, 5
make links between texts read and new information about the topic (Y2_ReadResp.3)	Units 1, 6, 7, 8, 9	Units 1, 2, 9, 10	Units 2, 4, 6, 8, 9	Units 2, 4, 6	Units 2, 4, 5, 8	Units 1, 3, 5, 7, 10
YEAR 3						
Reading: Strategies						
use a range of strategies to make meaning from words and sentences, including knowledge of phonics, word roots, word families, syntax, text organization and prior knowledge of context (Y3_ReadStrat.1)	All units	All units	All units	All units	All units	All units
read short information texts independently with concentration (Y3_ReadStrat.2)	All units	All units	All units	All units	All units	All units
with support, begin to recognize and understand the basic features of continuous and non-continuous texts in terms of language, structure and presentation, e.g. story structure, the layout of a letter (Y3_ReadStrat.3)	Units 2, 4, 9	Units 2, 4, 7, 9	Units 2, 4, 6, 8, 9	Units 2, 4, 6	Units 2, 4, 5, 8	Units 1, 3, 5, 7, 10
read aloud using punctuation to aid (Y3_ReadStrat.4)			Units 3, 7	Unit 9	Units 1, 6, 9	Units 4, 8, 9
skim to gain an overview of a text, e.g. topic, purpose (Y3_ReadStrat.5)			Units 5, 8, 9	Unit 2	Units 5, 8	Units 1, 5
look for specific information in texts using contents, indexes, glossaries, dictionaries (Y3_ReadStrat.6)	Units 2, 4, 9	Units 2, 4, 7, 9	Units 2, 3, 4, 5, 6, 7, 8, 9, 10	All units	All units	All units
identify different purposes of texts, e.g. to inform, instruct, explain (Y3_ReadStrat.7)	All units	All units	All units	All units	All units	All units

Curriculum for Wales (cont.)

	Book 1	Book 2	Book 3	Book 4	Book 5	Book 6
identify how texts are organised, e.g. lists, numbered points, diagrams with arrows, tables and bullet points (Y3_ReadStrat.8)			All units	All units	All units	All units
use visual clues, e.g. illustration, photographs, diagrams and charts, to enhance understanding (Y3_ReadStrat.9)	All units	All units	All units	All units	All units	All units
locate information on web pages using screen features, e.g. toolbars, side bars, headings, arrows (Y3_ReadStrat.10)	Units 2, 4, 9	Units 2, 4, 7, 9	Units 2, 4, 6, 8, 9	Units 2, 4, 6	Units 2, 4, 5, 8	Units 1, 3, 5, 7, 10
Reading: Comprehension						
accurately identify the topic and main ideas of a text, e.g. by highlighting, using key words of the text (Y3_ReadComp.1)	All units	All units	All units	All units	All units	All units
deduce ideas and information by linking explicit statements, e.g. cause and effect (Y3_ReadComp.2)	All units	All units	All units	All units	All units	All units
take an interest in information beyond their personal experience (Y3_ReadComp.3)	All units	All units	All units	All units	All units	All units
begin to make links between continuous and/or non-continuous texts (Y3_ReadComp.4)	Units 2, 4, 6, 9, 10	Units 2, 3, 4, 5, 6, 7, 9	Units 2, 4, 6, 8, 9	Units 2, 4, 6	Units 1, 2, 4, 5, 8	Units 1, 3, 5, 6, 8, 7, 9, 10
Reading: Response and Analysis						
use information from texts in their discussion or writing (Y3_ReadResp.1)	All units	All units	All units	All units	All units	All units
develop their ability to read continuous and non-continuous texts with fluency, accuracy, and enjoyment; respond to them orally and in writing (Y3_ReadResp.2)	All units	All units	All units	All units	All units	All units
with prompting, consider what they read/view, responding orally and in writing to the ideas, language and presentation (Y3_ReadResp.3)	All units	All units	All units	All units	All units	All units
understand that texts change when they are adapted for different media and audiences, e.g. a written text and a film/cartoon version (Y3_ReadResp.4)	All units	All units	All units	All units	All units	All units
make links between what they read and what they already know and believe about the topic (Y3_ReadResp.5)	All units	All units	All units	All units	All units	All units
YEAR 4						
Reading: Strategies						
use a range of strategies to make meaning from words and sentences, including knowledge of phonics, word roots, word families, syntax, text organization and prior knowledge of context (Y4_ReadStrat.1)						
read texts, including those with few visual clues, independently with concentration (Y4_ReadStrat.2)	All units	All units	All units	All units	All units	All units
with support, recognize and understand the features of continuous and non-continuous texts in terms of language, structure and presentation, e.g. traditional tales, a newspaper article (Y4_ReadStrat.3)	All units	All units	All units	All units	All units	All units

Curriculum for Wales (cont.)

	Book 1	Book 2	Book 3	Book 4	Book 5	Book 6
use understanding of sentence structure and punctuation to make meaning (Y4_ReadStrat.4)	All units	All units	All units	All units	All units	All units
skim to gain the gist of a text or the main idea in a chapter (Y4_ReadStrat.5)	Units 2, 4, 9	Units 2, 4, 7, 9	Units 2, 4, 5, 6, 8, 9	Units 2, 4, 6	Units 2, 4, 5, 8	Units 1, 3, 5, 7, 10
scan for specific information using a variety of features in texts, e.g. titles, illustrations, key words (Y4_ReadStrat.6)	Units 2, 4, 9	Units 2, 4, 7, 9	Units 2, 4, 5, 6, 8, 9	Units 2, 4, 6	Units 2, 4, 5, 8	Units 1, 3, 5, 7, 10
identify how texts differ in purpose, structure and layout (Y4_ReadStrat.7)	All units	All units	All units	All units	All units	All units
find information and ideas from web pages, using different search methods, considering which are the most efficient methods (Y4_ReadStrat.8)	Units 2, 4, 9	Units 2, 4, 7, 9	Units 2, 4, 6, 8, 9	Units 2, 4, 6	Units 2, 4, 5, 8	Units 1, 3, 5, 7, 10
Reading: Comprehension						
accurately identify the main points and supporting information in texts (Y4_ReadComp.1)	All units	All units	All units	All units	All units	All units
deduce connections between information, e.g. sequence, importance (Y4_ReadComp.2)	Units 1, 2, 3, 4, 5, 6, 7, 8, 10	Units 1, 3, 7, 9, 10	All units	All units	All units	All units
explore information and ideas beyond their personal experience (Y4_ReadComp.3)	All units	All units	All units	All units	All units	All units
identify similarities and differences between continuous and/or non-continuous texts (Y4_ReadComp.4)	Units 2, 4, 6, 9, 10	Units 2, 3, 4, 5, 6, 7, 9	Units 2, 4, 6, 8, 9	Units 2, 4, 6	Units 1, 2, 4, 5, 8	Units 1, 3, 5, 6, 8, 7, 9, 10
Reading: Response and Analysis						
select and use information and ideas from texts (Y4_ReadResp.1)	All units	All units	All units	All units	All units	All units
develop their ability to read a range of continuous and non-continuous texts with fluency, accuracy and enjoyment; respond to them orally and in writing (Y4_ReadResp.2)	All units	All units	All units	All units	All units	All units
consider what they read/view, responding orally and in writing to the ideas, language, tone and presentation/organization (Y4_ReadResp.3)	All units	All units	All units	All units	All units	All units
identify how texts change when they are adapted for different media and audiences (Y4_ReadResp.4)	All units	All units	All units	All units	All units	All units
understand how something can be represented in different ways, e.g. moving image, multi-modal and print (Y4_ReadResp.5)						
YEAR 5						
Reading: Strategies						
use a range of strategies to make meaning from words and sentences, including knowledge of phonics, word roots, word families, syntax, text organization and prior knowledge of context (Y5 ReadStrat.1)						
read extended texts independently for sustained periods (Y5_ReadStrat.2)	All units	All units	All units	All units	All units	All units

Curriculum for Wales (cont.)

	Book 1	Book 2	Book 3	Book 4	Book 5	Book 6
recognize and understand the characteristics of an increasing range of texts (continuous and non-continuous) in terms of language, structure and presentation, e.g. the language of an autobiography, the language of a speech (Y5_ReadStrat.3)	All units	All units	All units	All units	All units	All units
identify how punctuation relates to sentence structure and how meaning is constructed in complex sentences (Y5_ReadStrat.4)	All units	All units	All units	All units	All units	All units
use a range of strategies for skimming, e.g. finding key words, phrases, gist, main ideas, themes (Y5_ReadStrat.5)	Units 2, 4, 9	Units 2, 4, 7, 9	Units 2, 4, 5, 6, 8, 9	Units 2, 4, 6	Units 2, 4, 5, 8	Units 1, 3, 5, 7, 10
scan to find specific details using graphic and textual organisers, e.g. sub-headings, diagrams (Y5_ReadStrat.6)	Units 2, 4, 9	Units 2, 4, 7, 9	Units 2, 4, 5, 6, 8, 9	Units 2, 4, 6	Units 2, 4, 5, 8	Units 1, 3, 5, 7, 10
identify features of texts, e.g. introduction to topic, sequence, illustrations, degree of formality (Y5_ReadStrat.7)	All units	All units	All units	All units	All units	All units
use information from trusted sources, on-screen and on paper, selecting and downloading as necessary (Y5_ReadStrat.8)						
Reading: Comprehension						
show understanding of main ideas and significant details in texts, e.g. mindmapping showing hierarchy of ideas, flowchart identifying a process (Y5_ReadComp.1)	All units	All units	All units	All units	All units	All units
infer meaning which is not explicitly stated, e.g. what happens next?, why did he/she do that? (Y5_ReadComp.2)	Units 1, 2, 3, 4, 5, 6, 7, 8, 10	Units 1, 3, 7, 9, 10	Units 1, 3, 5, 7, 8, 10	Units 1, 2, 3, 5, 7, 8, 9, 10	Units 1, 2, 3, 5, 6, 7, 8, 9, 10	Units 1, 2, 4, 5, 6, 7, 8, 9
identify and explore ideas and information that interest them (Y5_ReadComp.3)	All units	All units	All units	All units	All units	All units
independently identify similarities and differences between continuous and/or non-continuous texts (Y5_ReadComp.4)	Units 2, 4, 6, 9, 10	Units 2, 3, 4, 5, 6, 7, 9	Units 2, 4, 6, 8, 9	Units 2, 4, 6	Units 1, 2, 4, 5, 8	Units 1, 3, 5, 6, 8, 7, 9, 10
Reading: Response and Analysis						
gather and organise information and ideas from different sources (Y5_ReadResp.1)	Units 1, 2, 4, 6, 7, 9, 10	Units 2,3, 4, 5, 6, 7, 9, 10	Units 2, 4, 5, 6, 8, 9	Units 1, 2, 3, 4, 6, 7, 8, 9, 10	All units	Units 1, 3, 4, 5, 6, 7, 8, 9, 10
identify what the writer thinks about the topic, e.g. admires a historical figure, only interested in facts (Y5_ReadResp.2)				Unit 2	Unit 8	Units 7,10
read an increasing range of continuous and non-continuous texts with fluency, accuracy, understanding and enjoyment; respond to them orally and in writing (Y5_ReadResp.3)	All units	All units	All units	All units	All units	All units
consider what they read/view, responding orally and in writing to the ideas, language, tone and presentation/organization; begin to select evidence to support their view (Y5_ReadResp.4)	All units	All units	All units	All units	All units	All units

Curriculum for Wales (cont.)

	Book 1	Book 2	Book 3	Book 4	Book 5	Book 6
begin to comment on how texts change when they are adapted for different media and audiences (Y5_ReadResp.5)	All units	All units	All units	All units	All units	All units
consider if the content is reliable, e.g. are photographs more reliable than drawings? (Y5_ReadResp.6)				Unit 2	Unit 8	Units 7,10
YEAR 6						
Reading: Strategies						
use a range of strategies to make meaning from words and sentences, including knowledge of phonics, word roots, word families, syntax, text organization and prior knowledge of context (Y6_ReadStrat.1)						
read complex texts independently for sustained periods (Y6_ReadStrat.2)	All units	All units	All units	All units	All units	All units
confidently recognize and understand the characteristics of a range of different texts (continuous and non-continuous) in terms of language, theme, structure and presentation (Y6_ReadStrat.3)	All units	All units	All units	All units	All units	All units
understand how punctuation can vary and so affect sentence structure and meaning, e.g. I had chocolate(,) cake and cheese for tea (Y6_ReadStrat.4)	All units	All units	All units	All units	All units	All units
use a range of strategies for finding information, e.g. skimming for gist, scanning for detail (Y6_ReadStrat.5)	All units	All units	All units	All units	All units	All units
read closely, annotating for specific purposes (Y6_ReadStrat.6)	All units	All units	All units	All units	All units	All units
use internet searches carefully, deciding which sources to read and believe (Y6_ReadStrat.7)				Unit 2	Unit 8	Units 7,10
Reading: Comprehension						
show understanding of main ideas and significant details in different texts on the same topic (Y6_ReadComp.1)	All units	All units	All units	All units	All units	All units
infer ideas which are not explicitly stated, e.g. writers' viewpoints or attitudes (Y6_ReadComp.2)	Units 1, 2, 3, 4, 5, 6, 7, 8, 10	Units 1, 3, 7, 9, 10	Units 1, 3, 5, 7, 8, 10	Units 1, 2, 3, 5, 7, 8, 9, 10	Units 1, 2, 3, 5, 6, 7, 8, 9, 10	Units 1, 2, 4, 5, 6, 7, 8, 9
identify ideas and information that interest them to develop further understanding (Y6_ReadComp.3)	All units	All units	All units	All units	All units	All units
identify and begin to comment on similarities and differences between continuous and/or non-continuous texts in terms of language, techniques, structure, character and form (Y6_ReadComp.4)	Units 2, 4, 6, 9, 10	Units 2, 3, 4, 5, 6, 7, 9	Units 2, 4, 6, 8, 9	Units 2, 4, 6	Units 1, 2, 4, 5, 8	Units 1, 3, 5, 6, 8, 7, 9, 10
Reading: Response and Analysis						
collate and make connections, e.g. prioritizing, categorizing, between information and ideas from different sources (Y6_ReadResp.1)	All units	All units	All units	All units	All units	All units
distinguish between facts, theories and opinions (Y6_ReadResp.2)				Unit 2	Unit 8	Units 7,10
compare the viewpoint of different writers on the same topic, e.g. rats are fascinating or a menace (Y6_ReadResp.3)	Units 6, 10	Units 3, 5, 6	Unit 8		Units 1, 8	Units 6, 8, 9

Curriculum for Wales (cont.)

	Book 1	Book 2	Book 3	Book 4	Book 5	Book 6
confidently read a range of continuous and non-continuous texts with fluency, accuracy, understanding and enjoyment; respond to them orally and in writing (Y6_ReadResp.4)	All units	All units	All units	All units	All units	All units
consider what they read/view, responding orally and in writing to the ideas, language, tone, style and presentation/organization; select evidence to support their views (Y6_ReadResp.5)	All units	All units	All units	All units	All units	All units
comment on how texts change when they are adapted for different media and audiences (Y6_ReadResp.6)	All units	All units	All units	All units	All units	All units
consider whether a text is effective in conveying information and ideas (Y6_ReadResp.7)	Units 1, 2, 4, 6, 7, 9	Units 3, 5, 6, 7, 9, 10	Units 1, 5, 7, 10	All units	All units	Units 2, 3, 4, 5, 6, 7, 8, 9, 10

Northern Ireland

Levels of Progression in Communication across the curriculum

	Book 1	Book 2	Book 3	Book 4	Book 5	Book 6
YEAR 1						
Level 1						
show understanding of the meaning carried by print, pictures and images (L1_com_read.1)	All units	All units	All units	All units	All units	All units
understand that words are made up of sounds and syllables and that sounds are represented by letters (L1_com_read.2i)						
use reading strategies (L1_com_read.2ii)	All units	All units	All units	All units	All units	All units
read and understand familiar words, signs and symbols in the environment (L1_com_read.3i)	All units	Units 1, 2, 3, 4, 5, 6, 7, 9, 10	All units	All units	All units	All units
use visual clues to locate information (L1_com_read.3ii)	Units 1, 2, 3, 4, 5, 6, 7, 10	Units 1, 3, 7, 9, 10	All units	All units	All units	All units
use language associated with texts (L1_com_read.4)						
talk about what they read and answer questions (L1_com_read.5)	All units	All units	All units	All units	All units	All units
Level 2						
understand, recount and sequence events and information (L2_com_read.1)	Units 1, 4, 7, 9	Unit 2				Units 1, 5
use a range of reading strategies (L2_com_read.2)	All units	All units	All units	All units	All units	All units
select information for a purpose (L2_com_read.3i)	Units 2, 4, 9	Units 2, 4, 7, 9	Units 2, 4, 6, 8, 9	Units 2, 4, 6	Units 2, 4, 5, 8	Units 1, 3, 5, 7, 10
use basic alphabetical knowledge and visual clues to locate information (L2_com_read.3ii)	Units 1, 2, 3, 4, 5, 6, 7, 10	Units 1, 3, 7, 9, 10	All units	All units	All units	All units
recognize some forms and features of texts (L2_com_read.4)	Units 2, 4, 9	Units 2, 4, 7, 9	Units 2, 4, 6, 8, 9	Units 2, 4, 6	Units 2, 4, 5, 8	Units 1, 3, 5, 7, 10
ask questions to seek clarification that develops understanding (L2_com_read.5i)	All units	All units	All units	All units	All units	All units
express opinions and make predictions (L2_com_read.5ii)	Units 1, 3, 6, 8	Units 1, 3	Units 1, 5, 7, 10	Units 1, 8, 9, 10	Units 1, 7, 9, 10	Units 2, 6
YEAR 2						
Level 2						
understand, recount and sequence events and information (L2_com_read.1)	Units 1, 4, 7, 9	Unit 2				Units 1, 5
use a range of reading strategies (L2_com_read.2)	All units	All units	All units	All units	All units	All units
follow discussions, make contributions and observe conventions of conversation (L2_com_talk.2i)	All units	All units	All units	All units	All units	All units
select information for a purpose (L2_com_read.3i)	Units 2, 4, 9	Units 2, 4, 7, 9	Units 2, 4, 6, 8, 9	Units 2, 4, 6	Units 2, 4, 5, 8	Units 1, 3, 5, 7, 10
use basic alphabetical knowledge and visual clues to locate information (L2_com.read.3ii)	Units 1, 2, 3, 4, 5, 6, 7, 10	Units 1, 3, 7, 9, 10	All units	All units	All units	All units
recognise some forms and features of texts (L2_com_read.4)	Units 2, 3, 4, 5, 9, 10	Units 2, 4, 5, 7, 9, 10	Units 2, 4, 6, 8, 9	Units 2, 4, 6	Units 2, 4, 5, 8	Units 1, 3, 5, 7, 10
ask questions to seek clarification that develops understanding (L2_com_read.5i)	All units	All units	All units	All units	All units	All units
express opinions and make predictions (L2_com_read.5ii)	Units 1, 3, 6, 8	Units 1, 3	Units 1, 5, 7, 10	Units 1, 8, 9, 10	Units 1, 7, 9, 10	Units 2, 6

Northern Ireland (cont.)

	Book 1	Book 2	Book 3	Book 4	Book 5	Book 6
YEAR 3						
understand, recount and sequence events and information (L2_com_read.1)	Units 1, 4, 7, 9	Unit 2				Units 1, 5
use a range of reading strategies (L2_com_read.2)	All units	All units	All units	All units	All units	All units
select information for a purpose (L2_com_read.3i)	Units 2, 4, 9	Units 2, 4, 7, 9	Units 2, 4, 6, 8, 9	Units 2, 4, 6	Units 2, 4, 5, 8	Units 1, 3, 5, 7, 10
use basic alphabetical knowledge and visual clues to locate information (L2_com_read.3ii)	Units 1, 2, 3, 4, 5, 6, 7, 10	Units 1, 3, 7, 9, 10	All units	All units	All units	All units
recognize some forms and features of texts (L2_com_read.4)	All units	All units	All units	All units	All units	All units
ask questions to seek clarification that develops understanding (L2_com_read.5i)	All units	All units	All units	All units	All units	All units
express opinions and make predictions (L2_com_read.5ii)	Units 1, 3, 6, 8	Units 1, 3	Units 1, 5, 7, 10	Units 1, 8, 9, 10	Units 1, 7, 9, 10	Units 2, 6
YEAR 4						
recognize, understand and sequence main points (L3_com_read.1i)	Units 1, 4, 7, 9	Unit 2				Units 1, 5
paraphrase with general accuracy (L3_com_read.1ii)	Units 1, 2, 3, 4, 5, 6, 7, 10	Units 1, 3, 7, 9, 10	Units 1, 3, 5, 7, 8, 9, 10	Units 1, 2, 3, 5, 7, 8, 9, 10	Units 1, 2, 3, 5, 6, 7, 8, 9, 10	Units 1, 2, 4, 5, 6, 7, 8, 9
choose and use reading strategies independently (L3_com_read.2)	All units	All units	All units	All units	All units	All units
use organizational features, including alphabetical order, to locate and obtain information (L3_com_read.3)	Units 1, 2, 3, 4, 5, 6, 7, 10	Units 1, 3, 7, 9, 10	All units	All units	All units	All units
understand that there are different forms and features of texts (L3_com_read.4i)	All units	All units	All units	All units	All units	All units
make deductions using information from the text (L3_com_read.4ii)	Units 1, 2, 3, 4, 5, 6, 7, 10	Units 1, 3, 7, 9, 10	Units 1, 3, 5, 7, 8, 10	Units 1, 2, 3, 5, 7, 8, 9, 10	Units 1, 2, 3, 6, 7, 8, 9, 10	Units 1, 2, 4, 5, 6, 7, 8, 9
ask and respond to questions to extend understanding (L3_com_read.5i)	All units	All units	All units	All units	All units	All units
express opinions and give reasons (L3_com_read.5ii)	Units 1, 2, 4, 6, 7, 9	Units 3, 5, 6, 7, 9, 10		Units 1, 2, 3, 4, 6, 7, 8, 9, 10	All units	Units 3, 4, 5, 6, 7, 8, 8, 9, 10
YEAR 5						
show understanding by identifying and recognize information (L4_com_read.1i)	All units	All units	All units	All units	All units	All units
paraphrase (L4_com_read.1ii)	All units	All units	All units	All units	All units	All units
read independently (L4_com_read.2)	All units	All units	All units	All units	All units	All units
locate relevant information and use it appropriately (L4_com_read.3)	All units	All units	All units	All units	All units	All units
recognize main features and understand how these are linked to form purpose (L4_com_read.4i)	Units 2, 4, 9	Units 2, 4, 7, 9	Units 2, 4, 6, 8, 9	Units 2, 4, 6	Units 2, 4, 5, 8	Units 1, 3, 5, 7, 10
understand explicit meanings and recognize some implicit meanings (L4_com_read.4ii)	Units 1, 2, 3, 4, 5, 6, 7, 10	Units 1, 3, 7, 9, 10	Units 1, 3, 5, 7, 8, 10	Units 1, 2, 3, 5, 7, 8, 9, 10	Units 1, 2, 3, 6, 7, 8, 9, 10	Units 1, 2, 4, 5, 6, 7, 8, 9
explain opinions about what they read (L4_com_read.5)	Units 1, 2, 4, 6, 7, 9	Units 3, 5, 6, 7, 9, 10		Units 1, 2, 3, 4, 6, 7, 8, 9, 10	All units	Units 3, 4, 5, 6, 7, 8, 8, 9, 10

Northern Ireland (cont.)

	Book 1	Book 2	Book 3	Book 4	Book 5	Book 6
YEAR 6						
show understanding by identifying and summarizing information, ideas and details (L5_com_read.1)	All units	All units	All units	All units	All units	All units
select and manage information from a range of sources (L5_com_read.2)	All units	All units	All units	All units	All units	All units
describe language, structure and presentation (L5_com_read.3i)	All units	All units	All units	All units	All units	All units
understand some implicit meanings and attitudes (L5_com_read.3ii)	Units 1, 2, 3, 4, 5, 6, 7, 8, 10	Units 1, 3, 7, 9, 10	Units 1, 3, 5, 7, 8, 10	Units 1, 2, 3, 5, 7, 8, 9, 10	Units 1, 2, 3, 6, 7, 8, 9, 10	Units 1, 2, 4, 5, 6, 7, 8, 9
differentiate between fact and opinion (L5_com_read.3iii)				Unit 2	Unit 8	Units 7, 10
make reference to text to support opinions and draw conclusions (L5_com_read.4)	All units	All units	All units	All units	All units	All units

The Cambridge International Primary Curriculum

		Book 1	Book 2	Book 3	Book 4	Book 5	Book 6
STAGE 1							
Demonstrate understanding of explicit meaning in texts							
1Rx1	Read labels, lists and captions to find information.	Units 2, 4, 9	Units 2, 4, 7, 9	Units 2, 4, 6, 8, 9	Units 2, 4, 6	Units 2, 4, 5, 8	Units 1, 3, 5, 7, 10
Demonstrate understanding of implicit meaning in texts							
1Ri1	Anticipate what happens next in a story.	Units 1, 3, 6, 8	Units 1, 3	Units 1, 5, 7, 10	Units 1, 8, 9, 10	Units 1, 7, 9, 10	Units 2, 6
1Ri2	Talk about events in a story and make simple inferences about characters and events to show understanding.	Units 1, 2, 3, 4, 5, 6, 7, 10	Units 1, 3, 7, 9, 10	Units 1, 3, 5, 7, 8, 10	Units 1, 2, 3, 5, 7, 8, 9, 10	Units 1, 2, 3, 6, 7, 8, 9, 10	Units 1, 2, 4, 5, 6, 7, 8, 9
Explain, comment on and analyse the way writers use stylistic and other features of language and structure in texts							
1Rw1	Talk about significant aspects of a story's language, e.g. repetitive refrain, rhyme, patterned language.	Units 3, 5, 10	Units 5, 10				
1Rw2	Recognise story elements, e.g. beginning, middle and end.	Units 1, 4, 7, 9	Unit 2				Units 1, 5
Recognise conventions and evaluate viewpoint, purpose, themes and ideas in texts							
1Rv1	Show awareness that texts for different purposes look different, e.g. use of photographs, diagrams.	Units 2, 4, 9	Units 2, 4, 7, 9	Units 2, 4, 6, 8, 9	Units 2, 4, 6	Units 2, 4, 5, 8	Units 1, 3, 5, 7, 10
1Rv2	Know the parts of a book, e.g. title page, contents.	Units 1, 5	Unit 2	Units 1, 2, 9	Units 3, 4, 7	Unit 8	
STAGE 2							
Demonstrate understanding of explicit meaning in texts							
2Rx1	Read and respond to question words, e.g. *what, where, when, who, why.*	All units	All units	All units	All units	All units	All units
2Rx2	Read and follow simple instructions, e.g. in a recipe.	Unit 4	Unit 2	Unit 6		Unit 4	
2Rx3	Find answers to questions by reading a section of text.	All units	All units	All units	All units	All units	All units
2Rx4	Find factual information from different formats, e.g. charts, labelled diagrams.	Units 2, 4, 9	Units 2, 4, 7, 9	Units 2, 4, 6, 8, 9	Units 2, 4, 6	Units 2, 4, 5, 8	Units 1, 3, 5, 7, 10
Demonstrate understanding of implicit meaning in texts							
2Ri1	Predict story endings.	Units 1, 3, 6, 8	Units 1, 3	Units 1, 5, 7, 10	Units 1, 8, 9, 10	Units 1, 7, 9, 10	Units 2, 6
2Ri2	Identify and describe story settings and characters, recognising that they may be from different times and places.	Units 3, 6, 8	Units 1, 3, 6	Units 1, 5, 7, 10	Units 1, 5, 8, 10	Units 1, 3, 7, 9, 10	Units 2, 6, 8
2Ri3	Make simple inferences from the words on the page, e.g. about feelings.	Units 1, 2, 3, 4, 5, 6, 7, 10	Units 1, 3, 7, 9, 10	Units 1, 3, 5, 7, 8, 10	Units 1, 2, 3, 5, 7, 8, 9, 10	Units 1, 2, 3, 6, 7, 8, 9, 10	Units 1, 2, 4, 5, 6, 7, 8, 9
Explain, comment on and analyse the way writers use stylistic and other features of language and structure in texts							
2Rw1	Comment on some vocabulary choices, e.g. adjectives.	Units 3, 5, 6, 7, 8, 9	Units 1, 3, 4, 6, 7	All units	All units	All units	All units
2Rw2	Talk about what happens at the beginning, in the middle or at the end of a story.	Units 1, 4, 7, 9	Unit 2				Units 1, 5

The Cambridge International Primary Curriculum (cont.)

		Book 1	Book 2	Book 3	Book 4	Book 5	Book 6
2Rw3	Read poems and comment on words and sounds, rhyme and rhythm.	Units 5, 10	Units 5, 10	Unit 3	Unit 3	Unit 6	Units 4, 9
Recognise conventions and evaluate viewpoint, purpose, themes and ideas in texts							
2Rv1	Show some awareness that texts have different purposes.	All units	All units	All units	All units	All units	All units
2Rv2	Identify general features of known text types.	All units	All units	All units	All units	All units	All units
STAGE 3							
Demonstrate understanding of explicit meaning in texts							
3Rx1	Answer questions with some reference to single points in a text.	All units	All units	All units	All units	All units	All units
3Rx2	Scan a passage to find specific information and answer questions.	All units	All units	All units	All units	All units	All units
3Rx3	Identify the main points or gist of a text.			Units 5, 8, 9	Unit 2	Units 5, 8	Units 1, 5
Demonstrate understanding of implicit meaning in texts							
3Ri1	Begin to infer meanings beyond the literal, e.g. about motives and character.	Units 1, 2, 3, 4, 5, 6, 7, 10	Units 1, 3, 7, 9, 10	Units 1, 3, 5, 7, 8, 10	Units 1, 2, 3, 5, 7, 8, 9, 10	Units 1, 2, 3, 6, 7, 8, 9, 10	Units 1, 2, 4, 5, 6, 7, 8, 9
3Ri2	Infer the meaning of unknown words from the context.	All units	All units	All units	All units	All units	All units
Explain, comment on and analyse the way writers use stylistic and other features of language and structure in texts							
3Rw1	Consider how choice of words can heighten meaning.		Units 1, 3, 4, 5, 6, 7, 10	Units 1, 5, 7, 10	Units 1, 3, 5, 7, 8, 10	Units 2, 3, 5, 6, 7, 9, 10	Units 2, 4, 8, 9
3Rw2	Consider words that make an impact, e.g. adjectives and powerful verbs.		Units 1, 3, 4, 5, 6, 7, 10	Units 1, 5, 7, 10	Units 1, 3, 5, 7, 8, 10	Units 2, 3, 5, 6, 7, 9, 10	Units 2, 4, 8, 9
3Rw3	Consider ways that information is set out on a page and on a screen, e.g. lists, charts, bullet points.	Units 2, 4, 9	Units 2, 4, 7, 9	Units 2, 4, 6, 8, 9	Units 2, 4, 6	Units 2, 4, 5, 8	Units 1, 3, 5, 7, 10
Recognise conventions and evaluate viewpoint, purpose, themes and ideas in texts							
3Rv1	Identify the main purpose of a text.			Unit 4	Unit 6	Units 3, 8	Units 3,5
3Rv2	Understand and use the terms 'fact', 'fiction' and 'non-fiction'.			Units 2, 8			
3Rv3	Identify different types of stories and typical story themes.	Units 3, 6, 8	Units 1, 3, 6	Units 1, 5, 7, 10	Units 1, 5, 8, 10	Units 1, 3, 7, 9, 10	Units 2, 6, 8
STAGE 4							
Demonstrate understanding of explicit meaning in texts							
4Rx1	Retell or paraphrase events from the text in response to questions.	All units	All units	All units	All units	All units	All units
4Rx2	Note key words and phrases to identify the main points in a passage.			Units 5, 8, 9	Unit 2	Units 5, 8	Units 1, 5
4Rx3	Distinguish between fact and opinion in print and IT sources.				Unit 2	Unit 8	Units 7,10
4Rx4	Explore explicit meanings within a text.	All units	All units	All units	All units	All units	All units

The Cambridge International Primary Curriculum (cont.)

		Book 1	Book 2	Book 3	Book 4	Book 5	Book 6
Demonstrate understanding of implicit meaning in texts							
4Ri1	Investigate how settings and characters are built up from details and identify key words and phrases.	Units 3, 6, 8	Units 1, 3, 6	Units 1, 5, 7, 10	Units 1, 5, 8, 10	Units 1, 3, 7, 9, 10	Units 2, 6, 8
4Ri2	Explore implicit meanings within a text.	Units 1, 2, 3, 4, 5, 6, 7, 10	Units 1, 3, 7, 9, 10	Units 1, 3, 5, 7, 8, 10	Units 1, 2, 3, 5, 7, 8, 9, 10	Units 1, 2, 3, 6, 7, 8, 9, 10	Units 1, 2, 4, 5, 6, 7, 8, 9
Explain, comment on and analyse the way writers use stylistic and other features of language and structure in texts							
4Rw1	Recognise meaning in figurative language.			Units 1, 5, 7, 10	Units 1, 3, 5, 7, 8, 10	Units 2, 3, 5, 6, 7, 9, 10	Units 2, 4, 8, 9
4Rw2	Understand the impact of imagery and figurative language in poetry, including alliteration and simile, e.g. *as … as a …* .	Units 5, 10	Units 5, 10	Unit 3	Unit 3	Unit 6	Units 4, 9
4Rw3	Understand how expressive and descriptive language creates mood.			Units 1, 5, 7, 10	Units 1, 3, 5, 7, 8, 10	Units 2, 3, 5, 6, 7, 9, 10	Units 2, 4, 8, 9
4Rw4	Identify adverbs and their impact on meaning.			Unit 5	Unit 8		
4Rw5	Understand the use of connectives to structure an argument, e.g. *if, although*.						
4Rw6	Understand how points are ordered to make a coherent argument.						
4Rw7	Understand the main stages in a story from introduction to resolution.	Units 1, 4, 7, 9	Unit 2				Units 1, 5
4Rw8	Explore narrative order and the focus on significant events.	Units 3, 6, 8	Units 1, 3, 6	Units 1, 5, 7, 10	Units 1, 5, 8, 10	Units 1, 3, 7, 9, 10	Units 2, 6, 8
4Rw9	Understand how paragraphs and chapters are used to organise ideas.						
4Rw10	Compare and contrast poems and investigate poetic features.	Units 5, 10	Units 5, 10	Unit 3	Unit 3	Unit 6	Units 4, 9
4Rw11	Investigate the grammar of different sentences: statements, questions and orders.						
Recognise conventions and evaluate viewpoint, purpose, themes and ideas in texts							
4Rv1	Identify different types of non-fiction text and their known key features.	Units 2, 4, 9	Units 2, 4, 7, 9	Units 2, 4, 6, 8, 9	Units 2, 4, 6	Units 2, 4, 5, 8	Units 1, 3, 5, 7, 10
4Rv2	Read newspaper reports and consider how they engage the reader.				Unit 2	Units 5, 8	Unit 7
4Rv3	Understand how persuasive writing is used to convince a reader.				Unit 7	Units 2, 8	Unit 3
STAGE 5							
Demonstrate understanding of explicit meaning in texts							
5Rx1	Look for information in non-fiction texts to build on what is already known.	Units 2, 4, 9	Units 2, 4, 7, 9	Units 2, 4, 6, 8, 9	Units 2, 4, 6	Units 2, 4, 5, 8	Units 1, 3, 5, 7, 10
5Rx2	Extract key points and group and link ideas.			Units 5, 8, 9	Unit 2	Units 5, 8	Units 1, 5

The Cambridge International Primary Curriculum (cont.)

		Book 1	Book 2	Book 3	Book 4	Book 5	Book 6
5Rx3	Locate information confidently and efficiently from different sources.						
Demonstrate understanding of implicit meaning in texts							
5Ri1	Provide accurate textual reference from more than one point in a story to support answers to questions.			Units 1, 5, 7, 10	Units 1, 5, 8, 10	Units 1, 3, 7, 9, 10	Units 2, 6, 8
5Ri2	Identify the point of view from which a story is told.				Unit 1	Unit 3	Units 2, 7, 10
Explain, comment on and analyse the way writers use stylistic and other features of language and structure in texts							
5Rw1	Comment on a writer's use of language and explain reasons for the writer's choices.			All units	All units	All units	All units
5Rw2	Begin to interpret imagery and techniques, e.g. metaphor, personification, simile, adding to understanding beyond the literal.			Units 1, 5, 7, 10	Units 1, 3, 5, 7, 8, 10	Units 2, 3, 5, 6, 7, 9, 10	Units 2, 4, 8, 9
5Rw3	Discuss metaphorical expressions and figures of speech.			Units 1, 5, 7, 10	Units 1, 3, 5, 7, 8, 10	Units 2, 3, 5, 6, 7, 9, 10	Units 2, 4, 8, 9
5Rw4	Investigate clauses within sentences and how they are connected.						
5Rw5	Compare the structure of different stories.						
5Rw6	Understand the difference between direct and reported speech.						
5Rw7	Learn how dialogue is set out and punctuated.						
5Rw8	Identify unfamiliar words, explore definitions and use new words in context.		Unit 7	Units 2, 3, 4, 5, 6, 7, 8, 9, 10	All units	All units	All units
5Rw9	Understand the use of impersonal style in explanatory texts.			Unit 6	Unit 6	Unit 4	Units 5, 7
5Rw10	Understand conventions of standard English, e.g. agreement of verbs.						
Recognise conventions and evaluate viewpoint, purpose, themes and ideas in texts							
5Rv1	Read and evaluate non-fiction texts for purpose, style, clarity and organisation.	Units 2, 4, 9	Units 2, 4, 7, 9	Units 2, 4, 6, 8, 9	Units 2, 4, 6	Units 2, 4, 5, 8	Units 1, 3, 5, 7, 10
5Rv2	Explore the features of texts which are about events and experiences, e.g. diaries.					Unit 5	Units 7, 10
5Rv3	Compare writing that informs and persuades.			Unit 9	Units 2, 4, 6, 7	Units 2, 5, 8	Units 3, 5, 7
5Rv4	Note the use of persuasive devices, words and phrases in print and other media.			Unit 9	Unit 7	Units 2, 8	Units 3, 7
5Rv5	Read and identify characteristics of myths, legends and fables.	Units 3, 6, 8	Unit 3	Units 1, 5	Unit 8	Units 1, 9, 10	Units 2, 6, 8
5Rv6	Read widely and explore the features of different fiction genres.	Units 3, 6, 8	Units 1, 3, 6	Units 1, 5, 7, 10	Units 1, 5, 8, 10	Units 1, 3, 7, 9, 10	Units 2, 6, 8
5Rv7	Consider how a writer expresses their own point of view, e.g. how characters are presented.	3, 6, 8	1, 3, 6	1, 5, 7, 9, 10	1, 5, 7, 8, 10	1, 2, 3, 7, 8, 9, 10	2, 3, 6, 7, 8

The Cambridge International Primary Curriculum (cont.)

		Book 1	Book 2	Book 3	Book 4	Book 5	Book 6
STAGE 6							
Demonstrate understanding of explicit meaning in texts							
6Rx1	Distinguish between fact and opinion in a range of texts and other media.				Unit 2	Unit 8	Units 7,10
6Rx2	Paraphrase explicit meanings based on information from more than one point in the text.			Units 5, 8, 9	Unit 2	Units 5, 8	Units 1, 5
Demonstrate understanding of implicit meaning in texts							
6Ri1	Consider how the author manipulates the reaction of the reader, e.g. how characters and settings are presented.			Units 1, 5, 7, 10	Units 1, 3, 5, 7, 8, 10	Units 2, 3, 5, 6, 7, 9, 10	Units 2, 4, 8, 9
6Ri2	Look for implicit meanings, and make plausible inferences from more than one point in the text.	Units 1, 2, 3, 4, 5, 6, 7, 10	Units 1, 3, 7, 9, 10	Units 1, 3, 5, 7, 8, 10	Units 1, 2, 3, 5, 7, 8, 9, 10	Units 1, 2, 3, 6, 7, 8, 9, 10	Units 1, 2, 4, 5, 6, 7, 8, 9
Explain, comment on and analyse the way writers use stylistic and other features of language and structure in texts							
6Rw1	Comment on a writer's use of language, demonstrating awareness of its impact on the reader.			Units 1, 5, 7, Unit 10	Units 1, 3, 5, Units 7, 8, 10	Units 2, 3, 5, Units 6, 7, 9, 10	Units 2, 4, 8, Unit 9
6Rw2	Explore proverbs, sayings and figurative expressions.			Units 1, 5, 7, 8	Units 1, 3	Units 1, 3, 6, 7, 9, 10	Units 4, 6, 8, 9
6Rw3	Analyse the success of writing in evoking particular moods, e.g. suspense.				Unit 8		Unit 8
6Rw4	Begin to show awareness of the impact of a writer's choices of sentence length and structure.						
6Rw5	Understand the use of conditionals, e.g. to express possibility.						
6Rw6	Discuss and express preferences in terms of language, style and themes.			Unit 8			Units 8, 9
6Rw7	Understand aspects of narrative structure, e.g. the handling of time.						
6Rw8	Analyse how paragraphs and chapters are structured and linked.						
6Rw9	Read and interpret poems in which meanings are implied or multilayered.				Unit 3	Unit 6	Units 4, 9
6Rw10	Explore how poets manipulate and play with words and their sounds.			Units 1, 5, 7, 10	Units 1, 3, 5, 7, 8, 10	Units 2, 3, 5, 6, 7, 9, 10	Units 2, 4, 8, 9
6Rw11	Explore use of active and passive verbs within a sentence.						
6Rw12	Understand changes over time in words and expressions and their use.						
6Rw13	Identify uses of the colon, semi-colon, parenthetic commas, dashes and brackets.						

Book 3 Scope and Sequence

Unit	Unit Focus	Texts	Oxford Level	Oxford Reading Criterion Scale	Genre / text type	Resources & Assessment Book Support	Resources & Assessment Book Extension
1	Looking at Settings	*The Laughing Snowman,* Anne Forsyth	11	standard 4, criteria 1, 4, 5, 6, 9, 10, 12, 14, 16, 17, 21, 22, 23	fiction: stories and settings	putting narrative events in the right order; cloze activity	interpreting pictures; personal responses to snow
		The Hodgeheg, Dick King-Smith	11			matching beginnings and endings of sentences; identifying images	predicting the outcome of the story; thinking about settings
		The Ugly Duckling, retold by Wendy Wren	11			identifying sentences as true or false; matching opposites	thinking about characters' feelings
2	Using the Contents Page and Index	Looking for Information	10	standard 4, criteria 1, 3, 5, 10, 12, 14, 17, 20	non-fiction	choosing the correct sentence endings; classifying words	completing sentences; making an index
		What's Out in Space?	9			matching questions and answers; writing chapter titles	planning and writing questions
		Sport for All!	10			multiple choice; identifying images	labelling and ordering words in an index
3	Understanding Shape Poems	'Cats Can', Coral Rumble	10	standard 4, criteria 1, 2, 9, 10, 12, 14, 17, 18, 19	poetry	identifying similes; sorting muddled words; matching rhyming words	using appropriate verbs in poems
		'Rhythm Machine', Trevor Harvey	11			matching verbs with nouns; matching rhyming words.	thinking about onomatopoeic words
		'Stereo Headphones', James Carter	10			cloze activity; drawing the shape of a poem; identifying onomatopoeic words	describing sounds
4	Retrieving Information	Walls and Towers	11	standard 4, criteria 1, 3, 5, 10, 12, 14, 17, 20	non-fiction	identifying walls and towers from sets of facts; finding proper nouns and adjectives	planning questions
		The World's Great Canals	11			grouping facts under correct headings; matching words and definitions	planning and writing questions
		Let's Find Out About Bridges	10			completing sentences; identifying verbs and nouns	writing questions and finding information
5	Features of Myths and Legends	*Perseus is Given the Quest*	10	standard 4, criteria 1, 3, 4, 6, 9, 10, 12, 14, 16, 17, 18, 19, 21, 22, 23	fiction: myths and legends	identifying who said what; using adjectives in cloze activity	predicting an outcome
		The Quest Begins	10			putting narrative events in the right order; identifying groups of words	predicting; writing notes
		Perseus Meets Medusa, all retold by Wendy Wren	10			identifying sentences as true or false; identifying adverbs	completing a story chart

6	Following Instructions	How to Play Charades	10	standard 4, criteria 1, 3, 10, 12, 14, 17, 20	non-fiction: instructions	answering questions about what instructions tell you to do; identifying and using imperative verbs	following instructions to play a game
		How to Make Chocolate Fudge Sauce	10			choosing the correct sentence endings; matching words and meanings; identifying adjectives	writing instructions
		How to Find Your Way!	11			identifying true and false statements; identifying vocabulary from images	writing directions
7	Speech in Narrative and Plays	*The Lion and the Mouse*, retold by Wendy Wren	11	standard 4, criteria 1, 2, 5, 6, 10, 12, 14, 16, 17, 22, 23	fiction: narratives and playscripts	multiple choice; cloze activity	preparing and performing a playscript
		What is a Friend? retold by Wendy Wren	10			cloze activity; identifying stage directions and dialogue	preparing and performing a playscript
		The Village Dinosaur, Phyllis Arkle	12			correcting words in sentences; choosing correct definitions	writing stage directions
8	Exploring Language in Letters	Writing About Books	10	standard 4, criteria 1, 3, 9, 10, 12, 14, 17, 20	non-fiction: letters	matching paragraphs to the correct summary; finding adjectives; interpreting text speech	exploring different methods of communicating through writing
		Have You Heard?	10			who wrote that?; adding missing words	making a plan to write an email
		What Do You Like to Read?	10			multiple choice; solving anagrams	writing notes about your favourite books; writing a letter
9	Looking at Reports and Notes	Planet in Danger!	11	standard 4, criteria 1, 3, 8, 10, 12, 14, 15, 17, 20	non-fiction: reports	completing a chart; choosing the correct definitions	interpreting images; drawing images for captions
		Save the Rainforests	11			completing a chart; choosing the correct definitions	thinking about different perspectives; asking and answering questions
		Recycle With Michael	10			categorising words; cloze activity	writing lists; categorising results
10	Understanding Characters' Feelings	'Wanted: a Real Dragon'	10	standard 4, criteria 1, 5, 9, 10, 12, 14, 17, 21, 23	fiction: fantasy	identifying sentences as true or false; writing sentences; matching words with definitions; matching adjectives to nouns	thinking about and predicting what happens next
		'Meeting the Dragon'	11			putting narrative events in the right order; matching words to their definitions	thinking and writing about a character's feelings
		'Flying With a Dragon', all from *Dragon Ride*, Helen Cresswell	10			identifying incorrect words in sentences; identifying adjectives; underlining correct definitions	imagining you are in the story and writing about what you would do

UNIT FOCUS: Looking at Settings

Investigating ...

- where stories take place
- how stories can have more than one setting as the narrative moves along
- how settings are described

TEACH

- Ask the children what they think 'setting' means in connection with stories.
- Talk about the children's favourite stories and their settings.
- Ask if they have read stories set in e.g. a wood, a castle, a cave, and talk about stories with similar settings.
- Discuss the children's attitude to snow. Do they like it when it snows? What do they do in the snow?
- Explain that they are going to read the beginning of a story called *The Laughing Snowman*. What does the title tell them about what may happen in the story?
- Read the extract to the class; ask individual children to read it aloud in turn; or read in silence individually.

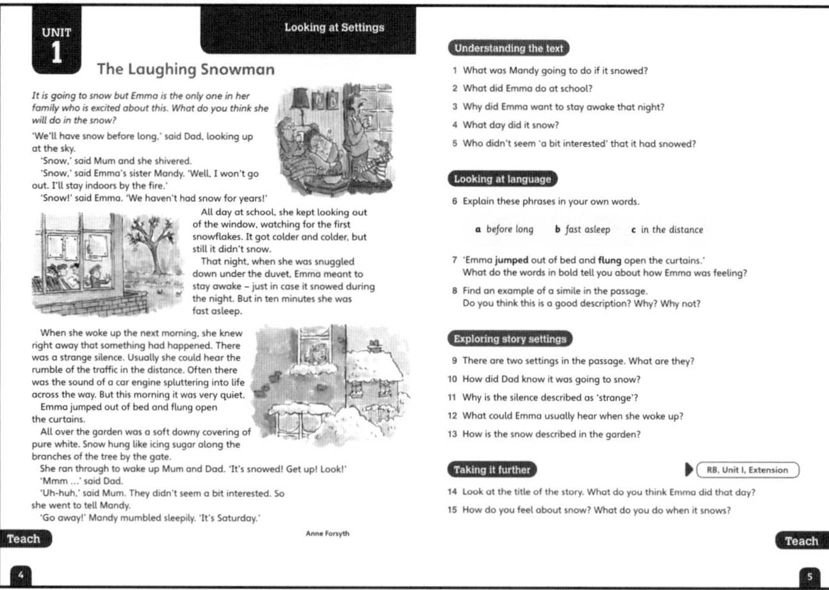

UNIT 1

Looking at Settings

The Laughing Snowman

It is going to snow but Emma is the only one in her family who is excited about this. What do you think she will do in the snow?

'We'll have snow before long,' said Dad, looking up at the sky.

'Snow,' said Mum and she shivered.

'Snow,' said Emma's sister Mandy. 'Well, I won't go out. I'll stay indoors by the fire.'

'Snow!' said Emma. 'We haven't had snow for years!'

All day at school, she kept looking out of the window, watching for the first snowflakes. It got colder and colder, but still it didn't snow.

That night, when she was snuggled down under the duvet, Emma meant to stay awake – just in case it snowed during the night. But in ten minutes she was fast asleep.

When she woke up the next morning, she knew right away that something had happened. There was a strange silence. Usually she could hear the rumble of the traffic in the distance. Often there was the sound of a car engine spluttering into life across the way. But this morning it was very quiet.

Emma jumped out of bed and flung open the curtains.

All over the garden was a soft downy covering of pure white. Snow hung like icing sugar along the branches of the tree by the gate.

She ran through to wake up Mum and Dad. 'It's snowed! Get up! Look!'

'Mmm ...' said Dad.

'Uh-huh,' said Mum. They didn't seem a bit interested. So she went to tell Mandy.

'Go away!' Mandy mumbled sleepily. 'It's Saturday.'

Anne Forsyth

Teach

4

Understanding the text

1 What was Mandy going to do if it snowed?
2 What did Emma do at school?
3 Why did Emma want to stay awake that night?
4 What day did it snow?
5 Who didn't seem 'a bit interested' that it had snowed?

Looking at language

6 Explain these phrases in your own words.

a *before long* **b** *fast asleep* **c** *in the distance*

7 'Emma **jumped** out of bed and **flung** open the curtains.'
What do the words in bold tell you about how Emma was feeling?

8 Find an example of a simile in the passage.
Do you think this is a good description? Why? Why not?

Exploring story settings

9 There are two settings in the passage. What are they?
10 How did Dad know it was going to snow?
11 Why is the silence described as 'strange'?
12 What could Emma usually hear when she woke up?
13 How is the snow described in the garden?

Taking it further RB, Unit I, Extension

14 Look at the title of the story. What do you think Emma did that day?
15 How do you feel about snow? What do you do when it snows?

Teach

5

RESOURCES & ASSESSMENT BOOK

- **Support** (comprehension support): narrative sequence: numbering sentences in order; (vocabulary support) cloze: choice of verbs to complete sentences.
- **Extension:** interpreting pictures; personal response to snow.

PUPIL BOOK ANSWERS

1. She was going to 'stay indoors by the fire'.
2. She 'kept looking out of the window, watching for the first snowflakes'.
3. She wanted to stay awake 'in case it snowed'.
4. Saturday.
5. Mum and Dad.
6. Answers that suggest the following: **a** very soon; **b** in a deep sleep; **c** far away
7. She was feeling excited and impatient to know if it had snowed.
8. Simile: 'like icing sugar'. Answers that suggest this is a good description because icing sugar is fine, soft and powdery like the snow.
9. Emma's home and her school.
10. He looked at the sky.
11. The silence is described as 'strange' because Emma could normally hear noises when she woke up.
12. When Emma woke up she could usually hear 'the rumble of the traffic in the distance' and often 'the sound of a car engine spluttering into life across the way'.
13. As 'a soft downy covering of pure white' and hanging 'like icing sugar'.
14. Answers that suggest that Emma may have played in the snow, had a snowball fight etc. Answers must include the fact that she built a snowman.
15. Individual answers. Encourage children to think about how they feel as well as what they do e.g. excited / happy when getting ready to play in the snow; cold / wet / miserable when it is time to go indoors.

RESOURCE SHEET SUPPORT ANSWERS

A

a 5 b 1 c 10 d 3 e 8
f 2 g 11 h 7 i 9 j 4
k 6

B

1. Emma snuggled under her duvet.
2. There was usually traffic rumbling in the distance.
3. She flung open the curtains.
4. She ran to wake everyone up.
5. Mandy mumbled, 'Go away!'

GOING DEEPER

- Go over the various settings in the extract so children understand that, when different things happen in a story, the setting often changes.

TALK

- Discuss where the children live. Do any of them live near a busy road? Where do they cross the road? Why is a busy road dangerous?
- Explain that they are going to read the beginning of a story called *The Hodgeheg* which is set near a very busy and dangerous road.
- Read the extract to the class; ask individual children to read it aloud in turn; or read in silence individually.

RESOURCES & ASSESSMENT BOOK

- **Support** (comprehension support): matching beginnings and endings of sentences; (vocabulary support): identifying vehicles from pictures.
- **Extension:** predicting the outcome of the story; thinking about the 'human crossing-place' setting.

PUPIL BOOK ANSWERS

1. At 'dusk'.
2. The 'darkest spot he could find' / 'in the shadow of a tall litterbin'.
3. On 'the narrow road on which he sat' i.e. the pavement.
4. The 'noisy monsters aren't allowed up here' i.e. on the pavement.
5. A 'human crossing place'.
6. **b** noisy
7. Answers that suggest that Max was frightened / nervous / even terrified.
8. Nocturnal.
9. **a** traffic / cars, lorries etc.
   b pavements
10. E.g. timid / inexperienced / frightened.
11. The road and pavement.
12. Answers that suggest that the noise was loud and all around him.
13. Because of the lights of the cars, motorcycles etc. and the street lamps.
14. The scene was very busy. Answers should cite evidence:
    'Cars and motorbikes, buses and lorries thundered past'
    'numbers of pedestrians passed close to him'

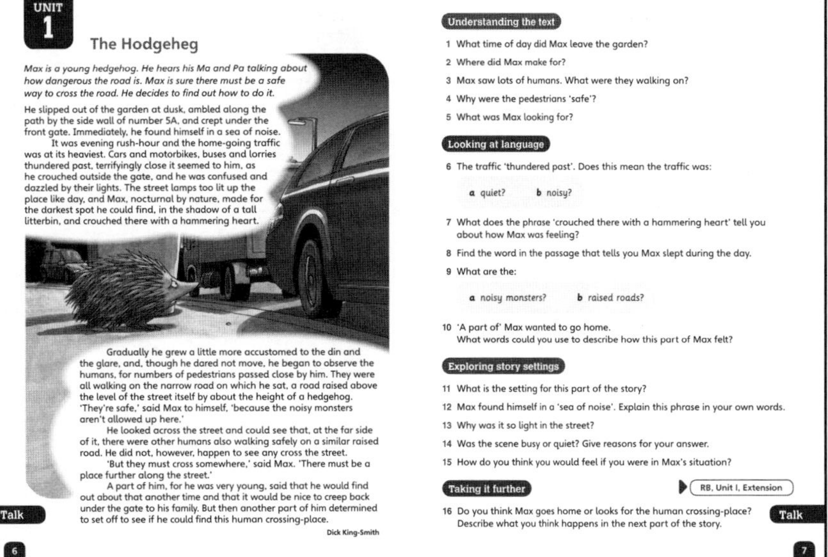

UNIT 1

The Hodgeheg

Max is a young hedgehog. He hears his Ma and Pa talking about how dangerous the road is. Max is sure there must be a safe way to cross the road. He decides to find out how to do it.

He slipped out of the garden at dusk, ambled along the path by the side wall of number 5A, and crept under the front gate. Immediately, he found himself in a sea of noise.

It was evening rush-hour and the home-going traffic was at its heaviest. Cars and motorbikes, buses and lorries thundered past, terrifyingly close it seemed to him, as he crouched outside the gate, and he was confused and dazzled by their lights. The street lamps too lit up the place like day, and Max, nocturnal by nature, made for the darkest spot he could find, in the shadow of a tall litterbin, and crouched there with a hammering heart.

Gradually he grew a little more accustomed to the din and the glare, and, though he dared not move, he began to observe the humans, for numbers of pedestrians passed close by him. They were all walking on the narrow road on which he sat, a road raised above the level of the street itself by about the height of a hedgehog. 'They're safe,' said Max to himself, 'because the noisy monsters aren't allowed up here.'

He looked across the street and could see that, at the far side of it, there were other humans also walking safely on a similar raised road. He did not, however, happen to see any cross the street.

'But they must cross somewhere,' said Max. 'There must be a place further along the street.'

A part of him, for he was very young, said that he would find out about that another time and that it would be nice to creep back under the gate to his family. But then another part of him determined to set off to see if he could find this human crossing-place.

Dick King-Smith

Talk

6

Understanding the text

1 What time of day did Max leave the garden?
2 Where did Max make for?
3 Max saw lots of humans. What were they walking on?
4 Why were the pedestrians 'safe'?
5 What was Max looking for?

Looking at language

6 The traffic 'thundered past'. Does this mean the traffic was:
a quiet? *b noisy?*
7 What does the phrase 'crouched there with a hammering heart' tell you about how Max was feeling?
8 Find the word in the passage that tells you Max slept during the day.
9 What are the:
a noisy monsters? *b raised roads?*
10 'A part of' Max wanted to go home.
What words could you use to describe how this part of Max felt?

Exploring story settings

11 What is the setting for this part of the story?
12 Max found himself in a 'sea of noise'. Explain this phrase in your own words.
13 Why was it so light in the street?
14 Was the scene busy or quiet? Give reasons for your answer.
15 How do you think you would feel if you were in Max's situation?

Taking it further

RB, Unit I, Extension

16 Do you think Max goes home or looks for the human crossing-place?
Describe what you think happens in the next part of the story.

Talk

7

15. Individual answers. Encourage children to explain why they may feel excited / frightened / curious.
16. Individual answers.

RESOURCE SHEET SUPPORT ANSWERS

A

1. at dusk.
2. thundered past.
3. a nocturnal animal.
4. outside the gate.
5. close by him.
6. allowed on the pavement.
7. must cross the street.
8. this human crossing-place.

B

1. car
2. motorbike
3. bus
4. lorry

GOING DEEPER

- Have any of the children read *The Hodgeheg*? What did they think of it? Would others like to read it? Why? Why not?

WRITE

- Explain to children that they are going to read a version of the fairy tale, *The Ugly Duckling.*
- Ask the children if they have read the story before.
- Read the extract to the class; ask individual children to read it aloud in turn; or read in silence individually.

RESOURCES & ASSESSMENT BOOK

- **Support** (comprehension support): assessing whether sentences about the story are true or false; (vocabulary support): matching words that are opposites.
- **Extension:** thinking about how the ugly duckling felt at different points in the story.

PUPIL BOOK ANSWERS

1 **b** summer

2 **c** bigger than the others

3 **a** to swim

4 **b** the swans

5 **c** beautiful

6 **a** finally **b** busy **c** miserable

7 **a** tall **b** ugly **c** better **d** gracefully **e** warmer **f** melted

8 Answer that suggests he almost couldn't believe it was true.

9 River, farmyard, riverbank.

10 **a** beautiful / sparkling / quiet **b** sweet / fluffy **c** beautiful / white

11 The river was quiet; the farmyard was noisy and busy.

12 **a** gentle breeze **b** bitter, cold

13 Answers that suggest he wanted to hide from everyone / felt frightened.

14 **a** Answers that suggest he felt afraid / unhappy.

b Answers that suggest he felt happy / surprised.

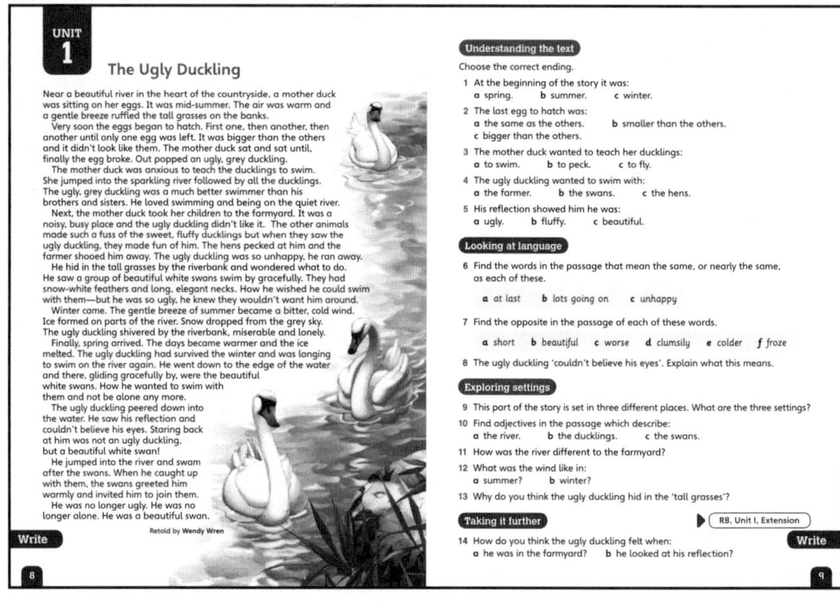

UNIT 1

The Ugly Duckling

Near a beautiful river in the heart of the countryside, a mother duck was sitting on her eggs. It was mid-summer. The air was warm and a gentle breeze ruffled the tall grasses on the banks.

Very soon the eggs began to hatch. First one, then another, then another until only one egg was left. It was bigger than the others and it didn't look like them. The mother duck sat and sat until, finally the egg broke. Out popped an ugly, grey duckling.

The mother duck was anxious to teach the ducklings to swim. She jumped into the sparkling river followed by all the ducklings. The ugly, grey duckling was a much better swimmer than his brothers and sisters. He loved swimming and being on the quiet river.

Next, the mother duck took her children to the farmyard. It was a noisy, busy place and the ugly duckling didn't like it. The other animals made such a fuss of the sweet, fluffy ducklings but when they saw the ugly duckling, they made fun of him. The hens pecked at him and the farmer shooed him away. The ugly duckling was so unhappy, he ran away.

He hid in the tall grasses by the riverbank and wondered what to do. He saw a group of beautiful white swans swim by gracefully. They had snow-white feathers and long, elegant necks. How he wished he could swim with them—but he was so ugly, he knew they wouldn't want him around.

Winter came. The gentle breeze of summer became a bitter, cold wind. Ice formed on parts of the river. Snow dropped from the grey sky. The ugly duckling shivered by the riverbank, miserable and lonely.

Finally, spring arrived. The days became warmer and the ice melted. The ugly duckling had survived the winter and was longing to swim on the river again. He went down to the edge of the water and there, gliding gracefully by, were the beautiful white swans. How he wanted to swim with them and not be alone any more.

The ugly duckling peered down into the water. He saw his reflection and couldn't believe his eyes. Staring back at him was not an ugly duckling, but a beautiful white swan!

He jumped into the river and swam after the swans. When he caught up with them, the swans greeted him warmly and invited him to join them.

He was no longer ugly. He was no longer alone. He was a beautiful swan.

Retold by **Wendy Wren**

Write

8

Understanding the text

Choose the correct ending.

1 At the beginning of the story it was:
a spring. **b** summer. **c** winter.

2 The last egg to hatch was:
a the same as the others. **b** smaller than the others. **c** bigger than the others.

3 The mother duck wanted to teach her ducklings:
a to swim. **b** to peck. **c** to fly.

4 The ugly duckling wanted to swim with:
a the farmer. **b** the swans. **c** the hens.

5 His reflection showed him he was:
a ugly. **b** fluffy. **c** beautiful.

Looking at language

6 Find the words in the passage that mean the same, or nearly the same, as each of these.

a *at last* **b** *lots going on* **c** *unhappy*

7 Find the opposite in the passage of each of these words.

a *short* **b** *beautiful* **c** *worse* **d** *clumsily* **e** *colder* **f** *froze*

8 The ugly duckling 'couldn't believe his eyes'. Explain what this means.

Exploring settings

9 This part of the story is set in three different places. What are the three settings?

10 Find adjectives in the passage which describe:
a the river. **b** the ducklings. **c** the swans.

11 How was the river different to the farmyard?

12 What was the wind like in:
a summer? **b** winter?

13 Why do you think the ugly duckling hid in the 'tall grasses'?

Taking it further RB, Unit 1, Extension

14 How do you think the ugly duckling felt when:
a he was in the farmyard? **b** he looked at his reflection?

Write

9

RESOURCE SHEET SUPPORT ANSWERS

A

1 The eggs hatched in winter. [F]

2 One of the eggs was bigger than the others. [T]

3 The ugly duckling could not swim very well. [F]

4 They visited the farmyard. [T]

5 The farmer was nice to the ugly duckling. [F]

6 The ugly duckling hid in the farmyard. [F]

7 It snowed in winter. [T]

8 The swans told the ugly duckling to go away. [F]

B

summer	winter
ugly	beautiful
loved	hated
unhappy	happy
gracefully	clumsily
colder	warmer
tall	short
dull	sparkling
froze	melted

GOING DEEPER

- Ask the children if they liked the story. How did it make them feel? Which setting did they like best? Why? How do they think the ugly duckling was treated by the other characters in the story? How do they think he should have been treated?

UNIT FOCUS: Using the Contents Page and Index

Investigating ...

- how to read and source information
- how to understand the features of an information text

TEACH

- Ask the children what they understand by the terms 'fiction' and 'non-fiction'.
- Ask the children what they would expect to find in a contents page / index and where they would find them.
- Discuss the children's favourite animals and why they like them.
- Explain to children that they are going to look at an index of a book called *All About Animals*.
- Read the text to the class; ask individual children to read it aloud in turn; or read in silence individually.

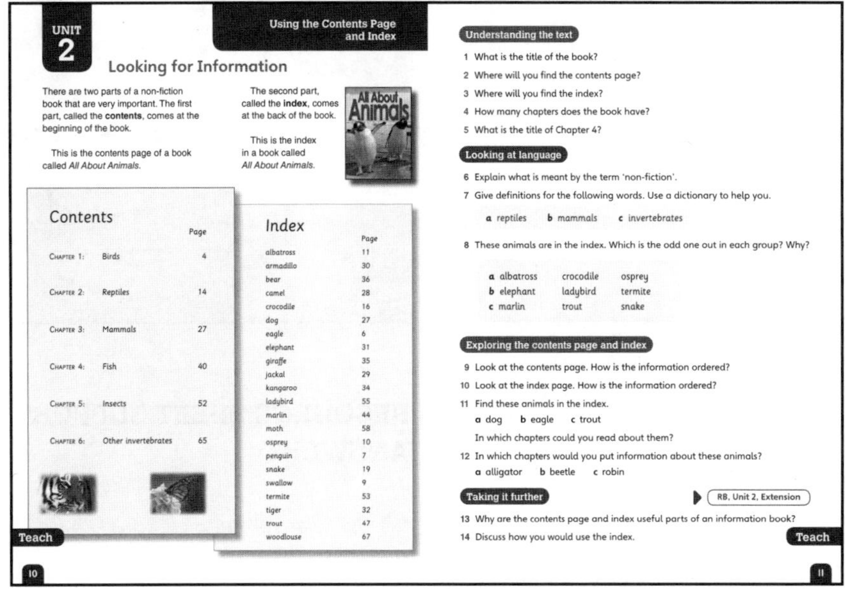

UNIT 2 Using the Contents Page and Index

Looking for Information

There are two parts of a non-fiction book that are very important. The first part, called the **contents**, comes at the beginning of the book.

This is the contents page of a book called *All About Animals*.

The second part, called the **index**, comes at the back of the book.

This is the index in a book called *All About Animals*.

Contents

		Page
Chapter 1:	Birds	4
Chapter 2:	Reptiles	14
Chapter 3:	Mammals	27
Chapter 4:	Fish	40
Chapter 5:	Insects	52
Chapter 6:	Other invertebrates	65

Index

	Page
albatross	11
armadillo	30
bear	36
camel	28
crocodile	16
dog	27
eagle	6
elephant	31
giraffe	35
jackal	29
kangaroo	34
ladybird	55
marlin	44
moth	58
osprey	10
penguin	7
snake	19
swallow	9
termite	53
tiger	32
trout	47
woodlouse	67

Understanding the text

1 What is the title of the book?
2 Where will you find the contents page?
3 Where will you find the index?
4 How many chapters does the book have?
5 What is the title of Chapter 4?

Looking at language

6 Explain what is meant by the term 'non-fiction'.
7 Give definitions for the following words. Use a dictionary to help you.
a reptiles b mammals c invertebrates
8 These animals are in the index. Which is the odd one out in each group? Why?
a albatross crocodile osprey
b elephant ladybird termite
c marlin trout snake

Exploring the contents page and index

9 Look at the contents page. How is the information ordered?
10 Look at the index page. How is the information ordered?
11 Find these animals in the index.
a dog b eagle c trout
In which chapters could you read about them?
12 In which chapters would you put information about these animals?
a alligator b beetle c robin

Taking it further ▶ RB, Unit 2, Extension

13 Why are the contents page and index useful parts of an information book?
14 Discuss how you would use the index.

Teach 10 Teach 11

RESOURCES & ASSESSMENT BOOK

- **Support** (comprehension support): choosing the correct sentence ending; (vocabulary support): classifying.
- **Extension:** completing sentences and making an index.

PUPIL BOOK ANSWERS

1. *All About Animals*
2. At the beginning of the book.
3. At the back of the book.
4. Six chapters.
5. Fish.
6. Non-fiction is factual / true writing.
7. **a** reptiles: cold blooded animals **b** mammals: animals that give birth to live young **c** invertebrates: animals without a backbone
8. **a** crocodile [the others are birds] **b** elephant [the others are insects] **c** snake [the others are fish]
9. In chapters.
10. Alphabetically.
11. **a** dog: chapter 3 **b** eagle: chapter 1 **c** trout: chapter 4
12. **a** alligator: chapter 2 **b** beetle: chapter 5 **c** robin: chapter 1
13. Answers that suggest they help you to find information quickly.
14. Answers that suggest that you would use the index to look for a particular topic.

RESOURCE SHEET SUPPORT ANSWERS

A

1. a
2. b
3. b
4. a

B

Birds	Reptiles	Mammals	Fish	Insects
osprey	crocodile	bear	trout	ladybird
albatross	snake	tiger	marlin	moth

C

Individual answers.

GOING DEEPER

- Recap the terms 'fiction' and 'non-fiction' and ask children to explain the difference between how a contents page and index page are arranged. Ask children why fiction books do not have an index.

TALK

- Ask the children what they understand by the term 'solar system'.
- Ask the children if they can name the planets in our solar system.
- Explain to children that they are going to look at the contents page of a book called *Our Solar System.*
- Ask the children what they think the book will be about.
- Read the text to the class; ask individual children to read it aloud in turn; or read in silence individually.

RESOURCES & ASSESSMENT BOOK

- **Support** (comprehension support): matching questions and answers; (vocabulary support): writing chapter titles from definitions.
- **Extension:** planning and writing questions.

PUPIL BOOK ANSWERS

1. *Our Solar System.*
2. Five.
3. Page 23.
4. Page 41.
5. Chapter 2.
6. Answers that suggest the Solar System is made up of the planets that orbit our sun.
7. **a** space: the universe outside of Earth's atmosphere **b** planet: large object that moves around our sun or another star **c** satellite: object orbiting Earth e.g. our Moon.
8. Because they are proper nouns.
9. Answers that suggest the numbers help the reader to find the part of the book they are interested in / the first page of the chapter.
10. Encourage each member of the group to make suggestions and take a vote.
11. Individual answers connected to the topic.
12. Encourage all members of the group to participate by making suggestions.
13. Encourage all members of the group to suggest questions, vote and research.

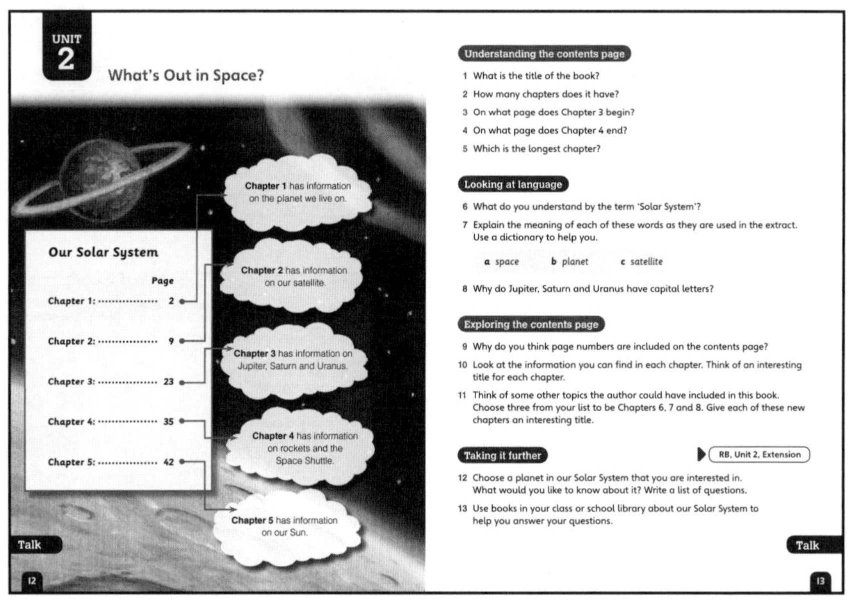

UNIT 2

What's Out in Space?

Our Solar System

	Page
Chapter 1:	2
Chapter 2:	9
Chapter 3:	23
Chapter 4:	35
Chapter 5:	42

Chapter 1 has information on the planet we live on.

Chapter 2 has information on our satellite.

Chapter 3 has information on Jupiter, Saturn and Uranus.

Chapter 4 has information on rockets and the Space Shuttle.

Chapter 5 has information on our Sun.

Talk

12

Understanding the contents page

1 What is the title of the book?
2 How many chapters does it have?
3 On what page does Chapter 3 begin?
4 On what page does Chapter 4 end?
5 Which is the longest chapter?

Looking at language

6 What do you understand by the term 'Solar System'?
7 Explain the meaning of each of these words as they are used in the extract. Use a dictionary to help you.

a *space* **b** *planet* **c** *satellite*

8 Why do Jupiter, Saturn and Uranus have capital letters?

Exploring the contents page

9 Why do you think page numbers are included on the contents page?
10 Look at the information you can find in each chapter. Think of an interesting title for each chapter.
11 Think of some other topics the author could have included in this book. Choose three from your list to be Chapters 6, 7 and 8. Give each of these new chapters an interesting title.

Taking it further RB, Unit 2, Extension

12 Choose a planet in our Solar System that you are interested in. What would you like to know about it? Write a list of questions.
13 Use books in your class or school library about our Solar System to help you answer your questions.

Talk

13

RESOURCE SHEET SUPPORT ANSWERS

A

1. *Our Solar System.*
2. five
3. page 23
4. page 41
5. chapter 2

B

Individual answers.

GOING DEEPER

- As a class, decide on a list of words that would go into the index of *Our Solar System.* Children should include important words from the extra chapters they have 'added'.

WRITE

- Discuss sport with the children and ask what their favourite sport is.
- Ask children to explain why they like their favourite sport so much.
- Explain to children that they are going to look at the contents page for a book called *Sport for All!*
- Ask if the children think the book will be about one type of sport or many different sorts and why they think so.
- Read the text to the class; ask individual children to read it aloud in turn; or read in silence individually.

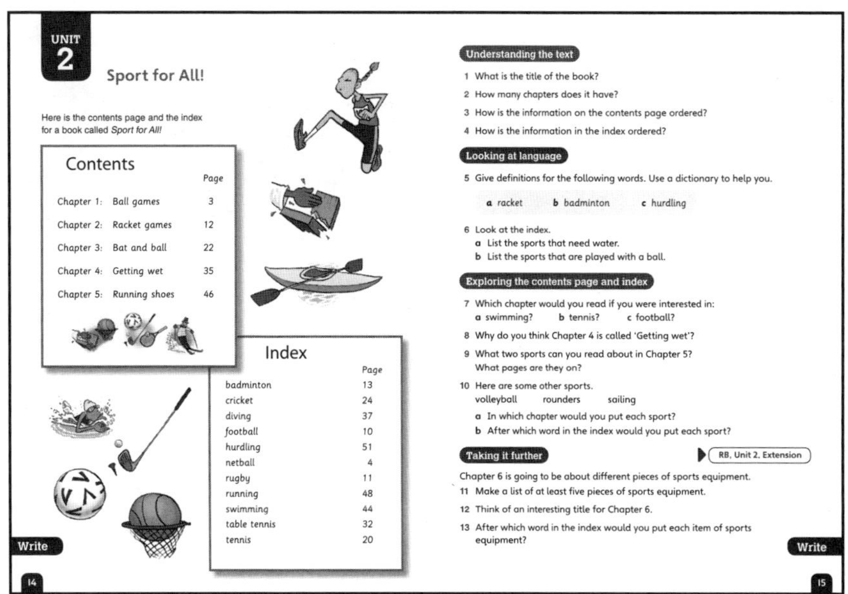

UNIT 2 Sport for All!

Here is the contents page and the index for a book called *Sport for All!*

Contents

Index

Understanding the text

1 What is the title of the book?
2 How many chapters does it have?
3 How is the information on the contents page ordered?
4 How is the information in the index ordered?

Looking at language

5 Give definitions for the following words. Use a dictionary to help you.
a *racket* **b** *badminton* **c** *hurdling*

6 Look at the index.
a List the sports that need water.
b List the sports that are played with a ball.

Exploring the contents page and index

7 Which chapter would you read if you were interested in:
a swimming? **b** tennis? **c** football?
8 Why do you think Chapter 4 is called 'Getting wet'?
9 What two sports can you read about in Chapter 5? What pages are they on?
10 Here are some other sports.
volleyball rounders sailing
a In which chapter would you put each sport?
b After which word in the index would you put each sport?

Taking it further RB, Unit 2, Extension

Chapter 6 is going to be about different pieces of sports equipment.
11 Make a list of at least five pieces of sports equipment.
12 Think of an interesting title for Chapter 6.
13 After which word in the index would you put each item of sports equipment?

Write 14 Write 15

RESOURCES & ASSESSMENT BOOK

- **Support** (comprehension support): multiple choice; (vocabulary support): identifying sport from picture stimulus.
- **Extension:** labelling and ordering words in an index.

PUPIL BOOK ANSWERS

1. *Sport for All!*
2. Five.
3. By chapter.
4. Alphabetically.
5. **a** racket: piece of equipment used for hitting a ball or other object **b** badminton: game played with rackets and shuttlecock over a high net **c** hurdling: running and jumping over hurdles
6. **a** diving / swimming **b** cricket / football / netball / rugby / table tennis / tennis
7. **a** swimming: chapter 4 **b** tennis: chapter 2 **c** football: chapter 1
8. Answers that suggest that the sports in this chapter involve water.
9. Running – page 48 / hurdling – page 51.
10. **a** volleyball: chapter 1 / rounders: chapter 3 / sailing: chapter 4 **b** volleyball after tennis / rounders after netball / sailing after running

11 12 13 Individual answers.

RESOURCE SHEET SUPPORT ANSWERS

A

1. b
2. a
3. b
4. a
5. b

B

1. football
2. cricket
3. hurdling
4. tennis

GOING DEEPER

- Recap on why contents pages and indexes are useful in non-fiction books. Ask children why these features save time and how they are arranged.

UNIT FOCUS: Understanding Shape Poems

Investigating …

- shape poems and calligrams through reading and reciting poems
- writing poems

TEACH

- Ask who has a pet cat, or knows a cat.
- Have they noticed how cats move and what they do?
- Tell the children that they're going to read a poem about cats that is written on the page in a special way.
- Read the poem to the class; ask individual children to read it aloud in turn; or read in silence individually.

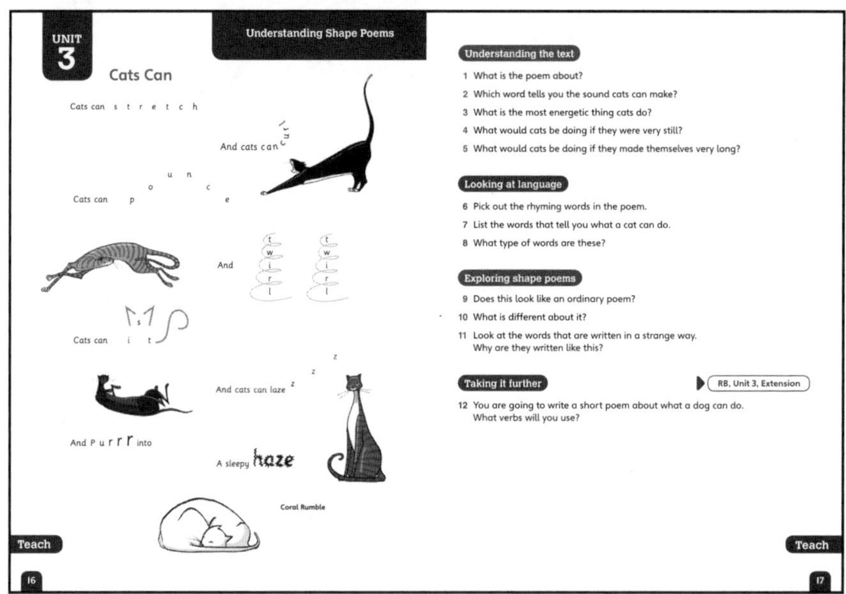

UNIT 3

Understanding Shape Poems

Cats Can

Cats can s t r e t c h

And cats can curl

Cats can p o u n c e

And twirl twirl

Cats can sit

And cats can laze z z z

And P u r r r into

A sleepy haze

Coral Rumble

Understanding the text

1 What is the poem about?
2 Which word tells you the sound cats can make?
3 What is the most energetic thing cats do?
4 What would cats be doing if they were very still?
5 What would cats be doing if they made themselves very long?

Looking at language

6 Pick out the rhyming words in the poem.
7 List the words that tell you what a cat can do.
8 What type of words are these?

Exploring shape poems

9 Does this look like an ordinary poem?
10 What is different about it?
11 Look at the words that are written in a strange way. Why are they written like this?

Taking it further RB, Unit 3, Extension

12 You are going to write a short poem about what a dog can do. What verbs will you use?

Teach 16 Teach 17

RESOURCES & ASSESSMENT BOOK

- **Support** (comprehension support): sorting muddled words; (vocabulary support): matching rhyming words, thinking of additional verbs.
- **Extension:** using appropriate verbs in poems.

PUPIL BOOK ANSWERS

1. It is about all the things that cats can do.
2. Purr.
3. Pounce.
4. Sitting or sleeping.
5. Stretching.
6. curl / twirl; laze / haze
7. stretch / curl / pounce / twirl / sit / laze / purr
8. Verbs.
9. No.
10. Answers that suggest that it is not 'line by line' but looks a different shape to normal poems, with different fonts etc.
11. Answers that suggest that some of the words have been made to look like the movement, sound etc. that they are describing.
12. Individual answers.

RESOURCE SHEET SUPPORT ANSWERS

A

1. twirl
2. stretch
3. purr
4. sit
5. laze
6. pounce

B

in / tin / pin, that / flat, laze / haze, twirl / curl

C

Individual answers.

GOING DEEPER

- Ask children to work in pairs or small groups to recite the poem to the class, using actions to emphasise the words.

TALK

- Discuss musical instruments with the children and ask if they play any. Which ones? For how long have they played?
- Ask what musical instruments make soft, gentle sounds.
- Ask what musical instruments make loud, strong sounds.
- Write the word 'calligram' on the board and explain that in these poems the letters and words are written in such a way that they resemble the thing they are describing.
- Explain that they are going to read a poem called 'Rhythm Machine', which is a calligram.
- Read the poem to the class; ask individual children to read it aloud in turn; or read in silence individually.

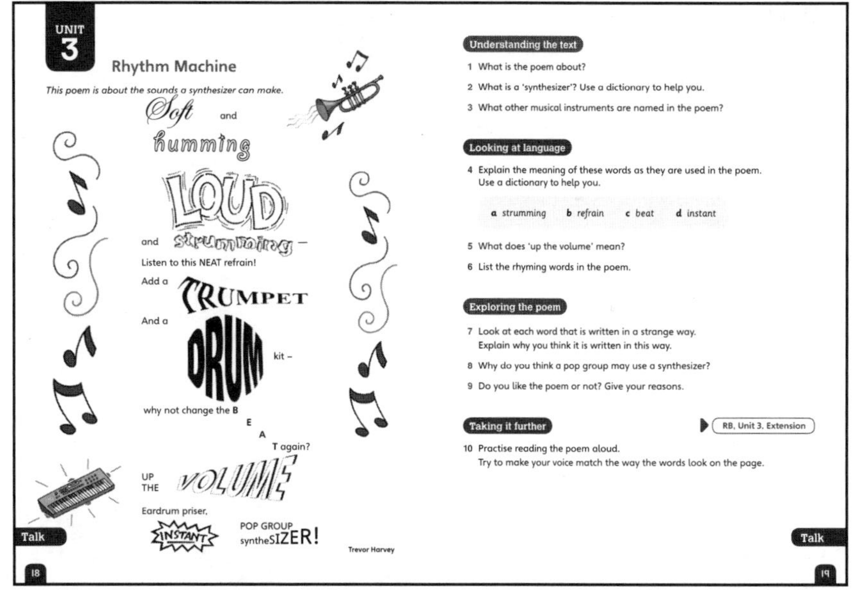
UNIT 3

Rhythm Machine

This poem is about the sounds a synthesizer can make.

Soft and
humming
LOUD
and strumming –
Listen to this NEAT refrain!
Add a
TRUMPET
And a
DRUM kit –
why not change the B
E
A
T again?
UP
THE
VOLUME
Eardrum priser,
INSTANT
POP GROUP
syntheSIZER!

Trevor Harvey

Talk

18

Understanding the text

1 What is the poem about?

2 What is a 'synthesizer'? Use a dictionary to help you.

3 What other musical instruments are named in the poem?

Looking at language

4 Explain the meaning of these words as they are used in the poem. Use a dictionary to help you.

a strumming **b** refrain **c** beat **d** instant

5 What does 'up the volume' mean?

6 List the rhyming words in the poem.

Exploring the poem

7 Look at each word that is written in a strange way. Explain why you think it is written in this way.

8 Why do you think a pop group may use a synthesizer?

9 Do you like the poem or not? Give your reasons.

Taking it further

RB, Unit 3, Extension

10 Practise reading the poem aloud. Try to make your voice match the way the words look on the page.

Talk

19

RESOURCES & ASSESSMENT BOOK

- **Support** (comprehension support): choosing the correct answer, identifying musical instruments; (vocabulary support): matching rhyming words.
- **Extension:** recognising onomatopoeic words.

PUPIL BOOK ANSWERS

1. The poem is about all the sounds a synthesizer can make.
2. An electronic machine that makes and combines musical sounds i.e. a machine that can sound like many different instruments.
3. trumpet / drum
4. **a** strumming: moving your fingers across the strings of a musical instrument e.g. a guitar **b** refrain: repeated words or tune / chorus **c** beat: rhythm / time **d** instant: immediate
5. Turn up the sound / make louder.
6. humming / strumming; trumpet / drum kit; refrain / again; priser / synthesizer
7. Answers that suggest: soft – the letters are curved and flowing, humming – flowing like a sound going on, loud – big and vibrating, strumming – shaken and broken up, trumpet – the shape of a trumpet, drum – the shape of a drum, volume – going from small [quiet] to large [loud].
8. Individual answers suggesting that pop groups can make a huge variety of music with a synthesizer even though they cannot play all of the instruments.
9. Individual answers supported by reasons.
10. Individual answers.

RESOURCE SHEET SUPPORT ANSWERS

A

1. a
2. a
3. b

B

1. flute
2. guitar
3. cymbal
4. triangle

C

humming / strumming, refrain / again, priser / synthesizer

GOING DEEPER

- Ask the children if they like the poem and, if so, why. Ask if they think it is written in an effective way, and encourage them to explain their answers.

WRITE

- Discuss why people sometimes use headphones when listening to music.
- Ask children if they see people outside with headphones on.
- Ask children how they listen to music.
- Explain to children that they are going to read a shape poem called 'Stereo Headphones'.
- Ask children what they expect the poem to look like.
- Read the poem to the class; ask individual children to read it aloud in turn; or read in silence individually.

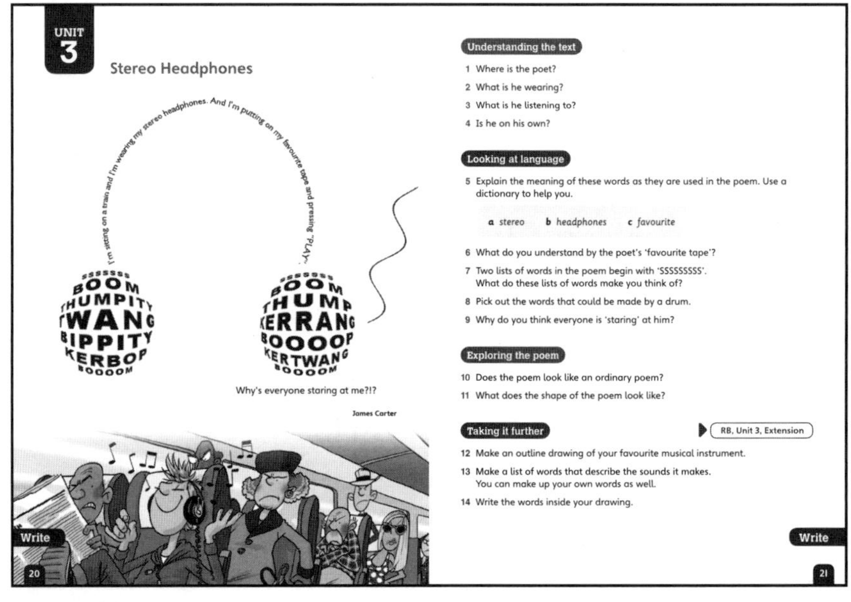

UNIT 3

Stereo Headphones

I'm sitting on a train and I'm wearing my stereo headphones. And I'm putting on my favourite tape and pressing "PLAY"

SSSSSSS BOOM THUMPITY TWANG BIPPITY KERBOP BOOOOM

SSSSSSS BOOM THUMP KERRANG BOOOOOP KERTWANG BOOOOM

Why's everyone staring at me?!?

James Carter

Understanding the text

1 Where is the poet?
2 What is he wearing?
3 What is he listening to?
4 Is he on his own?

Looking at language

5 Explain the meaning of these words as they are used in the poem. Use a dictionary to help you.

a stereo *b headphones* *c favourite*

6 What do you understand by the poet's 'favourite tape'?
7 Two lists of words in the poem begin with 'SSSSSSSSS'. What do these lists of words make you think of?
8 Pick out the words that could be made by a drum.
9 Why do you think everyone is 'staring' at him?

Exploring the poem

10 Does the poem look like an ordinary poem?
11 What does the shape of the poem look like?

Taking it further

RB, Unit 3, Extension

12 Make an outline drawing of your favourite musical instrument.
13 Make a list of words that describe the sounds it makes. You can make up your own words as well.
14 Write the words inside your drawing.

Write 20 Write 21

RESOURCES & ASSESSMENT BOOK

- **Support** (comprehension support): cloze activity, drawing the shape represented by the poem's layout; (vocabulary support): identifying onomatopoeic words.
- **Extension:** describing sounds.

PUPIL BOOK ANSWERS

1. Sitting on a train.
2. Stereo headphones.
3. His favourite tape.
4. No.
5. **a** stereo: where music comes in through two speakers **b** headphones: equipment to wear over your ears to listen to something **c** favourite: the best / most liked
6. Answers that suggest that this is the poet's most-liked music, stored on a tape that he's listening to.
7. Answers that suggest that the words represent sounds in a piece of music.
8. boom / thumpity / thump
9. Answers that suggest either that everyone can hear the music coming through the headphones OR they cannot hear the music but the poet is moving to or singing along to the music and looks odd.
10. No.
11. Answers that suggest the poem looks like the shape of headphones.

12 13 14 Individual answers.

RESOURCE SHEET SUPPORT ANSWERS

A

1. train
2. stereo headphones
3. tape
4. people
5. staring

B

1. boom, e.g. drum
2. twang e.g. guitar
3. thump, e.g. drum / piano

C

Children should draw a head with headphones on.

GOING DEEPER

- Recap on the poems the children have read and ask which of the poems they like the best. Encourage them to explain why. Ask children which type of poem they think is easier to write and why.

UNIT FOCUS: Retrieving Information

Investigating ...

- information through contents pages and indexes
- the features of factual writing
- how encyclopaedias and charts are organised

TEACH

- Discuss the term 'encyclopaedia' with the children and ask if they have ever used one.
- Ask children if they have ever used an online encyclopaedia and, if so, what for.
- Ask children if they have ever visited any famous walls or towers.
- Explain that they are going to read facts about some famous walls and towers, presented in an encyclopaedia and a chart.
- Read the text to the class; ask individual children to read it aloud in turn; or read in silence individually.

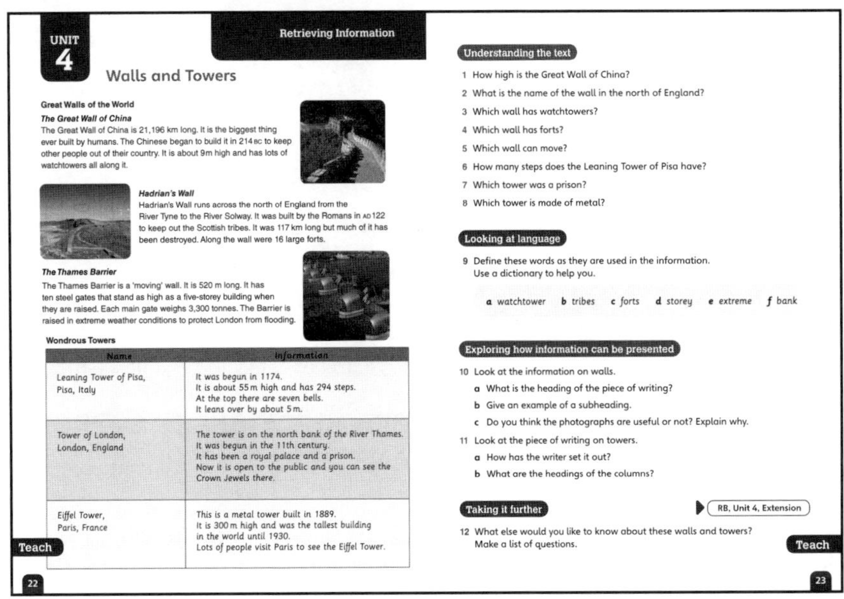

UNIT 4

Retrieving Information

Walls and Towers

Great Walls of the World

The Great Wall of China

The Great Wall of China is 21,196 km long. It is the biggest thing ever built by humans. The Chinese began to build it in 214 BC to keep other people out of their country. It is about 9m high and has lots of watchtowers all along it.

Hadrian's Wall

Hadrian's Wall runs across the north of England from the River Tyne to the River Solway. It was built by the Romans in AD 122 to keep out the Scottish tribes. It was 117 km long but much of it has been destroyed. Along the wall were 16 large forts.

The Thames Barrier

The Thames Barrier is a 'moving' wall. It is 520 m long. It has ten steel gates that stand as high as a five-storey building when they are raised. Each main gate weighs 3,300 tonnes. The Barrier is raised in extreme weather conditions to protect London from flooding.

Wondrous Towers

Name	Information
Leaning Tower of Pisa, Pisa, Italy	It was begun in 1174. It is about 55 m high and has 294 steps. At the top there are seven bells. It leans over by about 5 m.
Tower of London, London, England	The tower is on the north bank of the River Thames. It was begun in the 11th century. It has been a royal palace and a prison. Now it is open to the public and you can see the Crown Jewels there.
Eiffel Tower, Paris, France	This is a metal tower built in 1889. It is 300 m high and was the tallest building in the world until 1930. Lots of people visit Paris to see the Eiffel Tower.

Teach

22

Understanding the text

1 How high is the Great Wall of China?
2 What is the name of the wall in the north of England?
3 Which wall has watchtowers?
4 Which wall has forts?
5 Which wall can move?
6 How many steps does the Leaning Tower of Pisa have?
7 Which tower was a prison?
8 Which tower is made of metal?

Looking at language

9 Define these words as they are used in the information. Use a dictionary to help you.

a watchtower **b** tribes **c** forts **d** storey **e** extreme **f** bank

Exploring how information can be presented

10 Look at the information on walls.
 a What is the heading of the piece of writing?
 b Give an example of a subheading.
 c Do you think the photographs are useful or not? Explain why.

11 Look at the piece of writing on towers.
 a How has the writer set it out?
 b What are the headings of the columns?

Taking it further

RB, Unit 4, Extension

12 What else would you like to know about these walls and towers? Make a list of questions.

Teach

23

RESOURCES & ASSESSMENT BOOK

- **Support** (comprehension support): identifying the walls / towers from sets of facts; (vocabulary support): finding proper nouns and adjectives.
- **Extension:** planning questions.

PUPIL BOOK ANSWERS

1 Nine metres.

2 Hadrian's Wall.

3 The Great Wall of China.

4 Hadrian's Wall.

5 The Thames Barrier.

6 294 steps.

7 The Tower of London.

8 The Eiffel Tower.

9 **a** watchtower: a tower from which people can look at the surrounding land **b** tribes: a group of families or communities **c** forts: a building or group of buildings difficult to attack **d** storey: floor of a building **e** extreme: exceptionally bad **f** bank: side of a river

10 **a** Great Walls Of The World **b** Any one of: The Great Wall of China / Hadrian's Wall / The Thames Barrier **c** Answers suggesting that the photographs are useful because the reader can see what is being written about.

11 **a** as a chart **b** Name / Information

12 Individual answers.

RESOURCE SHEET SUPPORT ANSWERS

A

1 Hadrian's Wall

2 The Thames Barrier

3 The Great Wall Of China

B

1 The Tower Of London

2 The Eiffel Tower

3 The Leaning Tower Of Pisa

C

1 two proper nouns e.g. China / Hadrian / River Solway / Italy

2 two adjectives e.g. large / seven / royal / metal

GOING DEEPER

- As a class, set out the information about walls in chart form.

TALK

- Ask children what they understand by the term 'canal'.
- Ask if they know about any famous canals, and if they have ever been on a canal boat.
- Explain to children that they are going to read facts about two very famous canals.
- Read the text to the class; ask individual children to read it aloud in turn; or read in silence individually.

RESOURCES & ASSESSMENT BOOK

- **Support** (comprehension support): grouping facts under correct heading; (vocabulary support): matching words and definitions.
- **Extension:** plan and write questions about canals.

PUPIL BOOK ANSWERS

1. Egypt.
2. Central America.
3. The Mediterranean Sea and the Red Sea.
4. The Atlantic Ocean and the Pacific Ocean.
5. ships.
6. Not natural / something created by man.
7. **a** link: join **b** natural: not put there by man **c** connects: links / joins
8. The World's Great Canals.
9. Answers suggesting the italic writing is the introduction, explaining what the passage is about.
10. Answers that suggest the sub-headings divide the information into different parts of the topic and make it easier to find the information you're looking for.
11. Answers that suggest it is helpful to the reader to see where the canals are in relation to other parts of the world.
12. The age of the canals (when the canals were built).
13. Shorter. They are a shortcut rather than having to go along the coastline.
14. Encourage all members of the group to contribute.

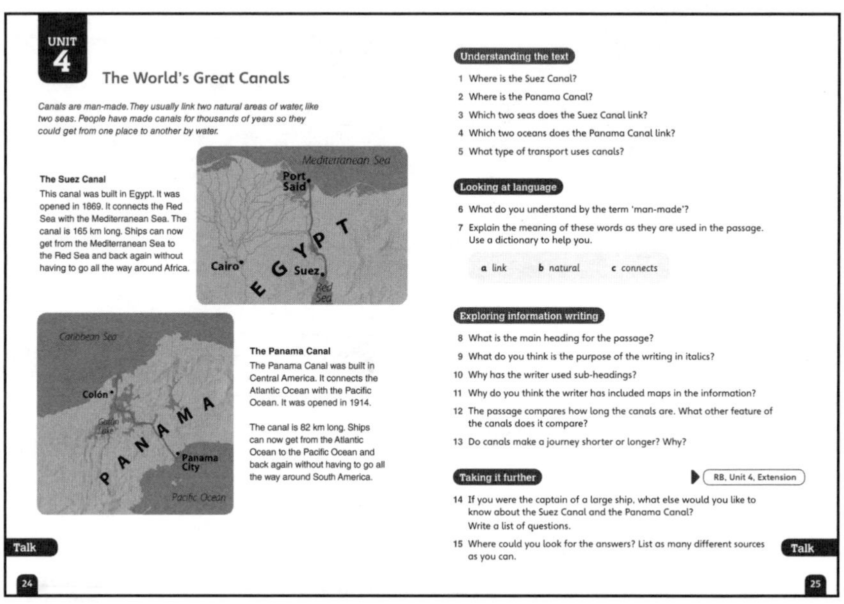
UNIT 4

The World's Great Canals

Canals are man-made. They usually link two natural areas of water, like two seas. People have made canals for thousands of years so they could get from one place to another by water.

The Suez Canal

This canal was built in Egypt. It was opened in 1869. It connects the Red Sea with the Mediterranean Sea. The canal is 165 km long. Ships can now get from the Mediterranean Sea to the Red Sea and back again without having to go all the way around Africa.

The Panama Canal

The Panama Canal was built in Central America. It connects the Atlantic Ocean with the Pacific Ocean. It was opened in 1914.

The canal is 82 km long. Ships can now get from the Atlantic Ocean to the Pacific Ocean and back again without having to go all the way around South America.

Talk

24

Understanding the text

1 Where is the Suez Canal?
2 Where is the Panama Canal?
3 Which two seas does the Suez Canal link?
4 Which two oceans does the Panama Canal link?
5 What type of transport uses canals?

Looking at language

6 What do you understand by the term 'man-made'?
7 Explain the meaning of these words as they are used in the passage. Use a dictionary to help you.

a link   b natural   c connects

Exploring information writing

8 What is the main heading for the passage?
9 What do you think is the purpose of the writing in italics?
10 Why has the writer used sub-headings?
11 Why do you think the writer has included maps in the information?
12 The passage compares how long the canals are. What other feature of the canals does it compare?
13 Do canals make a journey shorter or longer? Why?

Taking it further   RB, Unit 4, Extension

14 If you were the captain of a large ship, what else would you like to know about the Suez Canal and the Panama Canal? Write a list of questions.
15 Where could you look for the answers? List as many different sources as you can.

Talk

25

15. E.g. books / magazines / the internet.

RESOURCE SHEET SUPPORT ANSWERS

A

The Suez Canal	The Panama Canal
opened in 1869	connects Atlantic Ocean with Pacific Ocean
connects Red Sea with Mediterranean Sea	82 kilometres long
165 kilometres long	opened in 1914
built in Egypt	built in Central America

B

1. not put there by man – natural
2. connects – joins
3. ocean – large area of salt water
4. usually – most of the time

GOING DEEPER

- Use the children's ideas for 'Taking it further' as the basis for a discussion.

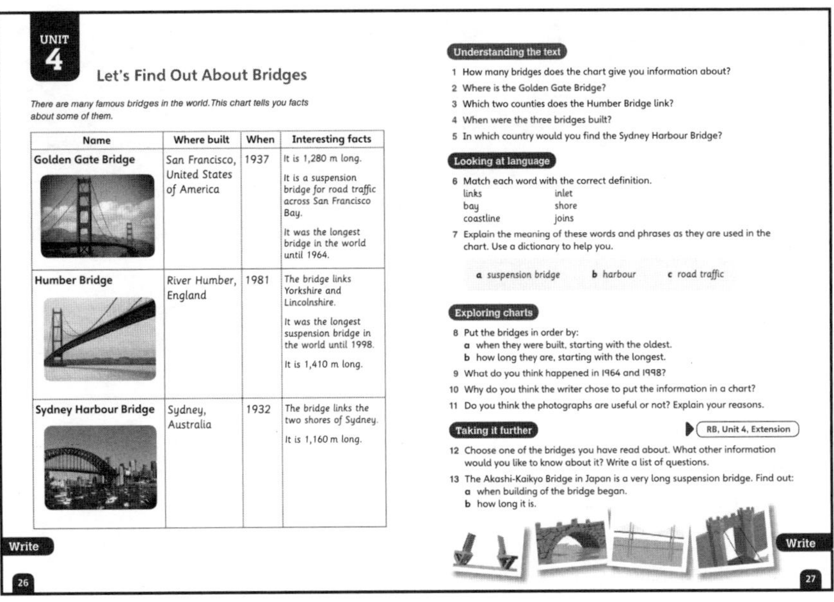

UNIT 4

Let's Find Out About Bridges

There are many famous bridges in the world. This chart tells you facts about some of them.

Name	Where built	When	Interesting facts
Golden Gate Bridge	San Francisco, United States of America	1937	It is 1,280 m long. It is a suspension bridge for road traffic across San Francisco Bay. It was the longest bridge in the world until 1964.
Humber Bridge	River Humber, England	1981	The bridge links Yorkshire and Lincolnshire. It was the longest suspension bridge in the world until 1998. It is 1,410 m long.
Sydney Harbour Bridge	Sydney, Australia	1932	The bridge links the two shores of Sydney. It is 1,160 m long.

Write

26

Understanding the text

1 How many bridges does the chart give you information about?
2 Where is the Golden Gate Bridge?
3 Which two counties does the Humber Bridge link?
4 When were the three bridges built?
5 In which country would you find the Sydney Harbour Bridge?

Looking at language

6 Match each word with the correct definition.
links inlet
bay shore
coastline joins
7 Explain the meaning of these words and phrases as they are used in the chart. Use a dictionary to help you.
a suspension bridge b harbour c road traffic

Exploring charts

8 Put the bridges in order by:
a when they were built, starting with the oldest.
b how long they are, starting with the longest.
9 What do you think happened in 1964 and 1998?
10 Why do you think the writer chose to put the information in a chart?
11 Do you think the photographs are useful or not? Explain your reasons.

Taking it further RB, Unit 4, Extension

12 Choose one of the bridges you have read about. What other information would you like to know about it? Write a list of questions.
13 The Akashi-Kaikyo Bridge in Japan is a very long suspension bridge. Find out:
a when building of the bridge began.
b how long it is.

Write

27

WRITE

- Ask children what they understand by the term 'bridge'.
- Ask if they know any famous bridges and if they have been across any big bridges. Do they cross bridges regularly? Why?
- Explain to children that they are going to read some facts about bridges presented in the form of a chart.
- Read the text to the class; ask individual children to read it aloud in turn; or read in silence individually.

RESOURCES & ASSESSMENT BOOK

- **Support** (comprehension support): completing sentences; (vocabulary support): identifying verbs and nouns.
- **Extension:** writing questions and finding information.

PUPIL BOOK ANSWERS

1. Three.
2. San Francisco, America.
3. Yorkshire and Lincolnshire.
4. Golden Gate Bridge: 1937 / Humber Bridge: 1981 / Sydney Harbour Bridge: 1932.
5. Australia.
6. Links – joins, bay – inlet, coastline – shore.
7. **a** suspension bridge: a type of bridge that hangs from strong steel ropes that are fixed to towers **b** harbour: an area of water near land where it is safe for boats to stay **c** road traffic: cars, lorries etc – vehicles that travel on roads
8. **a** Sydney Harbour Bridge, Golden Gate Bridge, Humber Bridge **b** Humber Bridge, Golden Gate Bridge, Sydney Harbour Bridge
9. 1964: a longer bridge than the Golden Gate Bridge was built.
   1998: a longer suspension bridge than the Humber Bridge was built.
10. Answers that suggest this way of presenting the information makes it clearer and easier to read and compare.
11. Answers that suggest the photographs are useful because they allow the reader to see the bridges that are being written about.
12. Individual answers.
13. **a** 1988 **b** 1,991 metres

RESOURCE SHEET SUPPORT ANSWERS

A

The Golden Gate Bridage:

1. San Francisco *[accept America]*
2. 1937
3. 1,280

The Humber Bridge:

1. River Humber
2. 1981
3. 1,410

Sydney Harbour Bridge:

1. Australia *[accept Sydney]*
2. 1932
3. 1,160

B

1. was / built / links
2. bridge / river / shores

GOING DEEPER

- Give children the opportunity to investigate the Akashi-Kaikyo Bridge and encourage them to use the internet. Compose a non-chronological report as a class.

UNIT FOCUS: Features of Myths and Legends

Investigating ...

- common features of myths and legends
- how stories unfold
- how to predict story endings

TEACH

- Discuss adventure stories / films with children.
- Ask children what they think the hero / heroine of the story / film usually has to do.
- Ask children if they understand the term 'quest'.
- Lead children to understand the features of many adventure stories involving a quest, i.e. something has to be found / dangers on the way / help from other people / battles with enemies.
- Ask children if they have heard of Perseus and / or Medusa and what they know about them.
- Explain that they are going to read about Perseus and his dangerous quest to bring back Medusa's head.
- Read the extract to the class; ask individual children to read it aloud in turn; or read in silence individually.

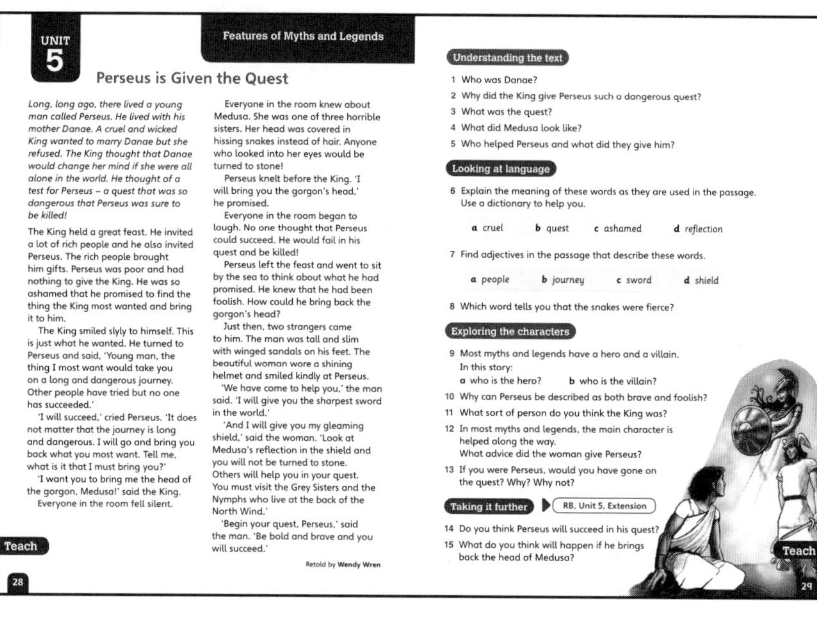

UNIT 5

Features of Myths and Legends

Perseus is Given the Quest

Long, long ago, there lived a young man called Perseus. He lived with his mother Danae. A cruel and wicked King wanted to marry Danae but she refused. The King thought that Danae would change her mind if she were all alone in the world. He thought of a test for Perseus – a quest that was so dangerous that Perseus was sure to be killed!

The King held a great feast. He invited a lot of rich people and he also invited Perseus. The rich people brought him gifts. Perseus was poor and had nothing to give the King. He was so ashamed that he promised to find the thing the King most wanted and bring it to him.

The King smiled slyly to himself. This is just what he wanted. He turned to Perseus and said, 'Young man, the thing I most want would take you on a long and dangerous journey. Other people have tried but no one has succeeded.'

'I will succeed,' cried Perseus. 'It does not matter that the journey is long and dangerous. I will go and bring you back what you most want. Tell me, what is it that I must bring you?'

'I want you to bring me the head of the gorgon, Medusa!' said the King.

Everyone in the room fell silent.

Everyone in the room knew about Medusa. She was one of three horrible sisters. Her head was covered in hissing snakes instead of hair. Anyone who looked into her eyes would be turned to stone!

Perseus knelt before the King. 'I will bring you the gorgon's head,' he promised.

Everyone in the room began to laugh. No one thought that Perseus could succeed. He would fail in his quest and be killed!

Perseus left the feast and went to sit by the sea to think about what he had promised. He knew that he had been foolish. How could he bring back the gorgon's head?

Just then, two strangers came to him. The man was tall and slim with winged sandals on his feet. The beautiful woman wore a shining helmet and smiled kindly at Perseus.

'We have come to help you,' the man said. 'I will give you the sharpest sword in the world.'

'And I will give you my gleaming shield,' said the woman. 'Look at Medusa's reflection in the shield and you will not be turned to stone. Others will help you in your quest. You must visit the Grey Sisters and the Nymphs who live at the back of the North Wind.'

'Begin your quest, Perseus,' said the man. 'Be bold and brave and you will succeed.'

Retold by **Wendy Wren**

Teach

28

Understanding the text

1 Who was Danae?
2 Why did the King give Perseus such a dangerous quest?
3 What was the quest?
4 What did Medusa look like?
5 Who helped Perseus and what did they give him?

Looking at language

6 Explain the meaning of these words as they are used in the passage. Use a dictionary to help you.
a *cruel* **b** *quest* **c** *ashamed* **d** *reflection*

7 Find adjectives in the passage that describe these words.
a *people* **b** *journey* **c** *sword* **d** *shield*

8 Which word tells you that the snakes were fierce?

Exploring the characters

9 Most myths and legends have a hero and a villain. In this story:
a who is the hero? **b** who is the villain?
10 Why can Perseus be described as both brave and foolish?
11 What sort of person do you think the King was?
12 In most myths and legends, the main character is helped along the way. What advice did the woman give Perseus?
13 If you were Perseus, would you have gone on the quest? Why? Why not?

Taking it further RB, Unit 5, Extension

14 Do you think Perseus will succeed in his quest?
15 What do you think will happen if he brings back the head of Medusa?

Teach

29

RESOURCES & ASSESSMENT BOOK

- **Support** (comprehension support): identifying the speaker; (vocabulary support): using adjectives in cloze activity.
- **Extension:** predicting an outcome.

PUPIL BOOK ANSWERS

1. Danae was the mother of Perseus.
2. The King wanted Perseus out of the way so he could marry the boy's mother, Danae.
3. The quest was to bring back the head of Medusa.
4. Medusa's head was covered with hissing snakes.
5. Perseus was helped by a tall, slim man with winged sandals, and a beautiful woman with a shining helmet. The woman gave him a 'gleaming shield' and the man gave him 'the sharpest sword in the world'.
6. **a** cruel: like to see or cause pain **b** quest: a search for something that usually involves danger **c** ashamed: sorry for something / embarrassed **d** reflection: as if looking in a mirror
7. **a** people: rich **b** journey: long / dangerous **c** sword: sharpest **d** shield: gleaming
8. 'hissing'.
9. **a** Perseus **b** The King
10. Answers that suggest that Perseus was:
    – brave because he went through with his promise in spite of the danger and probably certain death
    – foolish in making the promise to 'find the thing the King most wanted' without having any idea what that was.
11. Answers that suggest the King was cruel / sly / scheming and would stop at nothing to get what he wanted.
12. The woman told Perseus to 'Look at Medusa's reflection in the shield and you will not be turned to stone'.
13. Individual answers.
14. Individual answers.
15. Individual answers.

RESOURCE SHEET SUPPORT ANSWERS

A

1. the man
2. the King
3. Perseus
4. the woman

B

The King sent Perseus on a **dangerous** journey. He had to bring back the head of Medusa. The head was covered in **hissing** snakes. A **tall, slim** man gave him the **sharpest** sword in the world. A **beautiful** woman gave him her **gleaming** shield.

GOING DEEPER

- Remind children of the common features of a 'quest' story and ask them what they think happens next.

TALK

- Ask children to recap the story so far.
- Ask children to predict what they think may happen next.
- Read the extract to the class; ask individual children to read it aloud in turn; or read in silence individually.

RESOURCES & ASSESSMENT BOOK

- **Support** (comprehension support): narrative sequence; (vocabulary support): identifying groups of words.
- **Extension:** predicting and writing notes.

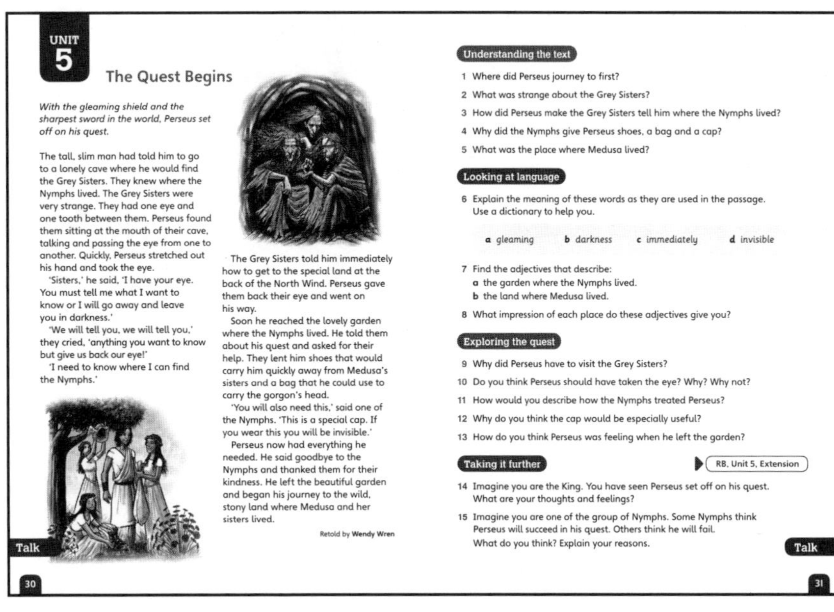

UNIT 5

The Quest Begins

With the gleaming shield and the sharpest sword in the world, Perseus set off on his quest.

The tall, slim man had told him to go to a lonely cave where he would find the Grey Sisters. They knew where the Nymphs lived. The Grey Sisters were very strange. They had one eye and one tooth between them. Perseus found them sitting at the mouth of their cave, talking and passing the eye from one to another. Quickly, Perseus stretched out his hand and took the eye.

'Sisters,' he said, 'I have your eye. You must tell me what I want to know or I will go away and leave you in darkness.'

'We will tell you, we will tell you,' they cried, 'anything you want to know but give us back our eye!'

'I need to know where I can find the Nymphs.'

The Grey Sisters told him immediately how to get to the special land at the back of the North Wind. Perseus gave them back their eye and went on his way.

Soon he reached the lovely garden where the Nymphs lived. He told them about his quest and asked for their help. They lent him shoes that would carry him quickly away from Medusa's sisters and a bag that he could use to carry the gorgon's head.

'You will also need this,' said one of the Nymphs. 'This is a special cap. If you wear this you will be invisible.'

Perseus now had everything he needed. He said goodbye to the Nymphs and thanked them for their kindness. He left the beautiful garden and began his journey to the wild, stony land where Medusa and her sisters lived.

Retold by **Wendy Wren**

Talk

30

Understanding the text

1 Where did Perseus journey to first?
2 What was strange about the Grey Sisters?
3 How did Perseus make the Grey Sisters tell him where the Nymphs lived?
4 Why did the Nymphs give Perseus shoes, a bag and a cap?
5 What was the place where Medusa lived?

Looking at language

6 Explain the meaning of these words as they are used in the passage. Use a dictionary to help you.

a *gleaming* **b** *darkness* **c** *immediately* **d** *invisible*

7 Find the adjectives that describe:
a the garden where the Nymphs lived.
b the land where Medusa lived.
8 What impression of each place do these adjectives give you?

Exploring the quest

9 Why did Perseus have to visit the Grey Sisters?
10 Do you think Perseus should have taken the eye? Why? Why not?
11 How would you describe how the Nymphs treated Perseus?
12 Why do you think the cap would be especially useful?
13 How do you think Perseus was feeling when he left the garden?

Taking it further RB, Unit 5, Extension

14 Imagine you are the King. You have seen Perseus set off on his quest. What are your thoughts and feelings?
15 Imagine you are one of the group of Nymphs. Some Nymphs think Perseus will succeed in his quest. Others think he will fail. What do you think? Explain your reasons.

Talk

31

PUPIL BOOK ANSWERS

1. Perseus first journeyed to the Grey Sisters.
2. The Grey Sisters only had one eye and one tooth between them.
3. Perseus took the eye and would only give it back if they told him where the Nymphs lived.
4. The Nymphs gave Perseus:
   – shoes 'to carry him quickly way from Medusa's sisters'
   – a bag to 'carry the gorgon's head'
   – a cap to make him invisible.
5. Medusa lived in a 'wild, stony land'.
6. **a** gleaming: shining / highly polished **b** darkness: inability to see **c** immediately: straight away / at once **d** invisible: not visible / not able to be seen
7. **a** lovely **b** wild / stony
8. Individual answers.
9. Perseus had to visit the Grey Sisters to find out where the Nymphs lived.
10. Individual answers suggesting that the information was vital to Perseus but his actions can be seen as cruel.
11. They treated him with great kindness and helped him with his quest.
12. Answers that suggest Perseus could use the cap to sneak up on the gorgons without being seen and he could make his escape without being seen.
13. Individual answers.
14. Individual answers that suggest the King is very sure he will never see Perseus again.
15. Encourage children in each group to take different sides. Some will be sure Perseus will succeed: others that he will fail. Children should think about:
   – why he will succeed e.g. he is brave / he has been given help by the strangers and the Nymphs / he has made a promise
   – why he will fail e.g. the gorgons are fearful creatures / how will he avoid being accidently turned to stone / he is one young man against three dangerous creatures.

RESOURCE SHEET SUPPORT ANSWERS

A

1. 4
2. 3
3. 1
4. 9
5. 6
6. 2
7. 5
8. 8
9. 10
10. 7

B

1. eye / tooth / hand / head
2. shoes / cap
3. a lonely cave / the land at the back of the North Wind *[accept lovely garden]* / wild, stony land

GOING DEEPER

- Use children's ideas for the 'Taking it further' activity as a basis for a class discussion.

WRITE

- Ask the children to recap on the story so far and to say what they think will happen next.
- Read the extract to the class; ask individual children to read it aloud in turn; or read in silence individually.

RESOURCES & ASSESSMENT BOOK

- **Support** (comprehension support): identifying True / False statements; (vocabulary support): identifying adverbs.
- **Extension:** completing a story chart, labelling drawings.

PUPIL BOOK ANSWERS

1 He knew which one was Medusa because her head was covered in hissing snakes.

2 He put on the cap so that he was invisible.

3 The snakes hissed loudly and woke up Medusa's sisters.

4 Perseus's mother had been made a slave by the King.

5 He was turned to stone.

6 **a** mighty: powerful / strong **b** rage: anger **c** escaped: got away **d** disbelief: couldn't believe what he saw

7 **a** quickly / quietly **b** loudly **c** swiftly

8 Individual answers.

9 'screaming with rage'.

10 The King would think Perseus was dead because it was such a dangerous quest, he didn't think there was any chance of Perseus surviving it.

11 12 13 Individual answers.

14

Place	What happened
by the sea	Perseus met two strangers. The man gave him 'the sharpest sword in the world' and the woman gave him a 'gleaming shield'.
the Cave of the Grey Sisters	Perseus stole their one eye and they told him where the Nymphs lived.
the land of the Nymphs	Perseus asked for help. The Nymphs gave him shoes, a bag and a cap to help him on his quest.
the land where the gorgons lived	Perseus slew Medusa, put her head in the bag and made his escape.
the palace	Perseus gave the king what he wanted – the head of Medusa – and the King turned to stone.

UNIT 5

Perseus Meets Medusa

After his long journey, Perseus finally arrived at the gorgons' lair.

As Perseus came near to where the gorgons lived, he saw statues of men and animals that had been turned to stone. Then he saw a frightening sight! The three gorgons were lying asleep in the sun. He knew which one was Medusa as her head was covered in hissing snakes.

Quickly and quietly, Perseus put on the cap that made him invisible. He held up the gleaming shield and looked at Medusa's reflection in it. He drew the sharpest sword in the world and with one mighty blow, cut off her head. He picked it up and put it into the bag.

The snakes hissed loudly and woke up Medusa's sisters. They saw what had happened and jumped up. As they tried to grab Perseus, he jumped into the air and the shoes took him swiftly away. They followed him, screaming with rage, but the shoes were too quick for them. Perseus escaped and returned to his homeland.

When he got there, he found that all was not well. His mother had been made a slave by the wicked King. Perseus knew what he had to do. The King would think Perseus was dead. He would not be expecting the young man to turn up at the palace.

Perseus visited the King at the palace. All those who had laughed at him were there. One of them said, 'Well, well, here is Perseus. Have you brought the gorgon's head with you?' And they all laughed again.

Perseus walked up to the King who said, 'So you have come back. Have you brought me my present?'

'Indeed I have,' said Perseus. He pulled Medusa's head out of the bag and held it up for all to see. Perseus made sure he did not look at it but those who did turned to stone. The King was one of them, and on his stone face was a look of fear and disbelief!

Retold by **Wendy Wren**

Write

32

Understanding the text

1 How did Perseus know which gorgon was Medusa?

2 What did Perseus do first? Why?

3 Why did Medusa's sisters wake up?

4 What had happened to Perseus's mother while he was away?

5 What happened to the King at the end of the story?

Looking at language

6 Explain the meaning of these words as they are used in the story. Use a dictionary to help you.

a *mighty* **b** *rage* **c** *escaped* **d** *disbelief*

7 Find adverbs in the story that tell you:
- a how Perseus put on the cap.
- b how the snakes hissed.
- c how the shoes took Perseus away.

Exploring the story ending

8 How do you think Perseus felt when he saw the three gorgons?

9 What phrase in the story tells you that Medusa's sisters were angry?

10 Why would the King think Perseus was dead?

11 How do you think Perseus felt when everyone laughed at him this time?

12 Do you think Perseus should have turned the King to stone? Why? Why not?

13 What do think happened to Perseus and his mother after the King was dead?

Taking it further RB, Unit 5, Extension

14 Make a list of the places Perseus went after he left the palace. Summarise what happened in each place.

15 Perseus's quest began and ended in the King's palace. Draw a map of his journey. Label it, showing where he went and who he met.

Write

33

15 Individual answers.

RESOURCE SHEET SUPPORT ANSWERS

A

1 True

2 False

3 False

4 True

5 True

6 False

7 True

8 False

9 True

10 False

B

1 a

2 b

3 a

GOING DEEPER

- Ask children if they enjoyed the story and why. Recap on the features of the story.

UNIT FOCUS: Following Instructions

Investigating …

- a variety of instructional text for playing a game, cooking and following directions
- common features of text types

TEACH

- Ask children what they know by the term 'instruction' and if they can give any examples.
- Ask children if they have ever used instructions and, if so, what for.
- Ask individual children to help you explain how to play a simple game.
- Explain that they are going to read a set of instructions for playing the game 'charades'.
- Read the extract to the class; ask individual children to read it aloud in turn; or read in silence individually.

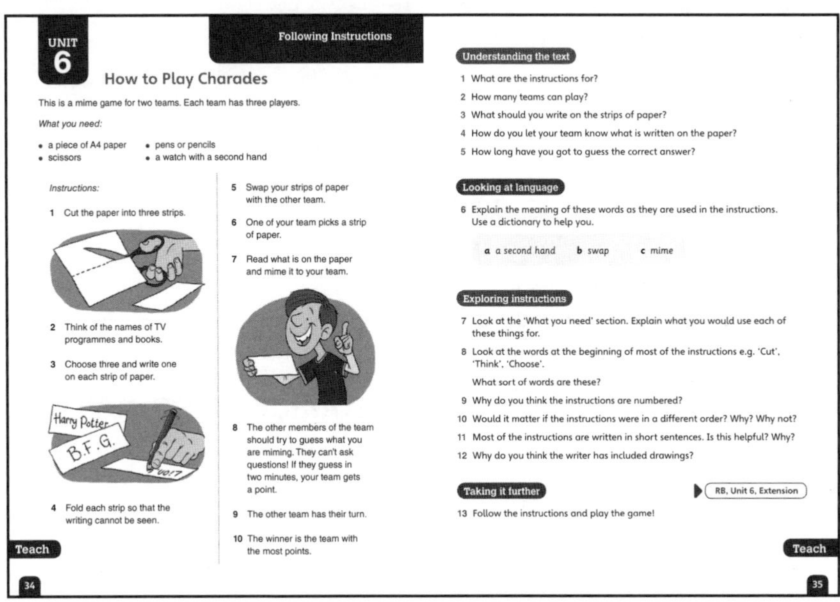

UNIT 6 Following Instructions

How to Play Charades

This is a mime game for two teams. Each team has three players.

What you need:

- a piece of A4 paper
- scissors
- pens or pencils
- a watch with a second hand

Instructions:

1 Cut the paper into three strips.

2 Think of the names of TV programmes and books.

3 Choose three and write one on each strip of paper.

4 Fold each strip so that the writing cannot be seen.

5 Swap your strips of paper with the other team.

6 One of your team picks a strip of paper.

7 Read what is on the paper and mime it to your team.

8 The other members of the team should try to guess what you are miming. They can't ask questions! If they guess in two minutes, your team gets a point.

9 The other team has their turn.

10 The winner is the team with the most points.

Teach 34

Understanding the text

1 What are the instructions for?
2 How many teams can play?
3 What should you write on the strips of paper?
4 How do you let your team know what is written on the paper?
5 How long have you got to guess the correct answer?

Looking at language

6 Explain the meaning of these words as they are used in the instructions. Use a dictionary to help you.

a a second hand **b** swap **c** mime

Exploring instructions

7 Look at the 'What you need' section. Explain what you would use each of these things for.
8 Look at the words at the beginning of most of the instructions e.g. 'Cut', 'Think', 'Choose'.

What sort of words are these?

9 Why do you think the instructions are numbered?
10 Would it matter if the instructions were in a different order? Why? Why not?
11 Most of the instructions are written in short sentences. Is this helpful? Why?
12 Why do you think the writer has included drawings?

Taking it further

RB, Unit 6, Extension

13 Follow the instructions and play the game!

Teach 35

RESOURCES & ASSESSMENT BOOK

- **Support** (comprehension support): explaining what to do; (vocabulary support): identifying and using imperative verbs.
- **Extension:** following instructions to play a game.

PUPIL BOOK ANSWERS

1. A game called Charades.
2. Two.
3. Book titles and TV programmes.
4. Through mime.
5. Two minutes.
6. **a** a second hand: a hand on a watch that moves every second **b** swap: exchange **c** mime: silently act
7. **a** piece of A4 paper: to write the titles of books and TV **b** programmes on pens or pencils: to write with **c** scissors: to cut the paper into strips **d** a watch with a second hand: to time the other team
8. Imperative verbs.
9. So they can be followed in the correct order.
10. Yes. The game would not work if the instructions were muddled up.
11. Yes. They are very easy to understand.
12. The drawings help you to see what you have to do.
13. Individual answers.

RESOURCE SHEET SUPPORT ANSWERS

A

1. to cut the paper into strips
2. the names of TV programmes and books
3. the names of TV programmes and books
4. the pieces of folded paper
5. mime what is on the paper

B

1. Fold each strip so that it cannot be seen.
2. Read what is on the paper.
3. Guess what they are miming.

C

Individual answers.

GOING DEEPER

- Recap on the features of: imperative verbs, numbering in order and short simple sentences. If time allows, children can work in groups, follow the instructions and play the game.

TALK

- Discuss cooking with children. Do they cook? Do they like cooking?
- If children do cook, ask what is their favourite thing to cook.
- Discuss what the children would expect to find in a recipe book.
- Explain that they are going to look at a recipe for making chocolate fudge sauce.
- Read the recipe to the class; ask individual children to read it aloud in turn; or read in silence individually.

RESOURCES & ASSESSMENT BOOK

- **Support** (comprehension support): choosing the correct sentence endings; (vocabulary support): matching words and meanings, identifying adjectives.
- **Extension:** writing instructions.

PUPIL BOOK ANSWERS

1. Making chocolate fudge sauce.
2. The chocolate and condensed milk.
3. The marshmallows.
4. Ice cream.
5. Hot or cold.
6. Put / Place / Cut / Stir / Beat / Serve.
7. **a** finely: very small, thin pieces **b** medium: moderate / not too high / not too low **c** mixture: things stirred together **d** smooth: even / not rough and lumpy
8. It tells you what ingredients you will need. You can get everything together before you begin.
9. **a** They make the instructions easier to understand. **b** They give you a good idea of what you should be doing and what the mixture should look like. **c** The numbers tell you the order in which you should do things.
10. Individual answers suggesting that Instruction Number 9 should be: Allow the sauce to cool before eating.
11. Individual answers. Encourage children to give reasons for their answer.
12. Individual answers. Encourage all members of the group to contribute. One child can take notes of the discussion.

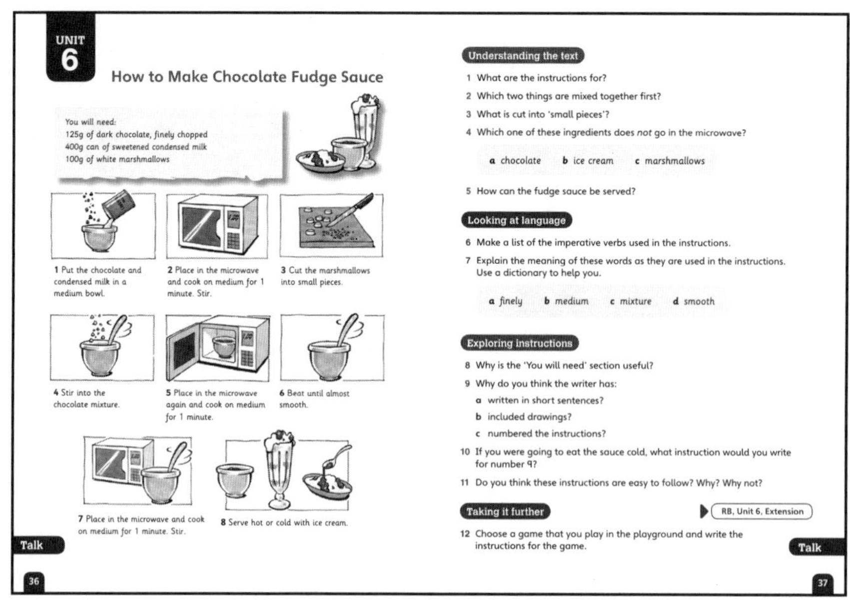

UNIT 6

How to Make Chocolate Fudge Sauce

You will need:
125g of dark chocolate, finely chopped
400g can of sweetened condensed milk
100g of white marshmallows

1 Put the chocolate and condensed milk in a medium bowl.

2 Place in the microwave and cook on medium for 1 minute. Stir.

3 Cut the marshmallows into small pieces.

4 Stir into the chocolate mixture.

5 Place in the microwave again and cook on medium for 1 minute.

6 Beat until almost smooth.

7 Place in the microwave and cook on medium for 1 minute. Stir.

8 Serve hot or cold with ice cream.

Talk

36

Understanding the text

1 What are the instructions for?
2 Which two things are mixed together first?
3 What is cut into 'small pieces'?
4 Which one of these ingredients does *not* go in the microwave?

a chocolate **b** ice cream **c** marshmallows

5 How can the fudge sauce be served?

Looking at language

6 Make a list of the imperative verbs used in the instructions.
7 Explain the meaning of these words as they are used in the instructions. Use a dictionary to help you.

a finely **b** medium **c** mixture **d** smooth

Exploring instructions

8 Why is the 'You will need' section useful?
9 Why do you think the writer has:
  a written in short sentences?
  b included drawings?
  c numbered the instructions?
10 If you were going to eat the sauce cold, what instruction would you write for number 9?
11 Do you think these instructions are easy to follow? Why? Why not?

Taking it further RB, Unit 6, Extension

12 Choose a game that you play in the playground and write the instructions for the game.

Talk

37

RESOURCE SHEET SUPPORT ANSWERS

A

1. into a bowl
2. cut them into small pieces
3. into the chocolate mixture
4. with ice cream

B

1. finely – very small, thin pieces
2. medium – not too high, not too low
3. mixture – things stirred together
4. smooth – even, not rough or lumpy

C

1. dark
2. sweetened
3. white

GOING DEEPER

- In groups, let children follow some of the instructions in the 'Taking it further' Pupil Book activity. The person or group who has written the instructions can watch and, if necessary, amend them where it is obvious they are not clear or if stages have been missed out.

WRITE

- Ask children what they would do if someone asked them for directions to their school from the street where they live.
- Encourage children to draw a map, write a list and / or tell you how they would get there.
- Explain they are going to read a set of instructions that give directions from one place to another.
- Read the instructions to the class; ask individual children to read it aloud in turn; or read in silence individually.

RESOURCES & ASSESSMENT BOOK

- **Support** (comprehension support): identifying True / False statements; (vocabulary support): identifying vocabulary from picture stimulus.
- **Extension:** writing a set of directions.

PUPIL BOOK ANSWERS

1. Greenly.
2. Bridgeton.
3. Right.
4. Five miles.
5. The first exit.
6. **a** the Internet: source of lots of information accessed through a computer **b** crossroads: where two roads cross each other **c** traffic lights: lights that tell vehicles when to stop and when to go **d** exit: way out **e** roundabout: circular traffic island where lots of roads meet **f** T-junction: where two roads meet to form 'T'
7. Any three of: Greenly / Park Road / Frog Lane / Grange Road / Bank Lane / Bridgeton.
8. Leave / Turn / Go / Take / Arrive.
9. The arrows help you to know the direction you are going in.
10. Individual answers suggesting that this makes them easier to follow.

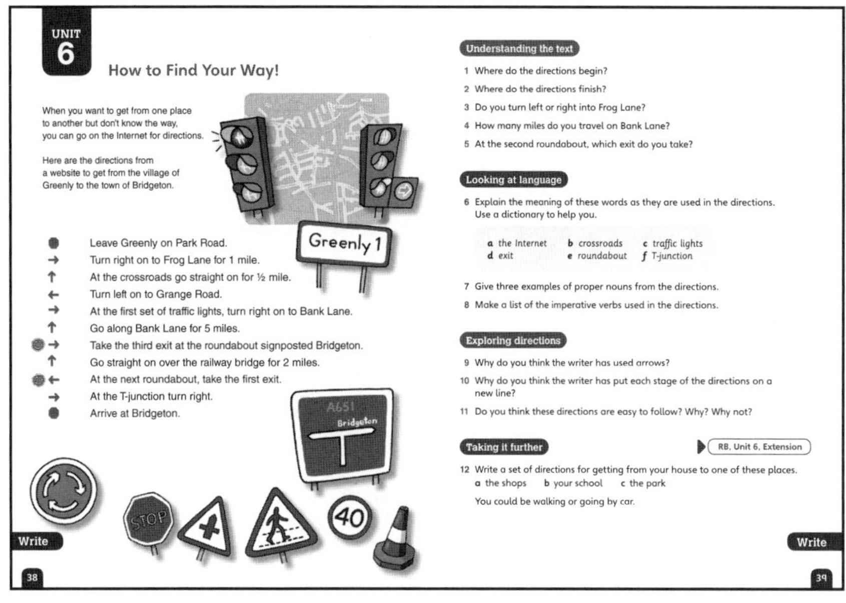

UNIT 6

How to Find Your Way!

When you want to get from one place to another but don't know the way, you can go on the Internet for directions.

Here are the directions from a website to get from the village of Greenly to the town of Bridgeton.

- Leave Greenly on Park Road.
- → Turn right on to Frog Lane for 1 mile.
- ↑ At the crossroads go straight on for ½ mile.
- ← Turn left on to Grange Road.
- → At the first set of traffic lights, turn right on to Bank Lane.
- ↑ Go along Bank Lane for 5 miles.
- → Take the third exit at the roundabout signposted Bridgeton.
- ↑ Go straight on over the railway bridge for 2 miles.
- ← At the next roundabout, take the first exit.
- → At the T-junction turn right.
- Arrive at Bridgeton.

Write

38

Understanding the text

1 Where do the directions begin?
2 Where do the directions finish?
3 Do you turn left or right into Frog Lane?
4 How many miles do you travel on Bank Lane?
5 At the second roundabout, which exit do you take?

Looking at language

6 Explain the meaning of these words as they are used in the directions. Use a dictionary to help you.
a the Internet **b** crossroads **c** traffic lights
d exit **e** roundabout **f** T-junction

7 Give three examples of proper nouns from the directions.
8 Make a list of the imperative verbs used in the directions.

Exploring directions

9 Why do you think the writer has used arrows?
10 Why do you think the writer has put each stage of the directions on a new line?
11 Do you think these directions are easy to follow? Why? Why not?

Taking it further RB, Unit 6, Extension

12 Write a set of directions for getting from your house to one of these places.
a the shops **b** your school **c** the park
You could be walking or going by car.

Write

39

11. Individual answers. Encourage children to give reasons for their answers.
12. Individual answers.

RESOURCE SHEET SUPPORT ANSWERS

A

1. True
2. False
3. True
4. True
5. False
6. True
7. True
8. False
9. False
10. True

B

1. crossroads
2. roundabout
3. T-junction
4. traffic lights

GOING DEEPER

- Re-cap on the features of instructional texts. Using some of the children's work from the 'Writing instructions' activities, discuss if they have used these features and assess whether they are easy to understand.

UNIT FOCUS: Speech in Narrative and Plays

Investigating ...

- dialogue in the form of narratives and playscripts
- converting parts of stories into playscripts
- writing plays

TEACH

- Discuss the idea of friendship with the children.
- Why do they need friends?
- What makes a good friend?
- Do their friends have to be human? Do they have to be the same age / gender?
- Explain to the children that they are going to read:
  - a narrative called *The Lion and the Mouse*
  - a play scene called *The Lion and the Mouse.*
- Read the extracts to the class; ask individual children to read them aloud; or read in silence individually.

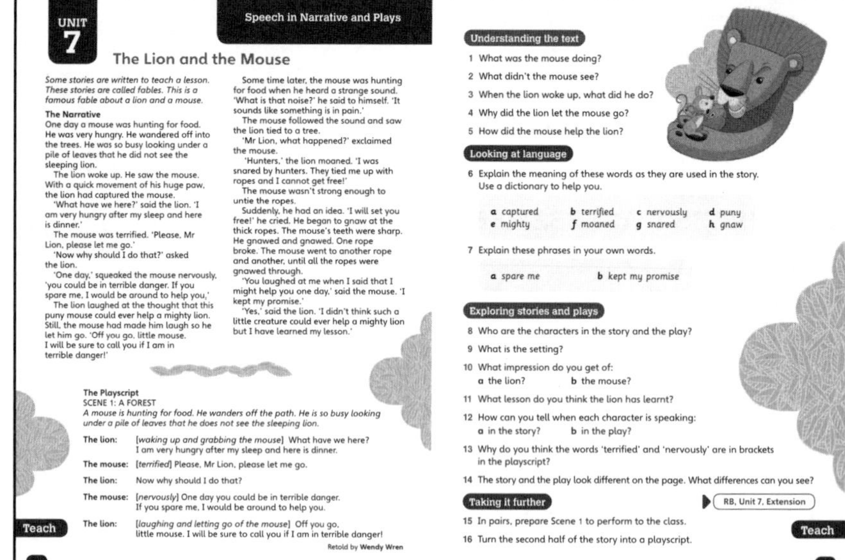
UNIT 7

Speech in Narrative and Plays

The Lion and the Mouse

Some stories are written to teach a lesson. These stories are called fables. This is a famous fable about a lion and a mouse.

The Narrative

One day a mouse was hunting for food. He was very hungry. He wandered off into the trees. He was so busy looking under a pile of leaves that he did not see the sleeping lion.

The lion woke up. He saw the mouse. With a quick movement of his huge paw, the lion had captured the mouse.

'What have we here?' said the lion. 'I am very hungry after my sleep and here is dinner.'

The mouse was terrified. 'Please, Mr Lion, please let me go.'

'Now why should I do that?' asked the lion.

'One day,' squeaked the mouse nervously, 'you could be in terrible danger. If you spare me, I would be around to help you,'

The lion laughed at the thought that this puny mouse could ever help a mighty lion. Still, the mouse had made him laugh so he let him go. 'Off you go, little mouse. I will be sure to call you if I am in terrible danger!'

Some time later, the mouse was hunting for food when he heard a strange sound. 'What is that noise?' he said to himself. 'It sounds like something is in pain.'

The mouse followed the sound and saw the lion tied to a tree.

'Mr Lion, what happened?' exclaimed the mouse.

'Hunters,' the lion moaned. 'I was snared by hunters. They tied me up with ropes and I cannot get free!'

The mouse wasn't strong enough to untie the ropes.

Suddenly, he had an idea. 'I will set you free!' he cried. He began to gnaw at the thick ropes. The mouse's teeth were sharp. He gnawed and gnawed. One rope broke. The mouse went to another rope and another, until all the ropes were gnawed through.

'You laughed at me when I said that I might help you one day,' said the mouse. 'I kept my promise.'

'Yes,' said the lion. 'I didn't think such a little creature could ever help a mighty lion but I have learned my lesson.'

The Playscript

SCENE 1: A FOREST

A mouse is hunting for food. He wanders off the path. He is so busy looking under a pile of leaves that he does not see the sleeping lion.

The lion: [*waking up and grabbing the mouse*] What have we here? I am very hungry after my sleep and here is dinner.

The mouse: [*terrified*] Please, Mr Lion, please let me go.

The lion: Now why should I do that?

The mouse: [*nervously*] One day you could be in terrible danger. If you spare me, I would be around to help you.

The lion: [*laughing and letting go of the mouse*] Off you go, little mouse. I will be sure to call you if I am in terrible danger!

Retold by **Wendy Wren**

Teach

40

Understanding the text

1 What was the mouse doing?
2 What didn't the mouse see?
3 When the lion woke up, what did he do?
4 Why did the lion let the mouse go?
5 How did the mouse help the lion?

Looking at language

6 Explain the meaning of these words as they are used in the story. Use a dictionary to help you.

a captured b terrified c nervously d puny e mighty f moaned g snared h gnaw

7 Explain these phrases in your own words.

a spare me b kept my promise

Exploring stories and plays

8 Who are the characters in the story and the play?
9 What is the setting?
10 What impression do you get of: a the lion? b the mouse?
11 What lesson do you think the lion has learnt?
12 How can you tell when each character is speaking: a in the story? b in the play?
13 Why do you think the words 'terrified' and 'nervously' are in brackets in the playscript?
14 The story and the play look different on the page. What differences can you see?

Taking it further

RB, Unit 7, Extension

15 In pairs, prepare Scene 1 to perform to the class.
16 Turn the second half of the story into a playscript.

Teach

41

RESOURCES & ASSESSMENT BOOK

- **Support** (comprehension support): choosing the correct answer; (vocabulary support): cloze activity for vocabulary reinforcement.
- **Extension:** preparing and performing a playscript.

PUPIL BOOK ANSWERS

1 Hunting for food.

2 The sleeping lion.

3 The lion captured the mouse with his huge paw.

4 The mouse had made him laugh.

5 The mouse gnawed through the ropes that the hunters had used to tie the lion to a tree.

6 **a** captured: caught **b** terrified: very frightened **c** nervously: worriedly / anxiously **d** puny: small, thin and weak **e** mighty: great and powerful **f** moaned: made a long, low sound due to pain **g** snared: trapped **h** gnaw: bite through

7 **a** spare me: let me go
b kept my promise: did what I said I would do

8 The mouse / the lion / [the hunters].

9 A forest.

10 **a** the lion: large and fierce but has a sense of humour **b** the mouse: small and weak but very determined / brave

11 Not to judge by appearances. Even a weak creature has talents that could help a strong one.

12 **a** speech marks at the beginning and end of the spoken words **b** the character's name on the left of the page – the words spoken on the right

13 They are instructions to the actor as to how to say the words.

14 Individual answers that consider:
– the story is written continuously using paragraphs
– the play is set out with characters' names on the left and speech on the right.

15 16 Pair work.

RESOURCE SHEET SUPPORT ANSWERS

A

1 b

2 a

3 b

4 c

5 b

B

When the lion saw the mouse, he **captured** him with his paw. The mouse was **terrified**. He squeaked **nervously**. The lion thought the mouse was **puny**. One day, the mouse heard the lion in pain. The lion **moaned**. He was **snared** by hunters. The mouse **gnawed** at the ropes and set the lion free.

GOING DEEPER

- Investigate the way in which dialogue is presented in the:
  - narrative: speech marks / new paragraph for new person speaking
  - the play: no speech marks / dialogue next to the character speaking.

  In pairs, children can prepare the scene. If time permits, ask some pairs to perform for the class.

TALK

- Discuss what sort of people the children choose as friends.
- Ask children the sort of things that may make people stop being friends.
- Explain to the children that they are going to read a short scene from a play where two friends are on a camping trip.
- Read the extract to the class; ask individual children to read it aloud; or read in silence individually.

RESOURCES & ASSESSMENT BOOK

- **Support** (comprehension support): cloze activity; (vocabulary support): identifying stage directions and dialogue.
- **Extension:** preparing and performing a playscript.

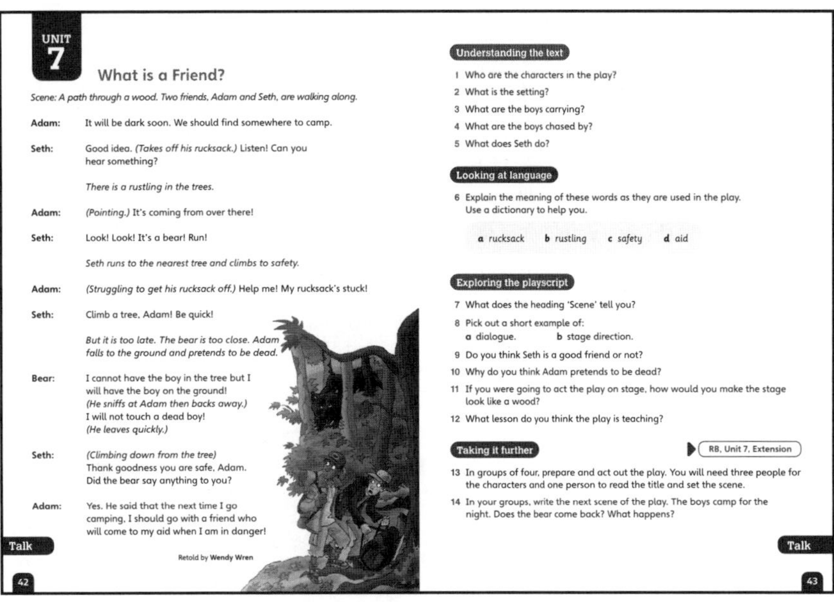

UNIT 7

What is a Friend?

Scene: A path through a wood. Two friends, Adam and Seth, are walking along.

Adam: It will be dark soon. We should find somewhere to camp.

Seth: Good idea. *(Takes off his rucksack.)* Listen! Can you hear something?

There is a rustling in the trees.

Adam: *(Pointing.)* It's coming from over there!

Seth: Look! Look! It's a bear! Run!

Seth runs to the nearest tree and climbs to safety.

Adam: *(Struggling to get his rucksack off.)* Help me! My rucksack's stuck!

Seth: Climb a tree, Adam! Be quick!

But it is too late. The bear is too close. Adam falls to the ground and pretends to be dead.

Bear: I cannot have the boy in the tree but I will have the boy on the ground! *(He sniffs at Adam then backs away.)* I will not touch a dead boy! *(He leaves quickly.)*

Seth: *(Climbing down from the tree)* Thank goodness you are safe, Adam. Did the bear say anything to you?

Adam: Yes. He said that the next time I go camping, I should go with a friend who will come to my aid when I am in danger!

Retold by **Wendy Wren**

Talk

42

Understanding the text

1 Who are the characters in the play?
2 What is the setting?
3 What are the boys carrying?
4 What are the boys chased by?
5 What does Seth do?

Looking at language

6 Explain the meaning of these words as they are used in the play. Use a dictionary to help you.

a *rucksack* **b** *rustling* **c** *safety* **d** *aid*

Exploring the playscript

7 What does the heading 'Scene' tell you?
8 Pick out a short example of:
a dialogue. **b** stage direction.
9 Do you think Seth is a good friend or not?
10 Why do you think Adam pretends to be dead?
11 If you were going to act the play on stage, how would you make the stage look like a wood?
12 What lesson do you think the play is teaching?

Taking it further RB, Unit 7, Extension

13 In groups of four, prepare and act out the play. You will need three people for the characters and one person to read the title and set the scene.
14 In your groups, write the next scene of the play. The boys camp for the night. Does the bear come back? What happens?

Talk

43

PUPIL BOOK ANSWERS

1. Seth / Adam / The Bear.
2. A wood.
3. Rucksacks.
4. A bear.
5. Seth 'runs to the nearest tree and climbs to safety'.
6. **a** rucksack: bag you carry on your back when walking long distances / camping **b** rustling: soft, crackling sound **c** safety: where there is no danger **d** aid: help / assistance
7. Where the action of the play takes place i.e. the setting.
8. Individual answers e.g. **a** It will be dark soon. **b** (pointing).
9. Individual answers that suggest he is not a good friend because he left Adam in danger and only thought of himself. Some children may consider it is difficult to make that judgement because Seth was probably terrified!
10. Individual answers suggesting that he pretends to be dead so the bear would leave him alone.
11. Individual answers. Encourage all members of the group to contribute ideas.
12. Individual answers reflecting the adage 'A friend in need is a friend indeed'.
13. Group work. Support preparation and comment on performance.
14. Group work. Encourage each group to discuss what may happen next before they begin to write the scene. Allow time for performance if possible.

RESOURCE SHEET SUPPORT ANSWERS

A

Adam and Seth are in a **wood**. They look for somewhere to **camp**. They are taking off their **rucksacks** when they hear a **rustling** in the trees. A **bear** runs towards them. Seth climbs a **tree** but Adam is not quick enough. Adam pretends to be **dead**. The bear **sniffs** at Adam and then leaves.

B

1. Takes off his rucksack – stage direction
2. Climb a tree, Adam! – dialogue
3. He leaves quickly – stage direction
4. Did the bear say anything to you? – dialogue
5. Good idea – dialogue

GOING DEEPER

- Look carefully at the script with the children and recap on how it would look differently on the page if it were written as a narrative story. If time allows, let some of the groups perform their plays for the class.

WRITE

- Ask what the children know about dinosaurs. Have they read any books or seen any films about them?
- Ask children why they think stories and films about dinosaurs are popular.
- Discuss what children would do if they actually saw a dinosaur. How would they feel? How would they react?
- Explain that they are going to read the beginning of a story where a boy called Jed actually meets a dinosaur.
- This is a challenging text for this year group, and you may wish to read it and discuss questions as a class or in groups before asking children to tackle it on their own.

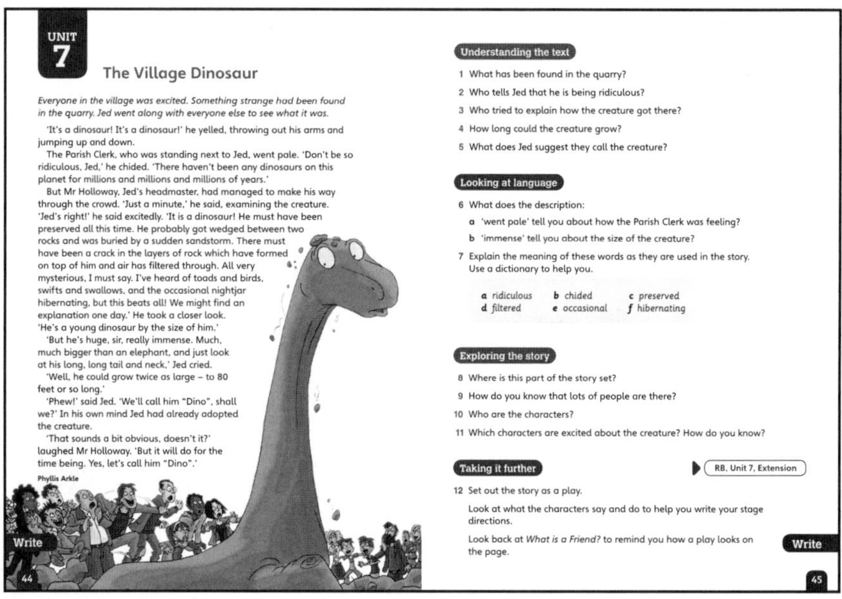

UNIT 7

The Village Dinosaur

Everyone in the village was excited. Something strange had been found in the quarry. Jed went along with everyone else to see what it was.

'It's a dinosaur! It's a dinosaur!' he yelled, throwing out his arms and jumping up and down.

The Parish Clerk, who was standing next to Jed, went pale. 'Don't be so ridiculous, Jed,' he chided. 'There haven't been any dinosaurs on this planet for millions and millions and millions of years.'

But Mr Holloway, Jed's headmaster, had managed to make his way through the crowd. 'Just a minute,' he said, examining the creature. 'Jed's right!' he said excitedly. 'It is a dinosaur! He must have been preserved all this time. He probably got wedged between two rocks and was buried by a sudden sandstorm. There must have been a crack in the layers of rock which have formed on top of him and air has filtered through. All very mysterious, I must say. I've heard of toads and birds, swifts and swallows, and the occasional nightjar hibernating, but this beats all! We might find an explanation one day.' He took a closer look. 'He's a young dinosaur by the size of him.'

'But he's huge, sir, really immense. Much, much bigger than an elephant, and just look at his long, long tail and neck,' Jed cried.

'Well, he could grow twice as large – to 80 feet or so long.'

'Phew!' said Jed. 'We'll call him "Dino", shall we?' In his own mind Jed had already adopted the creature.

'That sounds a bit obvious, doesn't it?' laughed Mr Holloway. 'But it will do for the time being. Yes, let's call him "Dino".'

Phyllis Arkle

Write

44

Understanding the text

1 What has been found in the quarry?
2 Who tells Jed that he is being ridiculous?
3 Who tried to explain how the creature got there?
4 How long could the creature grow?
5 What does Jed suggest they call the creature?

Looking at language

6 What does the description:
   a 'went pale' tell you about how the Parish Clerk was feeling?
   b 'immense' tell you about the size of the creature?
7 Explain the meaning of these words as they are used in the story. Use a dictionary to help you.

   a *ridiculous* b *chided* c *preserved*
   d *filtered* e *occasional* f *hibernating*

Exploring the story

8 Where is this part of the story set?
9 How do you know that lots of people are there?
10 Who are the characters?
11 Which characters are excited about the creature? How do you know?

Taking it further RB, Unit 7, Extension

12 Set out the story as a play.

Look at what the characters say and do to help you write your stage directions.

Look back at *What is a Friend?* to remind you how a play looks on the page.

Write

45

RESOURCES & ASSESSMENT BOOK

- **Support** (comprehension support): choosing the correct answer; (vocabulary support): choosing correct definitions.
- **Extension:** writing stage directions.

PUPIL BOOK ANSWERS

1. 'something strange' / a dinosaur.
2. The Parish Clerk.
3. Mr Holloway, the headmaster.
4. Up to 80 feet.
5. Dino.
6. **a** went pale: frightened / shocked
   b immense: huge
7. **a** ridiculous: silly / absurd **b** chided: told off **c** preserved: kept safe / alive
   d filtered: came through a little at a time
   e occasional: now and then / not very often **f** hibernating: sleeping through the winter
8. In a quarry.
9. Mr Holloway had to 'make his way through the crowd'.
10. Jed / The Parish Clerk / Mr Holloway / a crowd of villages / the dinosaur.
11. Jed: 'throwing out his arms and jumping up and down'
    Mr Holloway: 'he said excitedly'
12. Individual answers.

RESOURCE SHEET SUPPORT ANSWERS

A

1. <u>school</u> (quarry)
2. <u>Jed</u> (The Parish Clerk)
3. <u>nightjar</u> (dinosaur)
4. <u>old</u> (young)
5. <u>smaller</u> (bigger)
6. <u>short</u> (long)
7. <u>8</u> (80)
8. <u>Jed</u> (Dino)

B

1. ridiculous: silly
2. chided: told off
3. preserved: kept safe
4. filtered: seeped
5. occasional: now and then
6. hibernating: asleep in winter

GOING DEEPER

- Ask children if they would like to carry on reading *The Village Dinosaur,* and, if so, why. Recap on how speech in stories and speech in plays is set out differently. If time allows, ask the children to perform some of the plays written for the 'Taking it further' activity.

UNIT FOCUS: Exploring Language in Letters

Investigating ...

- various forms of written communication including letters, emails and texts
- letting other people know about books the children have read and enjoyed

TEACH

- Discuss why children think people send letters.
- Discuss why children think letter writing is no longer as popular as it was.
- Examine how we communicate with people if we cannot see them face-to-face.
- Ask children if they recommend books to one another.
- Ask why they think people tell others about books if they enjoy reading them.
- Ask children if they have read a book because someone said it was really good. Can they give an example?
- Read the letters to the class; ask individual children to read it aloud in turn; or read in silence individually.

UNIT 8 Exploring Language in Letters

Writing About Books

27 Farmway
Kenning
KG4 X33

Dear Ms Franks,

I have just finished reading your book, *The Adventurer*, and I am writing to tell you how much I enjoyed it.

I have read all of your books and I was given *The Adventurer* for my birthday. I couldn't put it down until I had finished it!

The Adventurer was a really frightening character at first, but then I realised he only frightened people who were evil and horrible.

I would love to be Sam and have all those amazing adventures with the Adventurer.

The way you describe the Adventurer's Castle Chaos is brilliant. Is it like a castle you've seen in real life or did you just make it up?

I do hope you will write some more *Adventurer* books. Are you going to? Are you writing one now? When will it be finished? I can't wait to read it.

Yours sincerely,
Mark Wood

Hi Liz - Hv u red the adventurer? Its gr8. U must read it. C U Mark

Mark W
Tom A
Subject: Hi Tom

Hi Tom,
Haven't heard from you for ages! What have you been up to? Just finished reading The Adventurer. It was ace! That Adventurer is really scary!!!!! Wish we could go to Castle Chaos – spooky or what????? Have you read it? Lend it to you when I see you. You coming over Sat like we planned? Mum says stay for tea,
Bye
Mark

Teach

46

Understanding the text

1 Who is Mark writing to?
2 What is he writing about?
3 Where does Mark live?
4 Where does the Adventurer live?
5 How do you know that Ms Franks is the author of *The Adventurer*?

Looking at language

6 What does Mark mean when he asks 'did you just make it up'?
7 What phrase tells you that Tom hasn't emailed Mark for a long time?
8 Explain these words as they are used in the letter and email. Use a dictionary to help you.

a *enjoyed* **b** *evil* **c** *spooky*

9 Write these 'words' from the text message in full.

a Hv **b** u **c** red **d** gr8 **e** c

Exploring letters, emails and text messages

10 Mark writes about *The Adventurer*. Did he like the book? How can you tell?
11 The letter is in six paragraphs. Summarise what each paragraph is about.
12 Mark is writing to three people. Which of these does he know? How can you tell?
13 What are the differences between the three pieces of writing?
Think about:
a the language.
b the way the writing is set out.
c the spelling.

RB, Unit 8, Extension

Taking it further

14 Who do you write to?
15 Which method do you use?

Teach

47

RESOURCES & ASSESSMENT BOOK

- **Support** (comprehension support): matching paragraphs to the correct summary; (vocabulary support): identifying adjectives, correcting text-speak.
- **Extension:** exploring different methods of communicating through writing.

PUPIL BOOK ANSWERS

1. Ms Franks / Tom / Liz.
2. a book called *The Adventurer.*
3. 27 Farmway, Kenning, KG4 X33.
4. Castle Chaos.
5. Mark writes: 'I have just finished reading **your** book', 'I have read all of **your** books', 'I do hope **you** will write some more'.
6. Did you imagine it?
7. 'for ages'.
8. **a** enjoyed: really liked **b** evil: very bad / wicked **c** spooky: frightening
9. **a** Hv: have **b** u: you **c** red: read **d** gr8: great **e** c: see
10. Yes, he liked the book:
    – letter: 'how much I enjoyed it' / 'I couldn't put it down until I had finished it' / 'I would love to be Sam' / 'amazing adventures' / 'brilliant'
    – email: 'It was ace' / 'Lend it to you when I see you'
    – text: 'Its gr8' / 'U must read it'
11. **Paragraph 1:** explains why he is writing **Paragraph 2:** says he has read *The Adventurer* **Paragraph 3:** says why he likes the main characters **Paragraph 4:** says he would like to be Sam **Paragraph 5:** says why he likes the setting **Paragraph 6:** says what he hopes will happen in the future
12. Mark knows Tom and Liz. You know this because he calls them by their first names. He writes a formal letter to Ms Franks and doesn't use her first name. The email and the text are more 'chatty' and informal.
13. Individual answers considering layout / paragraphing / formal – informal language / vocabulary / traditional – text spelling.
14. Individual answers.
15. Individual answers.

RESOURCE SHEET SUPPORT ANSWERS

A

Paragraph 1: explains why he is writing, **Paragraph 2:** says he has read the author's books, **Paragraph 3:** says what he thinks about the main character, **Paragraph 4:** says he would like to be Sam, **Paragraph 5:** is about the setting, **Paragraph 6:** says what he hopes will happen in the future.

B

1. frightening and scary
2. evil and horrible
3. amazing
4. spooky

C

Have you read *The Adventurer*? It's great. You must read it. See you, Mark

GOING DEEPER

- Discuss with the children when it is appropriate to write a letter, an email or a text. Look at the spelling in the text. Do children think it would be acceptable to write a letter in this way? Why / Why not?

TALK

- Discuss emails with the children. Do they send and receive emails?
- Ask children what they think the advantages of sending and receiving emails are. Do they think there are any disadvantages?
- Explain to children that they are going to read two emails that are written in a very different way from the letter. Can they spot the differences?
- Read the emails to the class; ask individual children to read them aloud in turn; or read in silence individually.

RESOURCES & ASSESSMENT BOOK

- **Support** (comprehension support): who wrote that?; (vocabulary support): adding missing words.
- **Extension:** making a plan to write an email.

PUPIL BOOK ANSWERS

1. Jake.
2. Information about a book competition.
3. *Black Beauty.*
4. *The Big Book of Football.*
5. *Jurassic Park.*
6. **a** competition: an event where people try to win prizes **b** fiction: made up **c** awesome: amazing
7. Really easy.
8. Jake is going to 'have a go at' writing about *Jurassic Park* and entering the competition.
9. **a** I **b** I am **c** The **d** You / We
10. Jake.
11. Dear.
12. 'See you'.
13. Yours faithfully.

14 15 Individual answers. Encourage each member of the group to offer suggestions. Group should vote on the book they will write about. One child can be the 'scribe' and write the competition entry.

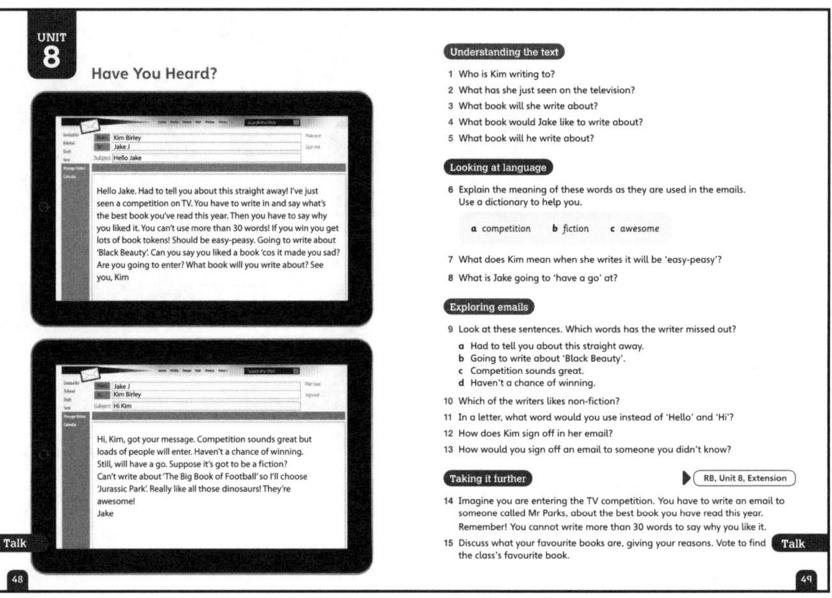

UNIT 8

Have You Heard?

From: Kim Birley
To: Jake J
Subject: Hello Jake

Hello Jake. Had to tell you about this straight away! I've just seen a competition on TV. You have to write in and say what's the best book you've read this year. Then you have to say why you liked it. You can't use more than 30 words! If you win you get lots of book tokens! Should be easy-peasy. Going to write about 'Black Beauty'. Can you say you liked a book 'cos it made you sad? Are you going to enter? What book will you write about? See you, Kim

From: Jake J
To: Kim Birley
Subject: Hi Kim

Hi, Kim, got your message. Competition sounds great but loads of people will enter. Haven't a chance of winning. Still, will have a go. Suppose it's got to be a fiction? Can't write about 'The Big Book of Football' so I'll choose 'Jurassic Park'. Really like all those dinosaurs! They're awesome!
Jake

Talk

48

Understanding the text

1 Who is Kim writing to?
2 What has she just seen on the television?
3 What book will she write about?
4 What book would Jake like to write about?
5 What book will he write about?

Looking at language

6 Explain the meaning of these words as they are used in the emails. Use a dictionary to help you.

a *competition* **b** *fiction* **c** *awesome*

7 What does Kim mean when she writes it will be 'easy-peasy'?
8 What is Jake going to 'have a go' at?

Exploring emails

9 Look at these sentences. Which words has the writer missed out?
- **a** Had to tell you about this straight away.
- **b** Going to write about 'Black Beauty'.
- **c** Competition sounds great.
- **d** Haven't a chance of winning.

10 Which of the writers likes non-fiction?
11 In a letter, what word would you use instead of 'Hello' and 'Hi'?
12 How does Kim sign off in her email?
13 How would you sign off an email to someone you didn't know?

Taking it further RB, Unit 8, Extension

14 Imagine you are entering the TV competition. You have to write an email to someone called Mr Parks, about the best book you have read this year. Remember! You cannot write more than 30 words to say why you like it.
15 Discuss what your favourite books are, giving your reasons. Vote to find the class's favourite book. Talk

49

RESOURCE SHEET SUPPORT ANSWERS

A

1. Kim
2. Jake
3. Jake
4. Kim
5. Jake
6. Kim
7. Kim
8. Jake

B

1. I
2. I am
3. The
4. I / You / We

GOING DEEPER

- Ask children to compare the letter and the emails. How many differences in style can they spot?

WRITE

- Ask children to say what type of book they like to read e.g. adventure / fantasy book.
- Discuss why they like it. What would they say to get others to read these types of books?
- Explain to children that they are going to read a letter from a teacher to a book magazine. She is writing about the kinds of books the children in her class like to read.
- Read the letter to the class; ask individual children to read it aloud in turn; or read in silence individually.

RESOURCES & ASSESSMENT BOOK

- **Support** (comprehension support): choosing the correct answer; (vocabulary support): sorting muddled words.
- **Extension:** making notes about favourite books.

PUPIL BOOK ANSWERS

1. Mrs P Richards.
2. The editor of *The World Of Books* magazine.
3. Primary school teacher.
4. Books the children in her class enjoy reading.
5. Animal stories / adventure and mystery stories / humorous books.
6. Books written about the same set of characters in different situations.
7. Books that readers find funny / amusing.
8. **a** editor: the person who chooses what goes into a magazine **b** article: a piece of writing in a magazine **c** suggestions: ideas **d** recommend: suggest in a positive way
9. The writer's address.
10. The first word is indented.
11. **Paragraph 1:** Mrs Richards explains who she is and why she is writing **Paragraph 2:** animal stories **Paragraph 3:** adventure and mystery stories **Paragraph 4:** humorous stories **Paragraph 5:** what she hopes will happen and what she will do
12. Answers suggesting that you need the author's name to find the book in the library / in a book shop / online.

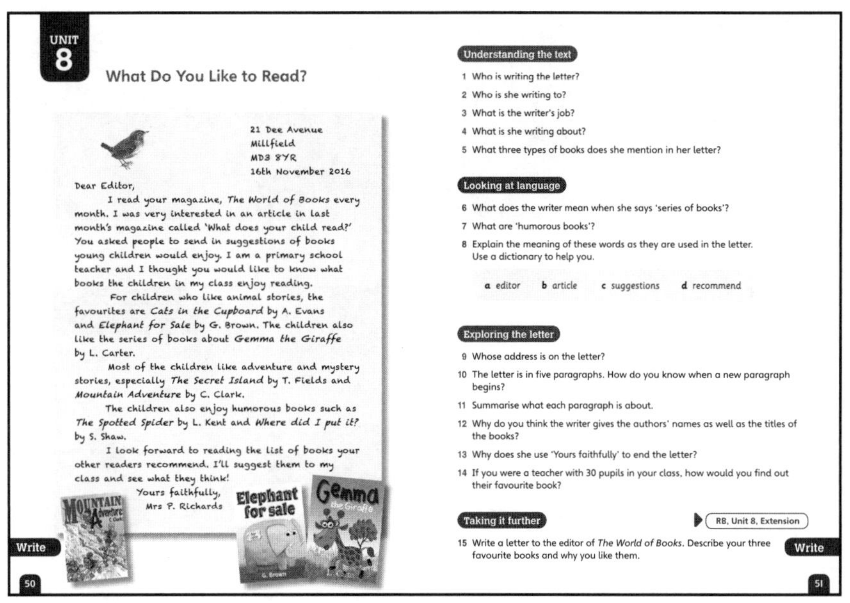

UNIT 8

What Do You Like to Read?

21 Dee Avenue
Millfield
MD3 8YR
16th November 2016

Dear Editor,

I read your magazine, *The World of Books* every month. I was very interested in an article in last month's magazine called 'What does your child read?' You asked people to send in suggestions of books young children would enjoy. I am a primary school teacher and I thought you would like to know what books the children in my class enjoy reading.

For children who like animal stories, the favourites are *Cats in the Cupboard* by A. Evans and *Elephant for Sale* by G. Brown. The children also like the series of books about *Gemma the Giraffe* by L. Carter.

Most of the children like adventure and mystery stories, especially *The Secret Island* by T. Fields and *Mountain Adventure* by C. Clark.

The children also enjoy humorous books such as *The Spotted Spider* by L. Kent and *Where did I put it?* by S. Shaw.

I look forward to reading the list of books your other readers recommend. I'll suggest them to my class and see what they think!

Yours faithfully,
Mrs P. Richards

Write

50

Understanding the text

1 Who is writing the letter?
2 Who is she writing to?
3 What is the writer's job?
4 What is she writing about?
5 What three types of books does she mention in her letter?

Looking at language

6 What does the writer mean when she says 'series of books'?
7 What are 'humorous books'?
8 Explain the meaning of these words as they are used in the letter. Use a dictionary to help you.

a editor **b** article **c** suggestions **d** recommend

Exploring the letter

9 Whose address is on the letter?
10 The letter is in five paragraphs. How do you know when a new paragraph begins?
11 Summarise what each paragraph is about.
12 Why do you think the writer gives the authors' names as well as the titles of the books?
13 Why does she use 'Yours faithfully' to end the letter?
14 If you were a teacher with 30 pupils in your class, how would you find out their favourite book?

Taking it further RB, Unit 8, Extension

15 Write a letter to the editor of *The World of Books*. Describe your three favourite books and why you like them. Write

51

13. She does not know the name of the person she is writing to.
14. Individual answers e.g. class vote / graph etc.
15. Individual answers. Remind children how to set out a letter and organise what they write into paragraphs.

RESOURCE SHEET SUPPORT ANSWERS

A

1. b
2. c
3. a
4. b
5. c

B

1. book
2. story
3. editor
4. read
5. readers

GOING DEEPER

- Use the discussion at the start of the lesson as a basis of: writing a list of book categories on the board; selecting a method for finding out the children's favourite books. Recap on purpose, audience and style of letters, emails and texts.

UNIT FOCUS: Looking at Reports and Notes

Investigating …
- factual information
- using facts in simple persuasive reports

TEACH

- Discuss what children understand by the term 'persuasion'.
- Discuss what children say and do in order to persuade others to do what they want or to agree with them.
- Ask children for acceptable methods of persuasion (e.g. discussing reasonably); and unacceptable methods of persuasion (e.g. bullying, physical violence).
- Explain to children that to succeed in persuading people, you have to be sure of your facts.
- Explain that the writer of 'Planet in Danger!' spoke to people to find out what they could do to save the planet and used these facts to persuade other people to do the same.
- Read the text to the class; ask individual children to read it aloud in turn; or read in silence individually.

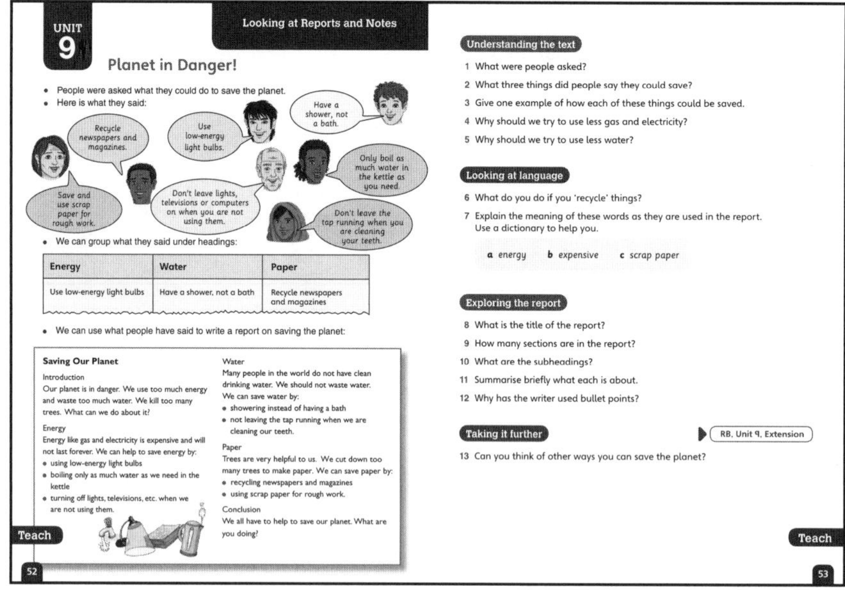
UNIT 9

Looking at Reports and Notes

Planet in Danger!

- People were asked what they could do to save the planet.
- Here is what they said:

- We can group what they said under headings:

Energy	Water	Paper
Use low-energy light bulbs	Have a shower, not a bath	Recycle newspapers and magazines

- We can use what people have said to write a report on saving the planet:

Saving Our Planet

Introduction
Our planet is in danger. We use too much energy and waste too much water. We kill too many trees. What can we do about it?

Energy
Energy like gas and electricity is expensive and will not last forever. We can help to save energy by:
- using low-energy light bulbs
- boiling only as much water as we need in the kettle
- turning off lights, televisions, etc. when we are not using them.

Water
Many people in the world do not have clean drinking water. We should not waste water. We can save water by:
- showering instead of having a bath
- not leaving the tap running when we are cleaning our teeth.

Paper
Trees are very helpful to us. We cut down too many trees to make paper. We can save paper by:
- recycling newspapers and magazines
- using scrap paper for rough work.

Conclusion
We all have to help to save our planet. What are you doing?

Teach

52

Understanding the text
1 What were people asked?
2 What three things did people say they could save?
3 Give one example of how each of these things could be saved.
4 Why should we try to use less gas and electricity?
5 Why should we try to use less water?

Looking at language
6 What do you do if you 'recycle' things?
7 Explain the meaning of these words as they are used in the report. Use a dictionary to help you.
a energy **b** expensive **c** scrap paper

Exploring the report
8 What is the title of the report?
9 How many sections are in the report?
10 What are the subheadings?
11 Summarise briefly what each is about.
12 Why has the writer used bullet points?

Taking it further
RB, Unit 9, Extension
13 Can you think of other ways you can save the planet?

Teach

53

RESOURCES & ASSESSMENT BOOK

- **Support** (comprehension support): completing a chart of information; (vocabulary support): choosing correct definition.
- **Extension:** identifying pictures.

PUPIL BOOK ANSWERS

1. What they could do to save the planet.
2. Energy, water and paper.
3. Energy: use low-energy light bulbs *or* switch things off when not in use *or* boil only as much water as you need.
   Water: take a shower instead of a bath *or* don't leave taps running.
   Paper: use scrap paper *or* recycle things.
4. These things are expensive and could run out.
5. Many people do not have clean water to drink. Making water safe to drink is expensive. We should realise it is precious and not waste it.
6. You re-use things, or put them in the recycling bin so that they can be made into something else.
7. **a** E.g. gas, electricity, fuel.
   b Costs a lot.
   c Odd bits of paper which may have already been used on one side.
8. Saving Our Planet.
9. Five.
10. Introduction / Energy / Water / Paper / Conclusion.
11. Section 1: explaining why the planet is in danger
    Section 2: energy and how we can save it
    Section 3: water and how we can save it
    Section 4: paper and how we can save it and trees
    Section 5: conclusion – asking the readers to help
12. Answers that suggest they make the suggestions very clear to focus on.
13. Individual answers.

RESOURCE SHEET SUPPORT ANSWERS

A

How can we save electricity?	How can we save water?	How can we save trees?
use low-energy light bulbs	shower	use scrap paper
switch things off when not in use	don't leave water running	recycle newspapers
	boil only the water you need	

B

1. to use again
2. costing a lot of money
3. notes and ideas
4. use badly

GOING DEEPER

- Discuss the report with children. How persuasive do they find it? If someone who had never thought about our planet being in danger read it, do the children think they would be persuaded to be more careful? Why / Why not?

TALK

- Ask children what they understand by the term 'rainforests'.
- Ask children if they know why rainforests are important and if they know what is happening to them.
- Explain to children that they are going to look at some facts that may persuade people that we should take more care of the rainforests.
- Read the text to the class; ask individual children to read it aloud in turn; or read in silence individually.

RESOURCES & ASSESSMENT BOOK

- **Support** (comprehension support) classifying information; (vocabulary support): choose correct definition.
- **Extension** persuasive writing.

PUPIL BOOK ANSWERS

1. rainforests
2. tropical regions near the equator / temperate regions
3. for timber / land for people to live on
4. West African rainforest
5. Any two from: two-thirds of world's plants / two-thirds of world's animals / natural medicines / timber / 28 per cent of world's oxygen.
6. Answers that suggest plants and shrubs that grow close to the ground.
7. Tourists visit places, usually on holiday.
8. **a** temperate: not very hot nor very cold **b** equator: an imaginary line around the centre of the Earth **c** shrinking: getting smaller **d** oxygen: one of the gases in air necessary for life
9. **a Paragraph 1:** tall, leafy trees / not much undergrowth due to lack of sunlight

   b Paragraph 2: tropical rainforests near the equator / temperate rainforests away from the equator e.g. North America

   c Paragraph 3: two-thirds of the world's plants and animals / natural medicines / 28% of the world's oxygen / timber / absorbs huge amounts of CO_2

   d Paragraph 4: world's rainforests are shrinking / trees cut down / land cleared for timber and people to live on

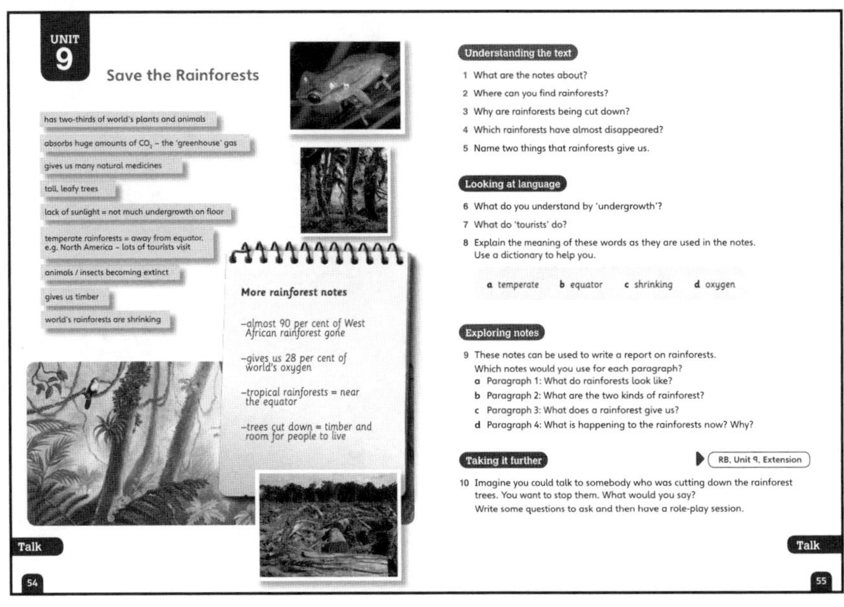

UNIT 9

Save the Rainforests

has two-thirds of world's plants and animals

absorbs huge amounts of CO_2 – the 'greenhouse' gas

gives us many natural medicines

tall, leafy trees

lack of sunlight = not much undergrowth on floor

temperate rainforests = away from equator, e.g. North America – lots of tourists visit

animals / insects becoming extinct

gives us timber

world's rainforests are shrinking

More rainforest notes

–almost 90 per cent of West African rainforest gone

–gives us 28 per cent of world's oxygen

–tropical rainforests = near the equator

–trees cut down = timber and room for people to live

Understanding the text

1 What are the notes about?
2 Where can you find rainforests?
3 Why are rainforests being cut down?
4 Which rainforests have almost disappeared?
5 Name two things that rainforests give us.

Looking at language

6 What do you understand by 'undergrowth'?
7 What do 'tourists' do?
8 Explain the meaning of these words as they are used in the notes. Use a dictionary to help you.

a temperate b equator c shrinking d oxygen

Exploring notes

9 These notes can be used to write a report on rainforests. Which notes would you use for each paragraph?
a Paragraph 1: What do rainforests look like?
b Paragraph 2: What are the two kinds of rainforest?
c Paragraph 3: What does a rainforest give us?
d Paragraph 4: What is happening to the rainforests now? Why?

Taking it further

RB, Unit 9, Extension

10 Imagine you could talk to somebody who was cutting down the rainforest trees. You want to stop them. What would you say? Write some questions to ask and then have a role-play session.

Talk 54

Talk 55

10. Encourage all members of the group to contribute. One child can make notes.

RESOURCE SHEET SUPPORT ANSWERS

A

What do they look like?	What kinds are there?	What do they give us / do for us?	What is happening to them?
not much undergrowth	tropical rainforests	absorb CO_2	rainforests are shrinking
tall, leafy trees	temperate rainforests	2/3 of world's plants and animals	animals becoming extinct
		many natural medicines	land cleared for building
			trees cut down for timber

B

1. not very hot or very cold
2. very hot

GOING DEEPER

- Focus on the element of 'hard facts' in persuasive writing to ensure children understand the need for research. Would the 'facts' be so persuasive if the writer had said: 'has *a lot* of the world's plants and animals'; '*quite a bit* of the West African rainforest has gone'; 'gives us *some* of the world's oxygen'?

WRITE

- Ask children what they understand by the term 'recycle'.
- Ask children if they recycle. If so, what do they recycle?
- Explain to children that many parts of the country have recycling schemes to persuade people to be more careful with their rubbish.
- Explain to children that they are going to read about a scheme in Wales called 'Recycle with Michael'.
- Read the text to the class; ask individual children to read it aloud in turn; or read in silence individually.

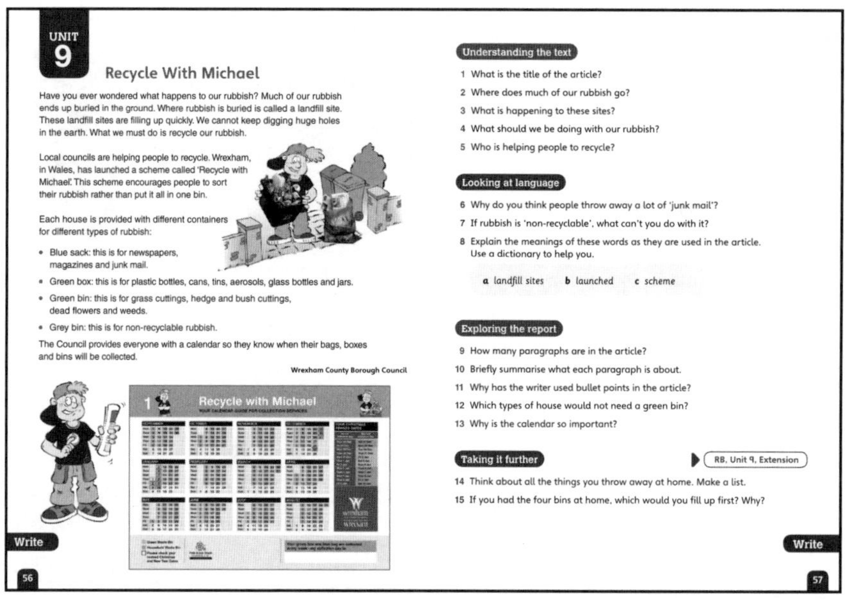

UNIT 9

Recycle With Michael

Have you ever wondered what happens to our rubbish? Much of our rubbish ends up buried in the ground. Where rubbish is buried is called a landfill site. These landfill sites are filling up quickly. We cannot keep digging huge holes in the earth. What we must do is recycle our rubbish.

Local councils are helping people to recycle. Wrexham, in Wales, has launched a scheme called 'Recycle with Michael'. This scheme encourages people to sort their rubbish rather than put it all in one bin.

Each house is provided with different containers for different types of rubbish:

- Blue sack: this is for newspapers, magazines and junk mail.
- Green box: this is for plastic bottles, cans, tins, aerosols, glass bottles and jars.
- Green bin: this is for grass cuttings, hedge and bush cuttings, dead flowers and weeds.
- Grey bin: this is for non-recyclable rubbish.

The Council provides everyone with a calendar so they know when their bags, boxes and bins will be collected.

Wrexham County Borough Council

Understanding the text

1 What is the title of the article?
2 Where does much of our rubbish go?
3 What is happening to these sites?
4 What should we be doing with our rubbish?
5 Who is helping people to recycle?

Looking at language

6 Why do you think people throw away a lot of 'junk mail'?
7 If rubbish is 'non-recyclable', what can't you do with it?
8 Explain the meanings of these words as they are used in the article. Use a dictionary to help you.

a *landfill sites* **b** *launched* **c** *scheme*

Exploring the report

9 How many paragraphs are in the article?
10 Briefly summarise what each paragraph is about.
11 Why has the writer used bullet points in the article?
12 Which types of house would not need a green bin?
13 Why is the calendar so important?

Taking it further

RB, Unit 9, Extension

14 Think about all the things you throw away at home. Make a list.
15 If you had the four bins at home, which would you fill up first? Why?

Write 56 Write 57

RESOURCES & ASSESSMENT BOOK

- **Support** (comprehension support): classifying information; (vocabulary support): cloze activity for vocabulary reinforcement.
- **Extension:** writing lists.

PUPIL BOOK ANSWERS

1. *Recycle With Michael.*
2. Landfill sites.
3. They are filling up quickly.
4. Recycling.
5. Local councils.
6. The clue is in the name! 'Junk mail' is not asked for and usually holds no interest for the people it is sent to. It is a form of advertising.
7. You cannot reuse it.
8. **a** landfill sites: huge holes in the ground where rubbish is buried **b** launched: started **c** scheme: plan
9. Four.
10. **Paragraph 1:** what we do and what we should do with our rubbish **Paragraph 2:** Wrexham's recycling scheme **Paragraph 3:** what the scheme provides for each house **Paragraph 4:** the calendar
11. The bullet points draw attention to what is provided and how it is to be used.
12. Houses / flats etc. that have no garden.
13. The calendar tells people when to leave each different bin to be emptied.
14. Individual answers. Compare lists in a class discussion.
15. Individual answers.

RESOURCE SHEET SUPPORT ANSWERS

A

1. newspapers / magazines / junk mail
2. cans / bottles / aerosols
3. grass cuttings / weeds / dead flowers
4. non-recyclable rubbish

B

A lot of our **rubbish** ends up in **landfill** sites. These are large **holes** in the ground where the rubbish is **buried**. The sites are filling up quickly. We must start to **recycle** our rubbish.

GOING DEEPER

- Recap on the stages needed for simple persuasive texts: research – know your facts; notes – order your notes so your report is easy to follow; write your report.

UNIT FOCUS: Understanding Characters' Feelings

Investigating …

- three extracts from the same adventure story in order to emphasis the 'need to know' element in good fiction writing
- 'cliff hangers' at the end of a text
- predicting the ending of a story

TEACH

- Ask children if they think dragons exist or have ever existed.
- Discuss what books and films they have seen dragons in.
- Explain to children that they are going to read the first instalment of an adventure story.
- Discuss the story so far: Jilly is about to have her seventh birthday. She has a poster of a dragon on her bedroom wall and the only present she wants is a real dragon. Her parents tell her that there are no such things as dragons. Jilly is not convinced and, next time the family goes to town, she takes her pocket money and goes to see Mr Pink in the Magic Shop!
- Read the extract to the class; ask individual children to read it aloud in turn; or read in silence individually.

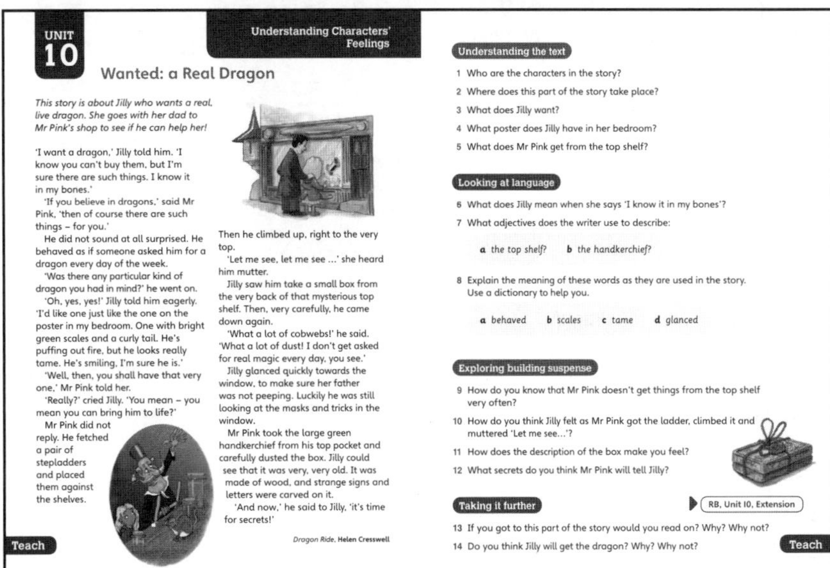

UNIT 10 Understanding Characters' Feelings

Wanted: a Real Dragon

This story is about Jilly who wants a real, live dragon. She goes with her dad to Mr Pink's shop to see if he can help her!

'I want a dragon,' Jilly told him. 'I know you can't buy them, but I'm sure there are such things. I know it in my bones.'

'If you believe in dragons,' said Mr Pink, 'then of course there are such things – for you.'

He did not sound at all surprised. He behaved as if someone asked him for a dragon every day of the week.

'Was there any particular kind of dragon you had in mind?' he went on.

'Oh, yes, yes!' Jilly told him eagerly. 'I'd like one just like the one on the poster in my bedroom. One with bright green scales and a curly tail. He's puffing out fire, but he looks really tame. He's smiling, I'm sure he is.'

'Well, then, you shall have that very one,' Mr Pink told her.

'Really?' cried Jilly. 'You mean – you mean you can bring him to life?'

Mr Pink did not reply. He fetched a pair of stepladders and placed them against the shelves.

Then he climbed up, right to the very top.

'Let me see, let me see ...' she heard him mutter.

Jilly saw him take a small box from the very back of that mysterious top shelf. Then, very carefully, he came down again.

'What a lot of cobwebs!' he said. 'What a lot of dust! I don't get asked for real magic every day, you see.'

Jilly glanced quickly towards the window, to make sure her father was not peeping. Luckily he was still looking at the masks and tricks in the window.

Mr Pink took the large green handkerchief from his top pocket and carefully dusted the box. Jilly could see that it was very, very old. It was made of wood, and strange signs and letters were carved on it.

'And now,' he said to Jilly, 'it's time for secrets!'

Dragon Ride, **Helen Cresswell**

Teach

58

Understanding the text

1 Who are the characters in the story?
2 Where does this part of the story take place?
3 What does Jilly want?
4 What poster does Jilly have in her bedroom?
5 What does Mr Pink get from the top shelf?

Looking at language

6 What does Jilly mean when she says 'I know it in my bones'?
7 What adjectives does the writer use to describe:
a *the top shelf?* **b** *the handkerchief?*
8 Explain the meaning of these words as they are used in the story. Use a dictionary to help you.
a *behaved* **b** *scales* **c** *tame* **d** *glanced*

Exploring building suspense

9 How do you know that Mr Pink doesn't get things from the top shelf very often?
10 How do you think Jilly felt as Mr Pink got the ladder, climbed it and muttered 'Let me see...'?
11 How does the description of the box make you feel?
12 What secrets do you think Mr Pink will tell Jilly?

Taking it further RB, Unit 10, Extension

13 If you got to this part of the story would you read on? Why? Why not?
14 Do you think Jilly will get the dragon? Why? Why not?

Teach

59

RESOURCES & ASSESSMENT BOOK

- **Support** (comprehension support): identifying True / False statements; (vocabulary support): matching words and definitions, adjectives.
- **Extension:** asking questions about the text, prediction.

PUPIL BOOK ANSWERS

1. Jilly / Jilly's father / Mr Pink.
2. In Mr Pink's shop.
3. A dragon.
4. A poster of a dragon.
5. 'a small box', 'made of wood' with 'strange signs and letters' on it.
6. Answers that suggest she cannot prove that dragons exist but she is absolutely convinced that they do.
7. **a** the top shelf: mysterious **b** the handkerchief: large / green.
8. **a** behaved: acted **b** scales: thin bony covering on fish and reptiles **c** tame: friendly / not wild **d** glanced: looked quickly
9. The top shelf is very dusty and has cobwebs.
10. Answers that suggest Jilly may have felt impatient as she wanted Mr Pink to get on with it. She probably felt excited.
11. Individual answers suggesting the reader is made to feel curious and impatient to know what is in the box.
12. Answers suggesting the secrets will lead to Jilly having a real dragon.
13. Individual answers suggesting that they would want to read on and see what happens.
14. Individual answers.

RESOURCE SHEET SUPPORT ANSWERS

A

1. True
2. False
3. False
4. True
5. False
6. True

B

1. Mr Pink is the shop owner. / Mr Pink is not Jilly's father.
2. Jilly had a poster of a dragon.
3. Mr Pink's handkerchief was large and green.

C

1. behaved: acted
2. scales: thin, bony covering on fish and reptiles
3. tame: friendly / not wild
4. glanced: looked quickly

D

The dragon: bright green / curly-tailed / tame
The box: carved / very old / dusty

GOING DEEPER

- Ask children if they are interested in the story. Why / Why not? Discuss what impression they get of Jilly.

TALK

- Ask children to recap the story so far.
- Read the extract to the class; ask individual children to read it aloud in turn; or read in silence individually.

RESOURCES & ASSESSMENT BOOK

- **Support** (comprehension support): narrative sequence; (vocabulary support): matching words and definitions.
- **Extension:** predicting, writing sentences.

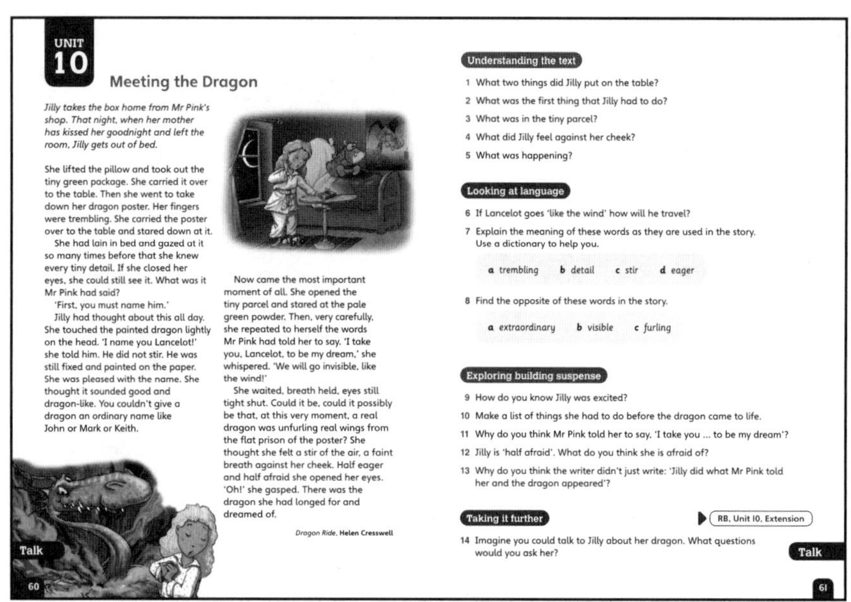

UNIT 10

Meeting the Dragon

Jilly takes the box home from Mr Pink's shop. That night, when her mother has kissed her goodnight and left the room, Jilly gets out of bed.

She lifted the pillow and took out the tiny green package. She carried it over to the table. Then she went to take down her dragon poster. Her fingers were trembling. She carried the poster over to the table and stared down at it.

She had lain in bed and gazed at it so many times before that she knew every tiny detail. If she closed her eyes, she could still see it. What was it Mr Pink had said?

'First, you must name him.'

Jilly had thought about this all day. She touched the painted dragon lightly on the head. 'I name you Lancelot!' she told him. He did not stir. He was still fixed and painted on the paper. She was pleased with the name. She thought it sounded good and dragon-like. You couldn't give a dragon an ordinary name like John or Mark or Keith.

Now came the most important moment of all. She opened the tiny parcel and stared at the pale green powder. Then, very carefully, she repeated to herself the words Mr Pink had told her to say. 'I take you, Lancelot, to be my dream,' she whispered. 'We will go invisible, like the wind!'

She waited, breath held, eyes still tight shut. Could it be, could it possibly be that, at this very moment, a real dragon was unfurling real wings from the flat prison of the poster? She thought she felt a stir of the air, a faint breath against her cheek. Half eager and half afraid she opened her eyes. 'Oh!' she gasped. There was the dragon she had longed for and dreamed of.

Dragon Ride, **Helen Cresswell**

Talk

60

Understanding the text

1 What two things did Jilly put on the table?
2 What was the first thing that Jilly had to do?
3 What was in the tiny parcel?
4 What did Jilly feel against her cheek?
5 What was happening?

Looking at language

6 If Lancelot goes 'like the wind' how will he travel?
7 Explain the meaning of these words as they are used in the story. Use a dictionary to help you.

a *trembling* **b** *detail* **c** *stir* **d** *eager*

8 Find the opposite of these words in the story.

a *extraordinary* **b** *visible* **c** *furling*

Exploring building suspense

9 How do you know Jilly was excited?
10 Make a list of things she had to do before the dragon came to life.
11 Why do you think Mr Pink told her to say, 'I take you ... to be my dream'?
12 Jilly is 'half afraid'. What do you think she is afraid of?
13 Why do you think the writer didn't just write: 'Jilly did what Mr Pink told her and the dragon appeared'?

Taking it further RB, Unit 10, Extension

14 Imagine you could talk to Jilly about her dragon. What questions would you ask her?

Talk

61

PUPIL BOOK ANSWERS

1. The tiny green package / the dragon poster.
2. She had to name the dragon.
3. Pale green powder.
4. 'a stir of air; a faint breath'.
5. The dragon was coming to life.
6. Very fast / unseen.
7. **a** trembling: shaking / shivering **b** detail: a small part of **c** stir: begin to move **d** eager: keen
8. **a** extraordinary: ordinary **b** visible: invisible **c** furling: unfurling
9. Answers based on details from the story e.g. 'Her fingers were trembling' / 'breath held' / 'half eager' / 'she gasped'.
10. She had to: give the dragon a name; open the tiny package; she had to say, 'I take you Lancelot, to be my dream. We will go invisible, like the wind.'
11. Answers suggesting that the words will make her dream come true.
12. Answers suggesting that Jilly is 'half afraid' that she will not get her dragon.
13. Answers suggesting that the way the writer has written it builds up the tension and makes the reader want to go on reading.
14. Encourage all members of the group to participate and to give reasons for the questions they would ask. One child can take notes.

RESOURCE SHEET SUPPORT ANSWERS

A

a 7 **b** 2 **c** 9 **d** 1 **e** 4 **f** 6 **g** 8 **h** 5 **i** 3

B

1. trembling: shaking / shivering
2. detail: a small part of
3. stir: begin to move
4. eager: keen

C

Individual answers.

GOING DEEPER

- Use the answers to the 'Taking it further' activity as a basis for a class discussion.

WRITE

- Ask children to recap on the story so far.
- Read the extract to the class; ask individual children to read it aloud in turn; or read in silence individually.

RESOURCES & ASSESSMENT BOOK

- **Support** (comprehension support): correcting statements; (vocabulary support): identifying adjectives, choosing correct definitions.
- **Extension:** expanding the text, explaining.

PUPIL BOOK ANSWERS

1. Through the window.
2. Jilly's father.
3. Puff some fire.
4. Puffed green smoke.
5. 'all they'd see is the moon coming up'
6. Rose quickly and travelled at speed.
7. 'danced and curled like scarlet snakes'. Answers suggesting it is a good description because the smoke curls and writhes like snakes moving.
8. **a** gasp: take a quick gulp of air **b** obeyed: did as he was asked **c** forking: going in different / many directions
9. Jilly and Lancelot were invisible.
10. Answers based on Jilly's reaction – 'Hurray!'.
11. 'They looked like toys'.
12. Answers based on the evidence 'it was just as she had dreamed it would be.'
13. Individual answers.
14. Individual answers.

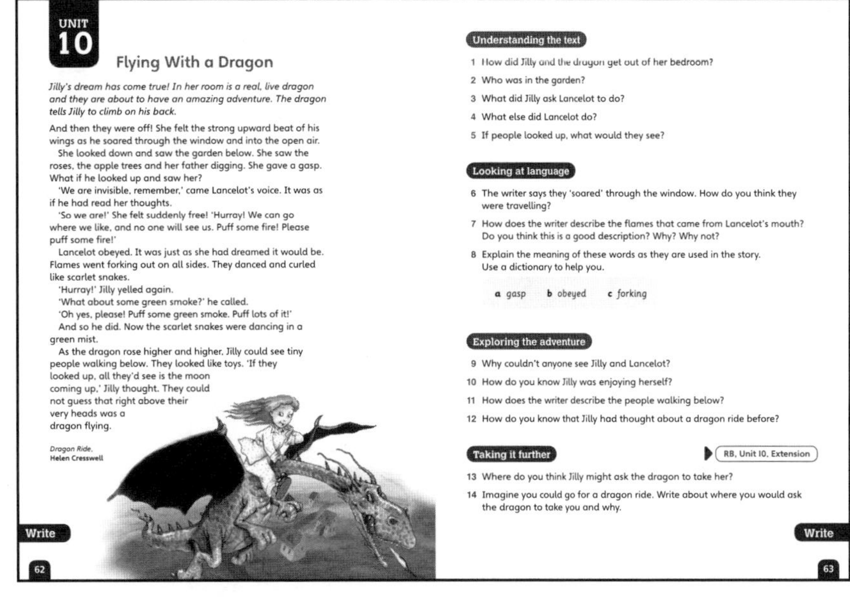

UNIT 10

Flying With a Dragon

Jilly's dream has come true! In her room is a real, live dragon and they are about to have an amazing adventure. The dragon tells Jilly to climb on his back.

And then they were off! She felt the strong upward beat of his wings as he soared through the window and into the open air.

She looked down and saw the garden below. She saw the roses, the apple trees and her father digging. She gave a gasp. What if he looked up and saw her?

'We are invisible, remember,' came Lancelot's voice. It was as if he had read her thoughts.

'So we are!' She felt suddenly free! 'Hurray! We can go where we like, and no one will see us. Puff some fire! Please puff some fire!'

Lancelot obeyed. It was just as she had dreamed it would be. Flames went forking out on all sides. They danced and curled like scarlet snakes.

'Hurray!' Jilly yelled again.

'What about some green smoke?' he called.

'Oh yes, please! Puff some green smoke. Puff lots of it!'

And so he did. Now the scarlet snakes were dancing in a green mist.

As the dragon rose higher and higher, Jilly could see tiny people walking below. They looked like toys. 'If they looked up, all they'd see is the moon coming up,' Jilly thought. They could not guess that right above their very heads was a dragon flying.

Dragon Ride, **Helen Cresswell**

Write

62

Understanding the text

1 How did Jilly and the dragon get out of her bedroom?
2 Who was in the garden?
3 What did Jilly ask Lancelot to do?
4 What else did Lancelot do?
5 If people looked up, what would they see?

Looking at language

6 The writer says they 'soared' through the window. How do you think they were travelling?
7 How does the writer describe the flames that came from Lancelot's mouth? Do you think this is a good description? Why? Why not?
8 Explain the meaning of these words as they are used in the story. Use a dictionary to help you.

a *gasp* **b** *obeyed* **c** *forking*

Exploring the adventure

9 Why couldn't anyone see Jilly and Lancelot?
10 How do you know Jilly was enjoying herself?
11 How does the writer describe the people walking below?
12 How do you know that Jilly had thought about a dragon ride before?

Taking it further RB, Unit 10, Extension

13 Where do you think Jilly might ask the dragon to take her?
14 Imagine you could go for a dragon ride. Write about where you would ask the dragon to take you and why.

Write

63

RESOURCE SHEET ANSWERS

A

1. door (window)
2. river (garden)
3. kneeling (digging)
4. visible (invisible)
5. snakes (fire)
6. smoke (toys)

B

1. beat: strong, upward
2. smoke: green
3. the people: tiny

C

1. gasp – take a sharp breath
2. obeyed – did do what was asked
3. forking – going in a different direction
4. invisible – not able to be seen

GOING DEEPER

- Ask children what they think happens to the dragon after the night ride. What do they think would be a happy ending to the story? What do they think would be a sad ending to the story?

Book 4 Scope and Sequence

Unit	Unit Focus	Texts	Oxford Level	Oxford Reading Criterion Scale	Genre / text type	Resources & Assessment Book Support	Resources & Assessment Book Extension
1	Characters' Points of View	'Leaving London' from *Carrie's War*, Nina Bawden	14	standard 5, criteria 2, 4, 7, 12, 13, 14, 18, 19, 23, 24	period fiction	underlining correct endings to sentences; identifying true statements; matching words with correct meanings	putting yourself in a character's position and writing about how you feel
		'Dad's Double' from *The War and Freddy*, Dennis Hamley	13			identifying who said what; cloze activity	thinking of questions to ask characters
		'The Crash' from *Blitz*, Robert Westall	14			putting narrative into correct sequence; predicting what characters might have said; labelling an illustration	putting yourself in a character's position and writing about how you feel
2	Exploring Journalistic Writing	Marathon Marvel Hangs up Her Running Shoes	14	standard 5, criteria 2, 4, 10, 12, 13, 18	non-fiction: sports journalism	completing a chart; underlining correct definitions	thinking of and writing down questions
		On Your Bike	14			matching paragraphs with correct summary; cloze activity	planning and creating a flyer
		Three Times the Pain!	14			matching beginnings and endings of sentences; finding adjectives; underlining correct definitions	comparing the three sports articles
3	Looking at Similes and Metaphors	'Quieter Than Snow', Berlie Doherty	14	standard 5, criteria 2, 4, 8, 12, 13, 14, 17, 18, 19	poetry	filling in a chart; identifying similes	thinking of questions to ask the poet
		'The Hills', Rachel Field	14			matching beginnings and endings of sentences; matching descriptions to illustrations; cloze activity.	thinking and writing about similes of your own
		'One Moment in Summer', David Harmer	15			completing a chart; completing similes; underlining correct definitions	writing your own poetic description
4	Understanding Information Writing	Let's Find Out About Argentina	15	standard 5, criteria 2, 4, 6, 10, 12, 13	non-fiction: information on countries	thinking of questions for answers; cloze activity	researching and writing about related topics
		Let's Find Out About China	15			identifying true statements; correcting false statements; matching words to definitions	writing questions about a country
		Let's Find Out About Australia	15				
						thinking of questions for answers; cloze activity; finding adjectives	writing questions about a city and researching to find the answers
5	Characters' Feelings and Actions	'Webbo' from *Chicken*, Alan Gibbons	14	standard 5, criteria 2, 4, 8, 12, 13, 14, 16, 17, 19, 22, 23	fiction	who said what; correcting sentences; matching words to definitions	putting yourself into a character's position and writing about what you would do
		'Trouble With Miss Gratwick' from *The Hallowe'en Cat*, Kenneth Lillington	14			putting narrative into correct sequence; who did what; writing out contractions in full	putting yourself into a character's position and writing about what you would do
		'The Balaclava Boys' from *The Balaclava Story*, George Layton	14			underlining correct endings and definitions	putting yourself into a character's position and writing about what you would do

6	Interpreting Explanation Texts	How Does Your Heart Work?	14	standard 5, criteria 2, 4, 7, 10, 12, 13	non-fiction	matching beginnings and endings of sentences; labelling a diagram; underlining correct definitions	thinking of and writing questions
		How Do We Move?	14			underlining the correct endings to sentences; labelling a diagram; underlining correct definitions	explaining diagram; drawing and explaining a labelled diagram
		How Do Our Lungs Work?	14			identifying true statements; correcting false statements; solving anagrams	thinking of and writing questions
7	Reading Persuasive Texts	*Bigfoot*	13	standard 5, criteria 2, 4, 12, 13, 18, 19, 21	book and film blurbs	correcting sentences; matching words to definitions	writing persuasive language
		Tripods Trilogy	13			identifying the correct endings to sentences; choosing adjectives	writing persuasive language
		Search for the Loch Ness Monster	13			writing questions for answers; matching words to definitions	writing persuasive language
8	How Settings Create Atmosphere	'Into the Forest' from *The Lord of the Rings*, J R R Tolkein	17	standard 5, criteria 2, 4, 7, 8, 12, 13, 14, 15, 16, 17, 19, 20, 21, 22	classic fiction	matching nouns to adjectives; identifying adjectives	writing about a character's thoughts and feelings
		'Down the Rabbit Hole' from *Alice in Wonderland*, Lewis Carroll	14			correcting sentences; matching words and definitions	writing about a character's thoughts and feelings
		'Lucy Looks into a Wardrobe' from *The Lion, the Witch and the Wardrobe*, C S Lewis	14			underlining correct answers; cloze activity	predicting what happens next
9	Exploring Stage Playscripts	'An Unexpected Meeting' adapted from *The Lion, the Witch and the Wardrobe*, C S Lewis	14	standard 5, criteria 2, 4, 7, 8, 10, 12, 13, 14, 19, 21	playscripts	cloze activity; matching words to definitions; understanding stage directions	thinking of and writing questions that characters may want to ask
		'The Threat' adapted from *Chicken*, Alan Gibbons	14			cloze activity; underlining correct endings to sentences; understanding stage directions	thinking about characters' actions and feelings; writing and performing a scene
		'Staying Together' adapted from *Carrie's War*, Nina Bawden	14			who said what; who does what; cloze activity	writing about a character's thoughts and feelings and writing a letter from their perspective
10	Looking at Settings	'Burning Heat' from *The Peacock Garden*, Anita Desai	16	standard 5, criteria 2, 4, 7, 8, 12, 13, 14, 16, 17, 19, 21, 24	fiction	matching phrases; matching adjectives to nouns	predicting what happens next
		'The Long Road' from *Journey to Jo'burg*, Beverley Naidoo	14			underlining correct answers; matching labels to illustrations	putting yourself in a character's position and thinking about their needs
		'My Home' from *The Most Beautiful Place in the World*, Ann Cameron	14			matching phrases to headings; underlining correct endings to sentences; matching adjectives to nouns	writing about what you think and why

UNIT FOCUS: Characters' Points of View

Investigating …

- fiction set during the Second World War
- using your imagination to relate to characters

TEACH

- Discuss what the terms 'evacuation' and 'evacuee' mean to the children.
- Ask children if they think it would be an easy or difficult decision for parents to send their children away in wartime.
- Ask children how they would feel if they had to be sent away.
- Read the extract to the class; ask individual children to read it aloud in turn; or read in silence individually.

RESOURCES & ASSESSMENT BOOK

- **Support** (comprehension support): choosing the correct ending, identifying True / False statements; (vocabulary support): matching words and definitions.
- **Extension:** understanding characters' points of view, making notes.

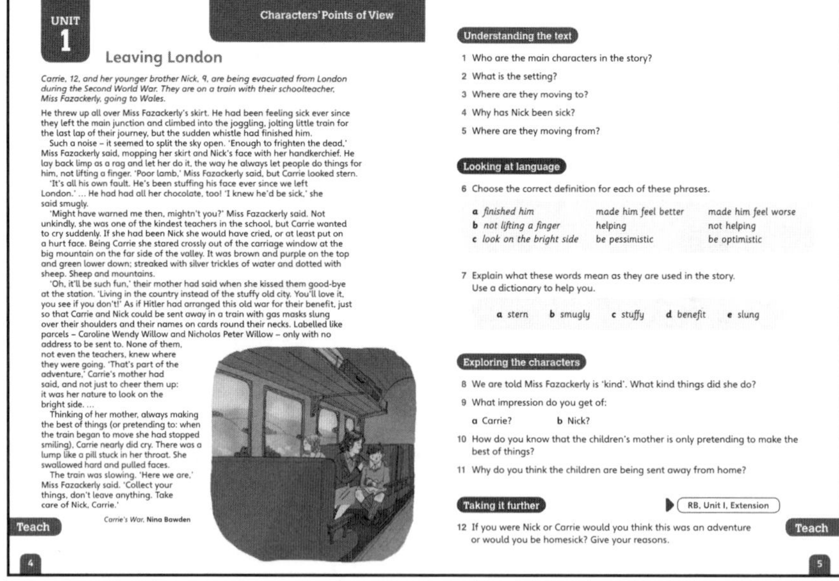

UNIT 1 — Characters' Points of View

Leaving London

Carrie, 12, and her younger brother Nick, 9, are being evacuated from London during the Second World War. They are on a train with their schoolteacher, Miss Fazackerly, going to Wales.

He threw up all over Miss Fazackerly's skirt. He had been feeling sick ever since they left the main junction and climbed into the joggling, jolting little train for the last lap of their journey, but the sudden whistle had finished him.

Such a noise – it seemed to split the sky open. 'Enough to frighten the dead,' Miss Fazackerly said, mopping her skirt and Nick's face with her handkerchief. He lay back limp as a rag and let her do it, the way he always let people do things for him, not lifting a finger. 'Poor lamb,' Miss Fazackerly said, but Carrie looked stern.

'It's all his own fault. He's been stuffing his face ever since we left London.' … He had had all her chocolate, too! 'I knew he'd be sick,' she said smugly.

'Might have warned me then, mightn't you?' Miss Fazackerly said. Not unkindly, she was one of the kindest teachers in the school, but Carrie wanted to cry suddenly. If she had been Nick she would have cried, or at least put on a hurt face. Being Carrie she stared crossly out of the carriage window at the big mountain on the far side of the valley. It was brown and purple on the top and green lower down; streaked with silver trickles of water and dotted with sheep. Sheep and mountains.

'Oh, it'll be such fun,' their mother had said when she kissed them good-bye at the station. 'Living in the country instead of the stuffy old city. You'll love it, you see if you don't!' As if Hitler had arranged this old war for their benefit, just so that Carrie and Nick could be sent away in a train with gas masks slung over their shoulders and their names on cards round their necks. Labelled like parcels – Caroline Wendy Willow and Nicholas Peter Willow – only with no address to be sent to. None of them, not even the teachers, knew where they were going. 'That's part of the adventure,' Carrie's mother had said, and not just to cheer them up: it was her nature to look on the bright side. …

Thinking of her mother, always making the best of things (or pretending to: when the train began to move she had stopped smiling), Carrie nearly did cry. There was a lump like a pill stuck in her throat. She swallowed hard and pulled faces.

The train was slowing. 'Here we are,' Miss Fazackerly said. 'Collect your things, don't leave anything. Take care of Nick, Carrie.'

Carrie's War, **Nina Bawden**

Teach

4

Understanding the text

1 Who are the main characters in the story?

2 What is the setting?

3 Where are they moving to?

4 Why has Nick been sick?

5 Where are they moving from?

Looking at language

6 Choose the correct definition for each of these phrases.

a *finished him*	*made him feel better*	*made him feel worse*
b *not lifting a finger*	helping	not helping
c *look on the bright side*	be pessimistic	be optimistic

7 Explain what these words mean as they are used in the story. Use a dictionary to help you.

a *stern* **b** *smugly* **c** *stuffy* **d** *benefit* **e** *slung*

Exploring the characters

8 We are told Miss Fazackerly is 'kind'. What kind things did she do?

9 What impression do you get of:

a Carrie? b Nick?

10 How do you know that the children's mother is only pretending to make the best of things?

11 Why do you think the children are being sent away from home?

Taking it further

RB, Unit I, Extension

12 If you were Nick or Carrie would you think this was an adventure or would you be homesick? Give your reasons.

Teach

5

PUPIL BOOK ANSWERS

1 Carrie / Nick / Miss Fazackerly / the children's mother.

2 A railway carriage.

3 They are moving to the country (Wales) but they are not sure exactly where they are going.

4 Nick has been 'stuffing his face'. He has even eaten his sister's chocolate. The 'joggling, jolting little train' and the 'sudden whistle' made him sick.

5 London.

6 **a** finished him: made him feel worse **b** not lifting a finger: not helping **c** look on the bright side: be optimistic

7 **a** stern: not sympathetic or understanding **b** smugly: pleased to be correct **c** stuffy: lacking space and fresh air / unpleasant **d** benefit: advantage or gain **e** carrying something hung off your body

8 She looked after Nick / was not cross when he was sick on her skirt.

9 **a** Carrie:

- She can be kind and thoughtful – she gives Nick her chocolate.
- She can be very impatient with her brother – she thinks it is his own fault that he is sick in the train.
- She doesn't like to show her true feelings – she wanted to cry but tried really hard not to.

b Nick:

- Easily frightened e.g. 'the sudden whistle had finished him'.
- He likes everything done for him – when he was sick he let Miss Fazackerly mop it up and wipe his face without helping her.

10 Their mother 'stopped smiling' when the train began to move.

11 Answers that suggest London would be unsafe because of enemy bombing.

12 Individual answers.

RESOURCE SHEET SUPPORT ANSWERS

A

1 a

2 b

3 a

4 b

5 b

B

1 True

2 True

3 False

4 False

5 True

C

jolting: moving suddenly, stern: serious, sympathy: understanding, smugly: in a satisfied way, stuffy: with no fresh air

GOING DEEPER

- Through discussion, help children to understand that Carrie and Nick would have no idea of where they were going to live or with whom. Ask children how they think the children in the story would be feeling at this point.

TALK

- Ask children what they understand by the term 'prisoner'.
- Discuss what they think happened to prisoners of war that were captured during the Second World War and brought to Britain.
- Explain that this extract from *The War and Freddy* is about a boy, Freddy, who is three years old when the war begins, experiences the departure of his father and the arrival of the prisoners of war.
- Read the extract to the class; ask individual children to read it aloud in turn; or read in silence individually.

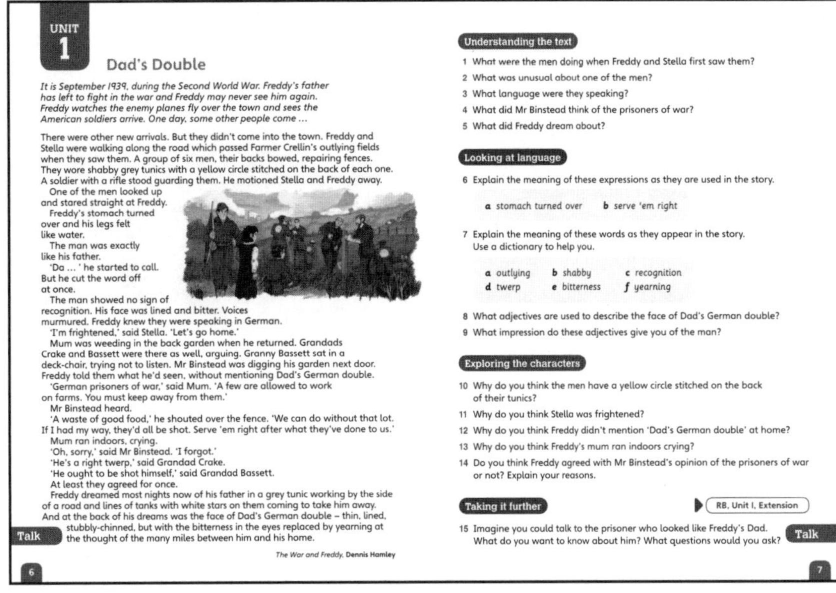

UNIT 1

Dad's Double

It is September 1939, during the Second World War. Freddy's father has left to fight in the war and Freddy may never see him again. Freddy watches the enemy planes fly over the town and sees the American soldiers arrive. One day, some other people come …

There were other new arrivals. But they didn't come into the town. Freddy and Stella were walking along the road which passed Farmer Crellin's outlying fields when they saw them. A group of six men, their backs bowed, repairing fences. They wore shabby grey tunics with a yellow circle stitched on the back of each one. A soldier with a rifle stood guarding them. He motioned Stella and Freddy away.

One of the men looked up and stared straight at Freddy.

Freddy's stomach turned over and his legs felt like water.

The man was exactly like his father.

'Da … ' he started to call. But he cut the word off at once.

The man showed no sign of recognition. His face was lined and bitter. Voices murmured. Freddy knew they were speaking in German.

'I'm frightened,' said Stella. 'Let's go home.'

Mum was weeding in the back garden when he returned. Grandads Crake and Bassett were there as well, arguing. Granny Bassett sat in a deck-chair, trying not to listen. Mr Binstead was digging his garden next door. Freddy told them what he'd seen, without mentioning Dad's German double.

'German prisoners of war,' said Mum. 'A few are allowed to work on farms. You must keep away from them.'

Mr Binstead heard.

'A waste of good food,' he shouted over the fence. 'We can do without that lot. If I had my way, they'd all be shot. Serve 'em right after what they've done to us.'

Mum ran indoors, crying.

'Oh, sorry,' said Mr Binstead. 'I forgot.'

'He's a right twerp,' said Grandad Crake.

'He ought to be shot himself,' said Grandad Bassett.

At least they agreed for once.

Freddy dreamed most nights now of his father in a grey tunic working by the side of a road and lines of tanks with white stars on them coming to take him away. And at the back of his dreams was the face of Dad's German double – thin, lined, stubbly-chinned, but with the bitterness in the eyes replaced by yearning at the thought of the many miles between him and his home.

Talk

The War and Freddy, **Dennis Hamley**

6

Understanding the text

1 What were the men doing when Freddy and Stella first saw them?
2 What was unusual about one of the men?
3 What language were they speaking?
4 What did Mr Binstead think of the prisoners of war?
5 What did Freddy dream about?

Looking at language

6 Explain the meaning of these expressions as they are used in the story.

a stomach turned over **b** serve 'em right

7 Explain the meaning of these words as they appear in the story. Use a dictionary to help you.

a outlying **b** shabby **c** recognition
d twerp **e** bitterness **f** yearning

8 What adjectives are used to describe the face of Dad's German double?
9 What impression do these adjectives give you of the man?

Exploring the characters

10 Why do you think the men have a yellow circle stitched on the back of their tunics?
11 Why do you think Stella was frightened?
12 Why do you think Freddy didn't mention 'Dad's German double' at home?
13 Why do you think Freddy's mum ran indoors crying?
14 Do you think Freddy agreed with Mr Binstead's opinion of the prisoners of war or not? Explain your reasons.

Taking it further

RB, Unit 1, Extension

15 Imagine you could talk to the prisoner who looked like Freddy's Dad. What do you want to know about him? What questions would you ask?

Talk

7

RESOURCES & ASSESSMENT BOOK

- **Support** (comprehension support): who said what?; (vocabulary support): cloze activity to reinforce vocabulary.
- **Extension:** understanding characters' points of view, writing questions.

PUPIL BOOK ANSWERS

1. Repairing fences.
2. He looked like Freddy's father.
3. German.
4. He thought that they were 'a waste of good food' and that they should 'all be shot'.
5. He dreamed about his father and the prisoner who looked like his father.
6. **a** stomach turned over: a strange feeling in the pit of your stomach when something shocks or surprises you. **b** serve 'em right: get what they deserve.
7. **a** outlying: away from areas where people live **b** shabby: worn / old / tatty **c** recognition: knowing him **d** twerp: silly / annoying person **e** bitterness: feelings of resentment and anger **f** yearning: longing / really wanting something
8. Lined / bitter / thin / stubbly-chinned.
9. Answers that suggest the man was underfed, under a lot of strain and not in a position to care about his appearance.
10. Answers that suggest it was to identify them as prisoners of war.
11. Answers that suggest the men were strangers / they spoke German / they were guarded.
12. Answers that suggest it would have upset his mother.
13. Answers that suggest Mr Binstead's opinion upset her because her husband may be a prisoner of war.
14. Answers that suggest Freddy did not agree with Mr Binstead. To Freddy they were not just 'the enemy'. In his dreams, it is his father who is the prisoner of war.
15. Encourage all members of the group to contribute. One child should take notes and include all the questions suggested in the discussion.

RESOURCE SHEET SUPPORT ANSWERS

A

1. Grandad Crake
2. Stella
3. Freddy
4. Mr Binstead
5. Mum

B

Stella and Freddy were near Farmer Crellin's **outlying** fields. They saw men in **shabby** grey uniforms. Freddy saw one that looked like his dad. He looked **bitter**. Freddy told his mum and grandad about the men. He didn't **mention** the one that looked like his dad. Mr Binstead **upset** Freddy's mum because he said **prisoners** of war should be shot. Freddy had dreams about his father working many **miles** away from home.

GOING DEEPER

- Ask children what they think about the prisoners of war in the extract. How do they think they should be treated? Do they see them as 'the enemy' or just soldiers doing their job?

WRITE

- Ask children what they understand by the term 'the Blitz'.
- Ask children how they think the Blitz affected the lives of ordinary people. How do they think children were affected by it?
- Explain to children that they are going to read an extract from a book of short stories called *Blitz*. It is set in Newcastle, Tyneside, during the Second World War, and the children's favourite pastime is playing pretend war games.
- Read the extract to the class; ask individual children to read it aloud in turn; or read in silence individually.

RESOURCES & ASSESSMENT BOOK

- **Support** (comprehension support): narrative sequencing, completing sentences; (vocabulary support): labelling drawings.
- **Extension:** understanding characters' feelings.

PUPIL BOOK ANSWERS

1. A plane that had crashed.
2. A lump of the tail had fallen off and it bore the British colours of red, white and blue.
3. Fighter planes.
4. There was a 'terrible smell of petrol' and Albert was afraid of a fire breaking out.
5. He saw the pilot with a ripped helmet and blood showing through.
6. 'horseshoe shapes' – they were bent out of shape.
7. Petrol could burn very easily.
8. **a** unsayable: too awful to be put into words **b** vanished: disappeared from view **c** baled out: jumped out **d** mocking him: making fun of him **e** edged up: went carefully and slowly **f** asphyxiating: making it very difficult to breathe
9. Answers that suggest the boys do not know what has happened or if the worst has happened:
   a cannot bring himself to say, 'He might be dead'. **b** They were expecting 'at every corner to see the crashed plane'.
10. Answers that suggest that below a certain height there would not be enough time for the parachute to open.

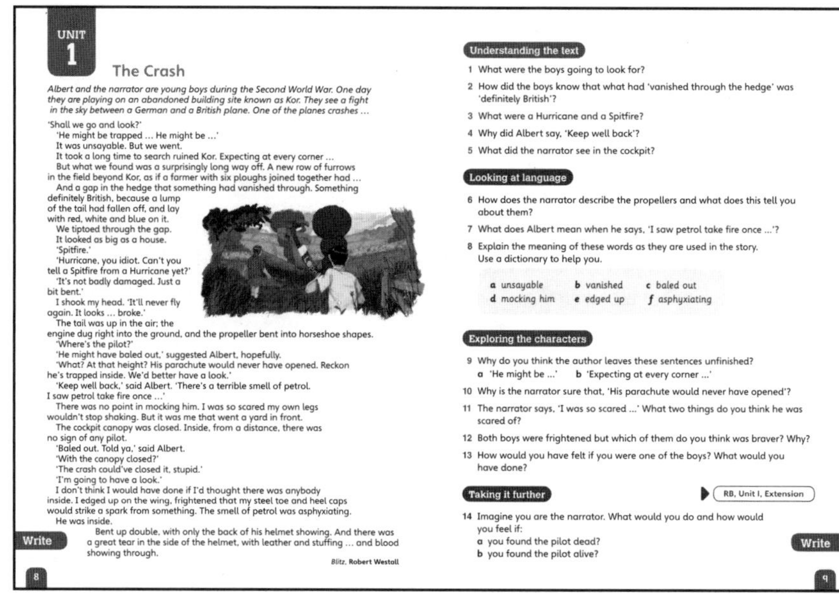
UNIT 1

The Crash

Albert and the narrator are young boys during the Second World War. One day they are playing on an abandoned building site known as Kor. They see a fight in the sky between a German and a British plane. One of the planes crashes …

'Shall we go and look?'

'He might be trapped … He might be …'

It was unsayable. But we went.

It took a long time to search ruined Kor. Expecting at every corner …

But what we found was a surprisingly long way off. A new row of furrows in the field beyond Kor, as if a farmer with six ploughs joined together had …

And a gap in the hedge that something had vanished through. Something definitely British, because a lump of the tail had fallen off, and lay with red, white and blue on it.

We tiptoed through the gap.

It looked as big as a house.

'Spitfire.'

'Hurricane, you idiot. Can't you tell a Spitfire from a Hurricane yet?'

'It's not badly damaged. Just a bit bent.'

I shook my head. 'It'll never fly again. It looks … broke.'

The tail was up in the air; the engine dug right into the ground, and the propeller bent into horseshoe shapes.

'Where's the pilot?'

'He might have baled out,' suggested Albert, hopefully.

'What? At that height? His parachute would never have opened. Reckon he's trapped inside. We'd better have a look.'

'Keep well back,' said Albert. 'There's a terrible smell of petrol. I saw petrol take fire once …'

There was no point in mocking him. I was so scared my own legs wouldn't stop shaking. But it was me that went a yard in front.

The cockpit canopy was closed. Inside, from a distance, there was no sign of any pilot.

'Baled out. Told ya,' said Albert.

'With the canopy closed?'

'The crash could've closed it, stupid.'

'I'm going to have a look.'

I don't think I would have done if I'd thought there was anybody inside. I edged up on the wing, frightened that my steel toe and heel caps would strike a spark from something. The smell of petrol was asphyxiating.

He was inside.

Bent up double, with only the back of his helmet showing. And there was a great tear in the side of the helmet, with leather and stuffing … and blood showing through.

Blitz, Robert Westall

Write

8

Understanding the text

1 What were the boys going to look for?

2 How did the boys know that what had 'vanished through the hedge' was 'definitely British'?

3 What were a Hurricane and a Spitfire?

4 Why did Albert say, 'Keep well back'?

5 What did the narrator see in the cockpit?

Looking at language

6 How does the narrator describe the propellers and what does this tell you about them?

7 What does Albert mean when he says, 'I saw petrol take fire once …'?

8 Explain the meaning of these words as they are used in the story. Use a dictionary to help you.

a unsayable b vanished c baled out
d mocking him e edged up f asphyxiating

Exploring the characters

9 Why do you think the author leaves these sentences unfinished?
a 'He might be …' b 'Expecting at every corner …'

10 Why is the narrator sure that, 'His parachute would never have opened'?

11 The narrator says, 'I was so scared …' What two things do you think he was scared of?

12 Both boys were frightened but which of them do you think was braver? Why?

13 How would you have felt if you were one of the boys? What would you have done?

Taking it further RB, Unit I, Extension

14 Imagine you are the narrator. What would you do and how would you feel if:
a you found the pilot dead?
b you found the pilot alive?

Write

9

11. Finding the pilot dead and the plane exploding.
12. Answer suggesting that the narrator was braver because, although he put himself in danger, he needed to see if he could help the pilot.
13. Individual answers.
14. Individual answers.

RESOURCE SHEET SUPPORT ANSWERS

A

They tiptoed through the gap. 6
He saw the pilot inside. 10
The boys were playing on a building site. 1
They searched the building site. 3
The narrator wanted to look in the cockpit. 7
They saw a new row of furrows in a field. 4
Albert wanted to stay back. 8
They saw a plane crash. 2
They saw a gap in the hedge and a lump of the plane's tail. 5
The narrator climbed on to the wing. 9

B

Individual answers.

C

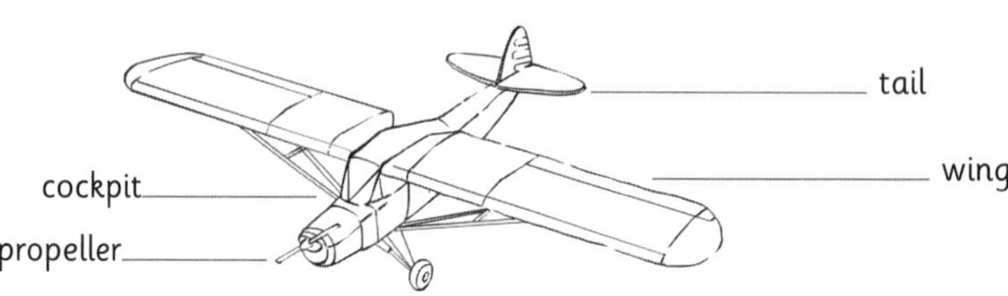

GOING DEEPER

- Discuss the three extracts with the children. How are the children in the stories and their situations similar and how are they different? Which extract made children appreciate the most what it must have been like to live in wartime? Why?

UNIT FOCUS: Exploring Journalistic Writing

Investigating …

- newspaper / magazine articles that have an element of 'recount' but also include biographical and factual information
- texts linked by the theme of sport

TEACH

- Discuss sport in general with the children. What are their favourite sports? Why? Do some of them not like any kind of sport? Why not?
- Discuss what children understand by the term 'marathon'.
- Ask children what they think about long-distance running.
- Explain to children that they are going to read a magazine article about one of the world's most famous and successful marathon runners, Paula Radcliffe.
- Read the article to the class; ask individual children to read it aloud in turn; or read in silence individually.

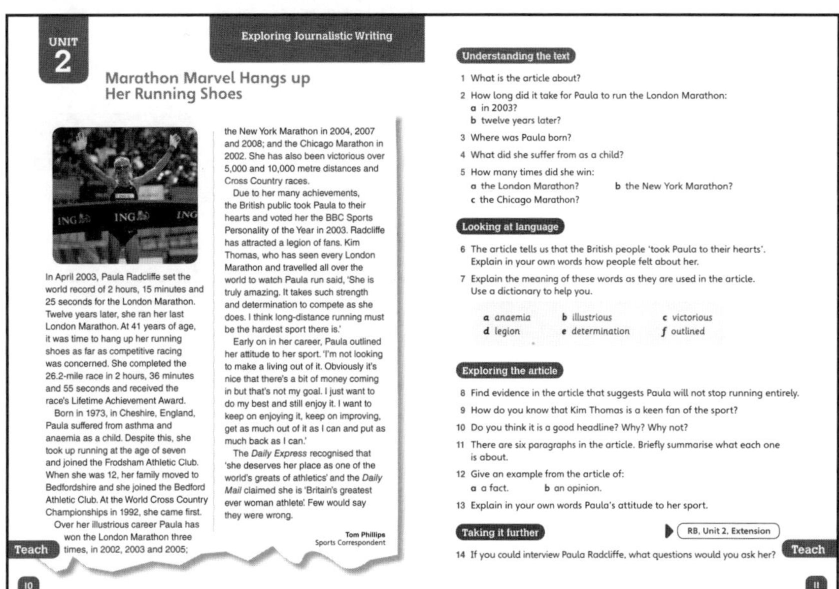
UNIT 2

Exploring Journalistic Writing

Marathon Marvel Hangs up Her Running Shoes

In April 2003, Paula Radcliffe set the world record of 2 hours, 15 minutes and 25 seconds for the London Marathon. Twelve years later, she ran her last London Marathon. At 41 years of age, it was time to hang up her running shoes as far as competitive racing was concerned. She completed the 26.2-mile race in 2 hours, 36 minutes and 55 seconds and received the race's Lifetime Achievement Award.

Born in 1973, in Cheshire, England, Paula suffered from asthma and anaemia as a child. Despite this, she took up running at the age of seven and joined the Frodsham Athletic Club. When she was 12, her family moved to Bedfordshire and she joined the Bedford Athletic Club. At the World Cross Country Championships in 1992, she came first.

Over her illustrious career Paula has won the London Marathon three times, in 2002, 2003 and 2005; the New York Marathon in 2004, 2007 and 2008; and the Chicago Marathon in 2002. She has also been victorious over 5,000 and 10,000 metre distances and Cross Country races.

Due to her many achievements, the British public took Paula to their hearts and voted her the BBC Sports Personality of the Year in 2003. Radcliffe has attracted a legion of fans. Kim Thomas, who has seen every London Marathon and travelled all over the world to watch Paula run said, 'She is truly amazing. It takes such strength and determination to compete as she does. I think long-distance running must be the hardest sport there is.'

Early on in her career, Paula outlined her attitude to her sport. 'I'm not looking to make a living out of it. Obviously it's nice that there's a bit of money coming in but that's not my goal. I just want to do my best and still enjoy it. I want to keep on enjoying it, keep on improving, get as much out of it as I can and put as much back as I can.'

The *Daily Express* recognised that 'she deserves her place as one of the world's greats of athletics' and the *Daily Mail* claimed she is 'Britain's greatest ever woman athlete'. Few would say they were wrong.

Tom Phillips
Sports Correspondent

Teach

10

Understanding the text

1 What is the article about?
2 How long did it take for Paula to run the London Marathon:
a in 2003?
b twelve years later?
3 Where was Paula born?
4 What did she suffer from as a child?
5 How many times did she win:
a the London Marathon? b the New York Marathon?
c the Chicago Marathon?

Looking at language

6 The article tells us that the British people 'took Paula to their hearts'. Explain in your own words how people felt about her.
7 Explain the meaning of these words as they are used in the article. Use a dictionary to help you.
a anaemia b illustrious c victorious
d legion e determination f outlined

Exploring the article

8 Find evidence in the article that suggests Paula will not stop running entirely.
9 How do you know that Kim Thomas is a keen fan of the sport?
10 Do you think it is a good headline? Why? Why not?
11 There are six paragraphs in the article. Briefly summarise what each one is about.
12 Give an example from the article of:
a a fact. b an opinion.
13 Explain in your own words Paula's attitude to her sport.

Taking it further

RB, Unit 2, Extension

14 If you could interview Paula Radcliffe, what questions would you ask her?

Teach

11

RESOURCES & ASSESSMENT BOOK

- **Support** (comprehension support): completing a chart with information from an article; (vocabulary support): choosing correct definition.
- **Extension:** writing questions for an interview.

PUPIL BOOK ANSWERS

1 Paula Radcliffe.

2 **a** 2 hours, 15 minutes and 25 seconds.
b 2 hours, 36 minutes and 55 seconds.

3 Cheshire, England.

4 Asthma and anaemia.

5 **a** Three times. **b** Three times. **c** Once.

6 Answers that suggest people were fond of her / wanted to support her / admired her.

7 **a** anaemia: medical condition where there are too few red blood cells
b illustrious: marked by respect and famous achievements **c** victorious: having won **d** legion: a huge number
e determination: refusal to be stopped from achieving what you set out to do
f outlined: summarised

8 Answers that cite evidence of retiring from 'competitive racing'. This suggests she would still run for fun / to keep fit / because she enjoys it.

9 She has seen every London Marathon and travelled all over the world to see Paula run.

10 Individual answers.

11 Paragraph 1: Paula's world record marathon and her last marathon.
Paragraph 2: her early years.
Paragraph 3: summary of her career.
Paragraph 4: Paula's fans.
Paragraph 5: Paula's attitude to her sport.
Paragraph 6: newspaper quotes about her.

12 **a** E.g. the timing of her races / the Marathons she won / her childhood illnesses.
b 'I think long-distance running must be the hardest sport there is' / 'she deserves her place as one of the world's greats of athletics' / 'Britain's greatest ever woman athlete'.

13 Answers that suggest Paula ran because she enjoyed it and wanted to get better at it rather than wanting fame and money.

14 Individual answers. Make notes on the board of all the suggested questions. Have a class vote on the five best.

RESOURCE SHEET SUPPORT ANSWERS

A

Date	What happened
1973	Paula Radcliffe born in Cheshire
1992	came first at World Cross Country Championships
2002	won the London Marathon / won the Chicago Marathon
2003	set world record of 2 hours, 15 minutes and 25 seconds for the London Marathon
2004	won New York Marathon
2005	won London Marathon
2007	won New York Marathon
2008	won New York Marathon
2015	ran in her last London Marathon

B

1 successful

2 strong-willed

3 won

GOING DEEPER

- Ask children what else they would like to know about Paula Radcliffe. What have they learnt about the features of newspapers? Discuss alternative headlines for the article.

TALK

- How many children cycle? Do they like it?
- What are the advantages of cycling?
- What are the disadvantages?
- Do they know the names of any famous cyclists?
- Explain to children that they are going to read a newspaper article about cycling called 'On Your Bike'.
- Read the article to the class; ask individual children to read it aloud in turn; or read in silence individually.

RESOURCES & ASSESSMENT BOOK

- **Support** (comprehension support): matching paragraphs to summaries; (vocabulary support): cloze activities for vocabulary reinforcement.
- **Extension:** planning to make a flyer.

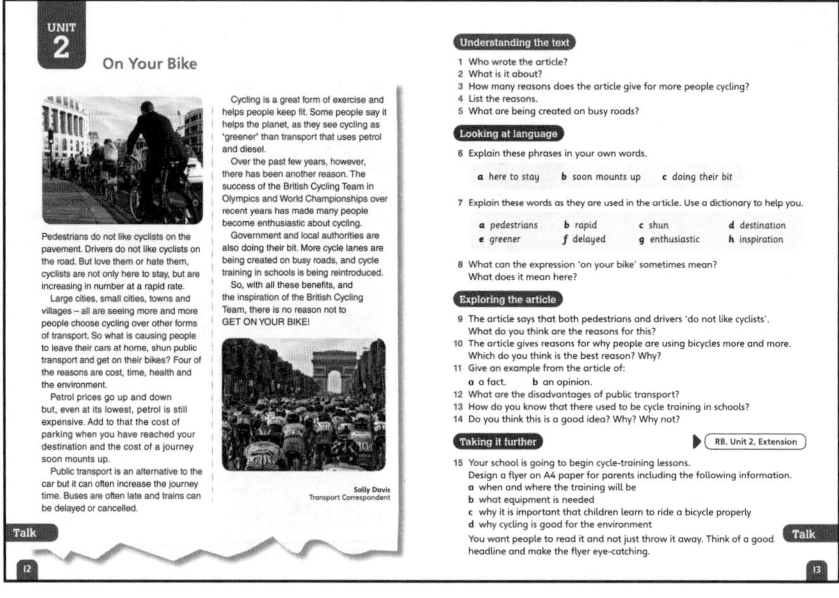

UNIT 2

On Your Bike

Pedestrians do not like cyclists on the pavement. Drivers do not like cyclists on the road. But love them or hate them, cyclists are not only here to stay, but are increasing in number at a rapid rate.

Large cities, small cities, towns and villages – all are seeing more and more people choose cycling over other forms of transport. So what is causing people to leave their cars at home, shun public transport and get on their bikes? Four of the reasons are cost, time, health and the environment.

Petrol prices go up and down but, even at its lowest, petrol is still expensive. Add to that the cost of parking when you have reached your destination and the cost of a journey soon mounts up.

Public transport is an alternative to the car but it can often increase the journey time. Buses are often late and trains can be delayed or cancelled.

Cycling is a great form of exercise and helps people keep fit. Some people say it helps the planet, as they see cycling as 'greener' than transport that uses petrol and diesel.

Over the past few years, however, there has been another reason. The success of the British Cycling Team in Olympics and World Championships over recent years has made many people become enthusiastic about cycling.

Government and local authorities are also doing their bit. More cycle lanes are being created on busy roads, and cycle training in schools is being reintroduced.

So, with all these benefits, and the inspiration of the British Cycling Team, there is no reason not to GET ON YOUR BIKE!

Sally Davis
Transport Correspondent

Talk

12

Understanding the text

1 Who wrote the article?
2 What is it about?
3 How many reasons does the article give for more people cycling?
4 List the reasons.
5 What are being created on busy roads?

Looking at language

6 Explain these phrases in your own words.
a *here to stay* b *soon mounts up* c *doing their bit*

7 Explain these words as they are used in the article. Use a dictionary to help you.
a *pedestrians* b *rapid* c *shun* d *destination*
e *greener* f *delayed* g *enthusiastic* h *inspiration*

8 What can the expression 'on your bike' sometimes mean? What does it mean here?

Exploring the article

9 The article says that both pedestrians and drivers 'do not like cyclists'. What do you think are the reasons for this?
10 The article gives reasons for why people are using bicycles more and more. Which do you think is the best reason? Why?
11 Give an example from the article of:
a a fact. b an opinion.
12 What are the disadvantages of public transport?
13 How do you know that there used to be cycle training in schools?
14 Do you think this is a good idea? Why? Why not?

Taking it further

RB, Unit 2, Extension

15 Your school is going to begin cycle-training lessons.
Design a flyer on A4 paper for parents including the following information.
a when and where the training will be
b what equipment is needed
c why it is important that children learn to ride a bicycle properly
d why cycling is good for the environment
You want people to read it and not just throw it away. Think of a good headline and make the flyer eye-catching.

Talk

13

PUPIL BOOK ANSWERS

1 Sally Davis.

2 Why cycling is becoming more popular.

3 Five.

4 Cost / time / health / environment / success of British Cycling Team.

5 Cycle lanes.

6 **a** here to stay: something that won't go away / disappear **b** soon mounts up: becomes more [expensive] very quickly **c** doing their bit: helping

7 **a** pedestrians: people who walk on the pavement **b** rapid: very quick **c** shun: avoid / have nothing to do with / stop using **d** destination: the end point of your journey **e** greener: more environmentally friendly **f** delayed: not arriving on time **g** enthusiastic: very interested / supportive **h** inspiration: example to follow

8 'Go away' / Here it means get cycling!

9 Answers that suggest cyclists on pavements can be a danger to pedestrians. If a driver gets stuck behind a cyclist on the road it can be very irritating. Drivers see them as a nuisance and a danger. Drivers often don't see cyclists and sometimes cyclists swerve in and out of traffic.

10 Individual answers that the group can debate.

11 **a** E.g. 'more and more people choose cycling over other forms of transport'. **b** E.g. 'Some people say it helps the planet, as they see cycling as "greener" than transport that uses petrol and diesel'.

12 It can be cancelled or delayed.

13 Answers that suggest the use of the word 'reintroduce' indicates that there was once cycle training in school but it had stopped.

14 Answers that suggest it is a good idea to ensure young people are aware of the dangers on the road and can handle their bicycles properly and with care.

15 Encourage all members of the group to participate. They should consider the layout and eye-catching qualities of the flyer e.g. font size / colour / illustration and the title.

RESOURCE SHEET SUPPORT ANSWERS

A

Paragraph 1: cyclists not liked but are here to stay **Paragraph 2:** asks questions – why people are cycling, gives 4 reasons **Paragraph 3:** cost of using a car **Paragraph 4:** disadvantages of public transport **Paragraph 5:** cycling as exercise, concern for the planet **Paragraph 6:** cycling's popularity due to success of team **Paragraph 7:** what government and local authorities are doing **Paragraph 8:** conclusion to 'get on your bike'

B

1 pedestrians

2 rapid

3 shun

4 destination

5 greener

6 delayed

7 enthusiastic

8 inspiration

GOING DEEPER

- Discuss the groups' responses to the reasons in the article why people cycle. If time permits, groups should produce their flyer for display.

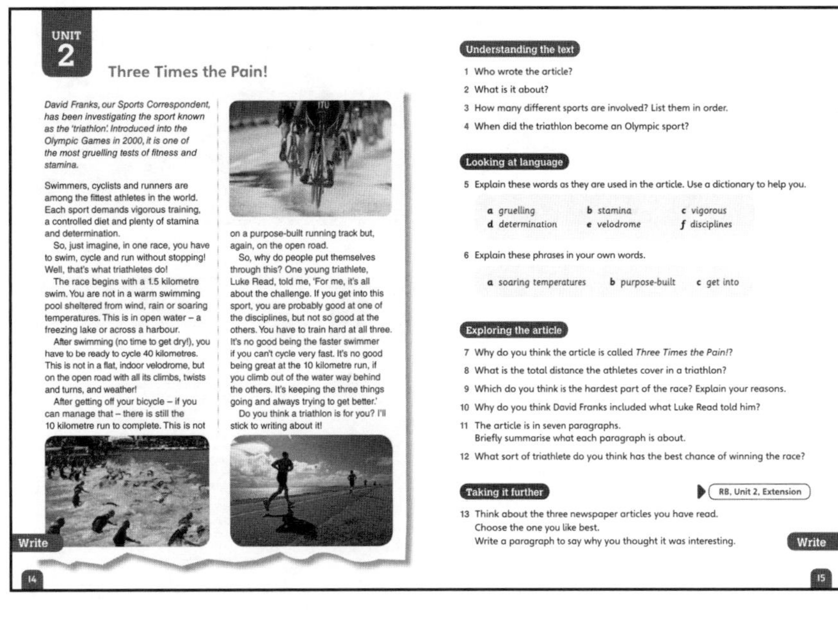

UNIT 2

Three Times the Pain!

David Franks, our Sports Correspondent, has been investigating the sport known as the 'triathlon'. Introduced into the Olympic Games in 2000, it is one of the most gruelling tests of fitness and stamina.

Swimmers, cyclists and runners are among the fittest athletes in the world. Each sport demands vigorous training, a controlled diet and plenty of stamina and determination.

So, just imagine, in one race, you have to swim, cycle and run without stopping! Well, that's what triathletes do!

The race begins with a 1.5 kilometre swim. You are not in a warm swimming pool sheltered from wind, rain or soaring temperatures. This is in open water – a freezing lake or across a harbour.

After swimming (no time to get dry!), you have to be ready to cycle 40 kilometres. This is not in a flat, indoor velodrome, but on the open road with all its climbs, twists and turns, and weather!

After getting off your bicycle – if you can manage that – there is still the 10 kilometre run to complete. This is not on a purpose-built running track but, again, on the open road.

So, why do people put themselves through this? One young triathlete, Luke Read, told me, 'For me, it's all about the challenge. If you get into this sport, you are probably good at one of the disciplines, but not so good at the others. You have to train hard at all three. It's no good being the faster swimmer if you can't cycle very fast. It's no good being great at the 10 kilometre run, if you climb out of the water way behind the others. It's keeping the three things going and always trying to get better.'

Do you think a triathlon is for you? I'll stick to writing about it!

Write

14

Understanding the text

1 Who wrote the article?

2 What is it about?

3 How many different sports are involved? List them in order.

4 When did the triathlon become an Olympic sport?

Looking at language

5 Explain these words as they are used in the article. Use a dictionary to help you.

a gruelling **b** stamina **c** vigorous
d determination **e** velodrome **f** disciplines

6 Explain these phrases in your own words.

a soaring temperatures **b** purpose-built **c** get into

Exploring the article

7 Why do you think the article is called *Three Times the Pain!*?

8 What is the total distance the athletes cover in a triathlon?

9 Which do you think is the hardest part of the race? Explain your reasons.

10 Why do you think David Franks included what Luke Read told him?

11 The article is in seven paragraphs.
Briefly summarise what each paragraph is about.

12 What sort of triathlete do you think has the best chance of winning the race?

Taking it further RB, Unit 2, Extension

13 Think about the three newspaper articles you have read.
Choose the one you like best.
Write a paragraph to say why you thought it was interesting. Write

15

WRITE

- Discuss the prefix 'tri' with the children. Can they give examples of 'tri' words e.g. triangle / tripod etc.
- Explain that a 'pentathlon' comprises five different sports and a heptathlon, seven different sports.
- How many sports do they think a 'triathlon' comprises?
- Explain they are going to read a newspaper article about the triathlon called 'Three Times the Pain!'
- Read the article to the class; ask individual children to read it aloud in turn; or read in silence individually.

RESOURCES & ASSESSMENT BOOK

- **Support** (comprehension support): matching sentence beginnings and endings; (vocabulary support): identifying adjectives, choosing correct definitions.
- **Extension:** choosing favourite article, writing notes.

PUPIL BOOK ANSWERS

1 David Franks.

2 Triathlons.

3 Three – swimming / cycling / running.

4 2000.

5 **a** gruelling: involving a lot of continuous effort **b** stamina: ability to work hard over a long period of time without getting tired **c** vigorous: energetic **d** determination: not letting anything stop you from what you want to do **e** velodrome: special building with a track for cycle racing **f** disciplines: type of sport

6 **a** soaring temperatures: temperatures that get very hot **b** purpose-built: built with a specific use in mind **c** get into: become involved with

7 Answers that suggest training for and competing in a sport can be physically painful. The triathlon involves three sports so there could be three times the pain!

8 51.5 kilometres.

9 Individual answers.

10 Answers that suggest readers would be interested in what an actual triathlete said about the sport.

11 **Paragraph 1:** swimming / cycling / running are demanding sports. **Paragraph 2:** asks reader to imagine doing all three. **Paragraph 3:** the swim. **Paragraph 4:** the cycle. **Paragraph 5:** the run. **Paragraph 6:** quotes form Luke Read who is a triathlete. **Paragraph 7:** question to the reader / decision of the writer.

12 Individual answers that may suggest e.g.:
- the athlete who is very good at all three disciplines
- the athlete who is strong in two and reasonable in another
- the athlete who can swim the faster and so leave all the others behind
- the athlete that can run the fastest and make up time lost etc.

13 Individual answers.

RESOURCE SHEET SUPPORT ANSWERS

A

1 and run without stopping.

2 a swim of 1.5 kilometres.

3 open water.

4 of 40 kilometres.

5 the open road.

6 a 10 kilometre run.

B

1 fittest

2 vigorous

3 warm

4 soaring

5 freezing

6 faster

C

1 hard work

2 keep going

3 energetic

4 a cycle track

GOING DEEPER

- Recap on what children have learned about newpaper / magazine articles.

UNIT FOCUS: Looking at Similes and Metaphors

Investigating ...

- how poets use their imagination to describe things they see
- how poets express experiences through similes and simple images

TEACH

- Ask children to imagine what it would be like to be in school on their own. What would the atmosphere be like? How would they feel?
- Explain to children that they are going to read a poem about a child who turns up to school 'a day too soon' and has a strange experience.
- Read the poem to the class; ask individual children to read it aloud in turn; or read in silence individually.

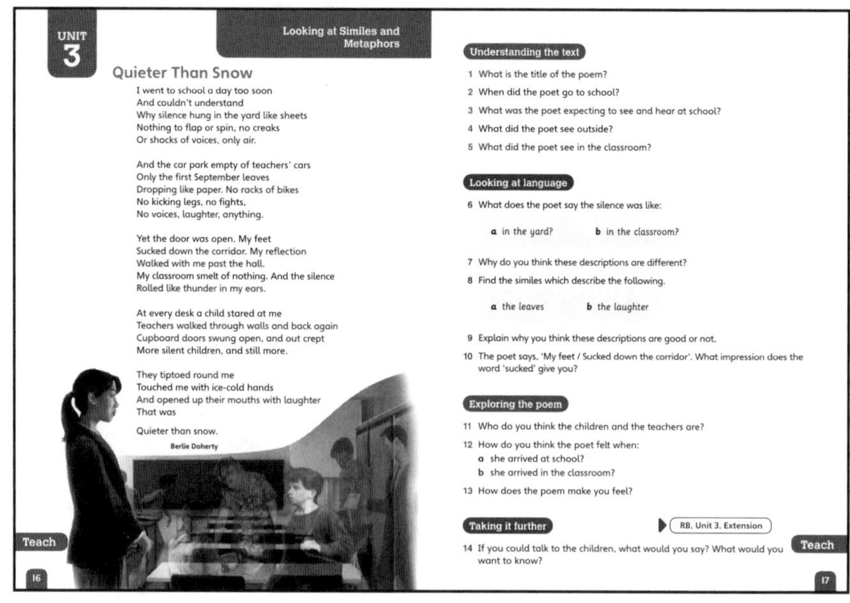

UNIT 3

Looking at Similes and Metaphors

Quieter Than Snow

I went to school a day too soon
And couldn't understand
Why silence hung in the yard like sheets
Nothing to flap or spin, no creaks
Or shocks of voices, only air.

And the car park empty of teachers' cars
Only the first September leaves
Dropping like paper. No racks of bikes
No kicking legs, no fights,
No voices, laughter, anything.

Yet the door was open. My feet
Sucked down the corridor. My reflection
Walked with me past the hall.
My classroom smelt of nothing. And the silence
Rolled like thunder in my ears.

At every desk a child stared at me
Teachers walked through walls and back again
Cupboard doors swung open, and out crept
More silent children, and still more.

They tiptoed round me
Touched me with ice-cold hands
And opened up their mouths with laughter
That was

Quieter than snow.

Berlie Doherty

Teach

16

Understanding the text

1 What is the title of the poem?
2 When did the poet go to school?
3 What was the poet expecting to see and hear at school?
4 What did the poet see outside?
5 What did the poet see in the classroom?

Looking at language

6 What does the poet say the silence was like:
a in the yard? b in the classroom?
7 Why do you think these descriptions are different?
8 Find the similes which describe the following.
a the leaves b the laughter
9 Explain why you think these descriptions are good or not.
10 The poet says, 'My feet / Sucked down the corridor'. What impression does the word 'sucked' give you?

Exploring the poem

11 Who do you think the children and the teachers are?
12 How do you think the poet felt when:
a she arrived at school?
b she arrived in the classroom?
13 How does the poem make you feel?

Taking it further

RB, Unit 3, Extension

14 If you could talk to the children, what would you say? What would you want to know?

Teach

17

RESOURCES & ASSESSMENT BOOK

- **Support** (comprehension support): completing a chart with details from the poem; (vocabulary support): identifying description from picture stimulus, completing descriptions.
- **Extension:** writing questions.

PUPIL BOOK ANSWERS

1. 'Quieter Than Snow'.
2. 'a day too soon' i.e. the day before term started.
3. See: a car park full of teachers' cars / racks of bikes / children fighting; hear: voices / laughter.
4. The poet saw an empty car park / empty bike racks / no children in the playground / falling leaves.
5. The poet saw: a child at every desk / teachers walking through walls / cupboard doors swinging open / more and more silent children.
6. **a** 'silence hung in the yard like sheets' **b** 'silence rolled like thunder in my ears'
7. Answers that suggest: there was no noise at all in the yard. The silence is likened to sheets on a washing line when there is no wind. They hang silent and unmoving; there was noise in the classroom but it seemed to come from a long way away, like thunder rolling in the distance.
8. **a** 'dropping like paper' **b** 'quieter than snow'
9. Individual answers that suggest these are good descriptions because: both leaves and paper are thin / they rustle / they would drop to the ground in the same way; the laughter of the children is like the 'silence' i.e. coming from far off [in time] and so almost silent.
10. 'Sucked' gives the impression of being pulled along strongly towards something, perhaps against your will.
11. Answers that suggest who the children and teachers are.
12. **a** Answers that suggest she felt puzzled / wary / couldn't understand. **b** Answers that suggest amazement / fear / wonder / curiosity.
13. Individual answers.
14. Individual answers e.g. Who are you? Where do you come from? Why are you here?

RESOURCE SHEET SUPPORT ANSWERS

A

What the poet sees and hears	What the poet does NOT see and hear
leaves dropping	laughter
her reflection	bikes
at every desk a child	fights
teachers	voices
open cupboard doors	teachers' cars

B

1. 'Why silence hung in the yard like sheets'
2. 'Only the first September leaves / Dropping like paper'

GOING DEEPER

- Ask children if they enjoyed the poem. Why / why not?
- Discuss what they would do if they were in the poet's situation. Invite the children to discuss the effects of some of the words and phrases that create strong images of what is happening in the poem.

TALK

- Show and discuss pictures that look like 'nothing' but, when you narrow your eyes, an image emerges, e.g. Escher / ink blots.
- Explain to children that they are going to read a poem that describes hills in an unusual way.
- Read the poem to the class; ask individual children to read it aloud in turn; or read in silence individually.

RESOURCES & ASSESSMENT BOOK

- **Support** (comprehension support): choosing the correct word to complete each sentence; (vocabulary support): identifying descriptions from picture stimulus, completing descriptions.
- **Extension:** using imagination to describe a given picture, completing a chart.

PUPIL BOOK ANSWERS

1 'sleeping dragons'.

2 'tufts of fur'.

3 'claws'.

4 'strange old battles'.

5 What would happen if the hills were really sleeping dragons and they woke up one day.

6 **a** loom: appear as a large, threatening shape **b** crouched: bent low **c** wisp: something with a long, thin, delicate shape **d** hollows: dips / indentations in the ground **e** stir: move **f** clustered: huddled together

7 Individual answers suggesting that the hills are at a distance because the poet cannot see them clearly so can imagine that they are dragons.

8 Less like dragons because the poet could see them more clearly.

9 Answers suggest that, as dragons breathe fire, the 'wisp' could be smoke from their mouths.

10 Smoke from the chimneys of the clustered houses.

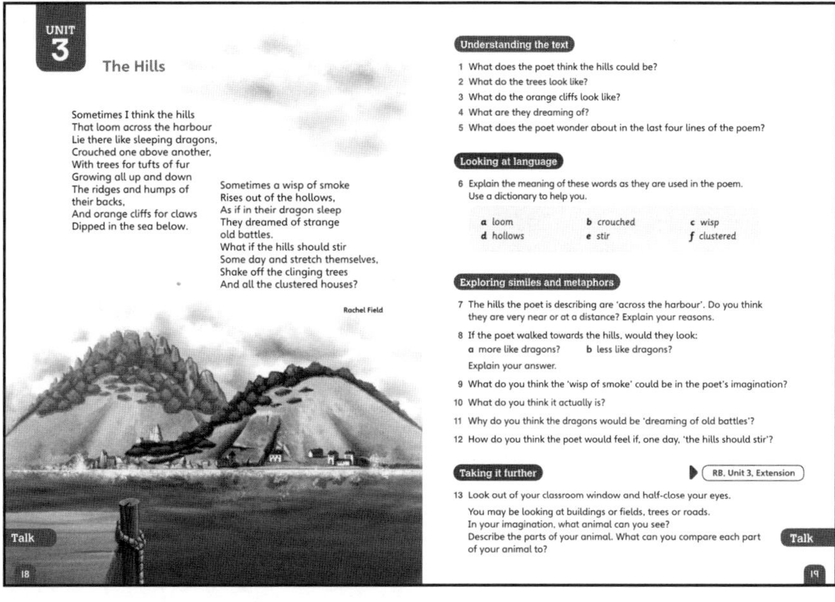

UNIT 3

The Hills

Sometimes I think the hills
That loom across the harbour
Lie there like sleeping dragons,
Crouched one above another,
With trees for tufts of fur
Growing all up and down
The ridges and humps of
their backs,
And orange cliffs for claws
Dipped in the sea below.

Sometimes a wisp of smoke
Rises out of the hollows,
As if in their dragon sleep
They dreamed of strange
old battles.
What if the hills should stir
Some day and stretch themselves,
Shake off the clinging trees
And all the clustered houses?

Rachel Field

Talk

18

Understanding the text

1 What does the poet think the hills could be?
2 What do the trees look like?
3 What do the orange cliffs look like?
4 What are they dreaming of?
5 What does the poet wonder about in the last four lines of the poem?

Looking at language

6 Explain the meaning of these words as they are used in the poem. Use a dictionary to help you.

a loom **b** crouched **c** wisp
d hollows **e** stir **f** clustered

Exploring similes and metaphors

7 The hills the poet is describing are 'across the harbour'. Do you think they are very near or at a distance? Explain your reasons.
8 If the poet walked towards the hills, would they look:
a more like dragons? **b** less like dragons?
Explain your answer.
9 What do you think the 'wisp of smoke' could be in the poet's imagination?
10 What do you think it actually is?
11 Why do you think the dragons would be 'dreaming of old battles'?
12 How do you think the poet would feel if, one day, 'the hills should stir'?

Taking it further RB, Unit 3, Extension

13 Look out of your classroom window and half-close your eyes.
You may be looking at buildings or fields, trees or roads.
In your imagination, what animal can you see?
Describe the parts of your animal. What can you compare each part of your animal to?

Talk

19

11 Answers that suggest in legends, dragons fought battles.

12 Individual answers suggesting amazement / fear / excitement / disbelief.

13 Children should do this individually then discuss it in their groups.

RESOURCE SHEET SUPPORT ANSWERS

A

1 The hills loom across the harbour.

2 They lie there like sleeping dragons.

3 The trees grow up and down the ridges.

4 A wisp of smoke rises out of the hollow.

5 The houses are clustered on the hills.

B

1 sleeping dragons

2 claws

C

The poet sometimes thinks the hills are sleeping **dragons**. She thinks the trees are **tufts** of fur. She thinks the cliffs are **claws**.

GOING DEEPER

- Discuss the groups' responses to what 'animals' they see when they half close their eyes, and particularly effective words and phrases used to describe them.

WRITE

- Ask children if they have ever experienced very hot weather. How does it make them feel? What does it make them want to do?
- Explain that this poem describes a moment in summer as perceived through the senses, by using strong metaphors and similes.
- Read the poem to the class; ask individual children to read it aloud in turn; or read in silence individually.

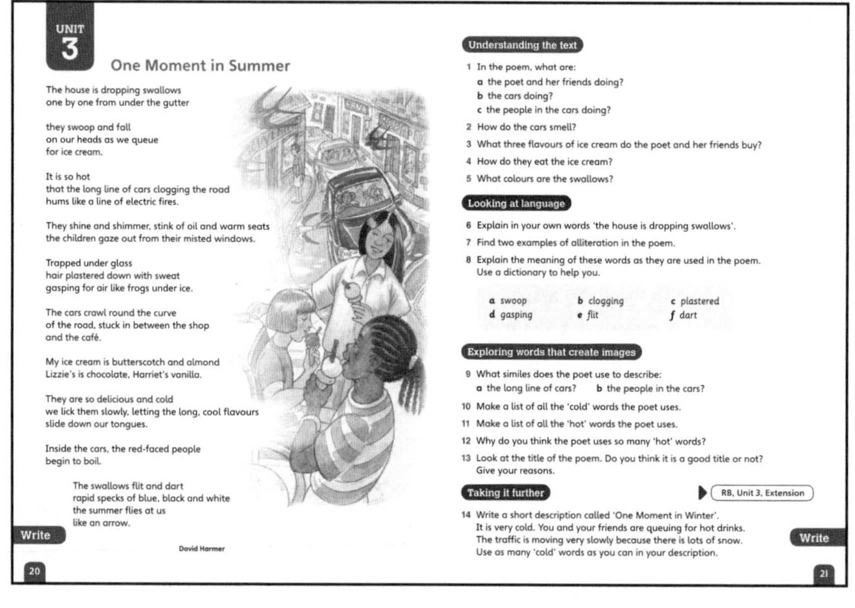

UNIT 3

One Moment in Summer

The house is dropping swallows
one by one from under the gutter

they swoop and fall
on our heads as we queue
for ice cream.

It is so hot
that the long line of cars clogging the road
hums like a line of electric fires.

They shine and shimmer, stink of oil and warm seats
the children gaze out from their misted windows.

Trapped under glass
hair plastered down with sweat
gasping for air like frogs under ice.

The cars crawl round the curve
of the road, stuck in between the shop
and the café.

My ice cream is butterscotch and almond
Lizzie's is chocolate, Harriet's vanilla.

They are so delicious and cold
we lick them slowly, letting the long, cool flavours
slide down our tongues.

Inside the cars, the red-faced people
begin to boil.

The swallows flit and dart
rapid specks of blue, black and white
the summer flies at us
like an arrow.

David Harmer

Write

20

Understanding the text

1 In the poem, what are:
a the poet and her friends doing?
b the cars doing?
c the people in the cars doing?
2 How do the cars smell?
3 What three flavours of ice cream do the poet and her friends buy?
4 How do they eat the ice cream?
5 What colours are the swallows?

Looking at language

6 Explain in your own words 'the house is dropping swallows'.
7 Find two examples of alliteration in the poem.
8 Explain the meaning of these words as they are used in the poem. Use a dictionary to help you.

a swoop b clogging c plastered
d gasping e flit f dart

Exploring words that create images

9 What similes does the poet use to describe:
a the long line of cars? b the people in the cars?
10 Make a list of all the 'cold' words the poet uses.
11 Make a list of all the 'hot' words the poet uses.
12 Why do you think the poet uses so many 'hot' words?
13 Look at the title of the poem. Do you think it is a good title or not? Give your reasons.

Taking it further

RB, Unit 3, Extension

14 Write a short description called 'One Moment in Winter'. It is very cold. You and your friends are queuing for hot drinks. The traffic is moving very slowly because there is lots of snow. Use as many 'cold' words as you can in your description.

Write

21

RESOURCES & ASSESSMENT BOOK

- **Support** (comprehension support): completing a chart with verbs from the poem; (vocabulary support): completing similes, choosing correct definitions.
- **Extension:** writing a description, using 'cold' adjectives.

PUPIL BOOK ANSWERS

1. **a** queuing for an ice cream / licking their ice creams **b** clogging the road / humming / shining / shimmering / stinking / crawling **c** sweating / gasping / boiling
2. They stink of 'oil and warm seats'.
3. Butterscotch and almond / chocolate / vanilla.
4. They 'lick them slowly'.
5. Blue / black / white.
6. Answers that suggest the swallows nest under the eaves of houses. As they fly out it looks as if the house is dropping them.
7. Any two from: long line / cars clogging / shine and shimmer / cars crawl.
8. **a** swoop: move quickly and suddenly downwards **b** clogging: blocking **c** plastered: stuck down **d** gasping: breathing quickly through lack of air **e** flit: move quickly from one place to another **f** dart: make a sudden quick movement
9. **a** 'like a line of electric fires' **b** 'like frogs under ice'
10. Ice cream / ice / cold / cool.
11. Hot / electric fires / warm / sweat / red-faced / boil.
12. To reflect the intensity of the heat people are experiencing.
13. Individual answers that suggest it is a good title as it describes a very short period of time in the heat of a summer's day.
14. Individual descriptions.

RESOURCE SHEET SUPPORT ANSWERS

A

People / Animals / Things	What do they do?
the house	dropping
the swallows	swoop / fall / flit / dart
the poet and friends	queue / lick
the cars	clogging / hum / crawl / shine / shimmer / stink
the people in the cars	gaze / gasp / boil

B

1. the long line of cars
2. the children

C

1. swoop: move downwards
2. clogging: blocking
3. plastered: stuck down
4. gasping: breathing quickly
5. flit: move quickly
6. dart: move suddenly

GOING DEEPER

- Ask the children to read out their descriptions for the 'Taking it further' activity. Discuss with the class, paying particular attention to their use of vocabulary.

UNIT FOCUS: Understanding Information Writing

Investigating ...

- information texts linked by the theme of countries around the world
- a variety of information through texts, maps and photographs
- 'reading' pictures

TEACH

- Ask children what they understand about Argentina.
- Ask children what they think people may like to know about Argentina. Where could they look for information?
- Read the information to the class; ask individual children to read it aloud in turn; or read in silence individually.

RESOURCES & ASSESSMENT BOOK

- **Support** (comprehension support): writing questions for given answers; (vocabulary support): cloze activity to reinforce vocabulary.
- **Extension:** finding information, making notes.

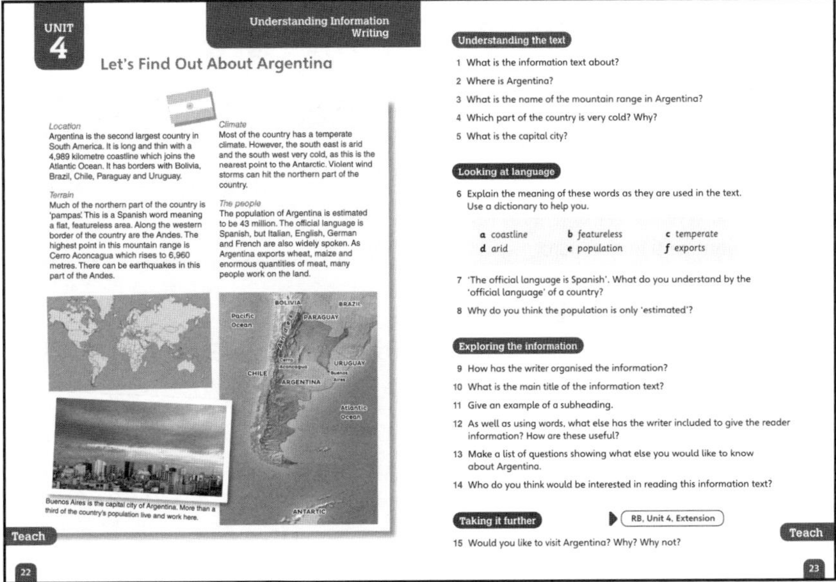

UNIT 4

Understanding Information Writing

Let's Find Out About Argentina

Location

Argentina is the second largest country in South America. It is long and thin with a 4,989 kilometre coastline which joins the Atlantic Ocean. It has borders with Bolivia, Brazil, Chile, Paraguay and Uruguay.

Terrain

Much of the northern part of the country is 'pampas'. This is a Spanish word meaning a flat, featureless area. Along the western border of the country are the Andes. The highest point in this mountain range is Cerro Aconcagua which rises to 6,960 metres. There can be earthquakes in this part of the Andes.

Climate

Most of the country has a temperate climate. However, the south east is arid and the south west very cold, as this is the nearest point to the Antarctic. Violent wind storms can hit the northern part of the country.

The people

The population of Argentina is estimated to be 43 million. The official language is Spanish, but Italian, English, German and French are also widely spoken. As Argentina exports wheat, maize and enormous quantities of meat, many people work on the land.

Buenos Aires is the capital city of Argentina. More than a third of the country's population live and work here.

Teach

22

Understanding the text

1 What is the information text about?
2 Where is Argentina?
3 What is the name of the mountain range in Argentina?
4 Which part of the country is very cold? Why?
5 What is the capital city?

Looking at language

6 Explain the meaning of these words as they are used in the text. Use a dictionary to help you.

a *coastline* **b** *featureless* **c** *temperate*
d *arid* **e** *population* **f** *exports*

7 'The official language is Spanish'. What do you understand by the 'official language' of a country?
8 Why do you think the population is only 'estimated'?

Exploring the information

9 How has the writer organised the information?
10 What is the main title of the information text?
11 Give an example of a subheading.
12 As well as using words, what else has the writer included to give the reader information? How are these useful?
13 Make a list of questions showing what else you would like to know about Argentina.
14 Who do you think would be interested in reading this information text?

Taking it further RB, Unit 4, Extension

15 Would you like to visit Argentina? Why? Why not?

Teach

23

PUPIL BOOK ANSWERS

1 Argentina.

2 South America.

3 The Andes.

4 The south west of Argentina is very cold as it is near to the Antarctic.

5 Buenos Aires.

6 **a** coastline: the land along the edge of the sea **b** featureless: having no features such as hills or valleys **c** temperate: never having extremely hot or extremely cold weather **d** arid: very dry **e** population: the number of people who live in a particular area **f** exports: sends goods to other countries

7 Answers that suggest it is the language most people speak and official documents, signs, laws etc. would be written in that language.

8 Answers that suggest it would be difficult to be exact when there are about 43 million people to count over such a large area.

9 In four sections, each with a sub-heading.

10 *Let's Find Out About Argentina.*

11 Any one of *Location / Terrain / Climate / The people.*

12 Answers that suggest the maps and photographs are useful. The world map allows the reader to locate the country relative to where he / she lives. The map of the country allows the reader to locate places mentioned in the text. The photograph gives a visual impression of the capital city.

13 Individual answers. Make a list of suggested questions on the board.

14 Answers that suggest people who are interested in South America / travel / world geography.

15 Individual answers.

RESOURCE SHEET SUPPORT ANSWERS

A

Question	Answer
1 How long is Argentina's coastline?	4,989 kilometres long
2 How high is the Cerro Aconcagua mountain range?	6,960 metres
3 What is the population of Argentina?	about 43 million

B

Argentina is the **second** largest country in South America. It has borders with **five** other countries. The **Andes** mountains are towards the west of the country and the **pampas** is in the north. Most of the country has a **temperate** climate. The south east is **arid** and the south west very cold. Argentina's official language is **Spanish**. Many people work on the **land**.

GOING DEEPER

- Recap on how information writing uses main headings, sub-headings and illustrations.
- Discuss what the children have learnt about Argentina.

TALK

- Ask children what they understand about China.
- Ask children what they think people may like to know about China. Where could they look for information?
- Read the information to the class; ask individual children to read it aloud in turn; or read in silence individually.

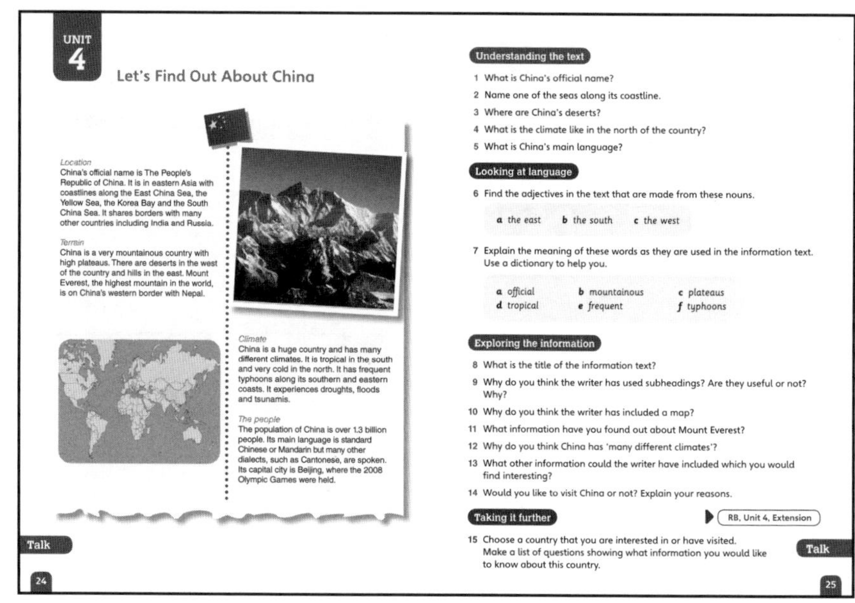

UNIT 4

Let's Find Out About China

Location
China's official name is The People's Republic of China. It is in eastern Asia with coastlines along the East China Sea, the Yellow Sea, the Korea Bay and the South China Sea. It shares borders with many other countries including India and Russia.

Terrain
China is a very mountainous country with high plateaus. There are deserts in the west of the country and hills in the east. Mount Everest, the highest mountain in the world, is on China's western border with Nepal.

Climate
China is a huge country and has many different climates. It is tropical in the south and very cold in the north. It has frequent typhoons along its southern and eastern coasts. It experiences droughts, floods and tsunamis.

The people
The population of China is over 1.3 billion people. Its main language is standard Chinese or Mandarin but many other dialects, such as Cantonese, are spoken. Its capital city is Beijing, where the 2008 Olympic Games were held.

Talk

24

Understanding the text

1 What is China's official name?
2 Name one of the seas along its coastline.
3 Where are China's deserts?
4 What is the climate like in the north of the country?
5 What is China's main language?

Looking at language

6 Find the adjectives in the text that are made from these nouns.

a *the east* **b** *the south* **c** *the west*

7 Explain the meaning of these words as they are used in the information text. Use a dictionary to help you.

a *official* **b** *mountainous* **c** *plateaus*
d *tropical* **e** *frequent* **f** *typhoons*

Exploring the information

8 What is the title of the information text?
9 Why do you think the writer has used subheadings? Are they useful or not? Why?
10 Why do you think the writer has included a map?
11 What information have you found out about Mount Everest?
12 Why do you think China has 'many different climates'?
13 What other information could the writer have included which you would find interesting?
14 Would you like to visit China or not? Explain your reasons.

Taking it further RB, Unit 4, Extension

15 Choose a country that you are interested in or have visited. Make a list of questions showing what information you would like to know about this country.

Talk

25

RESOURCES & ASSESSMENT BOOK

- **Support** (comprehension support): identifying true statements, correcting false statements; (vocabulary support): matching words and definitions.
- **Extension:** writing questions.

PUPIL BOOK ANSWERS

1. The People's Republic of China.
2. Any one of: East China Sea / Yellow Sea / Korea Bay / South China Sea.
3. In the west of the country.
4. Very cold.
5. Standard Chinese or Mandarin.
6. **a** eastern **b** southern **c** western
7. **a** official: formal **b** mountainous: covered with mountains **c** plateaus: large, flat areas of land that are higher than the land around them **d** tropical: very hot and humid **e** frequent: occurring often **f** typhoons: storms with very strong winds
8. *Let's Find Out About China.*
9. Answers that suggest sub-headings divide the information into different topics or types. They are useful for finding specific pieces of information without having to read the whole text.
10. Answers that suggest the world map allows the reader to see where China is in relation to where he / she lives.
11. Highest mountain in the world / situated on China's western border with Nepal.
12. Answers that suggest China is so big that the climate will differ from area to area.
13. Individual answers.
14. Individual answers.
15. Ensure groups choose countries other than Argentina / China / Australia.

RESOURCE SHEET SUPPORT ANSWERS

A

1. True
2. False
3. True
4. False
5. True
6. False
7. True

B

1. It has a coastline along [any from] the Yellow Sea, the East China Sea, the Korea Bay, the South China Sea.
2. China is very mountainous.
3. Mount Everest is in Nepal.
4. The population is more than 1 billion people.

C

1. covered in mountains
2. high, large, flat area of land
3. a storm with very strong winds
4. long period of time with no rain
5. large amount of water covering land
6. long, high sea wave caused by an earthquake

GOING DEEPER

- Discuss the children's answers to the last question and the 'Taking it further' activity. If time permits, allow each group to research their individual country and present a factual report on it.

WRITE

- Ask children what they understand about Australia.
- Ask children what they think people may like to know about Australia. Where could they look for information?
- Read the information to the class; ask individual children to read it aloud in turn; or read in silence individually.

RESOURCES & ASSESSMENT BOOK

- **Support** (comprehension support): writing questions for given answers, completing sentences; (vocabulary support): identifying adjectives.
- **Extension:** finding information, writing questions.

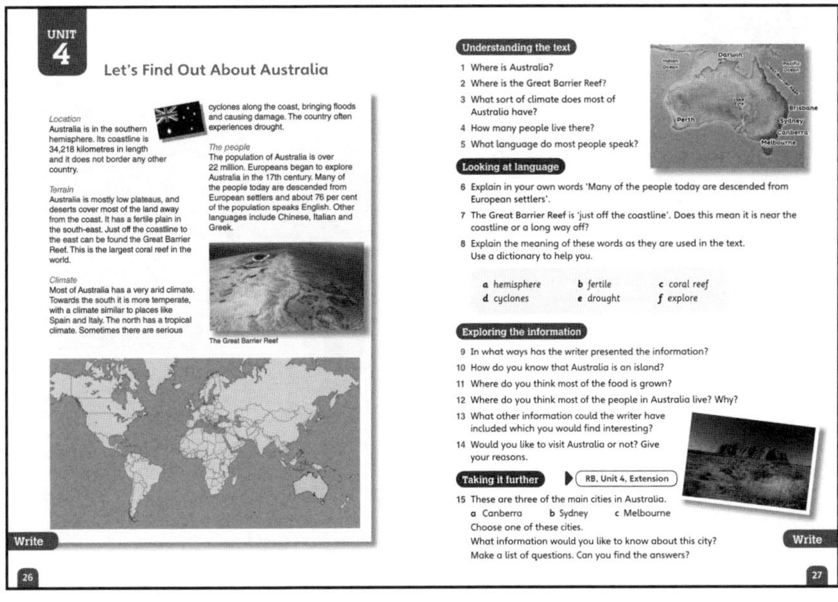

UNIT 4

Let's Find Out About Australia

Location
Australia is in the southern hemisphere. Its coastline is 34,218 kilometres in length and it does not border any other country.

Terrain
Australia is mostly low plateaus, and deserts cover most of the land away from the coast. It has a fertile plain in the south-east. Just off the coastline to the east can be found the Great Barrier Reef. This is the largest coral reef in the world.

Climate
Most of Australia has a very arid climate. Towards the south it is more temperate, with a climate similar to places like Spain and Italy. The north has a tropical climate. Sometimes there are serious cyclones along the coast, bringing floods and causing damage. The country often experiences drought.

The people
The population of Australia is over 22 million. Europeans began to explore Australia in the 17th century. Many of the people today are descended from European settlers and about 76 per cent of the population speaks English. Other languages include Chinese, Italian and Greek.

The Great Barrier Reef

Understanding the text

1 Where is Australia?
2 Where is the Great Barrier Reef?
3 What sort of climate does most of Australia have?
4 How many people live there?
5 What language do most people speak?

Looking at language

6 Explain in your own words 'Many of the people today are descended from European settlers'.
7 The Great Barrier Reef is 'just off the coastline'. Does this mean it is near the coastline or a long way off?
8 Explain the meaning of these words as they are used in the text. Use a dictionary to help you.

a hemisphere *b fertile* *c coral reef*
d cyclones *e drought* *f explore*

Exploring the information

9 In what ways has the writer presented the information?
10 How do you know that Australia is an island?
11 Where do you think most of the food is grown?
12 Where do you think most of the people in Australia live? Why?
13 What other information could the writer have included which you would find interesting?
14 Would you like to visit Australia or not? Give your reasons.

Taking it further ▶ RB, Unit 4, Extension

15 These are three of the main cities in Australia.
a Canberra b Sydney c Melbourne
Choose one of these cities.
What information would you like to know about this city?
Make a list of questions. Can you find the answers?

Write 26 Write 27

PUPIL BOOK ANSWERS

1. In the southern hemisphere.
2. Off the east coast of Australia.
3. Arid.
4. Over 22 million people.
5. English.
6. Answers that suggest the European settlers are their ancestors.
7. Near the coastline.
8. **a** hemisphere: half of Earth **b** fertile: land that can produce good crops and plants **c** coral reef: a hard, natural structure under the sea that is formed from the skeletons of small sea creatures **d** cyclones: severe storms with winds that spin in a circle **e** drought: very little rain **f** explore: travel around an area in order to find out about it
9. Answers should include use of a main heading; sub-headings; map and photograph.
10. Answers based on evidence of Australia's position on the map and the text 'does not border any other country'.
11. Answers that suggest most of the food is grown in the south where it is more temperate, especially on the fertile plain in the south-east of the country.
12. Answer that suggests that, based on the map and text, most people live along the coast because of the climate ('deserts cover most of the land away from the coast').
13. Individual answers.
14. Individual answers.
15. Individual answers.

RESOURCE SHEET SUPPORT ANSWERS

A

Question	Answer
1 How long is Australia's coastline?	34,218 kilometres
2 What is Australia's population?	over 22 million
3 What percentage of the population speak English?	76 per cent

B

1. Australia is in the southern hemisphere.
2. Deserts cover most of the land away from the coast.
3. The north of Australia has a tropical climate.
4. Cyclones bring floods and cause damage.
5. Europeans began to explore Australia in the 17th century.

C

1. **low** plateaus
2. **fertile** plain
3. **Great** Barrier Reef
4. **largest** coral reef
5. **arid / tropical** climate
6. **serious** cyclones

GOING DEEPER

- Discuss the children's answers to the 'Taking it further' activity.
- Recap on what they have learnt about the features of information writing.

UNIT FOCUS: Characters' Feelings and Actions

Investigating ...

- extracts from stories that deal with problems they may have encountered or witnessed in school
- main characters who face a dilemma they don't know how to deal with
- empathising with each character and using problem-solving skills to come up with a solution

TEACH

- Discuss the problem of bullying with the children.
- Ask why they think people bully others. How do they think they should react to a bully? What makes the situation better? What makes it worse?
- Explain to the children that they are going to read an extract from a story called *Chicken*.
- Explain the story so far: the narrator has just moved to a new school and a boy called Webbo has taken an instant dislike to him. The extract begins at the point where the narrator is trying to work out why Webbo dislikes him so much.
- Read the extract to the class; ask individual children to read it aloud in turn; or read in silence individually.

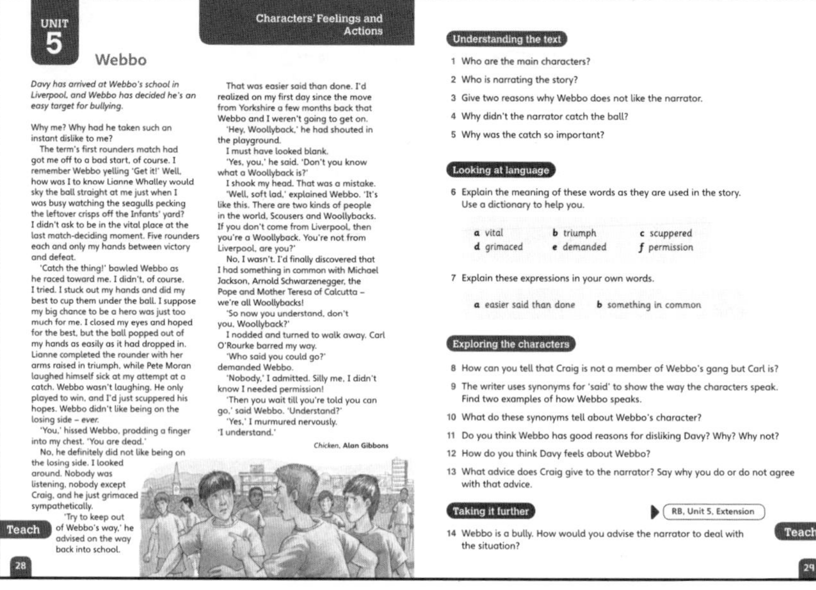

UNIT 5 Characters' Feelings and Actions

Webbo

Davy has arrived at Webbo's school in Liverpool, and Webbo has decided he's an easy target for bullying.

Why me? Why had he taken such an instant dislike to me?

The term's first rounders match had got me off to a bad start, of course. I remember Webbo yelling 'Get it!' Well, how was I to know Lianne Whalley would sky the ball straight at me just when I was busy watching the seagulls pecking the leftover crisps off the Infants' yard? I didn't ask to be in the vital place at the last match-deciding moment. Five rounders each and only my hands between victory and defeat.

'Catch the thing!' bawled Webbo as he raced toward me. I didn't, of course. I tried. I stuck out my hands and did my best to cup them under the ball. I suppose my big chance to be a hero was just too much for me. I closed my eyes and hoped for the best, but the ball popped out of my hands as easily as it had dropped in. Lianne completed the rounder with her arms raised in triumph, while Pete Moran laughed himself sick at my attempt at a catch. Webbo wasn't laughing. He only played to win, and I'd just scuppered his hopes. Webbo didn't like being on the losing side – *ever.*

'You,' hissed Webbo, prodding a finger into my chest. 'You are dead.'

No, he definitely did not like being on the losing side. I looked around. Nobody was listening, nobody except Craig, and he just grimaced sympathetically.

'Try to keep out of Webbo's way,' he advised on the way back into school.

That was easier said than done. I'd realized on my first day since the move from Yorkshire a few months back that Webbo and I weren't going to get on.

'Hey, Woollyback,' he had shouted in the playground.

I must have looked blank.

'Yes, you,' he said. 'Don't you know what a Woollyback is?'

I shook my head. That was a mistake.

'Well, soft lad,' explained Webbo. 'It's like this. There are two kinds of people in the world, Scousers and Woollybacks. If you don't come from Liverpool, then you're a Woollyback. You're not from Liverpool, are you?'

No, I wasn't. I'd finally discovered that I had something in common with Michael Jackson, Arnold Schwarzenegger, the Pope and Mother Teresa of Calcutta – we're all Woollybacks!

'So now you understand, don't you, Woollyback?'

I nodded and turned to walk away. Carl O'Rourke barred my way.

'Who said you could go?' demanded Webbo.

'Nobody,' I admitted. Silly me, I didn't know I needed permission!

'Then you wait till you're told you can go,' said Webbo. 'Understand?'

'Yes,' I murmured nervously. 'I understand.'

Chicken, **Alan Gibbons**

Teach 28

Understanding the text

1 Who are the main characters?
2 Who is narrating the story?
3 Give two reasons why Webbo does not like the narrator.
4 Why didn't the narrator catch the ball?
5 Why was the catch so important?

Looking at language

6 Explain the meaning of these words as they are used in the story. Use a dictionary to help you.

a vital **b** triumph **c** scuppered
d grimaced **e** demanded **f** permission

7 Explain these expressions in your own words.

a easier said than done **b** something in common

Exploring the characters

8 How can you tell that Craig is not a member of Webbo's gang but Carl is?
9 The writer uses synonyms for 'said' to show the way the characters speak. Find two examples of how Webbo speaks.
10 What do these synonyms tell about Webbo's character?
11 Do you think Webbo has good reasons for disliking Davy? Why? Why not?
12 How do you think Davy feels about Webbo?
13 What advice does Craig give to the narrator? Say why you do or do not agree with that advice.

Taking it further RB, Unit 5, Extension

14 Webbo is a bully. How would you advise the narrator to deal with the situation?

Teach 29

RESOURCES & ASSESSMENT BOOK

- **Support** (comprehension support): identifying the speaker, replacing incorrect words in sentences; (vocabulary support): matching words and definitions.
- **Extension:** empathising, listing advantages / disadvantages.

PUPIL BOOK ANSWERS

1. Davy and Webbo.
2. Davy.
3. He dropped the ball and lost the rounders match. / He doesn't come from Liverpool.
4. Davy didn't catch the ball because he closed his eyes.
5. It was important because he would have won the match for Webbo's team.
6. **a** vital: most important **b** triumph: victory **c** scuppered: ruined **d** grimaced: pulled a face **e** demanded: insisted / asked firmly **f** permission: being allowed to do something
7. **a** easier said than done: it is often harder to do something than to talk about doing something **b** something in common: having similarities to
8. Answers based on evidence:
   Craig: 'grimaced sympathetically' / gives advice to Davy, 'Try to keep out of Webbo's way'.
   Carl: stopped Davy from walking away from Webbo.
9. Any two from: yelling / bawled / hissed / shouted / explained.
10. Answers that suggest that Webbo is an aggressive, nasty character.
11. Answers that suggest the reader can understand why Webbo may be cross with Davy for dropping the ball, but he is wrong to dislike Davy just because he doesn't come from Liverpool.
12. Answers that suggest he is afraid of Webbo and nervous about what Webbo may do.
13. Craig advises Davy to keep out of Webbo's way. Individual answers.
14. Individual answers.

RESOURCE SHEET SUPPORT ANSWERS

A

1. Webbo
2. Davy
3. Craig

B

1. <u>liking</u> (dislike)
2. <u>Lianne</u> (Davy)
3. <u>losing</u> (winning)
4. <u>Liverpool</u> (Yorkshire)
5. <u>Craig</u> (Carl)

C

1. vital
2. triumph
3. scuppered
4. grimaced
5. demanded
6. permission

GOING DEEPER

- Discuss how Davy reacts to Webbo. Do the children think he should have stood up to Webbo? What would they have done?

TALK

- Ask what children understand by the term 'corporal punishment'? Do they agree or disagree with it?
- Explain to the children that they are going to read the opening of a story called *The Hallowe'en Cat,* where Mike appears to be in his teacher's bad books.
- Read the extract to the class; ask individual children to read it aloud in turn; or read in silence individually.

RESOURCES & ASSESSMENT BOOK

- **Support** (comprehension support): narrative sequence, identifying actions; (vocabulary support): writing contractions in full.
- **Extension:** empathising, listing advantages / disadvantages.

PUPIL BOOK ANSWERS

1. Calling out behind her back.
2. He had been trying to stop another boy from talking.
3. Chas.
4. He 'swiped at Chas's face'.
5. 'She gave Mike a painful knock on the head ... and made him stand behind the blackboard for the rest of the lesson'.
6. **a** suspicious by nature: naturally distrustful / her first thought is to be suspicious **b** got it in for you: seems determined to make his life difficult
7. **a** scathing: criticising in a strong way **b** ticked off: told off **c** ignored: took no notice of **d** bitterness: anger
8. Answers that suggest she is mean / unjust / cruel / distrustful.
9. Answers that suggest she treats him badly and unfairly.
10. Answers that suggest Chas comes across as quite unpleasant / he doesn't tell the truth about what happened / he seems to delight in Mike's situation.
11. Answers based on evidence. They leave school together talking.
12. It seems odd as you may expect that Mike would have nothing to do with Chas after what happened in class.
13. Answers that suggest Mike doesn't tell Chas what he is going to do because he doesn't yet know what he is going to do.

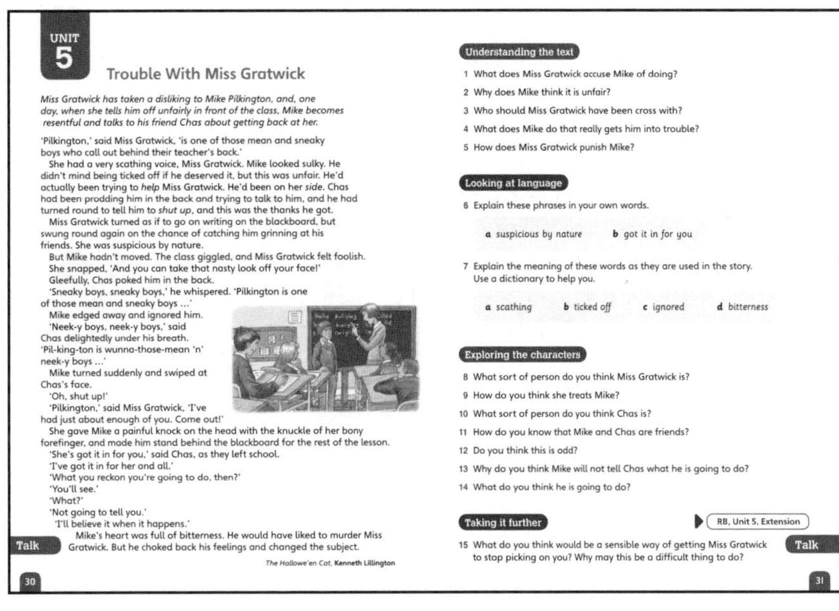

UNIT 5

Trouble With Miss Gratwick

Miss Gratwick has taken a disliking to Mike Pilkington, and, one day, when she tells him off unfairly in front of the class, Mike becomes resentful and talks to his friend Chas about getting back at her.

'Pilkington,' said Miss Gratwick, 'is one of those mean and sneaky boys who call out behind their teacher's back.'

She had a very scathing voice, Miss Gratwick. Mike looked sulky. He didn't mind being ticked off if he deserved it, but this was unfair. He'd actually been trying to *help* Miss Gratwick. He'd been on her *side*. Chas had been prodding him in the back and trying to talk to him, and he had turned round to tell him to *shut up*, and this was the thanks he got.

Miss Gratwick turned as if to go on writing on the blackboard, but swung round again on the chance of catching him grinning at his friends. She was suspicious by nature.

But Mike hadn't moved. The class giggled, and Miss Gratwick felt foolish.

She snapped, 'And you can take that nasty look off your face!'

Gleefully, Chas poked him in the back.

'Sneaky boys, sneaky boys,' he whispered. 'Pilkington is one of those mean and sneaky boys ...'

Mike edged away and ignored him.

'Neek-y boys, neek-y boys,' said Chas delightedly under his breath. 'Pil-king-ton is wunna-those-mean 'n' neek-y boys ...'

Mike turned suddenly and swiped at Chas's face.

'Oh, shut up!'

'Pilkington,' said Miss Gratwick, 'I've had just about enough of you. Come out!'

She gave Mike a painful knock on the head with the knuckle of her bony forefinger, and made him stand behind the blackboard for the rest of the lesson.

'She's got it in for you,' said Chas, as they left school.

'I've got it in for her and all.'

'What you reckon you're going to do, then?'

'You'll see.'

'What?'

'Not going to tell you.'

'I'll believe it when it happens.'

Talk

Mike's heart was full of bitterness. He would have liked to murder Miss Gratwick. But he choked back his feelings and changed the subject.

The Hallowe'en Cat, **Kenneth Lillington**

30

Understanding the text

1 What does Miss Gratwick accuse Mike of doing?

2 Why does Mike think it is unfair?

3 Who should Miss Gratwick have been cross with?

4 What does Mike do that really gets him into trouble?

5 How does Miss Gratwick punish Mike?

Looking at language

6 Explain these phrases in your own words.

a *suspicious by nature* **b** *got it in for you*

7 Explain the meaning of these words as they are used in the story. Use a dictionary to help you.

a *scathing* **b** *ticked off* **c** *ignored* **d** *bitterness*

Exploring the characters

8 What sort of person do you think Miss Gratwick is?

9 How do you think she treats Mike?

10 What sort of person do you think Chas is?

11 How do you know that Mike and Chas are friends?

12 Do you think this is odd?

13 Why do you think Mike will not tell Chas what he is going to do?

14 What do you think he is going to do?

Taking it further

RB, Unit 5, Extension

15 What do you think would be a sensible way of getting Miss Gratwick to stop picking on you? Why may this be a difficult thing to do?

Talk

31

14. Individual answers.
15. Individual answers.

RESOURCE SHEET SUPPORT ANSWERS

A

Miss Gratwick swung round again.	5
Miss Gratwick knocked Mike on the head.	11
Mike sulked.	2
Chas gleefully poked Mike in the back and whispered.	7
Miss Gratwick said Mike was a mean and sneaky boy.	1
Mike ignored him.	8
Mike was going to get his own back on Miss Gratwick.	12
Miss Gratwick turned back to write on the board.	4
Chas whispered again.	9
Mike had been telling Chas to shut up.	3
Mike swiped at Chas's face.	10
The class giggled.	6

B

1. the class
2. Mike
3. Miss Gratwick
4. Chas

C

1. did not
2. He had
3. had not
4. I have
5. She has
6. You will
7. I shall / I will

GOING DEEPER

- Use the answers to the 'Taking it further' activity as the basis of a class discussion.

WRITE

- Discuss the idea of friendship with the children. Why are people friends? Are they friends with people who are the same as them?
- Ask children if they like people who are different. What do they look for in a friend?
- Explain to children that they are going to read an extract from a story called *The Balaclava Story*.
- Explain the story so far: the extract is from near the beginning of the story and all we know so far is that at least half the people in the narrator's class have a balaclava. Some of them go around in a group known as the 'Balaclava Boys'. The narrator wants a balaclava so he can be in the group. However, his mum won't let him have one.
- Read the extract to the class; ask individual children to read it aloud in turn; or read in silence individually.

RESOURCES & ASSESSMENT BOOK

- **Support** (comprehension support): multiple choice; (vocabulary support): choosing correct definitions.
- **Extension:** persuasive writing.

PUPIL BOOK ANSWERS

1. He had earache.
2. Tony and Barry.
3. 'They just went around together, wearing their balaclavas.'
4. His mum wouldn't buy him one.
5. That he was losing all his friends.
6. **a** wasn't bothered: didn't care **b** go round with: keep company with **c** be a sport: be reasonable
7. **a** rotten: stupid **b** daft: silly / stupid **c** fed up: miserable / annoyed **d** handicraft: making things by hand
8. Answers that suggest Tony changed his mind when he saw that his friends wanted to wear it.
9. Answers that suggest they didn't do anything else but walk around, which didn't really make them a gang.
10. Answers that suggest they treated him unfairly. They were supposed to be his friends.

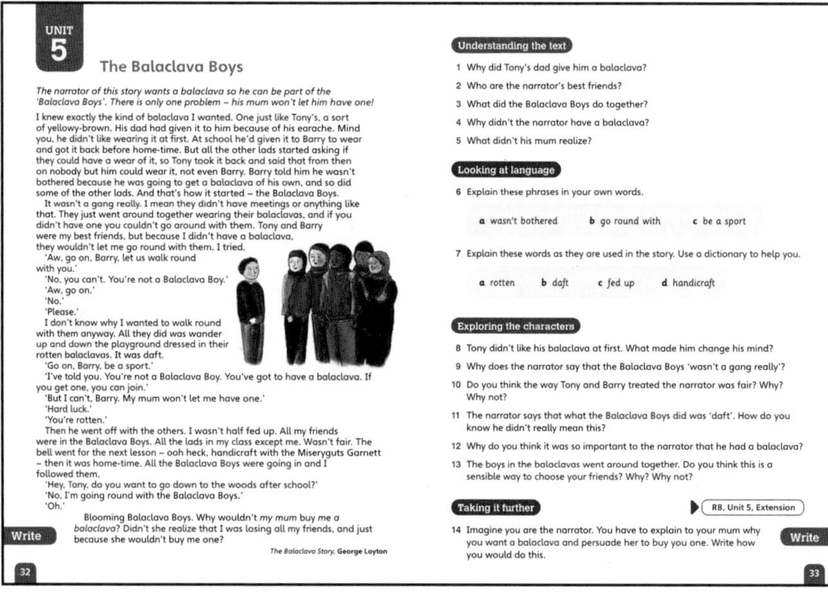

UNIT 5

The Balaclava Boys

The narrator of this story wants a balaclava so he can be part of the 'Balaclava Boys'. There is only one problem – his mum won't let him have one!

I knew exactly the kind of balaclava I wanted. One just like Tony's, a sort of yellowy-brown. His dad had given it to him because of his earache. Mind you, he didn't like wearing it at first. At school he'd given it to Barry to wear and got it back before home-time. But all the other lads started asking if they could have a wear of it, so Tony took it back and said that from then on nobody but him could wear it, not even Barry. Barry told him he wasn't bothered because he was going to get a balaclava of his own, and so did some of the other lads. And that's how it started – the Balaclava Boys.

It wasn't a gang really. I mean they didn't have meetings or anything like that. They just went around together wearing their balaclavas, and if you didn't have one you couldn't go around with them. Tony and Barry were my best friends, but because I didn't have a balaclava, they wouldn't let me go round with them. I tried.

'Aw, go on, Barry, let us walk round with you.'

'No, you can't. You're not a Balaclava Boy.'

'Aw, go on.'

'No.'

'Please.'

I don't know why I wanted to walk round with them anyway. All they did was wander up and down the playground dressed in their rotten balaclavas. It was daft.

'Go on, Barry, be a sport.'

'I've told you. You're not a Balaclava Boy. You've got to have a balaclava. If you get one, you can join.'

'But I can't, Barry. My mum won't let me have one.'

'Hard luck.'

'You're rotten.'

Then he went off with the others. I wasn't half fed up. All my friends were in the Balaclava Boys. All the lads in my class except me. Wasn't fair. The bell went for the next lesson – ooh heck, handicraft with the Miseryguts Garnett – then it was home-time. All the Balaclava Boys were going in and I followed them.

'Hey, Tony, do you want to go down to the woods after school?'

'No, I'm going round with the Balaclava Boys.'

'Oh.'

Write

Blooming Balaclava Boys. Why wouldn't *my mum* buy *me a balaclava*? Didn't she realize that I was losing all my friends, and just because she wouldn't buy me one?

The Balaclava Story, **George Layton**

32

Understanding the text

1 Why did Tony's dad give him a balaclava?

2 Who are the narrator's best friends?

3 What did the Balaclava Boys do together?

4 Why didn't the narrator have a balaclava?

5 What didn't his mum realize?

Looking at language

6 Explain these phrases in your own words.

a wasn't bothered **b** go round with **c** be a sport

7 Explain these words as they are used in the story. Use a dictionary to help you.

a rotten **b** daft **c** fed up **d** handicraft

Exploring the characters

8 Tony didn't like his balaclava at first. What made him change his mind?

9 Why does the narrator say that the Balaclava Boys 'wasn't a gang really'?

10 Do you think the way Tony and Barry treated the narrator was fair? Why? Why not?

11 The narrator says that what the Balaclava Boys did was 'daft'. How do you know he didn't really mean this?

12 Why do you think it was so important to the narrator that he had a balaclava?

13 The boys in the balaclavas went around together. Do you think this is a sensible way to choose your friends? Why? Why not?

Taking it further

RB, Unit 5, Extension

14 Imagine you are the narrator. You have to explain to your mum why you want a balaclava and persuade her to buy you one. Write how you would do this.

Write

33

11. Answers that suggest the narrator said this only because he couldn't be part of the 'gang'. He really wanted to go around with them and, when they wouldn't let him, he made out that the whole gang idea was silly.
12. Answers that suggest having a balaclava meant he could go around with his friends and not be left out.
13. Answers that suggest this is not a sensible way to choose your friends because it means friendship is dependent on what you wear rather than the sort of person you are.
14. Groups could write the conversation between the narrator and his mum as a play script.

RESOURCE SHEET SUPPORT ANSWERS

A

1. a
2. b
3. c
4. b
5. b
6. b

B

1. care
2. unhappy
3. with them
4. reasonable

GOING DEEPER

- Allow the groups to perform their plays from the 'Taking it further' activity to the class.
- Discuss the three extracts: Which character do the children think was in the worst situation? Why? How do the children think each character solved the problem?

UNIT FOCUS: Interpreting Explanation Texts

Investigating ...

- texts related by the common theme of the human body
- features of explanation texts, in both text and diagram form

TEACH

- Ask children what they understand by the term 'explanation'. What kinds of things can you explain? What 'explanations' have they read?
- Explain to the children that they are going to look at a text that explains what the heart is and how it works.
- Read the explanation to the class; ask individual children to read it aloud in turn; or read in silence individually.

RESOURCES & ASSESSMENT BOOK

- **Support** (comprehension support): matching sentence beginnings and endings; (vocabulary support): labelling diagrams for vocabulary reinforcement, choosing correct definitions.
- **Extension:** writing investigative questions.

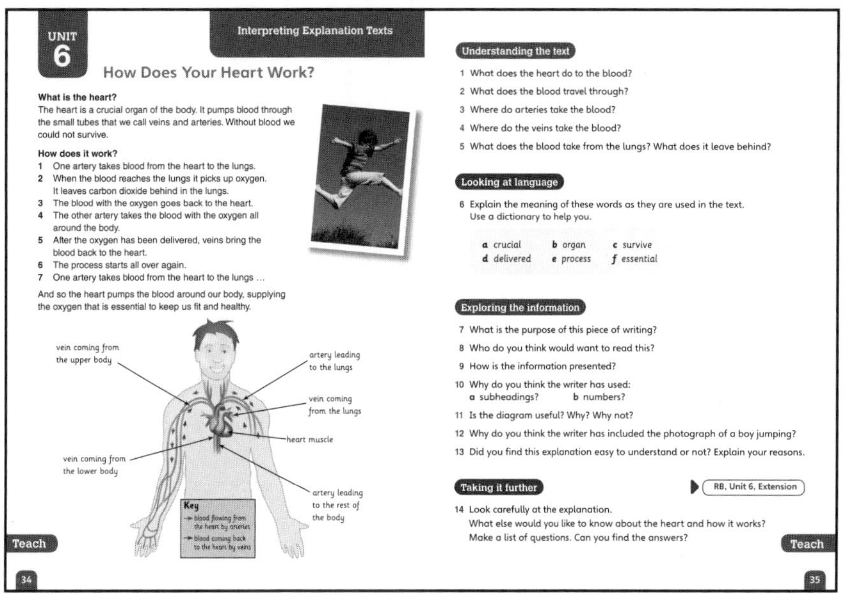

UNIT 6

Interpreting Explanation Texts

How Does Your Heart Work?

What is the heart?

The heart is a crucial organ of the body. It pumps blood through the small tubes that we call veins and arteries. Without blood we could not survive.

How does it work?

1. One artery takes blood from the heart to the lungs.
2. When the blood reaches the lungs it picks up oxygen. It leaves carbon dioxide behind in the lungs.
3. The blood with the oxygen goes back to the heart.
4. The other artery takes the blood with the oxygen all around the body.
5. After the oxygen has been delivered, veins bring the blood back to the heart.
6. The process starts all over again.
7. One artery takes blood from the heart to the lungs ...

And so the heart pumps the blood around our body, supplying the oxygen that is essential to keep us fit and healthy.

Teach

34

Understanding the text

1 What does the heart do to the blood?
2 What does the blood travel through?
3 Where do arteries take the blood?
4 Where do the veins take the blood?
5 What does the blood take from the lungs? What does it leave behind?

Looking at language

6 Explain the meaning of these words as they are used in the text. Use a dictionary to help you.

a crucial **b** organ **c** survive
d delivered **e** process **f** essential

Exploring the information

7 What is the purpose of this piece of writing?
8 Who do you think would want to read this?
9 How is the information presented?
10 Why do you think the writer has used:
a subheadings? **b** numbers?
11 Is the diagram useful? Why? Why not?
12 Why do you think the writer has included the photograph of a boy jumping?
13 Did you find this explanation easy to understand or not? Explain your reasons.

Taking it further

RB, Unit 6, Extension

14 Look carefully at the explanation.
What else would you like to know about the heart and how it works?
Make a list of questions. Can you find the answers?

Teach

35

PUPIL BOOK ANSWERS

1. Pumps it around the body.
2. Veins and arteries.
3. To the lungs from the heart / from the heart all around the body.
4. Back to the heart.
5. Takes oxygen / leaves carbon dioxide.
6. **a** crucial: very important **b** organ: part of the body that does a specific job **c** survive: stay alive **d** delivered: given **e** process: series of things that happen in a specific order **f** essential: very necessary
7. To explain how the heart works.
8. Answers that suggest anyone interested in how the body works.
9. Text / diagram / photograph.
10. **a** sub-headings: to divide the information **b** numbers: to show the steps of the process in the correct order
11. Individual answers that suggest the diagram is very useful as it shows what is happening and helps the reader see the process.
12. Individual answers suggesting that the boy represents a healthy body where the heart is working well.
13. Individual answers.
14. Compile a list of questions through class discussion.

RESOURCE SHEET SUPPORT ANSWERS

A

1. The heart pumps blood around the body.
2. The blood travels through veins and arteries.
3. One artery takes blood to the lungs.
4. The veins take blood to the heart.
5. The blood takes oxygen from the lungs.
6. The blood leaves carbon dioxide in the lungs.

B

blood
lungs
heart
vein
artery

C

1. very necessary
2. very important

GOING DEEPER

Recap on the features of the explanation. Discuss:

- the purpose of the text as a whole
- the purpose of the introductory paragraph
- organisation – introduction, bullet points
- presentation – illustrations, main heading, sub-heading
- language features – present tense, passive voice.

TALK

- Ask the children to move their arms up and down. Do they know how they can do this?
- Ask what type of text would tell them how they do this. Where would they find this type of text?
- Explain to the children that they are going to look at an explanation text that describes in detail how our arms move.
- Read the explanation to the class; ask individual children to read it aloud in turn; or read in silence individually.

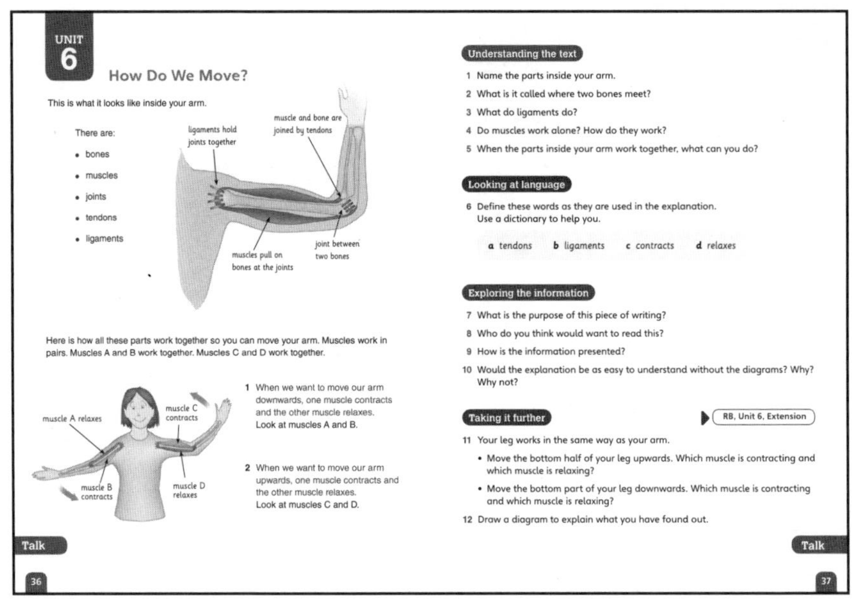

UNIT 6

How Do We Move?

This is what it looks like inside your arm.

There are:

- bones
- muscles
- joints
- tendons
- ligaments

Here is how all these parts work together so you can move your arm. Muscles work in pairs. Muscles A and B work together. Muscles C and D work together.

1 When we want to move our arm downwards, one muscle contracts and the other muscle relaxes. Look at muscles A and B.

2 When we want to move our arm upwards, one muscle contracts and the other muscle relaxes. Look at muscles C and D.

Talk

36

Understanding the text

1 Name the parts inside your arm.
2 What is it called where two bones meet?
3 What do ligaments do?
4 Do muscles work alone? How do they work?
5 When the parts inside your arm work together, what can you do?

Looking at language

6 Define these words as they are used in the explanation. Use a dictionary to help you.

a tendons **b** ligaments **c** contracts **d** relaxes

Exploring the information

7 What is the purpose of this piece of writing?
8 Who do you think would want to read this?
9 How is the information presented?
10 Would the explanation be as easy to understand without the diagrams? Why? Why not?

Taking it further

RB, Unit 6, Extension

11 Your leg works in the same way as your arm.
- Move the bottom half of your leg upwards. Which muscle is contracting and which muscle is relaxing?
- Move the bottom part of your leg downwards. Which muscle is contracting and which muscle is relaxing?

12 Draw a diagram to explain what you have found out.

Talk

37

RESOURCES & ASSESSMENT BOOK

- **Support** (comprehension support): multiple choice; (vocabulary support): labelling diagrams for vocabulary reinforcement, choosing correct definitions.
- **Extension:** writing explanatory text, drawing and labelling diagram.

PUPIL BOOK ANSWERS

1. Bones / muscles / joints / tendons / ligaments.
2. Joint.
3. Hold a joint together.
4. No. They work in pairs.
5. You can move your arm.
6. **a** tendons: strong bands of tissue that connect a muscle to bone **b** ligaments: strong bands of tissue holding joints together **c** contracts: shortens **d** relaxes: becomes less tight
7. To explain how we can move our arms.
8. Anyone interested in how the body works.
9. Text and diagrams.
10. Answers that suggest it would not be as easy to understand without diagrams. The diagrams show the reader what the text is explaining.

11 12 Encourage all members of the group to contribute to the experiment and explanation.

RESOURCE SHEET SUPPORT ANSWERS

A

 a

 b

3 c

B

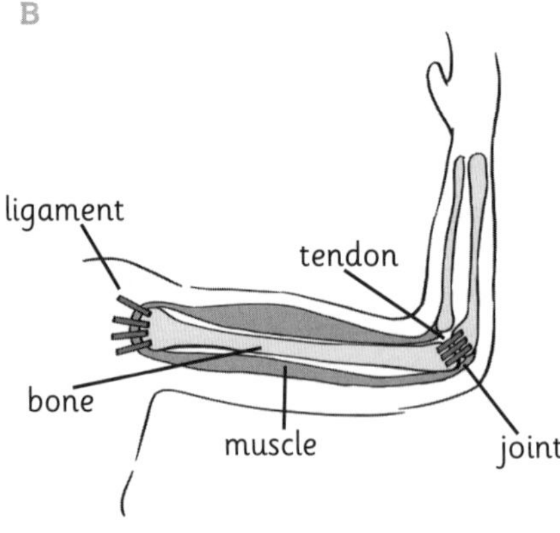

C

1 shortens

2 less tight

GOING DEEPER

- Use the answers to the 'Taking it further' activity as the basis of a class discussion, highlighting key features of the text type. Ask children in pairs to demonstrate and read their explanations.

WRITE

- Ask children to explain how we breathe. What parts of the body do we use?
- Explain to children that they are going to read an explanation of how humans breathe.
- Read the explanation to the class; ask individual children to read it aloud in turn; or read in silence individually.

RESOURCES & ASSESSMENT BOOK

- **Support** (comprehension support): identifying True / False statements, correcting false statements; (vocabulary support): sorting muddled words for vocabulary reinforcement.
- **Extension:** writing investigative questions.

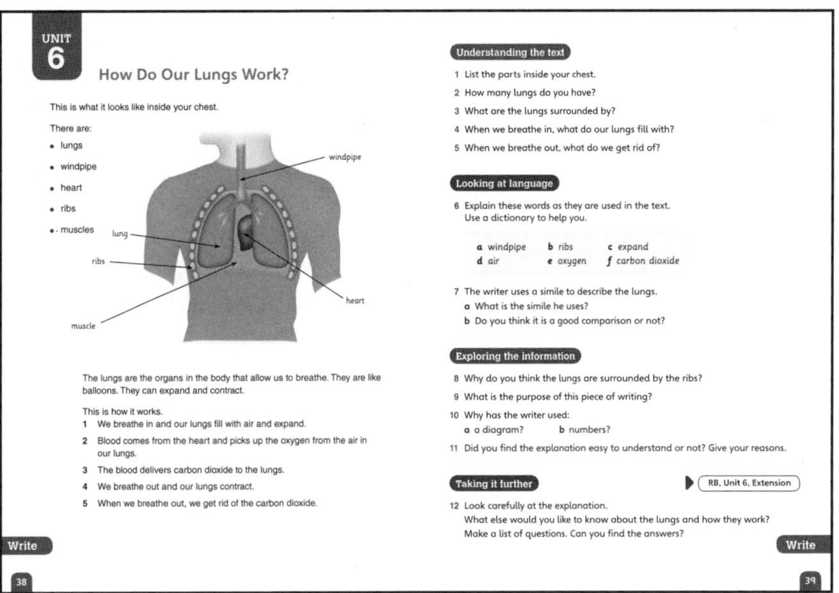

UNIT 6

How Do Our Lungs Work?

This is what it looks like inside your chest.

There are:

- lungs
- windpipe
- heart
- ribs
- muscles

The lungs are the organs in the body that allow us to breathe. They are like balloons. They can expand and contract.

This is how it works.

1 We breathe in and our lungs fill with air and expand.
2 Blood comes from the heart and picks up the oxygen from the air in our lungs.
3 The blood delivers carbon dioxide to the lungs.
4 We breathe out and our lungs contract.
5 When we breathe out, we get rid of the carbon dioxide.

Write

38

Understanding the text

1 List the parts inside your chest.
2 How many lungs do you have?
3 What are the lungs surrounded by?
4 When we breathe in, what do our lungs fill with?
5 When we breathe out, what do we get rid of?

Looking at language

6 Explain these words as they are used in the text. Use a dictionary to help you.
a *windpipe* **b** *ribs* **c** *expand* **d** *air* **e** *oxygen* **f** *carbon dioxide*
7 The writer uses a simile to describe the lungs.
a What is the simile he uses?
b Do you think it is a good comparison or not?

Exploring the information

8 Why do you think the lungs are surrounded by the ribs?
9 What is the purpose of this piece of writing?
10 Why has the writer used:
a a diagram? **b** numbers?
11 Did you find the explanation easy to understand or not? Give your reasons.

Taking it further

RB, Unit 6, Extension

12 Look carefully at the explanation.
What else would you like to know about the lungs and how they work?
Make a list of questions. Can you find the answers?

Write

39

PUPIL BOOK ANSWERS

1. Lungs / windpipe / heart / ribs / muscles.
2. Two.
3. Ribs.
4. Air.
5. Carbon dioxide.
6. **a** windpipe: a tube that carries air into the lungs from the nose and mouth **b** ribs: long curved bones in the chest **c** expand: get larger **d** air: the mixture of gases we breathe in **e** oxygen: a gas that is an important element in air **f** carbon dioxide: a gas we get rid of when we breathe out
7. **a** The lungs are 'like balloons'. **b** Answers that suggest this is a good comparison because both balloons and lungs expand and contract when air is put in and taken out. Also, they are a similar shape.
8. Answers that suggest the ribs protect the lungs.
9. To explain how the lungs work.
10. **a** It helps the reader to 'see' the process that is being explained. **b** To show the steps of the process in the correct order.
11. Individual answers.
12. Individual answers.

RESOURCE SHEET SUPPORT ANSWERS

A

1. True
2. False
3. False
4. True
5. True
6. False

B

1. Blood picks up oxygen from the air in our lungs.
2. When we breathe out, our lungs contract.
3. When we breathe out, we get rid of carbon dioxide.

C

1. windpipe
2. ribs
3. lungs
4. heart
5. muscles

GOING DEEPER

- Recap on why the writer has used a diagram (to help the reader 'see' the process, therefore making it easier to understand the text) and bullet points (to list items and to show the stages of the process).
- Use answers to 'Taking it further' activity as a basis for further class discussion.
- Discuss what causes our lungs to work less effectively, for example, air pollution, smoking, dust (miners and farm workers), asbestos.

UNIT FOCUS: Reading Persuasive Texts

Investigating …

- persuasive texts in the forms of film advertisements, book reviews and book blurbs
- features of hyperbolic language

TEACH

- Discuss how the children decide what films or programmes to watch and books to read. Do advertisements for films / books affect them? Do they listen to what friends say?
- Explain to the children that they are going to look at an advertisement for a new film, *Bigfoot*, which is based on a novel of the same name.
- Show the advertisement and book cover to the class; ask individual children to read it aloud in turn; or read in silence individually.

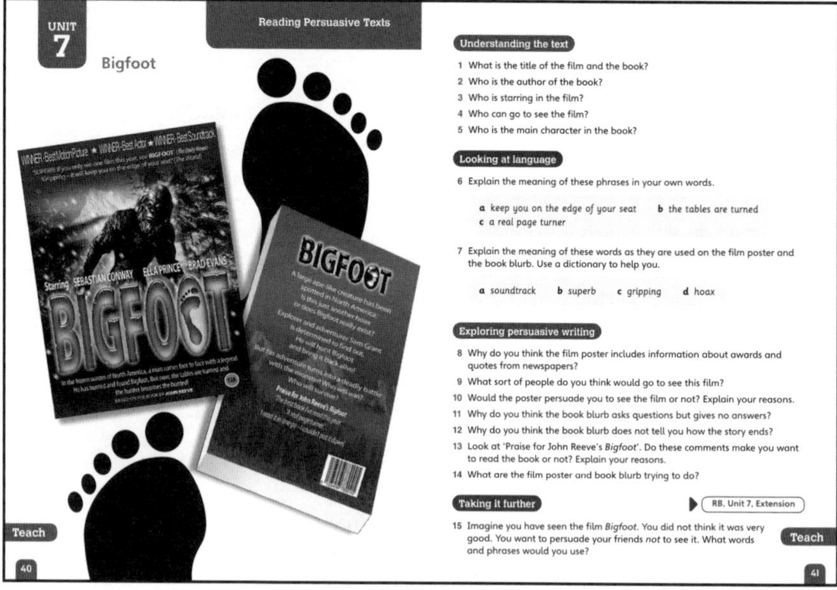
UNIT 7

Reading Persuasive Texts

Bigfoot

Understanding the text

1 What is the title of the film and the book?
2 Who is the author of the book?
3 Who is starring in the film?
4 Who can go to see the film?
5 Who is the main character in the book?

Looking at language

6 Explain the meaning of these phrases in your own words.

a keep you on the edge of your seat *b the tables are turned* *c a real page turner*

7 Explain the meaning of these words as they are used on the film poster and the book blurb. Use a dictionary to help you.

a soundtrack *b superb* *c gripping* *d hoax*

Exploring persuasive writing

8 Why do you think the film poster includes information about awards and quotes from newspapers?
9 What sort of people do you think would go to see this film?
10 Would the poster persuade you to see the film or not? Explain your reasons.
11 Why do you think the book blurb asks questions but gives no answers?
12 Why do you think the book blurb does not tell you how the story ends?
13 Look at 'Praise for John Reeve's *Bigfoot*'. Do these comments make you want to read the book or not? Explain your reasons.
14 What are the film poster and book blurb trying to do?

Taking it further

RB, Unit 7, Extension

15 Imagine you have seen the film *Bigfoot*. You did not think it was very good. You want to persuade your friends *not* to see it. What words and phrases would you use?

Teach 40 Teach 41

RESOURCES & ASSESSMENT BOOK

- **Support** (comprehension support): correcting incorrect facts; (vocabulary support): matching adjectives to correct definitions.
- **Extension:** making a plan for persuasive writing.

PUPIL BOOK ANSWERS

1 *Bigfoot*.

2 John Reeve.

3 Sebastian Conway / Ella Price / Brad Evans.

4 Anyone over 12. [Children under 12 are only allowed to see the film with an adult.]

5 Sam Grant.

6 **a** keep you on the edge of your seat: keep you interested / excited / wanting to know what is coming next **b** the tables are turned: the exact opposite of what has happened is now happening **c** a real page turner: so exciting that a reader just keep turning the pages

7 **a** soundtrack: music that is played during a film or TV programme **b** superb: excellent / of the highest quality **c** gripping: very exciting **d** hoax: lie or trick

8 Answers that suggest if the film has won awards, people have seen it and judged it to be very good. This encourages others to see it.

9 Answers that suggest people who like adventure films / films about monsters.

10 Individual answers.

11 Answers that suggest the questions get the reader thinking about the book but the only way to find the answers is to read it.

12 Answers that suggest if you already knew the ending of the book, you probably wouldn't read it.

13 Individual answers.

14 They are trying to persuade you to see the film / read the book.

15 Write suggested words and phrases on the board and choose the best through discussion.

RESOURCE SHEET SUPPORT ANSWERS

A

1 The film stars John Reeve. (Sebastian Conway / Ella Prince / Brad Evans)

2 The film is set in South America. (North America)

3 The film won a Best Actress award. (Actor)

4 The author of the book is Brad Evans. (John Reeve)

5 Sam Grant is an actor. (explorer and adventurer)

6 Bigfoot is a small creature. (large)

B

1 best – highest quality

2 superb – excellent

3 gripping – very exciting

4 frozen – turned to ice

5 large – very big

6 deadly – ending in death

GOING DEEPER

- Ask children to identify persuasive language in the advertisement and book blurb, for example, 'superb!', 'gripping', 'edge of your seat', 'best book', 'page turner', 'couldn't put it down'. Substitute these words and discuss the effect on the reader, for example, 'superb!' becomes 'OK!'; 'gripping' becomes 'boring', etc.

TALK

- Ask children what they look at first when they are given a book to read. Do they think the cover of a book is important? Why?
- Ask children what they think about the possibility of aliens coming to Earth.
- Explain to the children that they are going to look at the front and back covers of a book called *Tripods Trilogy*.
- Show the cover to the class; ask individual children to read it aloud in turn; or read in silence individually.

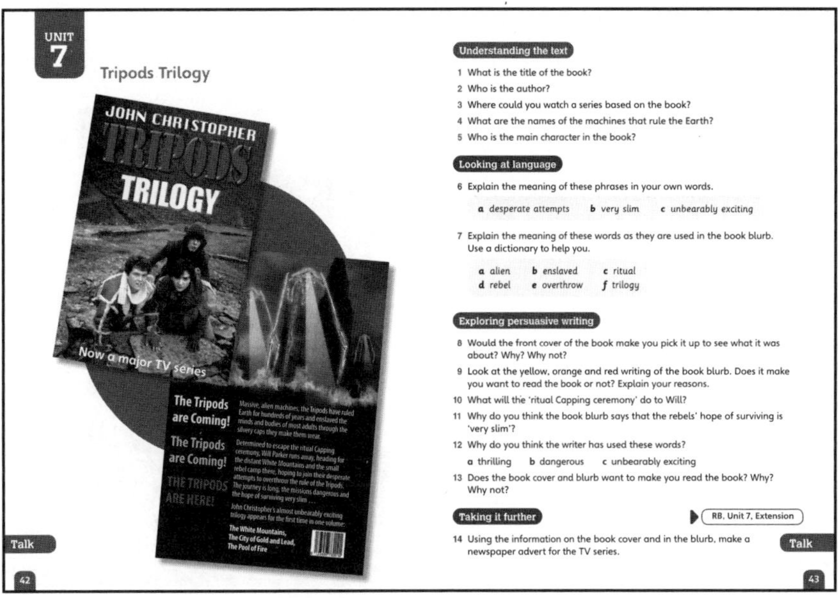

Understanding the text

1 What is the title of the book?
2 Who is the author?
3 Where could you watch a series based on the book?
4 What are the names of the machines that rule the Earth?
5 Who is the main character in the book?

Looking at language

6 Explain the meaning of these phrases in your own words.
a desperate attempts *b* very slim *c* unbearably exciting

7 Explain the meaning of these words as they are used in the book blurb. Use a dictionary to help you.
a alien *b* enslaved *c* ritual
d rebel *e* overthrow *f* trilogy

Exploring persuasive writing

8 Would the front cover of the book make you pick it up to see what it was about? Why? Why not?
9 Look at the yellow, orange and red writing of the book blurb. Does it make you want to read the book or not? Explain your reasons.
10 What will the 'ritual Capping ceremony' do to Will?
11 Why do you think the book blurb says that the rebels' hope of surviving is 'very slim'?
12 Why do you think the writer has used these words?
a thrilling b dangerous c unbearably exciting
13 Does the book cover and blurb want to make you read the book? Why? Why not?

Taking it further

RB, Unit 7, Extension

14 Using the information on the book cover and in the blurb, make a newspaper advert for the TV series.

Talk

43

RESOURCES & ASSESSMENT BOOK

- **Support** (comprehension support): identifying correct words to complete sentences; (vocabulary support): matching adjectives to correct nouns.
- **Extension:** making notes and creating own advert.

PUPIL BOOK ANSWERS

1. *Tripods Trilogy.*
2. John Christopher.
3. On TV.
4. The Tripods.
5. Will Parker.
6. **a** desperate attempts: try to make something happen even though it is unlikely **b** very slim: not much chance at all **c** unbearably exciting: so exciting you almost cannot go on reading
7. **a** alien: from another planet **b** enslaved: made a slave of **c** ritual: an event or ceremony, always done in the same way **d** rebel: someone who is against those who rule over them **e** overthrow: get rid of / take power away **f** trilogy: set of three
8. Individual answers.
9. Answers that suggest the lines of writing build up the tension and the reader will be keen to read the book.
10. Answers that suggest the 'capping' will make Will Parker a slave of the Tripods.
11. Answers that suggest this is a way of persuading you to read the book to find out whether they survive or not.
12. Answers that suggest these words are used to persuade you to read the book.
13. Individual answers.
14. Encourage all members of the group to contribute ideas and help with the design and wording of the advert.

RESOURCE SHEET SUPPORT ANSWERS

A

1. author
2. *Tripods Trilogy*
3. The Tripods
4. main character
5. not been capped

B

1	machines	massive, alien
2	caps	silvery
3	White Mountains	distant
4	rebel camp	small
5	attempts	desperate
6	journey	long
7	mission	dangerous
8	trilogy	exciting

GOING DEEPER

- Use the children's ideas for the 'Taking it further' activity as the basis of a class discussion.

WRITE

- Ask children what they know about the Loch Ness Monster. Do they believe it exists or doesn't exist? Why?
- Explain to the children that they are going to look at an advertisement for a film called *Search for the Loch Ness Monster*.
- Recap on the purpose of a film advertisement.
- Show the advertisement to the class; ask individual children to read it aloud in turn; or read in silence individually.

UNIT 7

Search for the Loch Ness Monster

A magical film that the whole family will enjoy. The scenery is beautiful and the monster so realistic you feel you could reach out and touch it!

Search for the LOCH NESS MONSTER

Starring the award-winning* Anne Grey and John Johnson

Maggie Brown's holiday on the banks of Loch Ness is more than she bargained for!

She sees the legendary Loch Ness Monster but no one believes her.

Can she convince people that she is not going mad?

Write

44

Understanding the text

1 What is the film being advertised?
2 Who are the stars of the film?
3 Where is the film set?
4 Who is the main character?
5 Who can go to see the film?

Looking at language

6 Explain these phrases in your own words.
a more than she bargained for **b** award-winning **c** not going mad

7 Explain these words as they are used in the poster. Use a dictionary to help you.
a realistic **b** legendary **c** convince

Exploring persuasive writing

8 Find the question in the poster. Why do you think it asks that question?
9 Why do you think the poster includes quotes from newspapers?
10 Why do you think it does not include quotes from people who did not like the film?
11 Why do you think it is important that the monster is 'realistic'?
12 Would the poster persuade you to see the film? Why? Why not?
13 Do you think that Maggie convinces people that she has seen the monster? Why? Why not?

Taking it further

RB, Unit 7, Extension

14 Imagine that *Search for the Loch Ness Monster* is a book. Write a book blurb to persuade people to read it. Write

45

RESOURCES & ASSESSMENT BOOK

- **Support** (comprehension support): writing questions for given answers; (vocabulary support): choosing correct definitions.
- **Extension**: making a plan for writing a blurb.

PUPIL BOOK ANSWERS

1. *Search for the Loch Ness Monster.*
2. Anne Grey / John Johnson.
3. 'on the banks of Loch Ness'.
4. Maggie Brown.
5. 'the whole family'.
6. **a** more than she bargained for: more than she expected **b** award-winning; someone who has won awards for their work **c** not going mad: she isn't seeing things / imagining things
7. **a** realistic: made to seem natural and real **b** legendary: very famous or well known for a long time **c** convince: make someone believe something
8. 'Can she convince people that she is not going mad?'
   Answers that suggest the only way to find the answer is to see the film.
9. Answers that suggest people who watch films and write about them for a living think the film is good. This encourages others to go and see it.
10. Answers that suggest, as the poster is trying to persuade people to see the film, it will not include anything that may persuade people *not* to see it (i.e. dissuade them).
11. Answers that suggest that it is important for the monster to be 'realistic' as people who watch the film must be convinced that the monster is 'real'.
12. Individual answers.
13. Individual answers.
14. Individual answers. Remind children to use the book blurb on p.42 as a model for their own writing.

RESOURCE SHEET SUPPORT ANSWERS

A

1. What is the title of the film?
2. Who stars in the film?
3. Who is the main character in the film?
4. What is she doing at Loch Ness?
5. What does she see?

B

1. the landscape / buildings of an area
2. made to seem very real and natural
3. look for
4. famous or well known for a long time
5. make someone believe something

GOING DEEPER

- Use the answers to the 'Taking it further' activity as the basis for a class discussion.
- Recap on what the children have learnt about persuasive writing.

UNIT FOCUS: How Settings Create Atmosphere

Investigating …

- fantasy settings
- how imagined worlds impact on characters' behaviour

TEACH

- Have children ever been in / walked through a wood or forest?
- If they have, or can imagine it, how do they think they would feel? Is it spooky or exciting?
- Explain to the children that they are going to read an extract from *The Lord of the Rings* where Frodo and the other hobbits have to journey through a mysterious and threatening forest.
- This is a challenging text for this year group, and you may wish to read it and discuss questions as a class or in groups before asking children to tackle it on their own.

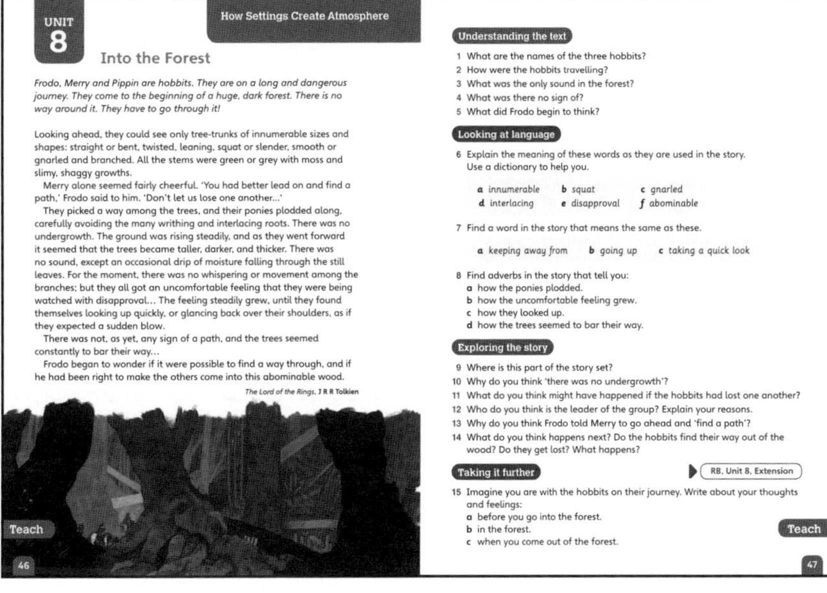

UNIT 8

How Settings Create Atmosphere

Into the Forest

Frodo, Merry and Pippin are hobbits. They are on a long and dangerous journey. They come to the beginning of a huge, dark forest. There is no way around it. They have to go through it!

Looking ahead, they could see only tree-trunks of innumerable sizes and shapes: straight or bent, twisted, leaning, squat or slender, smooth or gnarled and branched. All the stems were green or grey with moss and slimy, shaggy growths.

Merry alone seemed fairly cheerful. 'You had better lead on and find a path,' Frodo said to him. 'Don't let us lose one another...'

They picked a way among the trees, and their ponies plodded along, carefully avoiding the many writhing and interlacing roots. There was no undergrowth. The ground was rising steadily, and as they went forward it seemed that the trees became taller, darker, and thicker. There was no sound, except an occasional drip of moisture falling through the still leaves. For the moment, there was no whispering or movement among the branches; but they all got an uncomfortable feeling that they were being watched with disapproval... The feeling steadily grew, until they found themselves looking up quickly, or glancing back over their shoulders, as if they expected a sudden blow.

There was not, as yet, any sign of a path, and the trees seemed constantly to bar their way...

Frodo began to wonder if it were possible to find a way through, and if he had been right to make the others come into this abominable wood.

The Lord of the Rings, J R R Tolkien

Teach

46

Understanding the text

1 What are the names of the three hobbits?
2 How were the hobbits travelling?
3 What was the only sound in the forest?
4 What was there no sign of?
5 What did Frodo begin to think?

Looking at language

6 Explain the meaning of these words as they are used in the story. Use a dictionary to help you.

a *innumerable* **b** *squat* **c** *gnarled*
d *interlacing* **e** *disapproval* **f** *abominable*

7 Find a word in the story that means the same as these.

a *keeping away from* **b** *going up* **c** *taking a quick look*

8 Find adverbs in the story that tell you:
a how the ponies plodded.
b how the uncomfortable feeling grew.
c how they looked up.
d how the trees seemed to bar their way.

Exploring the story

9 Where is this part of the story set?
10 Why do you think 'there was no undergrowth'?
11 What do you think might have happened if the hobbits had lost one another?
12 Who do you think is the leader of the group? Explain your reasons.
13 Why do you think Frodo told Merry to go ahead and 'find a path'?
14 What do you think happens next? Do the hobbits find their way out of the wood? Do they get lost? What happens?

Taking it further

RB, Unit 8, Extension

15 Imagine you are with the hobbits on their journey. Write about your thoughts and feelings:
a before you go into the forest.
b in the forest.
c when you come out of the forest.

Teach

47

RESOURCES & ASSESSMENT BOOK

- **Support** (comprehension support): identifying descriptive detail; (vocabulary support): identifying adjectives.
- **Extension:** writing about thoughts and feelings.

PUPIL BOOK ANSWERS

1. Frodo / Merry / Pippin.
2. On ponies.
3. 'an occasional drip of moisture falling through the still leaves'.
4. A path.
5. 'if it were possible to find a way through, and if he had been right to make the others come into this abominable wood'.
6. **a** innumerable: too many to count **b** squat: wide but not very tall **c** gnarled: old, twisted and rough **d** interlacing: all tangled up together **e** disapproval: judging that someone's behaviour is not right or proper **f** abominable: extremely bad / horrible
7. **a** keeping away from: avoiding **b** going up: rising **c** taking a quick look: glancing
8. **a** how the ponies plodded: carefully **b** how the uncomfortable feeling grew: steadily **c** how they looked up: quickly **d** how the trees seemed to bar their way: constantly
9. In the forest.
10. Answers that suggest the trees grew so thickly that they hid the sun so no plants could grow on the forest floor.
11. Individual answers.
12. Answers that suggest Frodo is the leader based on evidence: He tells Merry to go ahead and find a path / He had made the others come into the wood.
13. Answers that suggest as 'Merry alone seemed fairly cheerful' it seemed sensible that he should go first.
14. Individual answers.
15. Individual answers.

RESOURCE SHEET SUPPORT ANSWERS

A

1. the trees
2. the moss on the stems
3. the roots
4. the trees
5. the wood

B

1. Merry
2. Frodo

C

1. the ponies
2. the feeling
3. the hobbits
4. the trees

D

1. **a** grey **b** green **c** gnarled
2. **a** straight **b** squat **c** slender **d** smooth **e** slimy **f** shaggy

GOING DEEPER

- What / Who do the children think were 'watching' the hobbits in the forest?
- Would the children like to have been with the hobbits in this part of the journey? Why? Why not?

TALK

- Ask children if they have ever heard of, or read, *Alice in Wonderland*. Can they give a brief retelling of their favourite part of it?
- Explain to the children that they are going to read an extract from near the beginning of *Alice in Wonderland.*
- Read the extract to the class; ask individual children to read it aloud in turn; or read in silence individually.

RESOURCES & ASSESSMENT BOOK

- **Support** (comprehension support): replacing incorrect words in sentences; (vocabulary support): matching words and definitions.
- **Extension:** answering questions to write own ending.

PUPIL BOOK ANSWERS

1. Alice saw a talking White Rabbit.
2. She followed the White Rabbit down the rabbit hole.
3. 'in a long, low hall'.
4. 'a tiny, golden key'.
5. 'a little door about fifteen inches high'.
6. **a** not a moment to be lost: to hurry and waste no time **b** like the wind: move very quickly **c** at any rate: in any case **d** out-of-the-way things: unusual / peculiar
7. **a** the passage: long **b** the hall: long / low / dark **c** the garden: loveliest
8. By the river / in the rabbit hole / in the passage / in the hall.
9. **a** surprised / curious **b** disappointed / sad / annoyed **c** hopeful / excited **d** disappointed / perhaps a little scared
10. Answers that use 'to her great delight' as evidence that she was pleased.
11. 'loveliest garden' / beds of bright flowers / cool fountains.
12. She wanted to 'shut up like a telescope'.
13. Answers that suggest she was curious / brave / not easily scared.
14. Encourage all members of the group to contribute ideas, consider each idea and vote on which may work best.

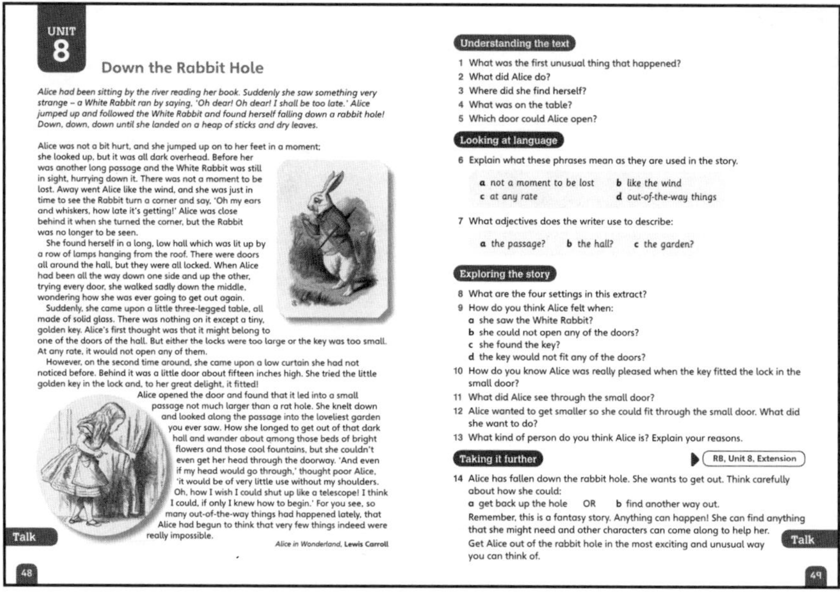

UNIT 8

Down the Rabbit Hole

Alice had been sitting by the river reading her book. Suddenly she saw something very strange – a White Rabbit ran by saying, 'Oh dear! Oh dear! I shall be too late.' Alice jumped up and followed the White Rabbit and found herself falling down a rabbit hole! Down, down, down until she landed on a heap of sticks and dry leaves.

Alice was not a bit hurt, and she jumped up on to her feet in a moment; she looked up, but it was all dark overhead. Before her was another long passage and the White Rabbit was still in sight, hurrying down it. There was not a moment to be lost. Away went Alice like the wind, and she was just in time to see the Rabbit turn a corner and say, 'Oh my ears and whiskers, how late it's getting!' Alice was close behind it when she turned the corner, but the Rabbit was no longer to be seen.

She found herself in a long, low hall which was lit up by a row of lamps hanging from the roof. There were doors all around the hall, but they were all locked. When Alice had been all the way down one side and up the other, trying every door, she walked sadly down the middle, wondering how she was ever going to get out again.

Suddenly, she came upon a little three-legged table, all made of solid glass. There was nothing on it except a tiny, golden key. Alice's first thought was that it might belong to one of the doors of the hall. But either the locks were too large or the key was too small. At any rate, it would not open any of them.

However, on the second time around, she came upon a low curtain she had not noticed before. Behind it was a little door about fifteen inches high. She tried the little golden key in the lock and, to her great delight, it fitted!

Alice opened the door and found that it led into a small passage not much larger than a rat hole. She knelt down and looked along the passage into the loveliest garden you ever saw. How she longed to get out of that dark hall and wander about among those beds of bright flowers and those cool fountains, but she couldn't even get her head through the doorway. 'And even if my head would go through,' thought poor Alice, 'it would be of very little use without my shoulders. Oh, how I wish I could shut up like a telescope! I think I could, if only I knew how to begin.' For you see, so many out-of-the-way things had happened lately, that Alice had begun to think that very few things indeed were really impossible.

Alice in Wonderland, **Lewis Carroll**

Talk

48

Understanding the text

1 What was the first unusual thing that happened?
2 What did Alice do?
3 Where did she find herself?
4 What was on the table?
5 Which door could Alice open?

Looking at language

6 Explain what these phrases mean as they are used in the story.
a *not a moment to be lost* **b** *like the wind*
c *at any rate* **d** *out-of-the-way things*

7 What adjectives does the writer use to describe:
a *the passage?* **b** *the hall?* **c** *the garden?*

Exploring the story

8 What are the four settings in this extract?
9 How do you think Alice felt when:
a she saw the White Rabbit?
b she could not open any of the doors?
c she found the key?
d the key would not fit any of the doors?
10 How do you know Alice was really pleased when the key fitted the lock in the small door?
11 What did Alice see through the small door?
12 Alice wanted to get smaller so she could fit through the small door. What did she want to do?
13 What kind of person do you think Alice is? Explain your reasons.

Taking it further RB, Unit 8, Extension

14 Alice has fallen down the rabbit hole. She wants to get out. Think carefully about how she could:
a get back up the hole OR **b** find another way out.
Remember, this is a fantasy story. Anything can happen! She can find anything that she might need and other characters can come along to help her. Get Alice out of the rabbit hole in the most exciting and unusual way you can think of.

Talk

49

RESOURCE SHEET SUPPORT ANSWERS

A

1. short (long)
2. candles (lamps)
3. open (locked)
4. gold (glass)
5. huge (little)
6. trees (flowers)

B

1. quickly and without warning – suddenly
2. really wanted – longed
3. up above – overhead
4. unhappily – sadly
5. cannot be done – impossible
6. most beautiful – loveliest

GOING DEEPER

- Use ideas for the 'Taking it further' activity as the basis for a class discussion.
- Ask the children to compare the setting for *Alice in Wonderland* with the one in *Into the Forest.* Even though they are both fantasy settings, what are the differences?

WRITE

- Ask children if they are familiar with the story of *The Lion, the Witch and the Wardrobe* through having read the book or seen the film. Can they explain what it is about?
- Explain to the children that they are going to read an extract from *The Lion, the Witch and the Wardrobe.*
- Read the extract to the class; ask individual children to read it aloud in turn; or read in silence individually.

RESOURCES & ASSESSMENT BOOK

- **Support** (comprehension support): multiple choice; (vocabulary support): completing sentences for vocabulary reinforcement.
- **Extension:** using imagination to answer questions.

PUPIL BOOK ANSWERS

1. She went in to hide because they were playing hide and seek.
2. Snow.
3. In a wood.
4. A lamp-post.
5. 'From the waist upwards he was like a man, but his legs were shaped like a goat's … and instead of feet he had goat's hooves.'
6. **a** discovers: finds **b** stooping: bending **c** exclaimed: said loudly and quickly because of surprise **d** inquisitive: curious / wanting to know **e** glimpse: a brief look **f** glossy: very shiny
7. **a** hard, smooth: the wooden floor of the wardrobe **b** powdery and extremely cold: the snow **c** hard and rough and even prickly: branches of trees **d** dark: tree trunks
8. The wardrobe / the wood.
9. Answers that suggest Lucy is really puzzled by what is happening but she wants to find out about it. She is excited because it is so strange.
10. Answers that suggest Lucy thought she could get back because she had left the wardrobe door open.
11. Answers that suggest she was curious and maybe a little startled but not afraid.
12. Individual answers.

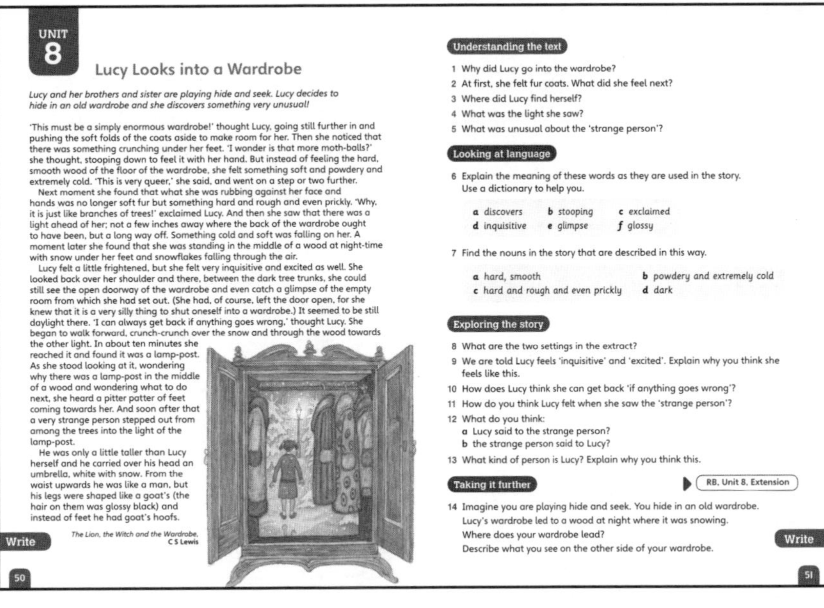

UNIT 8

Lucy Looks into a Wardrobe

Lucy and her brothers and sister are playing hide and seek. Lucy decides to hide in an old wardrobe and she discovers something very unusual!

'This must be a simply enormous wardrobe!' thought Lucy, going still further in and pushing the soft folds of the coats aside to make room for her. Then she noticed that there was something crunching under her feet. 'I wonder is that more moth-balls?' she thought, stooping down to feel it with her hand. But instead of feeling the hard, smooth wood of the floor of the wardrobe, she felt something soft and powdery and extremely cold. 'This is very queer,' she said, and went on a step or two further.

Next moment she found that what she was rubbing against her face and hands was no longer soft fur but something hard and rough and even prickly. 'Why, it is just like branches of trees!' exclaimed Lucy. And then she saw that there was a light ahead of her; not a few inches away where the back of the wardrobe ought to have been, but a long way off. Something cold and soft was falling on her. A moment later she found that she was standing in the middle of a wood at night-time with snow under her feet and snowflakes falling through the air.

Lucy felt a little frightened, but she felt very inquisitive and excited as well. She looked back over her shoulder and there, between the dark tree trunks, she could still see the open doorway of the wardrobe and even catch a glimpse of the empty room from which she had set out. (She had, of course, left the door open, for she knew that it is a very silly thing to shut oneself into a wardrobe.) It seemed to be still daylight there. 'I can always get back if anything goes wrong,' thought Lucy. She began to walk forward, crunch-crunch over the snow and through the wood towards the other light. In about ten minutes she reached it and found it was a lamp-post. As she stood looking at it, wondering why there was a lamp-post in the middle of a wood and wondering what to do next, she heard a pitter patter of feet coming towards her. And soon after that a very strange person stepped out from among the trees into the light of the lamp-post.

He was only a little taller than Lucy herself and he carried over his head an umbrella, white with snow. From the waist upwards he was like a man, but his legs were shaped like a goat's (the hair on them was glossy black) and instead of feet he had goat's hoofs.

The Lion, the Witch and the Wardrobe,
C S Lewis

Write

50

Understanding the text

1 Why did Lucy go into the wardrobe?
2 At first, she felt fur coats. What did she feel next?
3 Where did Lucy find herself?
4 What was the light she saw?
5 What was unusual about the 'strange person'?

Looking at language

6 Explain the meaning of these words as they are used in the story. Use a dictionary to help you.

a discovers *b* stooping *c* exclaimed
d inquisitive *e* glimpse *f* glossy

7 Find the nouns in the story that are described in this way.

a hard, smooth *b* powdery and extremely cold
c hard and rough and even prickly *d* dark

Exploring the story

8 What are the two settings in the extract?
9 We are told Lucy feels 'inquisitive' and 'excited'. Explain why you think she feels like this.
10 How does Lucy think she can get back 'if anything goes wrong'?
11 How do you think Lucy felt when she saw the 'strange person'?
12 What do you think:
a Lucy said to the strange person?
b the strange person said to Lucy?
13 What kind of person is Lucy? Explain why you think this.

Taking it further RB, Unit 8, Extension

14 Imagine you are playing hide and seek. You hide in an old wardrobe. Lucy's wardrobe led to a wood at night where it was snowing. Where does your wardrobe lead? Describe what you see on the other side of your wardrobe.

Write

51

13. Answers that suggest she is brave and curious, but not easily frightened.
14. Individual answers.

RESOURCE SHEET SUPPORT ANSWERS

A

1. a
2. c
3. b
4. b
5. c

B

1. Lucy **discovered** something very unusual about the wardrobe.
2. Lucy **stooped** down to feel what was on the floor.
3. She **exclaimed** in surprise when she felt the branches.
4. Lucy was **inquisitive** and wanted to know what was happening.
5. She looked back and **glimpsed** the empty room.
6. The hair on the strange person's legs was **glossy**.

GOING DEEPER

- Use answers to the 'Taking it further' activity as the basis for a class discussion.
- Discuss the three settings in the unit. Which setting can they see most clearly in their mind? Which setting would they like to visit? Which was the most unusual setting? Which one was most like the 'real' world?

UNIT FOCUS: Exploring Stage Playscripts

Investigating …

- playscripts based on the 'next instalment' of stories from previous units

TEACH

- Discuss plays with the children. Have they seen a play or acted in one?
- Ask children why they think people go to see plays.
- Remind the children of the extract from *The Lion, the Witch and the Wardrobe* they read in Unit 8.
- Recap on the story: Lucy has gone through the back of the wardrobe and found herself in a winter landscape. There she meets Mr Tumnus, a faun.
- Read the playscript to the class; ask individual children to read it aloud; or read in silence individually.

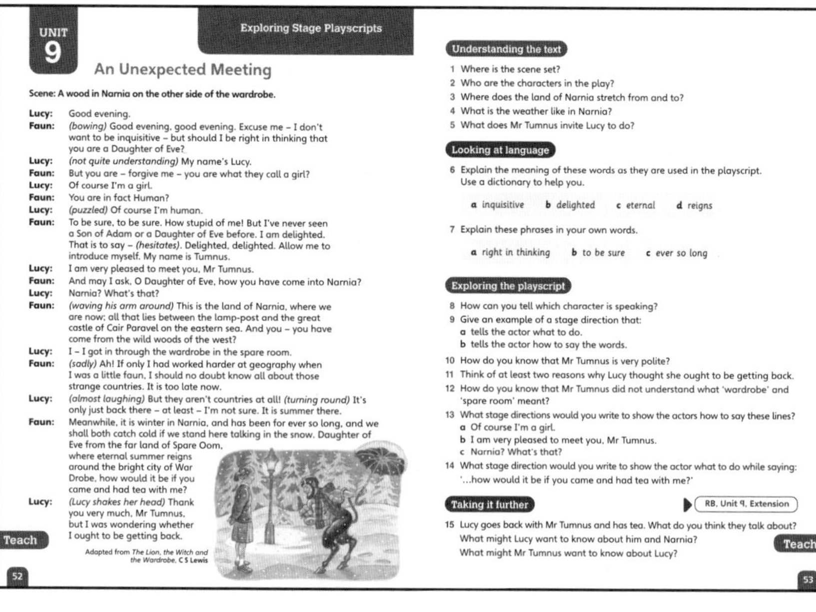

UNIT 9 Exploring Stage Playscripts

An Unexpected Meeting

Scene: A wood in Narnia on the other side of the wardrobe.

Lucy: Good evening.
Faun: *(bowing)* Good evening, good evening. Excuse me – I don't want to be inquisitive – but should I be right in thinking that you are a Daughter of Eve?
Lucy: *(not quite understanding)* My name's Lucy.
Faun: But you are – forgive me – you are what they call a girl?
Lucy: Of course I'm a girl.
Faun: You are in fact Human?
Lucy: *(puzzled)* Of course I'm human.
Faun: To be sure, to be sure. How stupid of me! But I've never seen a Son of Adam or a Daughter of Eve before. I am delighted. That is to say – *(hesitates)*. Delighted, delighted. Allow me to introduce myself. My name is Tumnus.
Lucy: I am very pleased to meet you, Mr Tumnus.
Faun: And may I ask, O Daughter of Eve, how you have come into Narnia?
Lucy: Narnia? What's that?
Faun: *(waving his arm around)* This is the land of Narnia, where we are now; all that lies between the lamp-post and the great castle of Cair Paravel on the eastern sea. And you – you have come from the wild woods of the west?
Lucy: I – I got in through the wardrobe in the spare room.
Faun: *(sadly)* Ah! If only I had worked harder at geography when I was a little faun, I should no doubt know all about those strange countries. It is too late now.
Lucy: *(almost laughing)* But they aren't countries at all! *(turning round)* It's only just back there – at least – I'm not sure. It is summer there.
Faun: Meanwhile, it is winter in Narnia, and has been for ever so long, and we shall both catch cold if we stand here talking in the snow. Daughter of Eve from the far land of Spare Oom, where eternal summer reigns around the bright city of War Drobe, how would it be if you came and had tea with me?
Lucy: *(Lucy shakes her head)* Thank you very much, Mr Tumnus, but I was wondering whether I ought to be getting back.

Adapted from *The Lion, the Witch and the Wardrobe*, C S Lewis

Teach

52

Understanding the text

1 Where is the scene set?
2 Who are the characters in the play?
3 Where does the land of Narnia stretch from and to?
4 What is the weather like in Narnia?
5 What does Mr Tumnus invite Lucy to do?

Looking at language

6 Explain the meaning of these words as they are used in the playscript. Use a dictionary to help you.
a *inquisitive* **b** *delighted* **c** *eternal* **d** *reigns*

7 Explain these phrases in your own words.
a *right in thinking* **b** *to be sure* **c** *ever so long*

Exploring the playscript

8 How can you tell which character is speaking?
9 Give an example of a stage direction that:
a tells the actor what to do.
b tells the actor how to say the words.
10 How do you know that Mr Tumnus is very polite?
11 Think of at least two reasons why Lucy thought she ought to be getting back.
12 How do you know that Mr Tumnus did not understand what 'wardrobe' and 'spare room' meant?
13 What stage directions would you write to show the actors how to say these lines?
a Of course I'm a girl.
b I am very pleased to meet you, Mr Tumnus.
c Narnia? What's that?
14 What stage direction would you write to show the actor what to do while saying: '...how would it be if you came and had tea with me?'

Taking it further RB, Unit 9, Extension

15 Lucy goes back with Mr Tumnus and has tea. What do you think they talk about? What might Lucy want to know about him and Narnia? What might Mr Tumnus want to know about Lucy?

Teach

53

RESOURCES & ASSESSMENT BOOK

- **Support** (comprehension support): completing sentences; (vocabulary support): choosing correct definitions, identifying stage directions.
- **Extension:** writing questions using imagination.

PUPIL BOOK ANSWERS

1. A wood in Narnia on the other side of the wardrobe.
2. Lucy / Mr Tumnus
3. From the lamp-post to the great castle of Cair Paravel on the eastern sea.
4. Winter – it is snowing.
5. To come and have tea with him.
6. **a** inquisitive: curious / wanting to know **b** delighted: really pleased **c** eternal: going on for ever **d** reigns: rules / dominates
7. **a** right in thinking: correct **b** to be sure: certainly **c** ever so long: for a very long time
8. The name of the character speaking is on the left hand side of the page.
9. **a** e.g. waving his arm around **b** e.g. sadly
10. Answers based on evidence: he bows and has manners; he says 'Good evening' and 'Excuse me'.
11. Answers that suggest Lucy is a little wary of Mr Tumnus / she is beginning to think she may not get back / her brothers and sister may be looking for her.
12. Answers based on evidence: he thinks Spare Oom is a country and War Drobe a city.
13. Individual answers e.g. **a** surprised **b** politely / warmly **c** puzzled / curious.
14. Individual answers e.g. pointing to the way he had come.
15. Individual answers.

RESOURCE SHEET SUPPORT ANSWERS

A

1. wood in Narnia.
2. Lucy and Mr Tumnus
3. the lamp-post / great castle of Cair Paravel
4. winter
5. tea

B

1. inquisitive: wanting to know something
2. delighted: really pleased
3. eternal: going on forever
4. reigns: rules
5. introduce: say who you are
6. eastern: towards the east

C

1. *(sadly)*
2. *(waving his arm around)*

GOING DEEPER

- Discuss how a playscript 'looks' different on the page from a story.

TALK

- Ask the children to retell what happened in the extract from *Chicken* that they read in Unit 5.
- Explain to the children that they are going to read a playscript of the next part of the story of *Chicken*. Mr Clarke, the teacher, is a new character. He senses that something is wrong and wants a word with Davy, the narrator of the story.
- Read the playscript to the class; ask individual children to read it aloud; or read in silence individually.

RESOURCES & ASSESSMENT BOOK

- **Support** (comprehension support): completing sentences; (vocabulary support): choosing correct definitions, identifying stage directions.
- **Extension:** understanding feelings. writing and perfoming a scene.

PUPIL BOOK ANSWERS

1. A teacher.
2. He thinks there may be something wrong as Davy doesn't 'seem very happy'.
3. Webbo and his mates.
4. Nothing.
5. 'What did Clarkey want?' / 'What did you say?'
6. **a** shrugs: moves shoulders up and down quickly **b** mumbling: speaking quickly and very quietly **c** not convinced: doesn't really believe him **d** menacingly: threateningly
7. **a** a sec: a second **b** a hard time: making life difficult **c** couple of weeks: two weeks **d** really get it: be in trouble
8. In a classroom.
9. Davy and Mr Clarke in the classroom / Webbo and his mates outside.
10. **a** e.g. mumbling / menacingly **b** e.g. Mr Clarke looks at Davy / Davy remains silent
11. Answers that suggest Mr Clarke is observant / kind / willing to help.
12. Answers that suggest children don't like to 'tell on' others in their class / Davy is frightened of what Webbo would do if he found out.

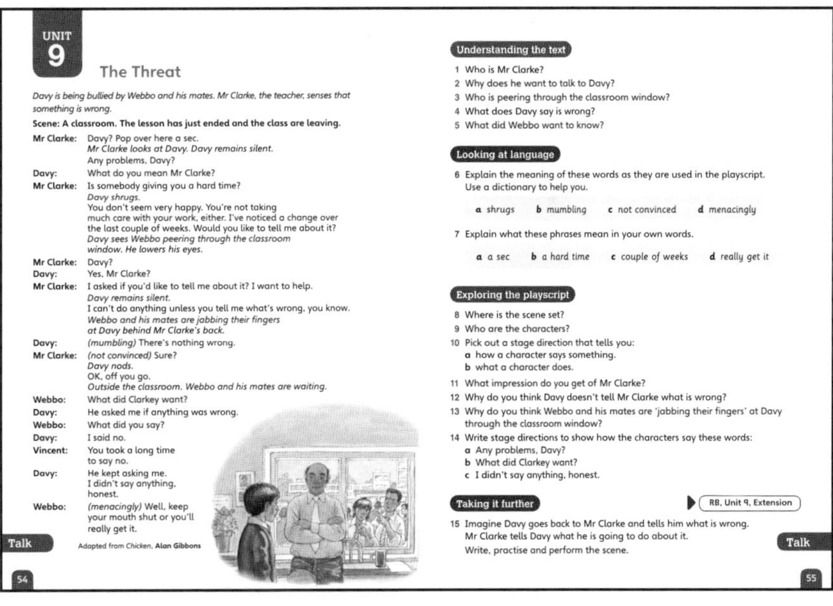

UNIT 9

The Threat

Davy is being bullied by Webbo and his mates. Mr Clarke, the teacher, senses that something is wrong.

Scene: A classroom. The lesson has just ended and the class are leaving.

Mr Clarke: Davy? Pop over here a sec.
Mr Clarke looks at Davy. Davy remains silent.
Any problems, Davy?
Davy: What do you mean Mr Clarke?
Mr Clarke: Is somebody giving you a hard time?
Davy shrugs.
You don't seem very happy. You're not taking much care with your work, either. I've noticed a change over the last couple of weeks. Would you like to tell me about it?
Davy sees Webbo peering through the classroom window. He lowers his eyes.
Mr Clarke: Davy?
Davy: Yes, Mr Clarke?
Mr Clarke: I asked if you'd like to tell me about it? I want to help.
Davy remains silent.
I can't do anything unless you tell me what's wrong, you know.
Webbo and his mates are jabbing their fingers at Davy behind Mr Clarke's back.
Davy: *(mumbling)* There's nothing wrong.
Mr Clarke: *(not convinced)* Sure?
Davy nods.
OK, off you go.
Outside the classroom. Webbo and his mates are waiting.
Webbo: What did Clarkey want?
Davy: He asked me if anything was wrong.
Webbo: What did you say?
Davy: I said no.
Vincent: You took a long time to say no.
Davy: He kept asking me. I didn't say anything, honest.
Webbo: *(menacingly)* Well, keep your mouth shut or you'll really get it.

Adapted from *Chicken*, **Alan Gibbons**

Talk

54

Understanding the text

1 Who is Mr Clarke?
2 Why does he want to talk to Davy?
3 Who is peering through the classroom window?
4 What does Davy say is wrong?
5 What did Webbo want to know?

Looking at language

6 Explain the meaning of these words as they are used in the playscript. Use a dictionary to help you.
a *shrugs* **b** *mumbling* **c** *not convinced* **d** *menacingly*
7 Explain what these phrases mean in your own words.
a *a sec* **b** *a hard time* **c** *couple of weeks* **d** *really get it*

Exploring the playscript

8 Where is the scene set?
9 Who are the characters?
10 Pick out a stage direction that tells you:
a how a character says something.
b what a character does.
11 What impression do you get of Mr Clarke?
12 Why do you think Davy doesn't tell Mr Clarke what is wrong?
13 Why do you think Webbo and his mates are 'jabbing their fingers' at Davy through the classroom window?
14 Write stage directions to show how the characters say these words:
a Any problems, Davy?
b What did Clarkey want?
c I didn't say anything, honest.

Taking it further RB, Unit 9, Extension

15 Imagine Davy goes back to Mr Clarke and tells him what is wrong. Mr Clarke tells Davy what he is going to do about it. Write, practise and perform the scene.

Talk

55

13. Answers that suggest they are making sure that Davy knows they are there and they are warning him to say nothing.
14. Individual answers e.g. **a** Any problems, Davy: kindly / sympathetically **b** What did Clarkey want?: threateningly / sneeringly **c** I didn't say anything, honest.: frightened / shakily
15. Encourage all members of the group to participate with suggestions and performance.

RESOURCE SHEET SUPPORT ANSWERS

A

1. the classroom
2. a teacher
3. a hard time
4. Webbo and his mates
5. said anything

B

1. move your shoulders up and down
2. speak quietly
3. disbelieve what is being said
4. threatening

C

1. *(mumbling)*
2. *He lowers his eyes.*

GOING DEEPER

- Allow the groups to act out their scene from the 'Taking it further' activity. Discuss the solutions they came up with.

WRITE

- Ask the children to retell what happened in the extract from *Carrie's War* they read in Unit 1.
- Explain to the children that they are going to read a playscript of the next part of the story of *Carrie's War*. A 'Woman' and Mrs Evans are new characters, and Carrie and the other children are now in a village hall waiting to find out where they are going to live.
- Read the playscript to the class; ask individual children to read it aloud; or read in silence individually.

RESOURCES & ASSESSMENT BOOK

- **Support** (comprehension support): who said what?, Who did what?; (vocabulary support): cloze activity for vocabulary reinforcement.
- **Extension:** empathising.

PUPIL BOOK ANSWERS

1. During the Second World War.
2. 'a village hall somewhere in Wales'.
3. Carrie / Nick / Albert / Mrs Evans / a woman.
4. They do not want to be separated.
5. He has bad dreams.
6. **a** bewildered: very puzzled and surprised **b** auction: where people buy and sell things **c** separated: split up **d** doubtful: not sure
7. Individual answers e.g. **a** sounding disgusted **b** Nick blinks in surprise.
8. Answers based on evidence: sounding disgusted / sits on his suitcase and begins to read a book making no attempt to get anyone to like him and take him home.
9. Answers that suggest she wants people to think he would be a nice boy to take home and would be no trouble.
10. Answers based on evidence: 'I always look after him' / 'he's no trouble at all'.
11. Answers that suggest: **a** Mrs Evans: kind / usually does what her brother tells her / is prepared to take a chance **b** her brother: strict / bossy / used to getting his own way.

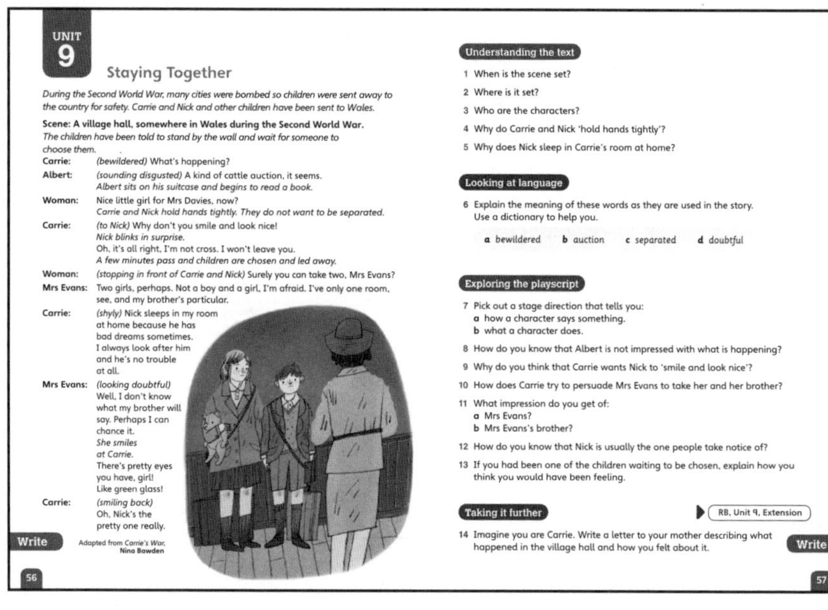

UNIT 9

Staying Together

During the Second World War, many cities were bombed so children were sent away to the country for safety. Carrie and Nick and other children have been sent to Wales.

Scene: A village hall, somewhere in Wales during the Second World War.
The children have been told to stand by the wall and wait for someone to choose them.

Carrie: *(bewildered)* What's happening?
Albert: *(sounding disgusted)* A kind of cattle auction, it seems.
Albert sits on his suitcase and begins to read a book.
Woman: Nice little girl for Mrs Davies, now?
Carrie and Nick hold hands tightly. They do not want to be separated.
Carrie: *(to Nick)* Why don't you smile and look nice!
Nick blinks in surprise.
Oh, it's all right, I'm not cross. I won't leave you.
A few minutes pass and children are chosen and led away.
Woman: *(stopping in front of Carrie and Nick)* Surely you can take two, Mrs Evans?
Mrs Evans: Two girls, perhaps. Not a boy and a girl, I'm afraid. I've only one room, see, and my brother's particular.
Carrie: *(shyly)* Nick sleeps in my room at home because he has bad dreams sometimes. I always look after him and he's no trouble at all.
Mrs Evans: *(looking doubtful)* Well, I don't know what my brother will say. Perhaps I can chance it.
She smiles at Carrie.
There's pretty eyes you have, girl! Like green glass!
Carrie: *(smiling back)* Oh, Nick's the pretty one really.

Write

Adapted from *Carrie's War*, **Nina Bawden**

56

Understanding the text

1 When is the scene set?
2 Where is it set?
3 Who are the characters?
4 Why do Carrie and Nick 'hold hands tightly'?
5 Why does Nick sleep in Carrie's room at home?

Looking at language

6 Explain the meaning of these words as they are used in the story. Use a dictionary to help you.
a *bewildered* **b** *auction* **c** *separated* **d** *doubtful*

Exploring the playscript

7 Pick out a stage direction that tells you:
a how a character says something.
b what a character does.
8 How do you know that Albert is not impressed with what is happening?
9 Why do you think that Carrie wants Nick to 'smile and look nice'?
10 How does Carrie try to persuade Mrs Evans to take her and her brother?
11 What impression do you get of:
a Mrs Evans?
b Mrs Evans's brother?
12 How do you know that Nick is usually the one people take notice of?
13 If you had been one of the children waiting to be chosen, explain how you think you would have been feeling.

Taking it further RB, Unit 9, Extension

14 Imagine you are Carrie. Write a letter to your mother describing what happened in the village hall and how you felt about it.

Write

57

12. Answers that suggest Carrie does not get many compliments as she says 'Nick's the pretty one, really'.
13. Individual answers.
14. Individual answers.

RESOURCE SHEET SUPPORT ANSWERS

A

1. Woman
2. Carrie
3. Mrs Evans
4. Albert

B

1. Albert
2. Mrs Evans
3. Woman
4. Carrie

C

Carrie and Nick are in a **village** hall. They are waiting to be **chosen** by someone who they will live with. Carrie is **bewildered** by it all. Albert is **disgusted**. Carrie and Nick do not want to be **separated**. Mrs Evans could take two **girls**. The woman **persuades** her to take Carrie and Nick. Mrs Evans doesn't know what her **brother** will say.

GOING DEEPER

- Discuss what the children have learned about playscripts, recapping on dialogue, stage directions, scene setting and layout.

UNIT FOCUS: Looking at Settings

Investigating ...

- extracts set in distant countries with unfamiliar settings
- child characters who are influenced by the setting they are in

TEACH

- Ask children what they understand by the term 'drought'. What effects do they think a drought will have on humans and on animals?
- Ask children where in the world they think droughts happen most frequently.
- Explain that they are going to read the beginning of a story called *The Peacock Garden*. It is the summer of 1947 and the rains are late.
- This is a challenging text for this year group, and you may wish to read it and discuss questions as a class or in groups before asking children to tackle it on their own.

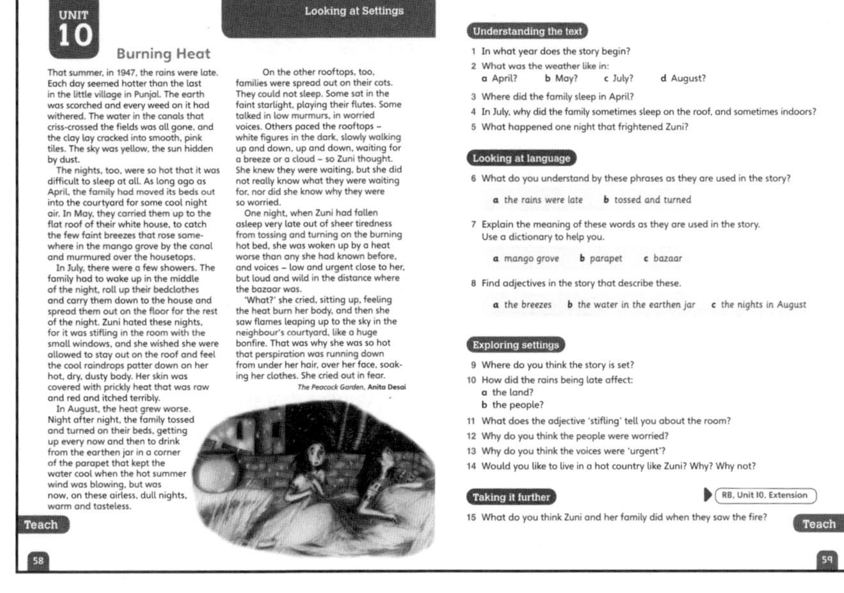

UNIT 10

Looking at Settings

Burning Heat

That summer, in 1947, the rains were late. Each day seemed hotter than the last in the little village in Punjal. The earth was scorched and every weed on it had withered. The water in the canals that criss-crossed the fields was all gone, and the clay lay cracked into smooth, pink tiles. The sky was yellow, the sun hidden by dust.

The nights, too, were so hot that it was difficult to sleep at all. As long ago as April, the family had moved its beds out into the courtyard for some cool night air. In May, they carried them up to the flat roof of their white house, to catch the few faint breezes that rose somewhere in the mango grove by the canal and murmured over the housetops.

In July, there were a few showers. The family had to wake up in the middle of the night, roll up their bedclothes and carry them down to the house and spread them out on the floor for the rest of the night. Zuni hated these nights, for it was stifling in the room with the small windows, and she wished she were allowed to stay out on the roof and feel the cool raindrops patter down on her hot, dry, dusty body. Her skin was covered with prickly heat that was raw and red and itched terribly.

In August, the heat grew worse. Night after night, the family tossed and turned on their beds, getting up every now and then to drink from the earthen jar in a corner of the parapet that kept the water cool when the hot summer wind was blowing, but was now, on these airless, dull nights, warm and tasteless.

On the other rooftops, too, families were spread out on their cots. They could not sleep. Some sat in the faint starlight, playing their flutes. Some talked in low murmurs, in worried voices. Others paced the rooftops – white figures in the dark, slowly walking up and down, up and down, waiting for a breeze or a cloud – so Zuni thought. She knew they were waiting, but she did not really know what they were waiting for, nor did she know why they were so worried.

One night, when Zuni had fallen asleep very late out of sheer tiredness from tossing and turning on the burning hot bed, she was woken up by a heat worse than any she had known before, and voices – low and urgent close to her, but loud and wild in the distance where the bazaar was.

'What?' she cried, sitting up, feeling the heat burn her body, and then she saw flames leaping up to the sky in the neighbour's courtyard, like a huge bonfire. That was why she was so hot that perspiration was running down from under her hair, over her face, soaking her clothes. She cried out in fear.

The Peacock Garden, **Anita Desai**

Understanding the text

1 In what year does the story begin?
2 What was the weather like in:
a April? b May? c July? d August?
3 Where did the family sleep in April?
4 In July, why did the family sometimes sleep on the roof, and sometimes indoors?
5 What happened one night that frightened Zuni?

Looking at language

6 What do you understand by these phrases as they are used in the story?
a the rains were late b tossed and turned
7 Explain the meaning of these words as they are used in the story. Use a dictionary to help you.
a mango grove b parapet c bazaar
8 Find adjectives in the story that describe these.
a the breezes b the water in the earthen jar c the nights in August

Exploring settings

9 Where do you think the story is set?
10 How did the rains being late affect:
a the land?
b the people?
11 What does the adjective 'stifling' tell you about the room?
12 Why do you think the people were worried?
13 Why do you think the voices were 'urgent'?
14 Would you like to live in a hot country like Zuni? Why? Why not?

Taking it further

RB, Unit 10, Extension

15 What do you think Zuni and her family did when they saw the fire?

Teach 58 Teach 59

RESOURCES & ASSESSMENT BOOK

- **Support** (comprehension support): identifying weather in different months; (vocabulary support): matching adjectives and nouns.
- **Extension:** writing a paragraph.

PUPIL BOOK ANSWERS

1. 1947.
2. **a** April: 'hot' / 'cool night air' **b** May: hotter / 'few faint breezes' **c** July: hotter / 'a few showers' **d** August: 'the heat grew worse'
3. In the courtyard.
4. On a night when there was a shower, the family moved their bedding indoors.
5. Zuni woke up because the heat was worse than usual. She saw there was a fire in the neighbour's courtyard.
6. **a** the rains were late: the rainy season did not begin when it should have done **b** tossed and turned: moved about in bed unable to get comfortable because of the heat
7. **a** mango grove: trees arranged in lines that grow mango fruit **b** parapet: low wall at the edge of a roof **c** bazaar: market
8. **a** the breezes: 'few, faint' **b** the water in the earthen jar: 'warm and tasteless' **c** the nights in August: 'airless, dull'
9. Answers showing that children have picked up on the climate and the area 'Punjal', to help them deduce that the story is set in a hot country [actually Pakistan].
10. Answers based on evidence: **a** the land: 'the earth was scorched' / 'every weed on it had withered' / 'the water in the canals ... all gone' / 'clay lay cracked into smooth, pink tiles' / 'sun hidden by dust' **b** the people: 'difficult to sleep' / 'moved beds out into the courtyard' / 'prickly heat' / 'tossed and turned on their beds'
11. Answers that suggest the room was very hot and airless.
12. Answers that suggest they may be worried about the drought and the possibility of fire.
13. Answers that suggest the voices were 'urgent' because of the situation i.e. a fire had broken out nearby.
14. Individual answers.
15. Individual answers.

RESOURCE SHEET SUPPORT ANSWERS

A

April: so hot / cool night air
May: few faint breezes
July: stifling / few showers
August: heat grew worse / airless, dull nights

B

1. little village
2. smooth tiles
3. cool night air
4. faint breezes / starlight
5. small windows
6. tasteless water
7. airless August nights
8. low voices

GOING DEEPER

- Discuss with the children how Zuni's life differs from their own.
- Discuss times when they have found it too hot to sleep. How does it feel? What goes through their minds as they lie awake?

TALK

- Ask the children to imagine they have to live with an uncle, aunt or grandparent because their parents have to work far away from home and are absent for long periods of time. How would they feel?
- Explain to children that they are going to read an extract from *Journey to Jo'burg*.
- Explain the story so far: Naledi, Tiro and their baby sister, Dineo, live with their granny. One day, Dineo falls ill. They have no money to pay for a doctor and the only hospital is miles away. Naledi and her brother Tiro decide that they must find their mother – they must walk to the city of Johannesburg (in South Africa).
- Read the extract to the class; ask individual children to read it aloud in turn; or read in silence individually.

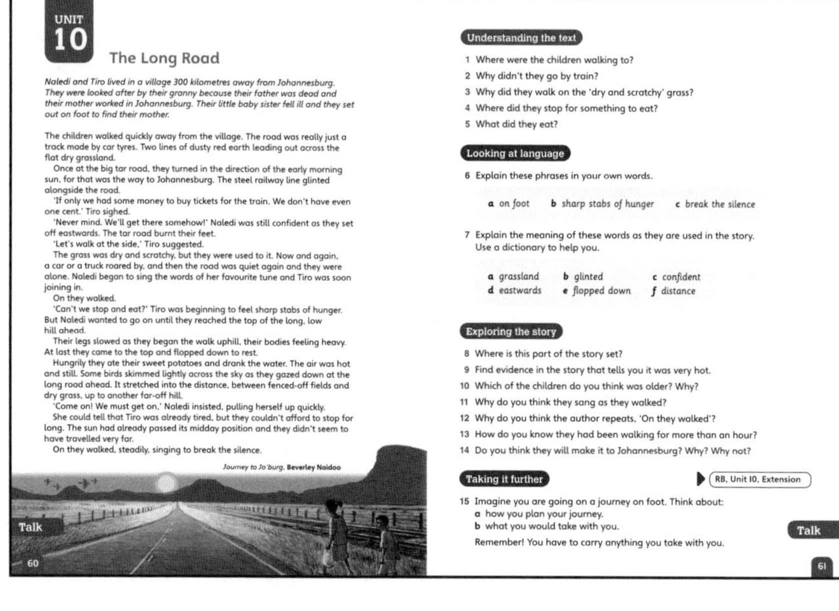

UNIT 10

The Long Road

Naledi and Tiro lived in a village 300 kilometres away from Johannesburg. They were looked after by their granny because their father was dead and their mother worked in Johannesburg. Their little baby sister fell ill and they set out on foot to find their mother.

The children walked quickly away from the village. The road was really just a track made by car tyres. Two lines of dusty red earth leading out across the flat dry grassland.

Once at the big tar road, they turned in the direction of the early morning sun, for that was the way to Johannesburg. The steel railway line glinted alongside the road.

'If only we had some money to buy tickets for the train. We don't have even one cent.' Tiro sighed.

'Never mind. We'll get there somehow!' Naledi was still confident as they set off eastwards. The tar road burnt their feet.

'Let's walk at the side,' Tiro suggested.

The grass was dry and scratchy, but they were used to it. Now and again, a car or a truck roared by, and then the road was quiet again and they were alone. Naledi began to sing the words of her favourite tune and Tiro was soon joining in.

On they walked.

'Can't we stop and eat?' Tiro was beginning to feel sharp stabs of hunger. But Naledi wanted to go on until they reached the top of the long, low hill ahead.

Their legs slowed as they began the walk uphill, their bodies feeling heavy. At last they came to the top and flopped down to rest.

Hungrily they ate their sweet potatoes and drank the water. The air was hot and still. Some birds skimmed lightly across the sky as they gazed down at the long road ahead. It stretched into the distance, between fenced-off fields and dry grass, up to another far-off hill.

'Come on! We must get on,' Naledi insisted, pulling herself up quickly.

She could tell that Tiro was already tired, but they couldn't afford to stop for long. The sun had already passed its midday position and they didn't seem to have travelled very far.

On they walked, steadily, singing to break the silence.

Journey to Jo'burg, **Beverley Naidoo**

Talk

60

Understanding the text

1 Where were the children walking to?
2 Why didn't they go by train?
3 Why did they walk on the 'dry and scratchy' grass?
4 Where did they stop for something to eat?
5 What did they eat?

Looking at language

6 Explain these phrases in your own words.

a *on foot* **b** *sharp stabs of hunger* **c** *break the silence*

7 Explain the meaning of these words as they are used in the story. Use a dictionary to help you.

a *grassland* **b** *glinted* **c** *confident*
d *eastwards* **e** *flopped down* **f** *distance*

Exploring the story

8 Where is this part of the story set?
9 Find evidence in the story that tells you it was very hot.
10 Which of the children do you think was older? Why?
11 Why do you think they sang as they walked?
12 Why do you think the author repeats, 'On they walked'?
13 How do you know they had been walking for more than an hour?
14 Do you think they will make it to Johannesburg? Why? Why not?

Taking it further

RB, Unit 10, Extension

15 Imagine you are going on a journey on foot. Think about:
a how you plan your journey.
b what you would take with you.
Remember! You have to carry anything you take with you.

Talk

61

RESOURCES & ASSESSMENT BOOK

- **Support** (comprehension support): choosing the correct sentence ending; (vocabulary support): matching descriptive phrases and pictures.
- **Extension:** making notes and lists.

PUPIL BOOK ANSWERS

1. Jo'burg [Johannesburg].
2. They had no money for tickets.
3. The tar road was so hot it burnt their feet.
4. On the top of a long low hill.
5. Sweet potatoes.
6. **a** on foot: walking **b** sharp stabs of hunger: stomach pains due to lack of food **c** break the silence: say something
7. **a** grassland: large area of land where wild grass grows **b** glinted: sparkled **c** confident: sure of herself and what she was doing **d** eastwards: towards the east **e** flopped down: let themselves fall **f** distance: far away
8. On the road to Johannesburg.
9. Answers based on evidence: 'The tar road burnt their feet.' / 'The air was hot and still.'
10. Answers that suggest Naledi was older because she made the decisions.
11. Answers that suggest it cheered them up and kept them going.
12. Answers that suggest this gives the reader the feeling of how far they have to go – there is nothing to do but walk on.
13. Answers based on evidence: when they walked away from the village 'the early morning sun' is mentioned. When they finished eating 'the sun had already passed its midday position'.
14. Individual answers.
15. Encourage all members of the group to contribute.

RESOURCE SHEET SUPPORT ANSWERS

A

1. Johannesburg
2. towards the sun
3. on foot
4. burnt their feet
5. stop and eat
6. after midday

B

1. flat, dry grassland
2. track made by tyres
3. big, tar road
4. long, low hill

GOING DEEPER

- Discuss whether the children think that walking to Johannesburg was the sensible and only thing to do? What would they have done?

WRITE

- Ask children what they know about South America. Have any children visited there? Do they think life is the same or different there?
- Explain to the children that they are going to read an extract from the beginning of a story called *The Most Beautiful Place in the World*. The narrator describes where he lives in great detail.
- Read the extract to the class; ask individual children to read it aloud in turn; or read in silence individually.

RESOURCES & ASSESSMENT BOOK

- **Support** (comprehension support): classifying; (vocabulary support): identifying adjectives, choosing correct answers for vocabulary reinforcement.
- **Extension:** making notes, writing to explain.

PUPIL BOOK ANSWERS

1. **a** Any two of: corn / garlic / onions
b Any two of eagles / orioles / owls / hummingbirds / wild parrots
c Any two of: jugs of water / baskets of bread / vegetables / babies / wooden beams.
2. By ferry-boat or canoe.
3. 'It's not a good one.'
4. At night the people 'stroll around town and have fun and tell stories and talk to their friends'.
5. It is where he was born.
6. **a** stray dogs: dogs that do not belong to anyone **b** strolled around: walked with no particular place to go **c** more or less: almost always
7. **a** zoom: move with speed and energy
b mules: mammals that have a donkey for a father and a horse for a mother
c beams: long, thick pieces of wood
d conversation: talking to one another
8. **a** the fields: steep / bright / green **b** the lake: big **c** the beams: huge / wooden
9. Children should pick up on the fact that San Pablo is surrounded by three volcanoes, and there is no indication in the passage that they are extinct.
10. Answer based on evidence: being able to grow coffee / tropical birds such as parrots and hummingbirds.

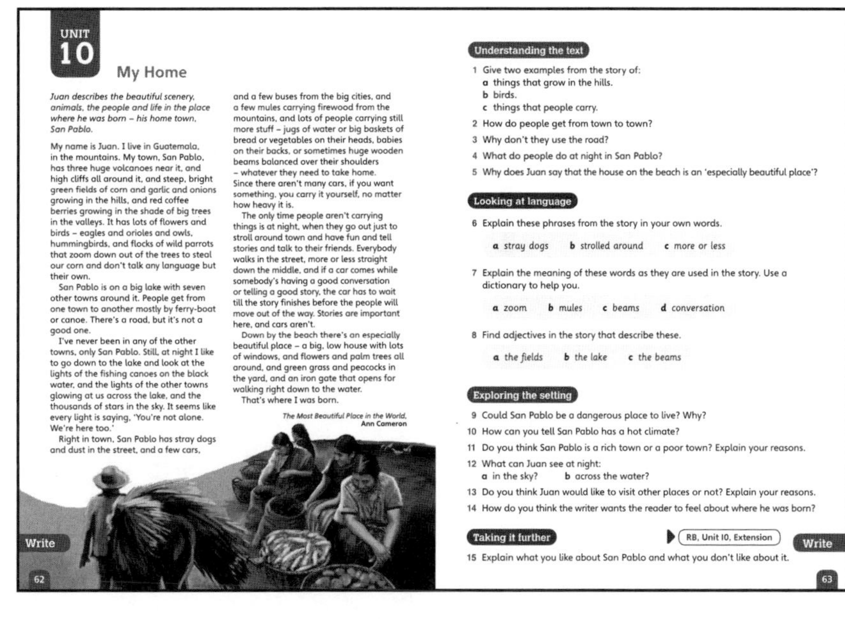

UNIT 10

My Home

Juan describes the beautiful scenery, animals, the people and life in the place where he was born – his home town, San Pablo.

My name is Juan. I live in Guatemala, in the mountains. My town, San Pablo, has three huge volcanoes near it, and high cliffs all around it, and steep, bright green fields of corn and garlic and onions growing in the hills, and red coffee berries growing in the shade of big trees in the valleys. It has lots of flowers and birds – eagles and orioles and owls, hummingbirds, and flocks of wild parrots that zoom down out of the trees to steal our corn and don't talk any language but their own.

San Pablo is on a big lake with seven other towns around it. People get from one town to another mostly by ferry-boat or canoe. There's a road, but it's not a good one.

I've never been in any of the other towns, only San Pablo. Still, at night I like to go down to the lake and look at the lights of the fishing canoes on the black water, and the lights of the other towns glowing at us across the lake, and the thousands of stars in the sky. It seems like every light is saying, 'You're not alone. We're here too.'

Right in town, San Pablo has stray dogs and dust in the street, and a few cars, and a few buses from the big cities, and a few mules carrying firewood from the mountains, and lots of people carrying still more stuff – jugs of water or big baskets of bread or vegetables on their heads, babies on their backs, or sometimes huge wooden beams balanced over their shoulders – whatever they need to take home. Since there aren't many cars, if you want something, you carry it yourself, no matter how heavy it is.

The only time people aren't carrying things is at night, when they go out just to stroll around town and have fun and tell stories and talk to their friends. Everybody walks in the street, more or less straight down the middle, and if a car comes while somebody's having a good conversation or telling a good story, the car has to wait till the story finishes before the people will move out of the way. Stories are important here, and cars aren't.

Down by the beach there's an especially beautiful place – a big, low house with lots of windows, and flowers and palm trees all around, and green grass and peacocks in the yard, and an iron gate that opens for walking right down to the water.

That's where I was born.

The Most Beautiful Place in the World, **Ann Cameron**

Write

62

Understanding the text

1 Give two examples from the story of:
a things that grow in the hills.
b birds.
c things that people carry.

2 How do people get from town to town?

3 Why don't they use the road?

4 What do people do at night in San Pablo?

5 Why does Juan say that the house on the beach is an 'especially beautiful place'?

Looking at language

6 Explain these phrases from the story in your own words.

a stray dogs b strolled around c more or less

7 Explain the meaning of these words as they are used in the story. Use a dictionary to help you.

a zoom b mules c beams d conversation

8 Find adjectives in the story that describe these.

a the fields b the lake c the beams

Exploring the setting

9 Could San Pablo be a dangerous place to live? Why?

10 How can you tell San Pablo has a hot climate?

11 Do you think San Pablo is a rich town or a poor town? Explain your reasons.

12 What can Juan see at night:
a in the sky? b across the water?

13 Do you think Juan would like to visit other places or not? Explain your reasons.

14 How do you think the writer wants the reader to feel about where he was born?

Taking it further

RB, Unit 10, Extension

Write

15 Explain what you like about San Pablo and what you don't like about it.

63

11. Answers that suggest it is relatively poor based on evidence: there are few cars / the road is not good / 'if you want something, you carry it yourself'.
12. **a** in the sky: 'thousands of stars' **b** across the water: 'the lights of the other towns'.
13. Answers that suggest he would probably like to visit other places as he goes down to the lake and looks at 'the lights of the other towns'.
14. Answers that suggest the writer wants the reader to feel that the place is 'especially beautiful' as he describes it as: 'big low house with lots of windows' / 'flowers and palm trees'/ 'green grass and peacocks'.
15. Individual answers.

RESOURCE SHEET SUPPORT ANSWERS

A

things that grow	birds	things people carry
corn	wild parrots	jugs of water
garlic	eagles	big baskets of bread
onions	orioles	babies
coffee	owls	vegetables
	hummingbirds	huge wooden beams

B

1. If parrots zoom, they move quickly.
2. A beam is a thick piece of wood.
3. A conversation is a chat.
4. If you stroll around, you walk.
5. Stray dogs have no owner.

C

1. steep / bright green
2. big
3. huge / wooden

GOING DEEPER

- Discuss living in San Pablo. Would the children like to live there? What are the advantages and disadvantages?
- Children have read extracts from stories set in Pakistan, South Africa and South America. Which of these places would they like to visit or live in?
- Which story would they like to read completely? Why?

Book 5 Scope and Sequence

Unit	Unit Focus	Texts	Oxford Level	Oxford Reading Criterion Scale	Genre / text type	Resources & Assessment Book Support	Resources & Assessment Book Extension
1	Understanding Playscripts	'Oliver Asks for More'	16	standard 6, criteria 4, 7, 8, 11, 16, 18, 19, 25, 26	playscripts	who said what; underlining correct definitions; cloze activity	writing a narrative from a playscript
		'Oliver and the Undertaker'	16			who did what; cloze activity	planning a scene for a playscript
		'Oliver Meets the Artful Dodger', all scenes based on *Oliver Twist*, Charles Dickens	16			choosing true statements; correcting sentences; underlining correct definitions	comparing the three playscripts in the unit
2	Looking at Advertisements	The Power of Advertising	15	standard 6, criteria 4, 10, 13, 19, 22	non-fiction: advertise-ments	matching advertisement to purpose; multiple choice; matching words to definitions	comparing advertisements
		The Copywriter's Job	15			underlining correct endings for sentences; underlining correct definitions	planning and creating an advertisement
		Sail Away to the Holiday of Your Dreams!	15			multiple choice; matching words to definitions	writing questions
3	Exploring Characters' Feelings	'Meeting Great-Aunt Dymphna' from *The Growing Summer*, Noel Streatfeild	16	standard 6, criteria 4, 6, 8, 11, 16, 18, 19, 24	fiction	underlining correct answers; defining words	planning and writing a letter
		'Miss Slighcarp' from *The Wolves of Willoughby Chase*, Joan Aiken	17			identifying true statements; correcting false statements; who said what	planning questions; role play
		'Bush Fire' from *Ash Road*, Ivan Southall	16			who said what; cloze activity	putting yourself in a character's position, writing about how you feel
4	Following Instructions	How to Use an Online Bookshop	14	standard 6, criteria 4, 10, 19, 22	non-fiction: instructions	putting instructions in correct order; underlining correct definitions	putting phrases under correct headings
		How to Download Photographs to Your Desktop	16			matching beginnings and endings of sentences; cloze activity	putting phrases under correct headings
		How to Set an Alarm Clock on a Mobile Phone	14			underlining correct answers; solving anagrams	writing instructions
5	Looking at Media Reports	An Egyptian Treasure!	18	standard 6, criteria 4, 10, 19, 22, 24	non-fiction: reports	writing questions for answers; cloze activity	putting yourself in a person's position, writing about how you feel
		Treasures of the Past	16			who did what; matching words to definitions	writing questions
		The Valley of the Kings	16			cloze activity; matching paragraphs to their summaries; underlining correct definitions	researching a topic and preparing a report

6	Telling Stories Through Poetry	'Jim, Who Ran Away From His Nurse and Was Eaten by a Lion', Hilaire Belloc	16	standard 6, criteria 4, 8, 9, 14, 16, 18, 19, 24, 25	poetry	putting narrative sequence in correct order; identifying correct adjectives	turning a verse into a playscript
		'The Apple-Raid', Vernon Scannell	16			correcting sentences; identifying adjectives; matching words to definitions	putting yourself in a character's position; role play
		'Early Last Sunday Morning', Ian Souter	16			multiple choice; matching verbs to sentences	putting yourself into a character's position and writing about their feelings
7	Stories From Around the World	'A New School' from *The White Giraffe*, Lauren St John	16	standard 6, criteria 4, 8, 9, 11, 16, 18, 19	fiction	putting narrative sequence in correct order; cloze activity	putting yourself into a character's position and writing about their feelings
		'Snowfall' from *Jeffie Lemmington and Me*, Merle Hodge	16			matching beginnings and endings of sentences; cloze activity	thinking of questions to ask a character
		Walkabout, James Vance Marshall	16			identifying true and false statements; correcting statements; finding adjectives	putting yourself into a character's position and predicting what they will do
8	Persuasive Language	You Are What You Eat	16	standard 6, criteria 4, 10, 13, 17, 19, 22	non-fiction	matching beginnings and endings of sentences; solving anagrams; matching words to definitions	planning and designing an advertisement
		Expressing an Opinion	16			identifying true and false statements; correcting statements; matching words with definitions	planning and drafting a letter
		Outlaw Sunbeds	16			cloze activity; underlining the correct answer	comparing two articles in the unit
9	Reading Older Novels	'A Breakfast Conversation' from *The Railway Children*, E Nesbit	16	standard 6, criteria 4, 8, 11, 16, 18, 19, 21, 23	classic fiction	who did what; underlining the correct answer	imagining what conversation may take place next
		'Christmas Presents' from *Little Women*, Louisa May Alcott	16			who said what; identifying correct adverbs	imagining what conversation may take place next; role play
		The Secret Garden, Frances Hodgson Burnett	16			putting narrative sentences in correct order	imagining what conversation may take place next
10	The Roles of Heroes and Heroines	*The Sword in the Stone*, retold by Wendy Wren	18	standard 6, criteria 4, 8, 11, 14, 18, 19, 24	fiction and fable	correcting sentences; matching words with definitions	imagining what conversation may take place next
		'Mowgli is Rescued' from *The Jungle Book*, Rudyard Kipling	17			matching summaries to paragraphs; underlining correct definitions	predicting what happens next in the story
		The Storm, retold by Wendy Wren	18			multiple choice; cloze activity	imagining what conversation may take place next

UNIT FOCUS: Understanding Playscripts

Investigating ...

- conventions of playscripts as a springboard to using these conventions in a non-fiction context
- characters and settings

TEACH

- Ask what children understand by the term 'workhouse'.
- Explain the concept of the workhouse in Victorian times to the children.
- Ask children what they know about the story *Oliver Twist.*
- Explain the story so far: Oliver is an orphan. His mother died in the workhouse when he was born and Oliver, having nowhere else to go, grows up there.
- Read the playscript to the class; ask individual children to read it aloud; or read in silence individually.

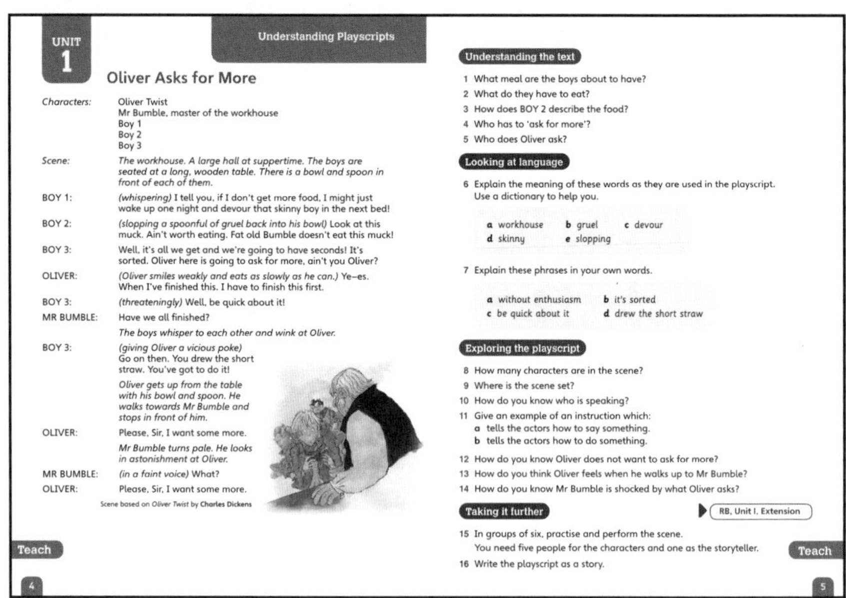
UNIT 1 Understanding Playscripts

Oliver Asks for More

Characters: Oliver Twist
Mr Bumble, master of the workhouse
Boy 1
Boy 2
Boy 3

Scene: *The workhouse. A large hall at suppertime. The boys are seated at a long, wooden table. There is a bowl and spoon in front of each of them.*

BOY 1: *(whispering)* I tell you, if I don't get more food, I might just wake up one night and devour that skinny boy in the next bed!

BOY 2: *(slopping a spoonful of gruel back into his bowl)* Look at this muck. Ain't worth eating. Fat old Bumble doesn't eat this muck!

BOY 3: Well, it's all we get and we're going to have seconds! It's sorted. Oliver here is going to ask for more, ain't you Oliver?

OLIVER: *(Oliver smiles weakly and eats as slowly as he can.)* Ye–es. When I've finished this. I have to finish this first.

BOY 3: *(threateningly)* Well, be quick about it!

MR BUMBLE: Have we all finished?

The boys whisper to each other and wink at Oliver.

BOY 3: *(giving Oliver a vicious poke)* Go on then. You drew the short straw. You've got to do it!

Oliver gets up from the table with his bowl and spoon. He walks towards Mr Bumble and stops in front of him.

OLIVER: Please, Sir, I want some more.

Mr Bumble turns pale. He looks in astonishment at Oliver.

MR BUMBLE: *(in a faint voice)* What?

OLIVER: Please, Sir, I want some more.

Scene based on *Oliver Twist* by **Charles Dickens**

Teach

4

Understanding the text

1 What meal are the boys about to have?
2 What do they have to eat?
3 How does BOY 2 describe the food?
4 Who has to 'ask for more'?
5 Who does Oliver ask?

Looking at language

6 Explain the meaning of these words as they are used in the playscript. Use a dictionary to help you.
a workhouse **b** gruel **c** devour **d** skinny **e** slopping

7 Explain these phrases in your own words.
a *without enthusiasm* **b** *it's sorted* **c** *be quick about it* **d** *drew the short straw*

Exploring the playscript

8 How many characters are in the scene?
9 Where is the scene set?
10 How do you know who is speaking?
11 Give an example of an instruction which:
a tells the actors how to say something.
b tells the actors how to do something.
12 How do you know Oliver does not want to ask for more?
13 How do you think Oliver feels when he walks up to Mr Bumble?
14 How do you know Mr Bumble is shocked by what Oliver asks?

Taking it further

RB, Unit I, Extension

15 In groups of six, practise and perform the scene. You need five people for the characters and one as the storyteller.
16 Write the playscript as a story.

Teach

5

RESOURCES & ASSESSMENT BOOK

- **Support** (comprehension support): who said what?, cloze activity; (vocabulary support): choosing correct definitions.
- **Extension:** writing part of a story.

PUPIL BOOK ANSWERS

1. Supper.
2. Gruel.
3. 'muck'.
4. Oliver.
5. Mr Bumble.
6. **a** a place where poor people and orphans lived **b** a thin soup of boiled grain **c** eat very quickly **d** very thin **e** throwing down so some spills
7. **a** with no eagerness or enjoyment **b** it has been agreed **c** get on with it **d** lose
8. Five.
9. A large hall in the workhouse at suppertime.
10. Character's name appears on the left of the page in capitals.
11. **a** E.g. *(whispering).*
    b *E.g. (Oliver smiles weakly and eats as slowly as he can).*
12. Oliver 'smiles weakly' / 'eats as slowly as he can'.
13. Frightened.
14. Stage directions*: [Mr Bumble turns pale. He looks in astonishment at Oliver] / (in a faint voice).*

15 16 Individual answers.

RESOURCE SHEET SUPPORT ANSWERS

A

1. Mr Bumble
2. Boy 1
3. Oliver
4. Boy 3
5. Boy 2

B

1. speaking quietly
2. with no interest
3. hardly smiles
4. nastily

C

1. gruel
2. devoured
3. skinny
4. slopping

GOING DEEPER

- Ask for volunteers to be Oliver and Mr Bumble. The class act as interviewers and ask them questions about the incident in the extract. Make notes on the questions asked and the responses given on the board. Children then write up the 'interview', setting it out like a playscript.

TALK

- Explain to the children that this scene shows what happens to Oliver after he asks for more – he is taken to be an apprentice to an undertaker.
- Ask children what they understand by the term 'undertaker'. How would they feel about working at an undertaker's?
- Ask children to recap on the scene *Oliver Asks for More.*
- Read the playscript to the class; ask individual children to read it aloud; or read in silence individually.

RESOURCES & ASSESSMENT BOOK

- **Support** (comprehension support): who did what?; (vocabulary support): cloze activity to reinforce vocabulary.
- **Extension:** planning a playscript.

PUPIL BOOK ANSWERS

1. Oliver Twist / Mr Bumble / Mr Sowerberry / Mrs Sowerberry.
2. The undertaker's shop at dusk.
3. Writing / doing accounts.
4. 'Oliver makes a small bow.'
5. 'rather small' / 'bag o' bones'.
6. **a** someone's whose job it is to arrange funerals **b** the end of the day, just before it gets dark **c** feeble / gloomy **d** in a worried voice / nervously **e** unkindly / bitterly **f** food
7. **a** anxiously / sharply / fearfully **b** pushing Oliver forward / Oliver bows again **c** Mr Sowerberry making some entries in his daybook by the light of a dismal candle
8. Apprehensive / nervous / scared for Oliver.
9. He is too scared or too unhappy to speak.
10. **a** he is worried that she won't take Oliver **b** doesn't want to give her the chance to refuse

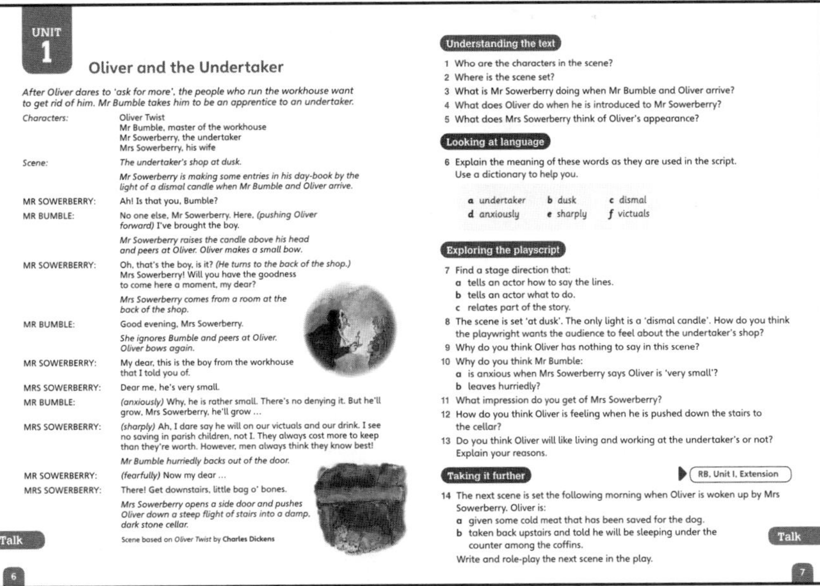

UNIT 1

Oliver and the Undertaker

After Oliver dares to 'ask for more', the people who run the workhouse want to get rid of him. Mr Bumble takes him to be an apprentice to an undertaker.

Characters:	Oliver Twist Mr Bumble, master of the workhouse Mr Sowerberry, the undertaker Mrs Sowerberry, his wife
Scene:	*The undertaker's shop at dusk.*
	Mr Sowerberry is making some entries in his day-book by the light of a dismal candle when Mr Bumble and Oliver arrive.
MR SOWERBERRY:	Ah! Is that you, Bumble?
MR BUMBLE:	No one else, Mr Sowerberry. Here, *(pushing Oliver forward)* I've brought the boy.
	Mr Sowerberry raises the candle above his head and peers at Oliver. Oliver makes a small bow.
MR SOWERBERRY:	Oh, that's the boy, is it? *(He turns to the back of the shop.)* Mrs Sowerberry! Will you have the goodness to come here a moment, my dear?
	Mrs Sowerberry comes from a room at the back of the shop.
MR BUMBLE:	Good evening, Mrs Sowerberry.
	She ignores Bumble and peers at Oliver. Oliver bows again.
MR SOWERBERRY:	My dear, this is the boy from the workhouse that I told you of.
MRS SOWERBERRY:	Dear me, he's very small.
MR BUMBLE:	*(anxiously)* Why, he is rather small. There's no denying it. But he'll grow, Mrs Sowerberry, he'll grow …
MRS SOWERBERRY:	*(sharply)* Ah, I dare say he will on our victuals and our drink. I see no saving in parish children, not I. They always cost more to keep than they're worth. However, men always think they know best!
	Mr Bumble hurriedly backs out of the door.
MR SOWERBERRY:	*(fearfully)* Now my dear …
MRS SOWERBERRY:	There! Get downstairs, little bag o' bones.
	Mrs Sowerberry opens a side door and pushes Oliver down a steep flight of stairs into a damp, dark stone cellar.

Scene based on *Oliver Twist* by **Charles Dickens**

Talk

6

Understanding the text

1 Who are the characters in the scene?
2 Where is the scene set?
3 What is Mr Sowerberry doing when Mr Bumble and Oliver arrive?
4 What does Oliver do when he is introduced to Mr Sowerberry?
5 What does Mrs Sowerberry think of Oliver's appearance?

Looking at language

6 Explain the meaning of these words as they are used in the script. Use a dictionary to help you.
a *undertaker* **b** *dusk* **c** *dismal* **d** *anxiously* **e** *sharply* **f** *victuals*

Exploring the playscript

7 Find a stage direction that:
a tells an actor how to say the lines.
b tells an actor what to do.
c relates part of the story.
8 The scene is set 'at dusk'. The only light is a 'dismal candle'. How do you think the playwright wants the audience to feel about the undertaker's shop?
9 Why do you think Oliver has nothing to say in this scene?
10 Why do you think Mr Bumble:
a is anxious when Mrs Sowerberry says Oliver is 'very small'?
b leaves hurriedly?
11 What impression do you get of Mrs Sowerberry?
12 How do you think Oliver is feeling when he is pushed down the stairs to the cellar?
13 Do you think Oliver will like living and working at the undertaker's or not? Explain your reasons.

Taking it further RB, Unit I, Extension

14 The next scene is set the following morning when Oliver is woken up by Mrs Sowerberry. Oliver is:
a given some cold meat that has been saved for the dog.
b taken back upstairs and told he will be sleeping under the counter among the coffins.
Write and role-play the next scene in the play.

Talk

7

11. She is cruel and has no pity for Oliver.
12. Scared / unhappy / relieved to be out of the workhouse.
13. Individual answers.
14. Individual answers.

RESOURCE SHEET SUPPORT ANSWERS

A

1. Mr Sowerberry
2. Mr Bumble
3. Oliver
4. Mr Sowerberry
5. Mrs Sowerberry
6. Mr Bumble
7. Mrs Sowerberry

B

Mr Sowerberry is an **undertaker**. Mr Bumble brings Oliver to Mr Sowerberry's shop at **dusk**. The only light is a **dismal** candle. Mrs Sowerberry thinks Oliver is very small.

'He'll grow,' says Mr Bumble **anxiously**.

Mrs Sowerberry says **sharply**, ' He'll grow eating our **victuals** and drinking our drink!'

GOING DEEPER

- Discuss children's ideas for the 'Taking it further' activity. Give time for group performances.

WRITE

- Ask children what they understand by the terms 'living on the street' / 'living rough'. How would they feel if they had to do this?
- Ask children to recap on Oliver's life so far.
- Read the playscript to the class; ask individual children to read it aloud; or read in silence individually.

RESOURCES & ASSESSMENT BOOK

- **Support** (comprehension support): identifying True / False statements, correcting false statements; (vocabulary support): choosing the correct definition.
- **Extension:** answering questions based on playscripts.

PUPIL BOOK ANSWERS

1. Sitting on a doorstep.
2. He thinks the law is after him.
3. Ham and bread.
4. 'some place to sleep tonight'.
5. 'Mr Fagin and the other lads'.
6. **a** what's the matter / what's wrong **b** running away to avoid capture by the police **c** you want food **d** don't worry
7. **a** crafty / deceitful **b** raggedly dressed child usually living by their wits **c** an officer of the law **d** very hungrily **e** craftily **f** seriously
8. He comes across as helpful and kind.
9. He seems to know too much about running away from the law and could lead Oliver into trouble.
10. He is too willing to take the Dodger's help and is not at all suspicious.
11. He probably hasn't eaten for a long time.
12. He is probably keeping an eye out for the police.
13. **a** *(slyly)* **b** *(looking around all the time)*
14. Individual answers.

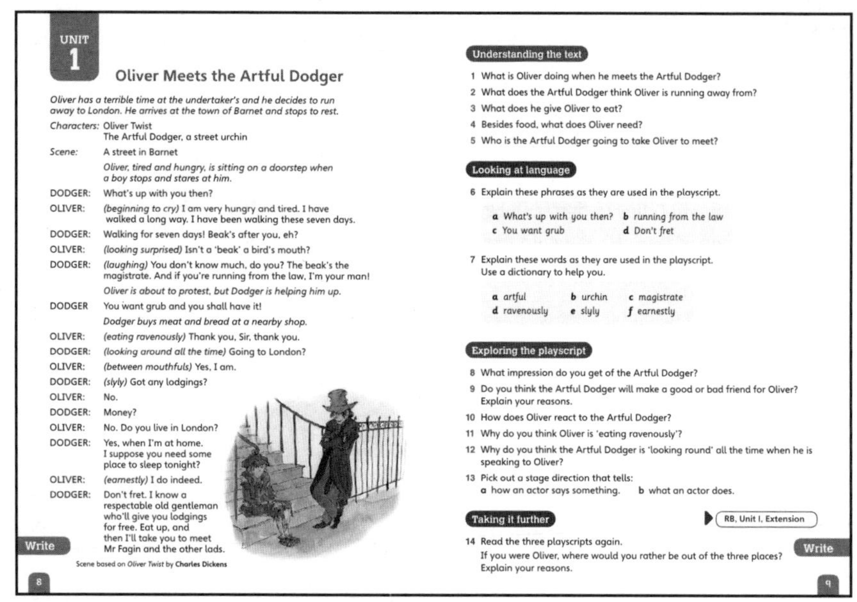

UNIT 1

Oliver Meets the Artful Dodger

Oliver has a terrible time at the undertaker's and he decides to run away to London. He arrives at the town of Barnet and stops to rest.

Characters: Oliver Twist
The Artful Dodger, a street urchin

Scene: A street in Barnet

Oliver, tired and hungry, is sitting on a doorstep when a boy stops and stares at him.

DODGER: What's up with you then?
OLIVER: *(beginning to cry)* I am very hungry and tired. I have walked a long way. I have been walking these seven days.
DODGER: Walking for seven days! Beak's after you, eh?
OLIVER: *(looking surprised)* Isn't a 'beak' a bird's mouth?
DODGER: *(laughing)* You don't know much, do you? The beak's the magistrate. And if you're running from the law, I'm your man!
Oliver is about to protest, but Dodger is helping him up.
DODGER You want grub and you shall have it!
Dodger buys meat and bread at a nearby shop.
OLIVER: *(eating ravenously)* Thank you, Sir, thank you.
DODGER: *(looking around all the time)* Going to London?
OLIVER: *(between mouthfuls)* Yes, I am.
DODGER: *(slyly)* Got any lodgings?
OLIVER: No.
DODGER: Money?
OLIVER: No. Do you live in London?
DODGER: Yes, when I'm at home. I suppose you need some place to sleep tonight?
OLIVER: *(earnestly)* I do indeed.
DODGER: Don't fret. I know a respectable old gentleman who'll give you lodgings for free. Eat up, and then I'll take you to meet Mr Fagin and the other lads.

Scene based on *Oliver Twist* by **Charles Dickens**

Write

8

Understanding the text

1 What is Oliver doing when he meets the Artful Dodger?
2 What does the Artful Dodger think Oliver is running away from?
3 What does he give Oliver to eat?
4 Besides food, what does Oliver need?
5 Who is the Artful Dodger going to take Oliver to meet?

Looking at language

6 Explain these phrases as they are used in the playscript.
a *What's up with you then?* **b** *running from the law*
c *You want grub* **d** *Don't fret*

7 Explain these words as they are used in the playscript. Use a dictionary to help you.
a *artful* **b** *urchin* **c** *magistrate*
d *ravenously* **e** *slyly* **f** *earnestly*

Exploring the playscript

8 What impression do you get of the Artful Dodger?
9 Do you think the Artful Dodger will make a good or bad friend for Oliver? Explain your reasons.
10 How does Oliver react to the Artful Dodger?
11 Why do you think Oliver is 'eating ravenously'?
12 Why do you think the Artful Dodger is 'looking round' all the time when he is speaking to Oliver?
13 Pick out a stage direction that tells:
a how an actor says something. **b** what an actor does.

Taking it further RB, Unit I, Extension

14 Read the three playscripts again.
If you were Oliver, where would you rather be out of the three places? Explain your reasons.

Write

9

RESOURCE SHEET SUPPORT ANSWERS

A

1. TRUE
2. FALSE
3. TRUE
4. TRUE
5. FALSE
6. FALSE

B

1. The Artful Dodger sees Oliver sitting on a doorstep.
2. Oliver has been walking for seven days.
3. The Artful Dodger lives in London.

B

1. crafty
2. raggedly dressed
3. an officer of the law
4. very hungry
5. tricky
6. serious

GOING DEEPER

- Use ideas for the 'Taking it further' activity as the basis for a class discussion.

UNIT FOCUS: Looking at Advertisements

Investigating …

- persuasive language
- the language of advertising
- how adverts are designed to persuade readers

TEACH

- Discuss what the children understand by the term 'advertising'.
- Ask what children think of advertising – pros and cons.
- Ask children which adverts they like / dislike.
- Have children ever been persuaded to buy something or do something because of an advert?
- Explain that the children are going to look at three advertisements that are designed to persuade people to do different things.
- Show the adverts to the class; ask individual children to read them aloud in turn; or read in silence individually.

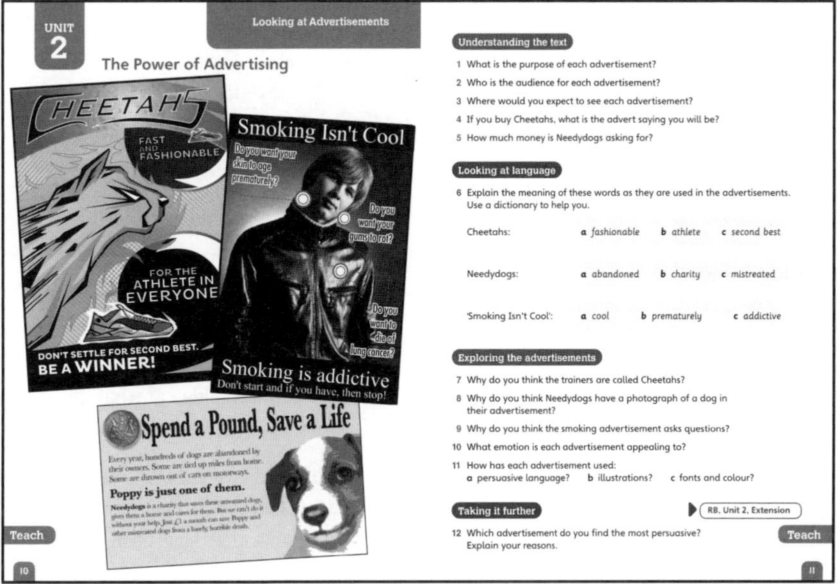
UNIT 2 Looking at Advertisements

The Power of Advertising

Understanding the text

1 What is the purpose of each advertisement?
2 Who is the audience for each advertisement?
3 Where would you expect to see each advertisement?
4 If you buy Cheetahs, what is the advert saying you will be?
5 How much money is Needydogs asking for?

Looking at language

6 Explain the meaning of these words as they are used in the advertisements. Use a dictionary to help you.

Cheetahs: a fashionable b athlete c second best

Needydogs: a abandoned b charity c mistreated

'Smoking Isn't Cool': a cool b prematurely c addictive

Exploring the advertisements

7 Why do you think the trainers are called Cheetahs?
8 Why do you think Needydogs have a photograph of a dog in their advertisement?
9 Why do you think the smoking advertisement asks questions?
10 What emotion is each advertisement appealing to?
11 How has each advertisement used: a persuasive language? b illustrations? c fonts and colour?

Taking it further RB, Unit 2, Extension

12 Which advertisement do you find the most persuasive? Explain your reasons.

Teach 10 Teach 11

RESOURCES & ASSESSMENT BOOK

- **Support** (comprehension support): matching adverts to their purpose, multiple choice; (vocabulary support): matching words and definitions.
- **Extension:** understanding persuasive language.

PUPIL BOOK ANSWERS

1. Persuade people to: buy Cheetahs / give money to save homeless dogs / give up smoking or not to start smoking.
2. Young sporty people / people who care about dogs / smokers or those thinking of taking it up.
3. Newspapers and magazines / *Needydogs* in a vet's surgery / *Smoking isn't cool* in a doctors surgery / hospital.
4. 'a winner'.
5. £1 a month.
6. Cheetahs: **a** a style popular at the time **b** someone good at sports **c** not as good as others Needydogs: **a** left alone **b** organisation that helps others **c** treated badly Smoking Isn't Cool: **a** to be admired / impressive **b** before it should do so normally **c** something that you want more and more and cannot do without
7. Cheetahs are the fastest land animal and the trainers will make you very fast like a cheetah.
8. People respond to dogs and will be more likely to read the advert.
9. Most people would answer 'no' to each of these questions that should lead them to conclude they should give up or not start.
10. Cheetahs: the need to have the best / be thought of as an athlete / win
    Needydogs: pity / 'warm' feeling that comes from doing good
    Smoking Isn't Cool: feeling of fear of the consequences
11. Individual answers.
12. Individual answers.

RESOURCE SHEET SUPPORT ANSWERS

A

1. persuades you to buy trainers
2. persuades you to give to a charity
3. persuades you not to smoke

B

1. Cheetahs
2. £1
3. your gums will rot

C

1. fashionable – a style popular at the time
2. athlete – someone good at sports
3. abandoned – left alone
4. mistreat – treat badly
5. prematurely – before it should do so normally
6. addictive – something you cannot do without

GOING DEEPER

- Discuss 'real' adverts that the children know. Can they identify how they are being persuaded, and what emotion the adverts are appealing to?

TALK

- Ask children what they understand by the term 'copywriter'.
- Explain, if necessary, that a copywriter writes the text for advertisements.
- Ask children if they think it would be an interesting job. Why? Why not?
- Explain to the children that they are going to look at some ideas a copywriter has for advertising *Fun City Theme Park*.
- Show the piece to the class; ask individual children to read it aloud in turn; or read in silence individually.

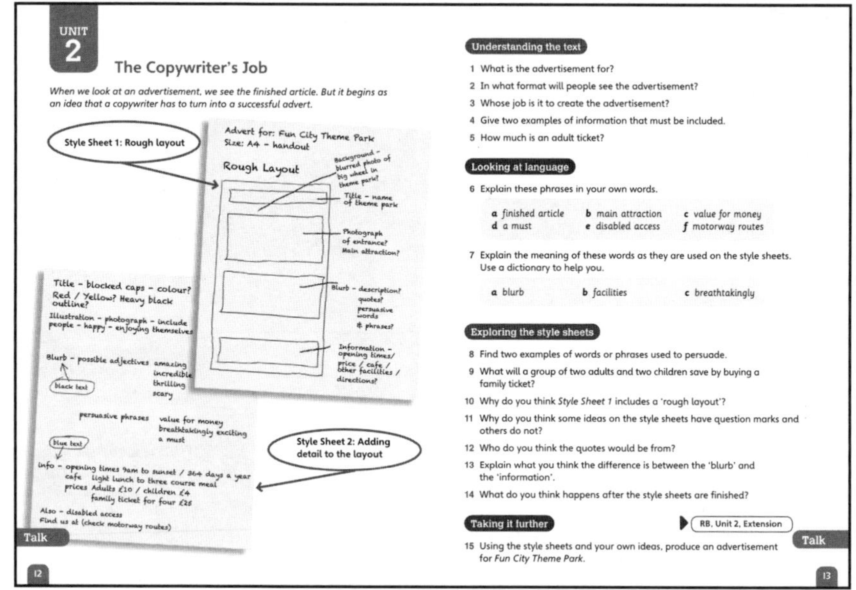

UNIT 2

The Copywriter's Job

When we look at an advertisement, we see the finished article. But it begins as an idea that a copywriter has to turn into a successful advert.

Talk

12

Understanding the text

1 What is the advertisement for?
2 In what format will people see the advertisement?
3 Whose job is it to create the advertisement?
4 Give two examples of information that must be included.
5 How much is an adult ticket?

Looking at language

6 Explain these phrases in your own words.

a *finished article* **b** *main attraction* **c** *value for money*
d *a must* **e** *disabled access* **f** *motorway routes*

7 Explain the meaning of these words as they are used on the style sheets. Use a dictionary to help you.

a *blurb* **b** *facilities* **c** *breathtakingly*

Exploring the style sheets

8 Find two examples of words or phrases used to persuade.
9 What will a group of two adults and two children save by buying a family ticket?
10 Why do you think *Style Sheet 1* includes a 'rough layout'?
11 Why do you think some ideas on the style sheets have question marks and others do not?
12 Who do you think the quotes would be from?
13 Explain what you think the difference is between the 'blurb' and the 'information'.
14 What do you think happens after the style sheets are finished?

Taking it further RB, Unit 2, Extension

15 Using the style sheets and your own ideas, produce an advertisement for *Fun City Theme Park*.

Talk

13

RESOURCES & ASSESSMENT BOOK

- **Support** (comprehension support): choosing correct sentence endings; (vocabulary support): choosing correct definitions.
- **Extension:** completing a style sheet, creating an advert.

PUPIL BOOK ANSWERS

1. *Fun City Theme Park.*
2. As a handout.
3. The copywriter's.
4. Opening times / price / other facilities / directions.
5. £10.
6. **a** the final draft **b** the things that attract the most people to visit **c** worth what is paid **d** can't be missed **e** ways of getting into and around the theme park for people who use wheelchairs **f** ways to get to the theme park using motorways
7. **a** writing that is designed to persuade people **b** things for people to use **c** takes your breath away
8. Amazing / incredible / thrilling / scary / value for money / breathtakingly exciting / a must / family ticket.
9. £3.
10. To give people an idea of what the finished advertisement will look like.
11. Text followed by a question mark are just 'ideas' at this point – those not followed by a question mark have been decided on.
12. People who run the theme park / satisfied customers of the theme park.
13. The 'blurb' is written to persuade; the 'information' gives factual details.
14. Individual answers.
15. Individual answers.

RESOURCE SHEET SUPPORT ANSWERS

A

1. a theme park
2. as a handout
3. the copywriter
4. an adult ticket costs £10
5. £3

B

1. the best thing in the theme park
2. complete
3. worth the money paid
4. it shouldn't be missed
5. wheelchairs

GOING DEEPER

- Discuss the finished adverts for the 'Taking it further' activity. Choose the most persuasive by a class vote. Voters should be able to give reasons.

WRITE

- Discuss holiday advertisements with the children. What do they usually look like / tell you?
- Ask children what they understand by the term 'cruise'.
- Ask children if they know where the Caribbean is.
- Explain to the children that they are going to look at an advertisement for a Caribbean cruise.
- Show the advert to the class; ask individual children to read it aloud in turn; or read in silence individually.

RESOURCES & ASSESSMENT BOOK

- **Support** (comprehension support): choosing the correct sentence endings; (vocabulary support): matching words and definitions.
- **Extension:** writing questions.

PUPIL BOOK ANSWERS

1. To persuade people to book a cruise.
2. The *Olympia.*
3. The Caribbean.
4. St Lucia / Antigua / Barbados.
5. 25 days / nights.
6. **a** something that only comes along once in a lifetime **b** bathed in sunlight **c** known all over the world
7. **a** expensive and high-quality surroundings **b** beautiful in a simple way / not fussy **c** very roomy **d** impressive / expensive **e** rest **f** only so many
8. Adults who are fairly well off.
9. **a** it makes a good visual impression on the reader / suggests what the advert is for **b** it looks good value for money and will persuade people to read the rest of the advert
10. These words are persuasive.
11. The islands are not overrun with tourists / they have not been changed in any way that makes them less beautiful.
12. 'an outside cabin' will have a sea view.
13. Individual answers.
14. Individual answers.

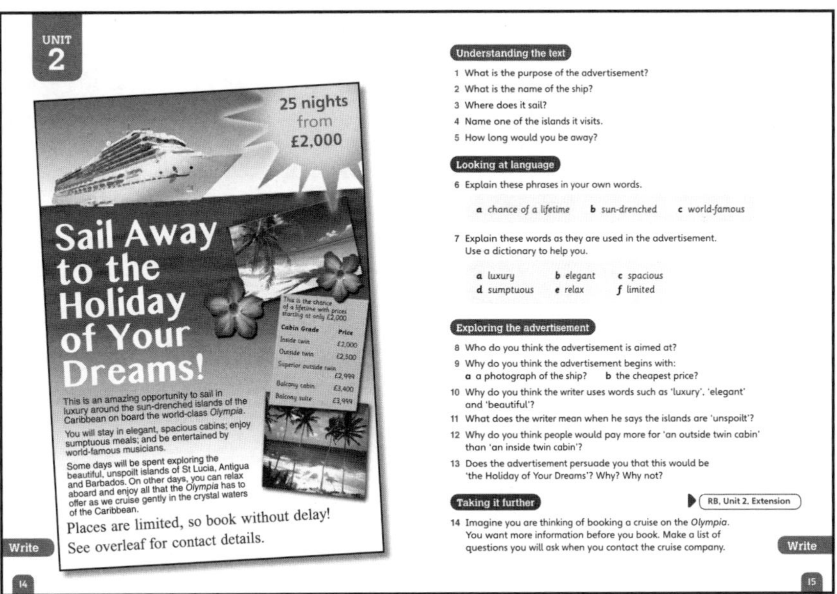

UNIT 2

25 nights
from
£2,000

Sail Away to the Holiday of Your Dreams!

This is an amazing opportunity to sail in luxury around the sun-drenched islands of the Caribbean on board the world-class *Olympia*.

You will stay in elegant, spacious cabins; enjoy sumptuous meals; and be entertained by world-famous musicians.

Some days will be spent exploring the beautiful, unspoilt islands of St Lucia, Antigua and Barbados. On other days, you can relax aboard and enjoy all that the *Olympia* has to offer as we cruise gently in the crystal waters of the Caribbean.

This is the chance of a lifetime with prices starting at only £2,000

Cabin Grade	Price
Inside twin	£2,000
Outside twin	£2,500
Superior outside twin	£2,999
Balcony cabin	£3,400
Balcony suite	£3,999

Places are limited, so book without delay!
See overleaf for contact details.

Write

14

Understanding the text

1 What is the purpose of the advertisement?
2 What is the name of the ship?
3 Where does it sail?
4 Name one of the islands it visits.
5 How long would you be away?

Looking at language

6 Explain these phrases in your own words.
a chance of a lifetime *b sun-drenched* *c world-famous*

7 Explain these words as they are used in the advertisement. Use a dictionary to help you.
a luxury *b elegant* *c spacious*
d sumptuous *e relax* *f limited*

Exploring the advertisement

8 Who do you think the advertisement is aimed at?
9 Why do you think the advertisement begins with:
a a photograph of the ship? b the cheapest price?
10 Why do you think the writer uses words such as 'luxury', 'elegant' and 'beautiful'?
11 What does the writer mean when he says the islands are 'unspoilt'?
12 Why do you think people would pay more for 'an outside twin cabin' than 'an inside twin cabin'?
13 Does the advertisement persuade you that this would be 'the Holiday of Your Dreams'? Why? Why not?

Taking it further RB, Unit 2, Extension

14 Imagine you are thinking of booking a cruise on the *Olympia*. You want more information before you book. Make a list of questions you will ask when you contact the cruise company.

Write

15

RESOURCE SHEET SUPPORT ANSWERS

A

1. *Olympia*
2. the Caribbean
3. Antigua
4. 25 nights
5. £2,000

B

1. luxury – expensive and high quality
2. elegant – stylish
3. spacious – very roomy
4. sumptuous – impressive / expensive
5. relax – rest
6. limited – only so many

GOING DEEPER

- Use children's ideas for the 'Taking it further' activity as a basis for a class discussion.
- Recap on what children have learned about persuasive writing in advertisements.

UNIT FOCUS: Exploring Characters' Feelings

Investigating …

- stories by long-established children's authors
- character portrayal
- how authors create characters and manipulate reader response through description, dialogue and actions

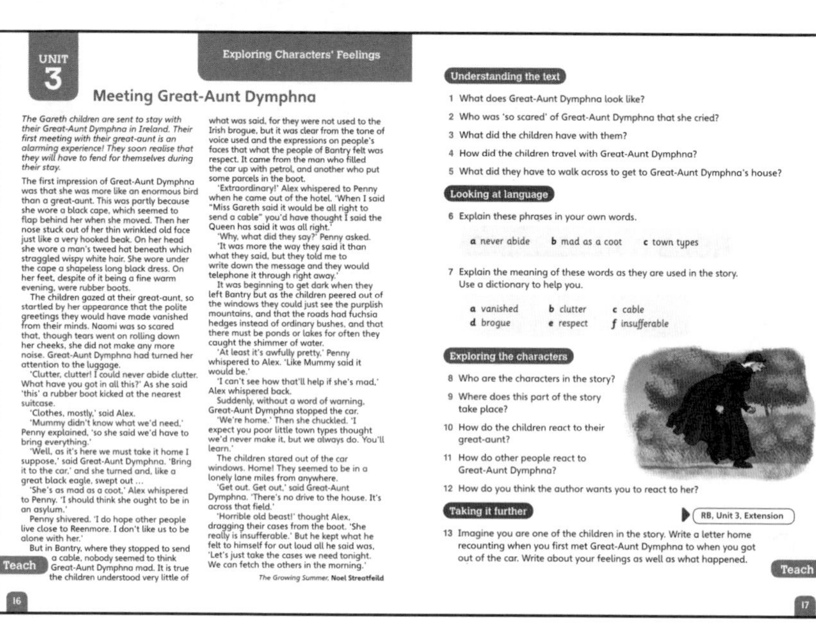

UNIT 3

Exploring Characters' Feelings

Meeting Great-Aunt Dymphna

The Gareth children are sent to stay with their Great-Aunt Dymphna in Ireland. Their first meeting with their great-aunt is an alarming experience! They soon realise that they will have to fend for themselves during their stay.

The first impression of Great-Aunt Dymphna was that she was more like an enormous bird than a great-aunt. This was partly because she wore a black cape, which seemed to flap behind her when she moved. Then her nose stuck out of her thin wrinkled old face just like a very hooked beak. On her head she wore a man's tweed hat beneath which straggled wispy white hair. She wore under the cape a shapeless long black dress. On her feet, despite of it being a fine warm evening, were rubber boots.

The children gazed at their great-aunt, so startled by her appearance that the polite greetings they would have made vanished from their minds. Naomi was so scared that, though tears went on rolling down her cheeks, she did not make any more noise. Great-Aunt Dymphna had turned her attention to the luggage.

'Clutter, clutter! I could never abide clutter. What have you got in all this?' As she said 'this' a rubber boot kicked at the nearest suitcase.

'Clothes, mostly,' said Alex.

'Mummy didn't know what we'd need,' Penny explained, 'so she said we'd have to bring everything.'

'Well, as it's here we must take it home I suppose,' said Great-Aunt Dymphna. 'Bring it to the car,' and she turned and, like a great black eagle, swept out …

'She's as mad as a coot,' Alex whispered to Penny. 'I should think she ought to be in an asylum.'

Penny shivered. 'I do hope other people live close to Reenmore. I don't like us to be alone with her.'

But in Bantry, where they stopped to send a cable, nobody seemed to think Great-Aunt Dymphna mad. It is true the children understood very little of what was said, for they were not used to the Irish brogue, but it was clear from the tone of voice used and the expressions on people's faces that what the people of Bantry felt was respect. It came from the man who filled the car up with petrol, and another who put some parcels in the boot.

'Extraordinary!' Alex whispered to Penny when he came out of the hotel. 'When I said "Miss Gareth said it would be all right to send a cable" you'd have thought I said the Queen has said it was all right.'

'Why, what did they say?' Penny asked.

'It was more the way they said it than what they said, but they told me to write down the message and they would telephone it through right away.'

It was beginning to get dark when they left Bantry but as the children peered out of the windows they could just see the purplish mountains, and that the roads had fuchsia hedges instead of ordinary bushes, and that there must be ponds or lakes for often they caught the shimmer of water.

'At least it's awfully pretty,' Penny whispered to Alex. 'Like Mummy said it would be.'

'I can't see how that'll help if she's mad,' Alex whispered back.

Suddenly, without a word of warning, Great-Aunt Dymphna stopped the car.

'We're home.' Then she chuckled. 'I expect you poor little town types thought we'd never make it, but we always do. You'll learn.'

The children stared out of the car windows. Home! They seemed to be in a lonely lane miles from anywhere.

'Get out. Get out,' said Great-Aunt Dymphna. 'There's no drive to the house. It's across that field.'

'Horrible old beast!' thought Alex, dragging their cases from the boot. 'She really is insufferable.' But he kept what he felt to himself for out loud all he said was, 'Let's just take the cases we need tonight. We can fetch the others in the morning.'

The Growing Summer, **Noel Streatfeild**

Teach

16

Understanding the text

1 What does Great-Aunt Dymphna look like?

2 Who was 'so scared' of Great-Aunt Dymphna that she cried?

3 What did the children have with them?

4 How did the children travel with Great-Aunt Dymphna?

5 What did they have to walk across to get to Great-Aunt Dymphna's house?

Looking at language

6 Explain these phrases in your own words.

a never abide **b** mad as a coot **c** town types

7 Explain the meaning of these words as they are used in the story. Use a dictionary to help you.

a vanished **b** clutter **c** cable
d brogue **e** respect **f** insufferable

Exploring the characters

8 Who are the characters in the story?

9 Where does this part of the story take place?

10 How do the children react to their great-aunt?

11 How do other people react to Great-Aunt Dymphna?

12 How do you think the author wants you to react to her?

Taking it further

RB, Unit 3, Extension

13 Imagine you are one of the children in the story. Write a letter home recounting when you first met Great-Aunt Dymphna to when you got out of the car. Write about your feelings as well as what happened.

Teach

17

TEACH

- Discuss what children understand by the term 'characters' in stories.
- Discuss how readers get to know a character through author description (appearance, personality); by what a character says and does; by how a character relates to other characters.
- Ask children to give examples of favourite characters from their own reading and say why they like them.
- Explain to children that they are going to read an extract from a story called *The Growing Summer*.
- Explain the story so far: The Gareth children – Alex, Penny, Robin and Naomi – are sent to stay with their great-aunt Dymphna in Ireland. They very much have to fend for themselves during their stay and they find the first meeting with their great-aunt an alarming experience.
- Read the extract to the class; ask individual children to read it aloud in turn; or read in silence individually.

RESOURCES & ASSESSMENT BOOK

- **Support** (comprehension support): multiple choice; (vocabulary support): writing synonyms.
- **Extension:** empathising, making notes.

PUPIL BOOK ANSWERS

1. 'an enormous bird' / 'a great black eagle'.
2. Naomi.
3. Suitcases.
4. By car.
5. A field.
6. **a** can't put up with / doesn't like **b** very odd **c** people who live in the town
7. **a** disappeared **b** lots of things – usually untidy and unnecessary **c** an old fashioned way of sending a message / telegram **d** accent / way of speaking **e** admiration / liking **f** difficult to put up with
8. Great-Aunt Dymphna / Alex / Penny / Robin / Naomi.
9. Loading and getting into the car / Bantry / a field.
10. Alex: considerate / realises the difficult situation but doesn't want to upset the others by speaking out.

    Penny: slightly nervous about the situation / tries to make the best of it.

    Robin: outspoken / doesn't necessarily think before he speaks.

    Naomi: frightened and upset.
11. Alex: thinks she is 'as mad as a coot'.

    Penny: very wary: 'I don't like us to be alone with her'.

    Robin: thinks she is so odd that nobody would ever visit her.

    Naomi: very scared.
12. Other people react with great respect and seem to like and admire her.
13. Find her scary / comic / interesting.
14. Individual answers.

RESOURCE SHEET SUPPORT ANSWERS

A

1. an enormous bird
2. cried
3. the suitcase
4. a cable
5. mountains

B

1. vanished: disappeared
2. clutter: lots of things, usually untidy
3. insufferable: difficult to be around / put up with

GOING DEEPER

- Discuss how children have found out about the various characters. Ensure children understand not only to look at what the author tells them, but also to examine what characters say and do in order to build up a picture of personality.

TALK

- Ask children what they understand by the term 'governess'.
- What do they think are the advantages / disadvantages of having a governess and being taught at home, as opposed to going to school?
- Ask children if they have read other stories where there is a governess.
- Explain to children they are going to read an extract from a story called *The Wolves of Willoughby Chase*. The story is set in 1832 when wolves roamed the countryside in the north of England. Sylvia is an orphan who comes to stay with her cousin Bonnie. One day, Bonnie's parents go away in a ship and Miss Slighcarp, an evil woman, arrives to look after the children. Her aim is to get rid of them but Bonnie and Sylvia are not going quietly!
- Read the extract to the class; ask individual children to read it aloud in turn; or read in silence individually.

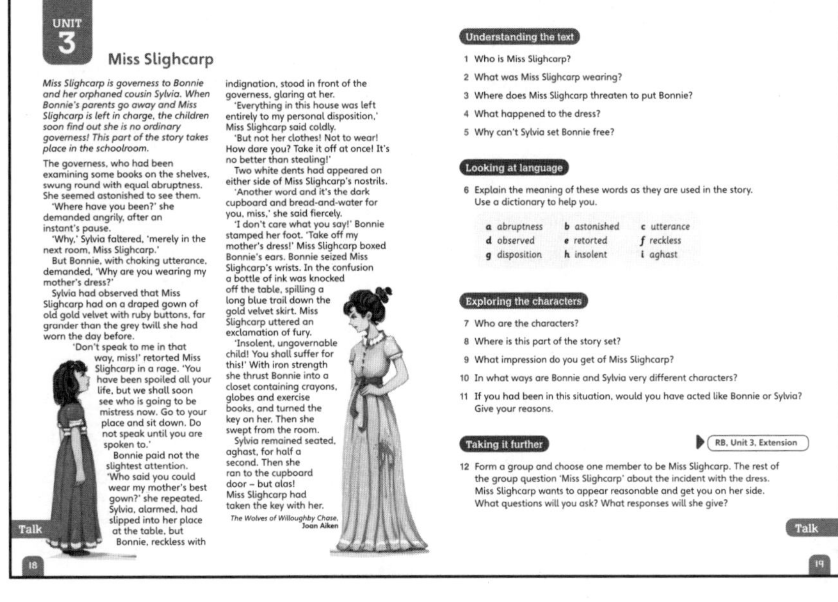

UNIT 3

Miss Slighcarp

Miss Slighcarp is governess to Bonnie and her orphaned cousin Sylvia. When Bonnie's parents go away and Miss Slighcarp is left in charge, the children soon find out she is no ordinary governess! This part of the story takes place in the schoolroom.

The governess, who had been examining some books on the shelves, swung round with equal abruptness. She seemed astonished to see them.

'Where have you been?' she demanded angrily, after an instant's pause.

'Why,' Sylvia faltered, 'merely in the next room, Miss Slighcarp.'

But Bonnie, with choking utterance, demanded, 'Why are you wearing my mother's dress?'

Sylvia had observed that Miss Slighcarp had on a draped gown of old gold velvet with ruby buttons, far grander than the grey twill she had worn the day before.

'Don't speak to me in that way, miss!' retorted Miss Slighcarp in a rage. 'You have been spoiled all your life, but we shall soon see who is going to be mistress now. Go to your place and sit down. Do not speak until you are spoken to.'

Bonnie paid not the slightest attention. 'Who said you could wear my mother's best gown?' she repeated. Sylvia, alarmed, had slipped into her place at the table, but Bonnie, reckless with indignation, stood in front of the governess, glaring at her.

'Everything in this house was left entirely to my personal disposition,' Miss Slighcarp said coldly.

'But not her clothes! Not to wear! How dare you? Take it off at once! It's no better than stealing!'

Two white dents had appeared on either side of Miss Slighcarp's nostrils.

'Another word and it's the dark cupboard and bread-and-water for you, miss,' she said fiercely.

'I don't care what you say!' Bonnie stamped her foot. 'Take off my mother's dress!' Miss Slighcarp boxed Bonnie's ears. Bonnie seized Miss Slighcarp's wrists. In the confusion a bottle of ink was knocked off the table, spilling a long blue trail down the gold velvet skirt. Miss Slighcarp uttered an exclamation of fury.

'Insolent, ungovernable child! You shall suffer for this!' With iron strength she thrust Bonnie into a closet containing crayons, globes and exercise books, and turned the key on her. Then she swept from the room.

Sylvia remained seated, aghast, for half a second. Then she ran to the cupboard door – but alas! Miss Slighcarp had taken the key with her.

The Wolves of Willoughby Chase, Joan Aiken

Talk 18

Understanding the text

1 Who is Miss Slighcarp?

2 What was Miss Slighcarp wearing?

3 Where does Miss Slighcarp threaten to put Bonnie?

4 What happened to the dress?

5 Why can't Sylvia set Bonnie free?

Looking at language

6 Explain the meaning of these words as they are used in the story. Use a dictionary to help you.

a abruptness **b** astonished **c** utterance
d observed **e** retorted **f** reckless
g disposition **h** insolent **i** aghast

Exploring the characters

7 Who are the characters?

8 Where is this part of the story set?

9 What impression do you get of Miss Slighcarp?

10 In what ways are Bonnie and Sylvia very different characters?

11 If you had been in this situation, would you have acted like Bonnie or Sylvia? Give your reasons.

Taking it further RB, Unit 3, Extension

12 Form a group and choose one member to be Miss Slighcarp. The rest of the group question 'Miss Slighcarp' about the incident with the dress. Miss Slighcarp wants to appear reasonable and get you on her side. What questions will you ask? What responses will she give?

Talk 19

RESOURCES & ASSESSMENT BOOK

- **Support** (comprehension support): identifying True / False statements, correcting false statements; (vocabulary support): choosing correct words to describe characters.
- **Extension:** writing questions and answers.

PUPIL BOOK ANSWERS

1. The governess.
2. Bonnie's mother's dress.
3. In 'the dark cupboard'.
4. Ink was spilled on it.
5. Miss Slighcarp has the key.
6. **a** suddenness **b** very surprised **c** something spoken **d** noticed **e** replied angrily **f** not thinking about the consequences **g** the power to do as one wants with something **h** offensive / arrogant / insulting **i** horrified
7. Miss Slighcarp / Bonnie / Sylvia.
8. In the schoolroom.
9. Answers that suggest she expects to be obeyed – 'Don't speak to me that way, miss!' / 'Do not speak until you are spoken to', and that she is cruel and violent – 'Miss Slighcarp boxed Bonnie's ears.' / 'she thrust Bonnie into a closet'.
10. Bonnie: brave and confronts Miss Slighcarp – 'Why are you wearing my mother's dress?'

    Sylvia: too scared to do or say anything
11. Individual answers.
12. Individual answers

RESOURCE SHEET SUPPORT ANSWERS

A

1. TRUE
2. FALSE
3. FALSE
4. TRUE
5. TRUE
6. FALSE

B

1. Miss Slighcarp was wearing a 'draped gown of old gold velvet with ruby buttons'.
2. Bonnie did not do as she was told.
3. Bonnie and Miss Slighcarp fought and 'in the confusion a bottle of ink was knocked off the table'.

C

Miss Slighcarp: governess / wearing a beautiful dress

Bonnie: doesn't obey / put in the closet

Sylvia: doesn't say anything / doesn't have the key

GOING DEEPER

- Ask children how they made their judgements about the characters. Do they think Sylvia was more or less sensible than Bonnie in the circumstances?

WRITE

- Ask children what they understand by 'a bush fire'. Where do bush fires happen? Why are they so dangerous?
- Ask children if they have seen pictures on television or in magazines that show raging bush fires. How did they feel when they looked at these pictures?
- Explain to children they are going to read an extract from a story called *Ash Road.*
- Read the extract to the class; ask individual children to read it aloud in turn; or read in silence individually.

Bush Fire!

Three boys are camping in the Australian bush. The weather is very hot and there is a dry north wind. In the middle of the night, Graham accidentally knocks over a bottle of methylated spirits, which catches fire.

'It's burning,' howled Graham.

A blue flame snaked from the little heater up through the rocks towards the bottle in the boy's hand; or at least that was how it seemed to happen. It happened so swiftly it may have deceived the eye. Instinctively, to protect himself, Graham threw the bottle away. There was a shower of fire from its neck, as from the nozzle of a hose.

'Oh my gosh,' yelled Wallace and tore off his sleeping-bag. 'Harry!' he screamed. 'Wake up, Harry!'

They tried to stamp on the fire, but their feet were bare and they couldn't find their shoes. They tried to smother it with their sleeping-bags, but it seemed to be everywhere. Harry couldn't even escape from his bag; he couldn't find the zip fastener, and for a few awful moments in his confusion between sleep and wakefulness he thought he was in his bed at home and the house had burst into flames around him. He couldn't come to grips with the situation; he knew only dismay and the wildest kind of alarm. Graham and Wallace, panicking, were throwing themselves from place to place, almost sobbing, beating futilely at the widening arc of fire. Every desperate blow they made seemed to fan the fire, to scatter it farther, to feed it.

'Put it out,' shouted Graham. 'Put it out.'

It wasn't dark any longer. It was a flickering world of tree trunks and twisted boughs, of scrub and saplings and stones, of shouts and wind and smoke and frantic fear. It was so quick. It was terrible.

'Put it out,' cried Graham, and Harry fought out of his sleeping-bag, knowing somehow that they'd never get it out by beating at it, that they'd have to get water up from the creek. But all they had was a four-pint billy-can.

Write

The fire was getting away from them in all directions, crackling through the scrub down-wind, burning fiercely back into the wind. Even the ground was burning: grass, roots and fallen leaves were burning, humus was burning. There were flames on the trees, bark was burning, foliage was flaring, flaring like a whip-crack; and the heat was savage and searing and awful to breathe.

'We can't, we can't,' cried Wallace. 'What are we going to do?'

'Oh, gee,' sobbed Graham. He was crying and he hadn't cried since he was twelve years old. 'What have I done? *We've got to get it out!*'

Harry was scrambling around wildly, bundling all their things together. It was not just that he was more level-headed than the others; it was just that he could see the end more clearly, the hopelessness of it, the absolute certainty of it, the imminent danger of encirclement, the possibility that they might be burnt alive. He could see all this because he hadn't been in it at the start. He wasn't responsible; he hadn't done it; and now he was wide awake he could see more clearly. He screamed at them, 'Grab your stuff and run for it.' But they didn't hear him or didn't want to hear him. They were blackened, their feet were cut, even their hair was singed. They beat and beat, and the fire was leaping into the tree-tops, and there were no black shadows left, only bright light, red light, yellow light, light that was hard and cruel and terrifying, and there was a rushing sound, a roaring sound, explosions, and smoke, smoke like a hot red fog.

'No,' cried Graham. 'No, no, no.' His arms dropped to his sides and he shook with sobs and Wallace dragged him away. 'Oh, Wally,' he sobbed. 'What have I done?'

'We've got to get out of here,' shouted Harry. 'Grab the things and run.'

'Our shoes!' cried Wallace. 'Where are they?' ...

'For Pete's sake run!' shouted Harry.

Ash Road, Ivan Southall

20

Understanding the text

1 What did Graham throw away? Why?

2 At first, how did the boys try to put out the fire?

3 When Harry woke up, what did he think had happened?

4 What did Harry know they needed to put out the fire?

5 What did Harry tell the others to do?

Looking at language

6 Explain these phrases in your own words.

a deceived the eye b come to grips with
c level-headed d in it at the start

7 Explain the meaning of these words as they are used in the story. Use a dictionary to help you.

a *instinctively* b *futilely* c *humus*
d *foliage* e *imminent* f *encirclement*

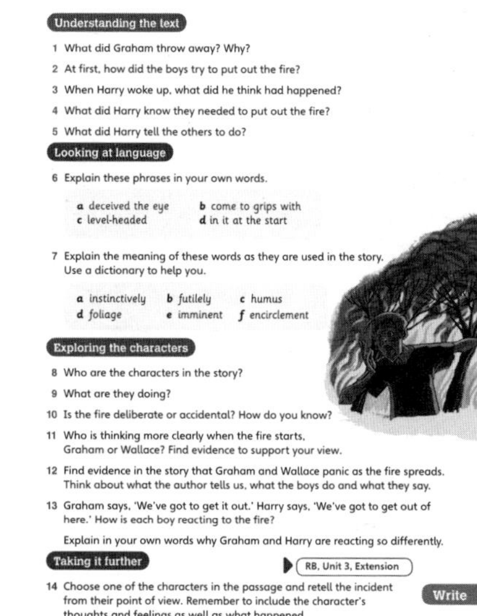

Exploring the characters

8 Who are the characters in the story?

9 What are they doing?

10 Is the fire deliberate or accidental? How do you know?

11 Who is thinking more clearly when the fire starts, Graham or Wallace? Find evidence to support your view.

12 Find evidence in the story that Graham and Wallace panic as the fire spreads. Think about what the author tells us, what the boys do and what they say.

13 Graham says, 'We've got to get it out.' Harry says, 'We've got to get out of here.' How is each boy reacting to the fire?

Explain in your own words why Graham and Harry are reacting so differently.

Taking it further

RB, Unit 3, Extension

14 Choose one of the characters in the passage and retell the incident from their point of view. Remember to include the character's thoughts and feelings as well as what happened.

Write

21

RESOURCES & ASSESSMENT BOOK

- **Support** (comprehension support): who said what?; (vocabulary support): cloze activity to reinforce vocabulary.
- **Extension:** understanding character feelings, empathising.

PUPIL BOOK ANSWERS

1 A bottle of methylated spirits. / It was on fire.

2 'They tried to stamp on the fire' / 'They tried to smother it with their sleeping bags'.

3 He thought he was at home and that the house was on fire.

4 He knew they needed water.

5 'Grab the things and run.'

6 **a** made them think they had seen something that had not actually happened **b** fully realise what was happening **c** sensible / calm in a crisis **d** there at the beginning

7 **a** without thinking **b** uselessly **c** decayed plants and leaves on the ground **d** leaves of a plant or tree **e** likely to happen very soon **f** being surrounded

8 Wallace / Graham / Harry.

9 Camping in the Australian bush.

10 Accidental. Graham accidentally knocks over a bottle of methylated spirits / their reaction to the fire.

11 Graham is not thinking clearly as he throws the burning bottle away from him. Wallace is thinking clearly enough at this time to wake Harry up.

12 What the author tells us – 'Graham and Wallace panicking' / Graham 'was crying'; what the boys do – 'throwing themselves from place to place' / 'beating futilely' / 'running around in circles'; what the boys say – 'Put it out' / 'What are we going to do?' / 'What have I done?' / 'They'll kill us.'

13 Graham's words show that he is only thinking of putting right what he has done wrong. Harry's words show that he is thinking ahead.

14 Individual answers.

RESOURCE SHEET SUPPORT ANSWERS

A

1 Graham

2 Harry

3 Wallace

4 Harry

5 Wallace

6 Graham

B

1 The bottle was on fire. Graham didn't think. He **instinctively** threw the bottle away.

2 The boys beat **futilely** at the flames. It didn't make any difference.

3 There was **imminent** danger of the flames being all round them.

4 The **foliage** on the trees was burning fiercely.

GOING DEEPER

- Use the three extracts as a basis for a class discussion to investigate how children made judgements about the characters.

UNIT FOCUS: Following Instructions

Investigating ...

- instructional writing in the context of ICT
- the features of instructions

TEACH

- Ask children what they can remember about the features of instructional writing, i.e. imperative verbs; present tense; numbered / short simple sentences, supported by diagrams.
- Ask children what they use the internet for. Have they (their family) ever bought anything on the internet?
- Explain to children they are going to read a set of instructions for buying a book from an online bookshop.
- Read the text to the class; ask individual children to read it aloud in turn; or read in silence individually.

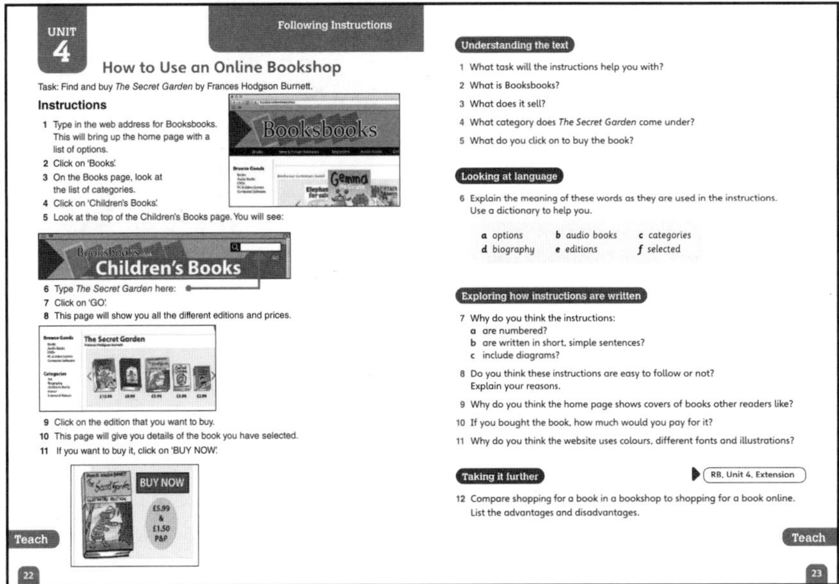

UNIT 4 Following Instructions

How to Use an Online Bookshop

Task: Find and buy *The Secret Garden* by Frances Hodgson Burnett.

Instructions

1 Type in the web address for Booksbooks. This will bring up the home page with a list of options.
2 Click on 'Books'.
3 On the Books page, look at the list of categories.
4 Click on 'Children's Books'.
5 Look at the top of the Children's Books page. You will see:

6 Type *The Secret Garden* here:
7 Click on 'GO'.
8 This page will show you all the different editions and prices.

9 Click on the edition that you want to buy.
10 This page will give you details of the book you have selected.
11 If you want to buy it, click on 'BUY NOW'.

Teach

22

Understanding the text

1 What task will the instructions help you with?
2 What is Booksbooks?
3 What does it sell?
4 What category does *The Secret Garden* come under?
5 What do you click on to buy the book?

Looking at language

6 Explain the meaning of these words as they are used in the instructions. Use a dictionary to help you.

a options **b** audio books **c** categories
d biography **e** editions **f** selected

Exploring how instructions are written

7 Why do you think the instructions:
a are numbered?
b are written in short, simple sentences?
c include diagrams?
8 Do you think these instructions are easy to follow or not? Explain your reasons.
9 Why do you think the home page shows covers of books other readers like?
10 If you bought the book, how much would you pay for it?
11 Why do you think the website uses colours, different fonts and illustrations?

Taking it further RB, Unit 4, Extension

12 Compare shopping for a book in a bookshop to shopping for a book online. List the advantages and disadvantages.

Teach

23

RESOURCES & ASSESSMENT BOOK

- **Support** (comprehension support): numbering instructions; (vocabulary support): choosing correct definitions.
- **Extension:** organising advantages and disadvantages.

PUPIL BOOK ANSWERS

1. Find and buy *The Secret Garden* by Francis Hodgson Burnett.
2. An online bookshop.
3. Books / audio books / DVDs / PC & video games / computer software.
4. Children's books.
5. BUY NOW.
6. **a** choices **b** books read by someone, recorded on to disc **c** group **d** account of someone's life written by another person **e** copies of a book that is published at different times **f** something that has been chosen
7. **a** to show the order in which they must be followed **b** to make them easier to understand **c** to help the reader see what the screen should look like at each stage of the instructions
8. Individual answers.
9. It is acting as a form of advertising.
10. £7.49 [£5.99 for the book + £1.50 postage and packing].
11. It needs to look attractive and inviting so people will be interested and keep going back to it.
12. Online:

    Advantages – online carries bigger stock / often cheaper / usually offer both new and second-hand editions.

    Disadvantages – have to pay postage and packing / have to wait for book to be delivered.

    Bookshop:

    Advantages – if the book is in stock, you can have it immediately / you can browse and handle the books / you don't have to pay postage and packing.

    Disadvantages – if not in stock, book has to be ordered / often more expensive.

RESOURCE SHEET SUPPORT ANSWERS

A

Click on 'Children's books'. 2

Click on the edition you want to buy. 5

Click on 'Books'. 1

Type in the title of the book you want. 3

If you want to buy the book, click on BUY NOW. 6

Click on GO. 4

B

1. choice
2. listened to
3. a group
4. about someone else

C

Individual answers.

GOING DEEPER

- Discuss what is easy to sell online and what is more difficult.

TALK

- Ask children where they (their family) store their photographs.
- Explain to children that they are going to read a set of instructions for downloading photographs and storing them on a computer.
- Read the text to the class; ask individual children to read it aloud in turn; or read in silence individually.

RESOURCES & ASSESSMENT BOOK

- **Support** (comprehension support): matching sentence beginnings and endings; (vocabulary support): cloze activity to reinforce vocabulary.
- **Extension:** organising advantages and disadvantages.

PUPIL BOOK ANSWERS

1. Downloading photographs from your digital camera to your desktop.
2. 11.
3. A PC / a digital camera memory card / a USB card reader.
4. Personal computer.
5. The photographs you have taken.
6. **a** way of connecting different devices **b** to choose something **c** to save something onto your computer **d** an image that represents a feature or application **e** the screen you see when you switch on your computer
7. Numbers / short, simple sentences / imperative verbs / present tense.
8. Number: e.g. 1 / 2 / 3; short, simple sentences e.g. 'Switch on the computer'; imperative verbs e.g. Press / Select / Plug; present tense e.g. Select the photograph.
9. Use the mouse to click on what you want.
10. Individual answers.
11. Individual answers e.g. print / email.

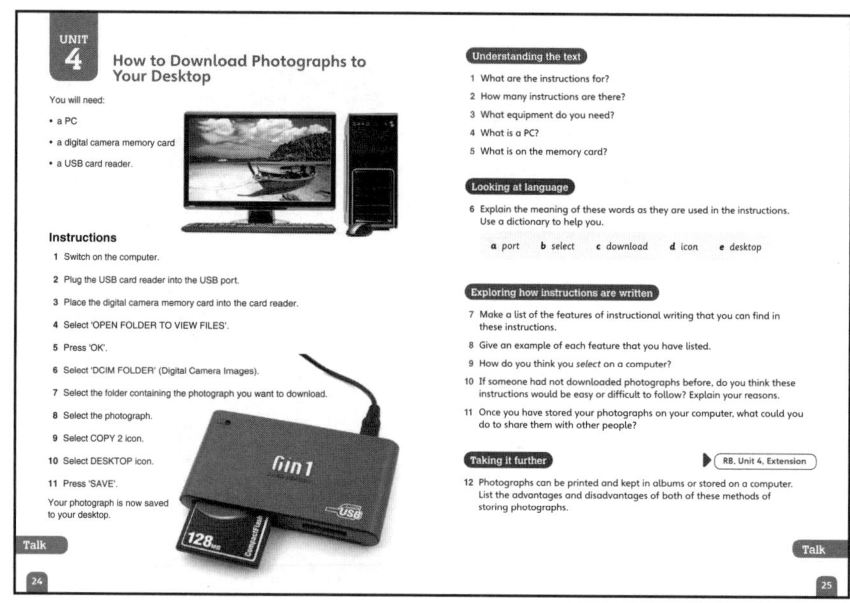

UNIT 4

How to Download Photographs to Your Desktop

You will need:

- a PC
- a digital camera memory card
- a USB card reader.

Instructions

1. Switch on the computer.
2. Plug the USB card reader into the USB port.
3. Place the digital camera memory card into the card reader.
4. Select 'OPEN FOLDER TO VIEW FILES'.
5. Press 'OK'.
6. Select 'DCIM FOLDER' (Digital Camera Images).
7. Select the folder containing the photograph you want to download.
8. Select the photograph.
9. Select COPY 2 icon.
10. Select DESKTOP icon.
11. Press 'SAVE'.

Your photograph is now saved to your desktop.

Talk

24

Understanding the text

1 What are the instructions for?
2 How many instructions are there?
3 What equipment do you need?
4 What is a PC?
5 What is on the memory card?

Looking at language

6 Explain the meaning of these words as they are used in the instructions. Use a dictionary to help you.

a *port* **b** *select* **c** *download* **d** *icon* **e** *desktop*

Exploring how instructions are written

7 Make a list of the features of instructional writing that you can find in these instructions.
8 Give an example of each feature that you have listed.
9 How do you think you *select* on a computer?
10 If someone had not downloaded photographs before, do you think these instructions would be easy or difficult to follow? Explain your reasons.
11 Once you have stored your photographs on your computer, what could you do to share them with other people?

Taking it further

RB, Unit 4, Extension

12 Photographs can be printed and kept in albums or stored on a computer. List the advantages and disadvantages of both of these methods of storing photographs.

Talk

25

12. <u>On the computer:</u>

    Advantages – you can edit – crop/ enlarge / copy photos.

    Disadvantages – have to be at the computer to look at them.

    <u>Albums:</u>

    Advantages – ability to look at them away from a computer.

    Disadvantages – cost of printing / space for storage.

RESOURCE SHEET SUPPORT ANSWERS

A

1. The instructions tell you how to download photographs to your desktop.
2. There are eleven instructions.
3. You need a PC, a memory card and a USB reader.
4. A PC is a personal computer.
5. The photographs are on the memory card.

B

A camera has a **memory** card. This card **stores** the **photographs** you take. If you put the memory card into the card **reader**, you can see your photographs on your **computer** screen. You can then **copy** and **save** your photographs onto your computer.

GOING DEEPER

- Use groups' answers to the last question in 'Exploring how instructions are written' and the 'Taking it further' activity as a basis for a class discussion.

WRITE

- Ask how many children have a mobile phone. Do children think they are a good idea? Why? Why not?
- Ask children what they can do on a mobile phone besides make phone calls.
- Ask children what they mainly use their mobile phone for.
- Explain to children that they are going to read a set of instructions about setting an alarm clock on a mobile phone.
- Read the instructions to the class; ask individual children to read it aloud in turn; or read in silence individually.

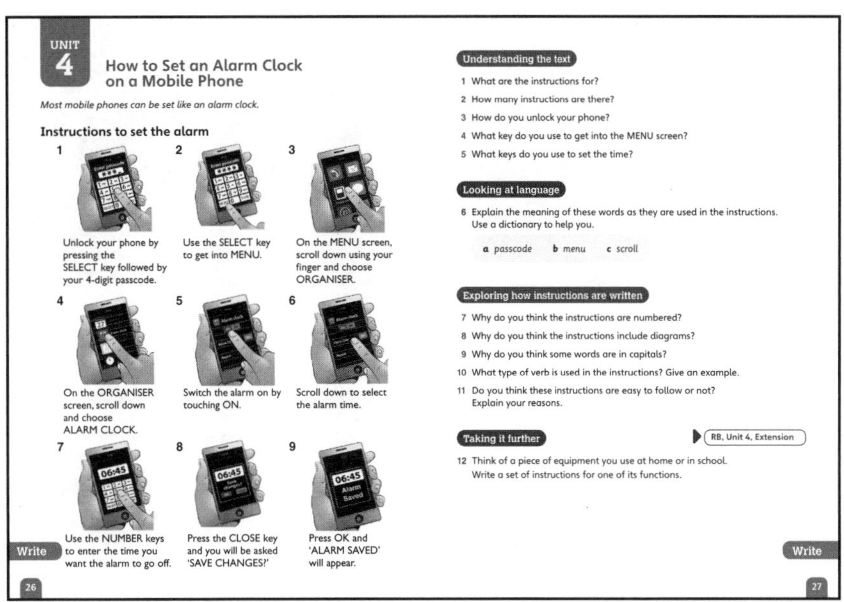

UNIT 4

How to Set an Alarm Clock on a Mobile Phone

Most mobile phones can be set like an alarm clock.

Instructions to set the alarm

1 Unlock your phone by pressing the SELECT key followed by your 4-digit passcode.

2 Use the SELECT key to get into MENU.

3 On the MENU screen, scroll down using your finger and choose ORGANISER.

4 On the ORGANISER screen, scroll down and choose ALARM CLOCK.

5 Switch the alarm on by touching ON.

6 Scroll down to select the alarm time.

7 Use the NUMBER keys to enter the time you want the alarm to go off.

8 Press the CLOSE key and you will be asked 'SAVE CHANGES?'

9 Press OK and 'ALARM SAVED' will appear.

Write

26

Understanding the text

1 What are the instructions for?
2 How many instructions are there?
3 How do you unlock your phone?
4 What key do you use to get into the MENU screen?
5 What keys do you use to set the time?

Looking at language

6 Explain the meaning of these words as they are used in the instructions. Use a dictionary to help you.

a *passcode* **b** *menu* **c** scroll

Exploring how instructions are written

7 Why do you think the instructions are numbered?
8 Why do you think the instructions include diagrams?
9 Why do you think some words are in capitals?
10 What type of verb is used in the instructions? Give an example.
11 Do you think these instructions are easy to follow or not? Explain your reasons.

Taking it further

RB, Unit 4, Extension

12 Think of a piece of equipment you use at home or in school. Write a set of instructions for one of its functions.

Write

27

RESOURCES & ASSESSMENT BOOK

- **Support** (comprehension support): multiple choice; (vocabulary support): sorting muddled words.
- **Extension:** writing a set of instructions.

PUPIL BOOK ANSWERS

1. Setting an alarm on a mobile phone.
2. Nine.
3. Press SELECT key followed by your 4-digit passcode.
4. SELECT key.
5. Number keys.
6. **a** a combination of numbers used as a password
   b selection of things to choose from
   c move down the screen
7. To show the order in which they must be followed.
8. To help the reader see what should be on the screen at each stage.
9. To suggest that these are options on the phone.
10. Imperative verbs e.g. Unlock / Use / Switch.
11. Individual answers.
12. Individual answers.

RESOURCE SHEET SUPPORT ANSWERS

A

1. setting the alarm
2. 9 instructions
3. the SELECT key and your 4-digit passcode
4. ORGANISER
5. set the alarm

B

1. CLOSE
2. SELECT
3. NUMBER

GOING DEEPER

- Go over the features of instructional writing, e.g. numbered instructions, short, simple sentences, use of diagrams, imperative verbs.

UNIT FOCUS: Looking at Media Reports

Investigating ...

- recount texts in the context of the media
- articles connected by the theme of Tutankhamen
- charting chronology, devising questions and conducting research

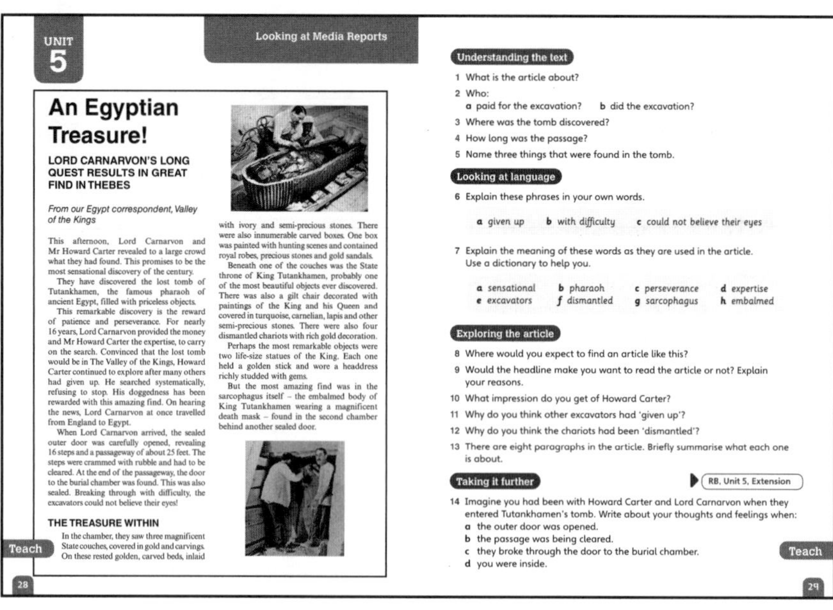

UNIT 5

Looking at Media Reports

An Egyptian Treasure!

LORD CARNARVON'S LONG QUEST RESULTS IN GREAT FIND IN THEBES

From our Egypt correspondent, Valley of the Kings

This afternoon, Lord Carnarvon and Mr Howard Carter revealed to a large crowd what they had found. This promises to be the most sensational discovery of the century.

They have discovered the lost tomb of Tutankhamen, the famous pharaoh of ancient Egypt, filled with priceless objects.

This remarkable discovery is the reward of patience and perseverance. For nearly 16 years, Lord Carnarvon provided the money and Mr Howard Carter the expertise, to carry on the search. Convinced that the lost tomb would be in The Valley of the Kings, Howard Carter continued to explore after many others had given up. He searched systematically, refusing to stop. His doggedness has been rewarded with this amazing find. On hearing the news, Lord Carnarvon at once travelled from England to Egypt.

When Lord Carnarvon arrived, the sealed outer door was carefully opened, revealing 16 steps and a passageway of about 25 feet. The steps were crammed with rubble and had to be cleared. At the end of the passageway, the door to the burial chamber was found. This was also sealed. Breaking through with difficulty, the excavators could not believe their eyes!

THE TREASURE WITHIN

In the chamber, they saw three magnificent State couches, covered in gold and carvings. On these rested golden, carved beds, inlaid with ivory and semi-precious stones. There were also innumerable carved boxes. One box was painted with hunting scenes and contained royal robes, precious stones and gold sandals.

Beneath one of the couches was the State throne of King Tutankhamen, probably one of the most beautiful objects ever discovered. There was also a gilt chair decorated with paintings of the King and his Queen and covered in turquoise, carnelian, lapis and other semi-precious stones. There were also four dismantled chariots with rich gold decoration.

Perhaps the most remarkable objects were two life-size statues of the King. Each one held a golden stick and wore a headdress richly studded with gems.

But the most amazing find was in the sarcophagus itself – the embalmed body of King Tutankhamen wearing a magnificent death mask – found in the second chamber behind another sealed door.

Teach

28

Understanding the text

1 What is the article about?
2 Who:
a paid for the excavation? b did the excavation?
3 Where was the tomb discovered?
4 How long was the passage?
5 Name three things that were found in the tomb.

Looking at language

6 Explain these phrases in your own words.
a given up b with difficulty c could not believe their eyes
7 Explain the meaning of these words as they are used in the article. Use a dictionary to help you.
a sensational b pharaoh c perseverance d expertise
e excavators f dismantled g sarcophagus h embalmed

Exploring the article

8 Where would you expect to find an article like this?
9 Would the headline make you want to read the article or not? Explain your reasons.
10 What impression do you get of Howard Carter?
11 Why do you think other excavators had 'given up'?
12 Why do you think the chariots had been 'dismantled'?
13 There are eight paragraphs in the article. Briefly summarise what each one is about.

Taking it further RB, Unit 5, Extension

14 Imagine you had been with Howard Carter and Lord Carnarvon when they entered Tutankhamen's tomb. Write about your thoughts and feelings when:
a the outer door was opened.
b the passage was being cleared.
c they broke through the door to the burial chamber.
d you were inside.

Teach

29

TEACH

- Ask children what they understand by the term 'archaeology'.
- Ask children what they know about Tutankhamen / Tutankhamun?
- Examine these words: Egypt, Egyptology, Egyptological.
- Explain that Howard Carter was the archaeologist who discovered the tomb of King Tutankhamen. The money for the excavation came from Lord Carnarvon.
- Explain to the children that they are going to read part of a newspaper report that was written only days after Carter made his discovery in the 1920s.
- This is a challenging text for this year group, and you may wish to read it and discuss questions as a class or in groups before asking children to tackle it on their own.

RESOURCES & ASSESSMENT BOOK

- **Support** (comprehension support): writing questions for given answers; (vocabulary support): cloze activity to reinforce vocabulary.
- **Extension:** using imagination to write thoughts and feelings.

PUPIL BOOK ANSWERS

1. The discovery of Tutankhamen's tomb.
2. **a** Lord Carnarvon **b** Howard Carter
3. The Valley of the Kings / Egypt.
4. 25 feet.
5. State couches / beds / boxes / royal robes / precious stones / golden sandals / state throne / gilt chair / chariots / life-size statues / sarcophagus / embalmed body of King Tutankhamen.
6. **a** stopped **b** not easily **c** could not believe what they were seeing because it was so amazing
7. **a** exciting and surprising **b** a ruler in ancient Egypt **c** to keep on going **d** special skill or knowledge **e** people who dig in the ground to find things **f** taken apart **g** stone coffin **h** preserved with bandages / chemicals
8. Newspaper / Magazine.
9. Individual answers.
10. Individual answers.
11. They found nothing and ran out of patience, money or ideas. / They thought there was nothing left to find.
12. They were too big to get into the tomb in one piece.
13. Paragraph 1: introduction to Howard Carter and his discovery Paragraph 2: the discovery Paragraph 3: background to the discovery Paragraph 4: getting into the tomb Paragraph 5: details of the first treasure seen Paragraph 6: more treasure Paragraph 7: details of life-size statues Paragraph 8: the sarcophagus.
14. Individual answers.

RESOURCE SHEET SUPPORT ANSWERS

A

1. Who found the tomb?
2. Who paid for Howard Carter's work?
3. Where did he find the tomb?
4. How long was the passageway?
5. What was the most remarkable find?

B

Howard Carter made a **sensational** discovery in the Valley of the Kings. He found the tomb of the **pharaoh** Tutankhamen. Many others **excavators** had given up but Carter's **perseverance** paid off. Among the things he found in the tomb were four **dismantled** chariots and the **sarcophagus** of Tutankhamen himself.

GOING DEEPER

- Using answers to the last 'Exploring the article' question, discuss the chronological structure of the article.

TALK

- Discuss interviews with the children. What interviews have they heard / seen / read? Why are people interviewed?
- Explain to children that they are going to read the transcript of a radio programme where an expert on Ancient Egypt is being interviewed. A transcript is a written copy of what was actually said.
- Read the transcript to the class; ask individual children to read it aloud; or read in silence individually.

RESOURCES & ASSESSMENT BOOK

- **Support** (comprehension support): who did what?; (vocabulary support): choosing correct word definitions.
- **Extension:** writing interview questions.

PUPIL BOOK ANSWERS

1. Fiona Jacobs.
2. Professor Simon Black.
3. 'Treasures of the Past'.
4. The discovery of Tutankhamen's tomb.
5. Nine feet.
6. **a** amazing / surprising **b** a personal account of your own life **c** body of a human being or animal embalmed for burial **d** take down / destroy **e** equipment with ropes used for lifting heavy objects **f** cloths wrapped around a dead body **g** model of someone **h** very interesting
7. 'There was no coffin or trace of a mummy' in the first chamber.
8. The doorway had a hole in it.
9. The lid was extremely heavy.
10. Individual answers **a** e.g. 'there was no coffin or trace of a mummy' **b** e.g. 'Carter said that it took 84 days'.
11. The objects were in a jumbled heap.
12. The shrines were inside of each other.
13. 'a gasp of wonderment escaped our lips' – everyone felt amazed.
14. Individual answers.
15. Individual answers.

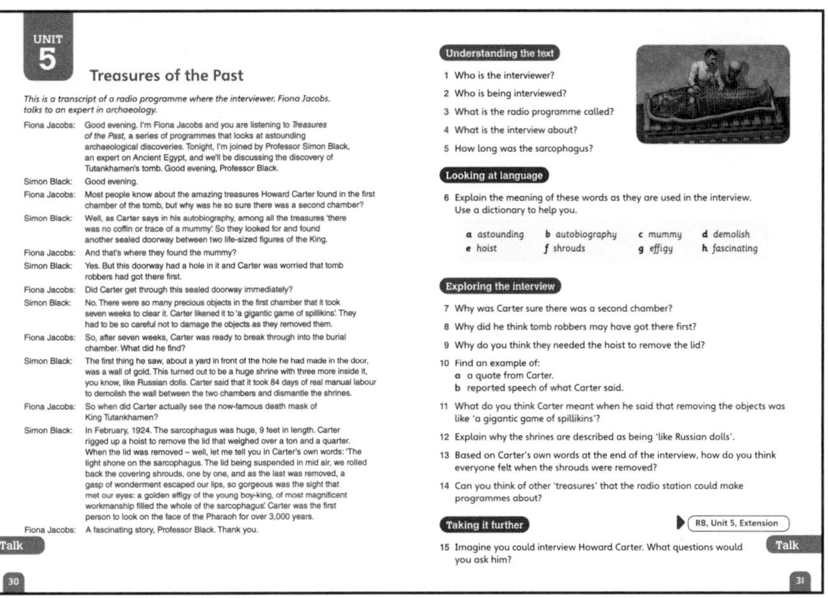

UNIT 5

Treasures of the Past

This is a transcript of a radio programme where the interviewer, Fiona Jacobs, talks to an expert in archaeology.

Fiona Jacobs: Good evening. I'm Fiona Jacobs and you are listening to *Treasures of the Past*, a series of programmes that looks at astounding archaeological discoveries. Tonight, I'm joined by Professor Simon Black, an expert on Ancient Egypt, and we'll be discussing the discovery of Tutankhamen's tomb. Good evening, Professor Black.

Simon Black: Good evening.

Fiona Jacobs: Most people know about the amazing treasures Howard Carter found in the first chamber of the tomb, but why was he so sure there was a second chamber?

Simon Black: Well, as Carter says in his autobiography, among all the treasures 'there was no coffin or trace of a mummy'. So they looked for and found another sealed doorway between two life-sized figures of the King.

Fiona Jacobs: And that's where they found the mummy?

Simon Black: Yes. But this doorway had a hole in it and Carter was worried that tomb robbers had got there first.

Fiona Jacobs: Did Carter get through this sealed doorway immediately?

Simon Black: No. There were so many precious objects in the first chamber that it took seven weeks to clear it. Carter likened it to 'a gigantic game of spillikins'. They had to be so careful not to damage the objects as they removed them.

Fiona Jacobs: So, after seven weeks, Carter was ready to break through into the burial chamber. What did he find?

Simon Black: The first thing he saw, about a yard in front of the hole he had made in the door, was a wall of gold. This turned out to be a huge shrine with three more inside it, you know, like Russian dolls. Carter said that it took 84 days of real manual labour to demolish the wall between the two chambers and dismantle the shrines.

Fiona Jacobs: So when did Carter actually see the now-famous death mask of King Tutankhamen?

Simon Black: In February, 1924. The sarcophagus was huge, 9 feet in length. Carter rigged up a hoist to remove the lid that weighed over a ton and a quarter. When the lid was removed – well, let me tell you in Carter's own words: 'The light shone on the sarcophagus. The lid being suspended in mid air, we rolled back the covering shrouds, one by one, and as the last was removed, a gasp of wonderment escaped our lips, so gorgeous was the sight that met our eyes: a golden effigy of the young boy-king, of most magnificent workmanship filled the whole of the sarcophagus.' Carter was the first person to look on the face of the Pharaoh for over 3,000 years.

Fiona Jacobs: A fascinating story, Professor Black. Thank you.

Talk

30

Understanding the text

1. Who is the interviewer?
2. Who is being interviewed?
3. What is the radio programme called?
4. What is the interview about?
5. How long was the sarcophagus?

Looking at language

6. Explain the meaning of these words as they are used in the interview. Use a dictionary to help you.

a *astounding* **b** *autobiography* **c** *mummy* **d** *demolish*
e *hoist* **f** *shrouds* **g** *effigy* **h** *fascinating*

Exploring the interview

7. Why was Carter sure there was a second chamber?
8. Why did he think tomb robbers may have got there first?
9. Why do you think they needed the hoist to remove the lid?
10. Find an example of:
    a a quote from Carter.
    b reported speech of what Carter said.
11. What do you think Carter meant when he said that removing the objects was like 'a gigantic game of spillikins'?
12. Explain why the shrines are described as being 'like Russian dolls'.
13. Based on Carter's own words at the end of the interview, how do you think everyone felt when the shrouds were removed?
14. Can you think of other 'treasures' that the radio station could make programmes about?

Taking it further RB, Unit 5, Extension

15. Imagine you could interview Howard Carter. What questions would you ask him?

Talk

31

RESOURCE SHEET SUPPORT ANSWERS

A

Fiona Jacobs interviewed **Professor Simon Black** on a radio programme called **'Treasures of the Past'**. He is an expert on **Ancient Egypt**. The tomb was found by **Howard Carter** and he looked on the **Tutankhamen** death mask in **February**, 1924.

B

1. astounding
2. autobiography
3. demolish
4. mummy
5. hoist
6. shrouds
7. effigy
8. fascinating

GOING DEEPER

- Ask each group to read out their questions, and explain why they chose them.
- Ask children what they notice about the way the transcript is set out, and the use of direct and reported speech.

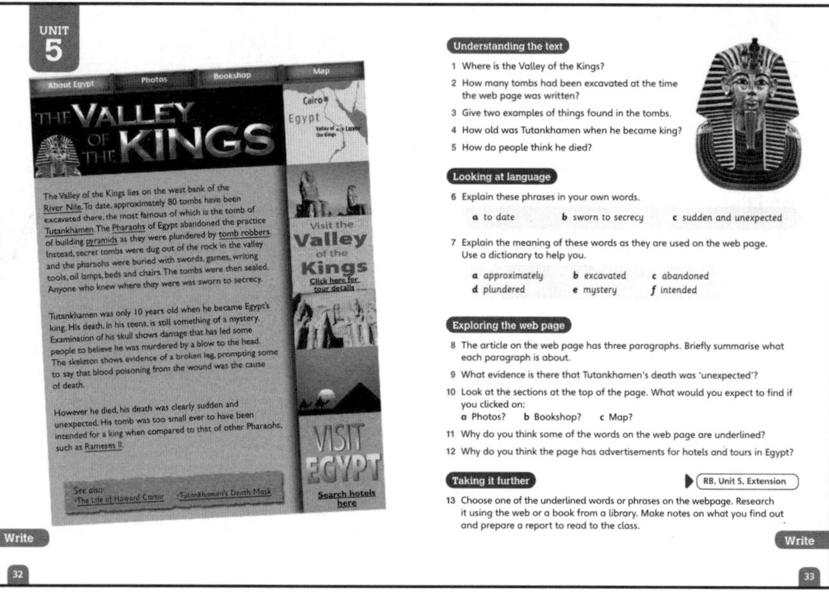

UNIT 5

About Egypt | Photos | Bookshop | Map

THE VALLEY OF THE KINGS

The Valley of the Kings lies on the west bank of the River Nile. To date, approximately 80 tombs have been excavated there, the most famous of which is the tomb of Tutankhamen. The Pharaohs of Egypt abandoned the practice of building pyramids as they were plundered by tomb robbers. Instead, secret tombs were dug out of the rock in the valley and the pharaohs were buried with swords, games, writing tools, oil lamps, beds and chairs. The tombs were then sealed. Anyone who knew where they were was sworn to secrecy.

Tutankhamen was only 10 years old when he became Egypt's king. His death, in his teens, is still something of a mystery. Examination of his skull shows damage that has led some people to believe he was murdered by a blow to the head. The skeleton shows evidence of a broken leg, prompting some to say that blood poisoning from the wound was the cause of death.

However he died, his death was clearly sudden and unexpected. His tomb was too small ever to have been intended for a king when compared to that of other Pharaohs, such as Rameses II.

See also:
-The Life of Howard Carter -Tutankhamen's Death Mask

Cairo
Egypt
Valley of the Kings
Luxor

Visit the Valley of the Kings
Click here for tour details

VISIT EGYPT
Search hotels here

Write

32

Understanding the text

1 Where is the Valley of the Kings?
2 How many tombs had been excavated at the time the web page was written?
3 Give two examples of things found in the tombs.
4 How old was Tutankhamen when he became king?
5 How do people think he died?

Looking at language

6 Explain these phrases in your own words.
a to date *b* sworn to secrecy *c* sudden and unexpected

7 Explain the meaning of these words as they are used on the web page. Use a dictionary to help you.
a approximately *b* excavated *c* abandoned
d plundered *e* mystery *f* intended

Exploring the web page

8 The article on the web page has three paragraphs. Briefly summarise what each paragraph is about.
9 What evidence is there that Tutankhamen's death was 'unexpected'?
10 Look at the sections at the top of the page. What would you expect to find if you clicked on:
a Photos? b Bookshop? c Map?
11 Why do you think some of the words on the web page are underlined?
12 Why do you think the page has advertisements for hotels and tours in Egypt?

Taking it further RB, Unit 5, Extension

13 Choose one of the underlined words or phrases on the webpage. Research it using the web or a book from a library. Make notes on what you find out and prepare a report to read to the class.

Write

33

WRITE

- Discuss what children use the internet for. Do they find it easy to use / complicated to use / useful, etc?
- Explain to children they are going to look at a web page about The Valley of the Kings.
- Read the web page to the class; ask individual children to read it aloud in turn; or read in silence individually.

RESOURCES & ASSESSMENT BOOK

- **Support** (comprehension support): cloze activity, matching paragraphs to content; (vocabulary support): choosing correct verb definitions.
- **Extension:** conducting research.

PUPIL BOOK ANSWERS

1. The west bank of the River Nile.
2. Approximately 80 tombs.
3. Swords / games / writing tools / oil lamps / beds / chairs.
4. 10 years old.
5. Either by a blow to the head or blood poisoning.
6. **a** so far **b** made to promise they would tell no one **c** happening quickly without warning
7. **a** about **b** dug up **c** stopped / gave up **d** robbed **e** with no answer **f** meant
8. Paragraph 1: introduction to the Valley of the Kings / Tutankhamen / pyramids / secret tombs and their contents. Paragraph 2: details of Tutankhamen and possible causes of death. Paragraph 3: Tutankhamen's tomb.
9. The tomb he was buried in was too small for a king.
10. **a** Photos: images connected with the information e.g. Valley of the Kings / the Nile / the tomb of Tutankhamen. **b** Bookshop: books about Egypt / The Nile / Valley of the Kings / Tutankhamen / other related Egyptian subjects. **c** Map: layout of the Valley of the Kings with tombs marked.
11. By clicking on the underlined words you will be taken to other pages and articles related to this topic.
12. People interested in reading this page may be interested in visiting Egypt; money from advertising pays for putting information on the web.
13. Individual answers.

RESOURCE SHEET SUPPORT ANSWERS

A

1. Egypt
2. 80
3. Swords / oil lamps
4. ten
5. head / blood

B

Paragraph 1: Introduction to the Valley of the Kings / Tutankhamen / pyramids / secret tombs **Paragraph 2:** Tutankhamen / possible causes of death **Paragraph 3:** Tutankhamen's tomb

C

1. dug up
2. robbed
3. gave up
4. meant

GOING DEEPER

- Discuss features of recounted text, e.g. chronological sequence / supporting illustration / degree of formality adopted. Children should be given the opportunity to read their reports to the class.

UNIT FOCUS: Telling Stories Through Poetry

Investigating ...

- narrative poetry
- poetry that doesn't 'tell a story' in a traditional way
- features of narratives, including characters, plot and setting

TEACH

- Ask children what they understand by the term 'cautionary tale'.
- Ask children what they understand by the term 'narrative'.
- Investigate what cautionary tales the children know.
- Explain that children are going to read a 'cautionary tale' told in the form of a 'narrative' poem. It is called 'Jim – Who Ran Away From His Nurse, and Was Eaten by a Lion'. Based on the title, what lesson do they think it is teaching?
- Read the poem to the class; ask individual children to read it aloud in turn; or read in silence individually.

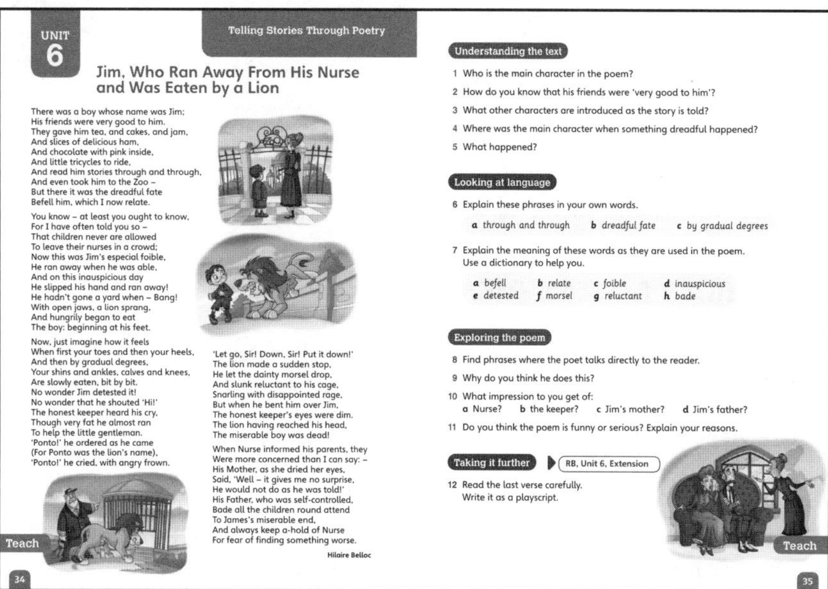

UNIT 6

Telling Stories Through Poetry

Jim, Who Ran Away From His Nurse and Was Eaten by a Lion

There was a boy whose name was Jim;
His friends were very good to him.
They gave him tea, and cakes, and jam,
And slices of delicious ham,
And chocolate with pink inside,
And little tricycles to ride,
And read him stories through and through,
And even took him to the Zoo –
But there it was the dreadful fate
Befell him, which I now relate.

You know – at least you ought to know,
For I have often told you so –
That children never are allowed
To leave their nurses in a crowd;
Now this was Jim's especial foible,
He ran away when he was able,
And on this inauspicious day
He slipped his hand and ran away!
He hadn't gone a yard when – Bang!
With open jaws, a lion sprang,
And hungrily began to eat
The boy: beginning at his feet.

Now, just imagine how it feels
When first your toes and then your heels,
And then by gradual degrees,
Your shins and ankles, calves and knees,
Are slowly eaten, bit by bit.
No wonder Jim detested it!
No wonder that he shouted 'Hi!'
The honest keeper heard his cry,
Though very fat he almost ran
To help the little gentleman.
'Ponto!' he ordered as he came
(For Ponto was the lion's name),
'Ponto!' he cried, with angry frown.
'Let go, Sir! Down, Sir! Put it down!'
The lion made a sudden stop,
He let the dainty morsel drop,
And slunk reluctant to his cage,
Snarling with disappointed rage.
But when he bent him over Jim,
The honest keeper's eyes were dim.
The lion having reached his head,
The miserable boy was dead!

When Nurse informed his parents, they
Were more concerned than I can say: –
His Mother, as she dried her eyes,
Said, 'Well – it gives me no surprise,
He would not do as he was told!'
His Father, who was self-controlled,
Bade all the children round attend
To James's miserable end,
And always keep a-hold of Nurse
For fear of finding something worse.

Hilaire Belloc

Teach

34

Understanding the text

1 Who is the main character in the poem?

2 How do you know that his friends were 'very good to him'?

3 What other characters are introduced as the story is told?

4 Where was the main character when something dreadful happened?

5 What happened?

Looking at language

6 Explain these phrases in your own words.

a *through and through* **b** *dreadful fate* **c** *by gradual degrees*

7 Explain the meaning of these words as they are used in the poem. Use a dictionary to help you.

a *befell* **b** *relate* **c** *foible* **d** *inauspicious*
e *detested* **f** *morsel* **g** *reluctant* **h** *bade*

Exploring the poem

8 Find phrases where the poet talks directly to the reader.

9 Why do you think he does this?

10 What impression to you get of:
a Nurse? **b** the keeper? **c** Jim's mother? **d** Jim's father?

11 Do you think the poem is funny or serious? Explain your reasons.

Taking it further ▶ RB, Unit 6, Extension

12 Read the last verse carefully. Write it as a playscript.

Teach

35

RESOURCES & ASSESSMENT BOOK

- **Support** (comprehension support): narrative sequence; (vocabulary support): adjectives and noun reinforcement.
- **Extension:** writing dialogue and stage directions.

PUPIL BOOK ANSWERS

1. Jim.
2. His friends 'gave him tea and cakes and jam' / 'slices of delicious ham' / 'chocolate with pink inside' / 'little tricycles to ride' / 'read him stories' / 'took him to the zoo'.
3. The Nurse / Ponto the lion / the Keeper / Jim's mother and father.
4. At the zoo.
5. He was eaten by a lion.
6. **a** over and over again **b** something awful that will happen **c** bit by bit
7. **a** happened to him **b** tell **c** weakness / bad habit **d** unlucky **e** hated **f** very small piece **g** not wanting to **h** ordered
8. e.g. 'You know – at least you ought to know, For I have often told you so ...' / 'Now, just imagine how it feels ...'
9. The poem is teaching something and the poet wants to create the impression that he is telling this face-to-face.
10. **a** careless / not very concerned about Jim **b** kind / tries to help / upset when he can't save Jim **c** upset but not as much as you would expect **d** doesn't seem upset at all
11. Individual answers.
12. Individual answers.

RESOURCE SHEET SUPPORT ANSWERS

A

a The lion began to eat Jim. 4 **b** Nurse told Jim's parents what had happened to him. 8 **c** Jim was taken to the zoo. 1 **d** A lion sprang out at him. 3 **e** The keeper ordered the lion to let go. 6 **f** Jim ran away from his nurse. 2 **g** The lion slunk back to his cage. 7 **h** The keeper ran to see what was happening. 5

B

1. little tricycles
2. dreadful fate
3. inauspicious day
4. open jaws
5. honest keeper
6. dainty morsel
7. disappointed rage
8. miserable end

GOING DEEPER

- Ask children if they enjoyed the poem. Why? Why not? Were they right about what the poem is teaching?

TALK

- Explain to children that a narrative poem, as well as having a plot, characters and dialogue, can also capture a short event or moment in time that lives in the memory.
- Ask children if they can think of something they have done that would make a good narrative poem.
- Explain to children that they are going to read a narrative poem called 'The Apple-Raid'. In it, the poet tells the story of a vivid memory from childhood.
- Read the poem to the class; ask individual children to read it aloud in turn; or read in silence individually.

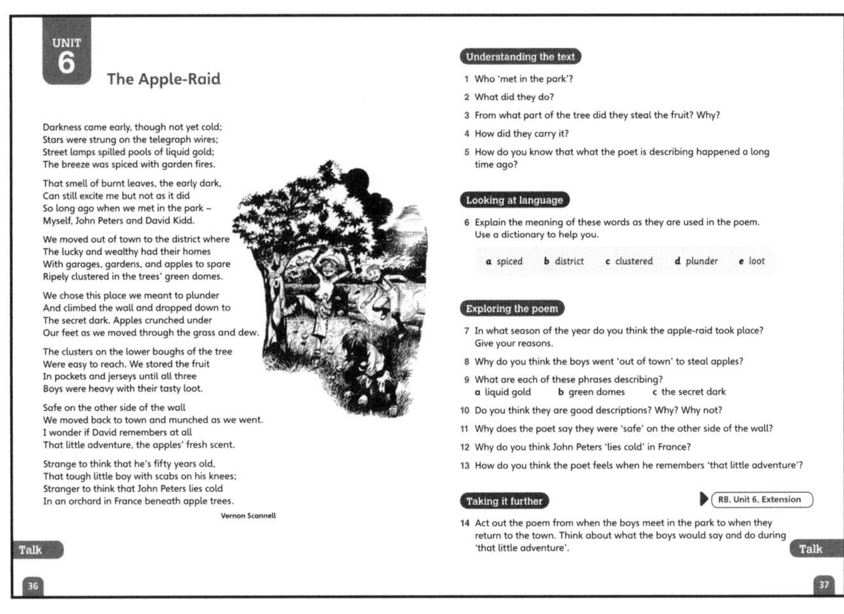

UNIT 6

The Apple-Raid

Darkness came early, though not yet cold;
Stars were strung on the telegraph wires;
Street lamps spilled pools of liquid gold;
The breeze was spiced with garden fires.

That smell of burnt leaves, the early dark,
Can still excite me but not as it did
So long ago when we met in the park –
Myself, John Peters and David Kidd.

We moved out of town to the district where
The lucky and wealthy had their homes
With garages, gardens, and apples to spare
Ripely clustered in the trees' green domes.

We chose this place we meant to plunder
And climbed the wall and dropped down to
The secret dark. Apples crunched under
Our feet as we moved through the grass and dew.

The clusters on the lower boughs of the tree
Were easy to reach. We stored the fruit
In pockets and jerseys until all three
Boys were heavy with their tasty loot.

Safe on the other side of the wall
We moved back to town and munched as we went.
I wonder if David remembers at all
That little adventure, the apples' fresh scent.

Strange to think that he's fifty years old,
That tough little boy with scabs on his knees;
Stranger to think that John Peters lies cold
In an orchard in France beneath apple trees.

Vernon Scannell

Understanding the text

1 Who 'met in the park'?
2 What did they do?
3 From what part of the tree did they steal the fruit? Why?
4 How did they carry it?
5 How do you know that what the poet is describing happened a long time ago?

Looking at language

6 Explain the meaning of these words as they are used in the poem. Use a dictionary to help you.

a spiced **b** district **c** clustered **d** plunder **e** loot

Exploring the poem

7 In what season of the year do you think the apple-raid took place? Give your reasons.
8 Why do you think the boys went 'out of town' to steal apples?
9 What are each of these phrases describing?
a liquid gold **b** green domes **c** the secret dark
10 Do you think they are good descriptions? Why? Why not?
11 Why does the poet say they were 'safe' on the other side of the wall?
12 Why do you think John Peters 'lies cold' in France?
13 How do you think the poet feels when he remembers 'that little adventure'?

Taking it further

RB, Unit 6, Extension

14 Act out the poem from when the boys meet in the park to when they return to the town. Think about what the boys would say and do during 'that little adventure'.

Talk

36 37

RESOURCES & ASSESSMENT BOOK

- **Support** (comprehension support): identifying wrong words in sentences, correcting sentences; (vocabulary support): identifying adjectives, choosing correct definitions.
- **Extension**: writing actions and speech, acting out part of poem.

PUPIL BOOK ANSWERS

1. The poet, John Peters and David Kidd.
2. Left the town and went to a 'smarter' district, chose a garden and stole apples.
3. 'the lower boughs of the tree' as they were 'easy to reach'.
4. 'in pockets and jerseys'.
5. 'strange to think he's [David] fifty years old' / 'John Peters lies cold'.
6. **a** made to smell spicy / tangy **b** area **c** grouped together **d** rob **e** things that have been stolen
7. Autumn –'Darkness came early, though not cold' / 'burnt leaves' / apples on trees.
8. The houses in the town did not have gardens so there were no apple trees.
9. **a** light from the street lamps **b** the leafy branches of the apple trees **c** the garden
10. Individual answers.
11. Once they are out of the garden they were safe from being caught.
12. He went to live in / other reasons for dying in a foreign country i.e. in war.
13. He feels nostalgic / enjoys reliving the adventure / sad to think so many years have passed.
14. Individual answers.

RESOURCE SHEET SUPPORT ANSWERS

A

1. warm / cold
2. garden / park
3. gate / wall
4. higher / lower
5. John / David

B

1 **liquid** gold

2 **green** domes

1 **early / secret** dark

3 **lower** boughs

5 **little** adventure

6 **fresh** scent

7 **tough / little** boy

8 **apple** trees

C

1. tangy
2. area
3. grouped together
4. rob
5. things stolen

GOING DEEPER

- Let each group act out the poem for the class.

WRITE

- Discuss what children do on a Sunday.
- Explain to children that they are going to read a poem called 'Early Last Sunday Morning', in which the poet narrates a trip to the park with his Dad.
- Read the poem to the class; ask individual children to read it aloud in turn; or read in silence individually.

RESOURCES & ASSESSMENT BOOK

- **Support** (comprehension support): multiple choice; (vocabulary support): identifying correct verbs to complete sentences.
- **Extension:** empathising, writing notes.

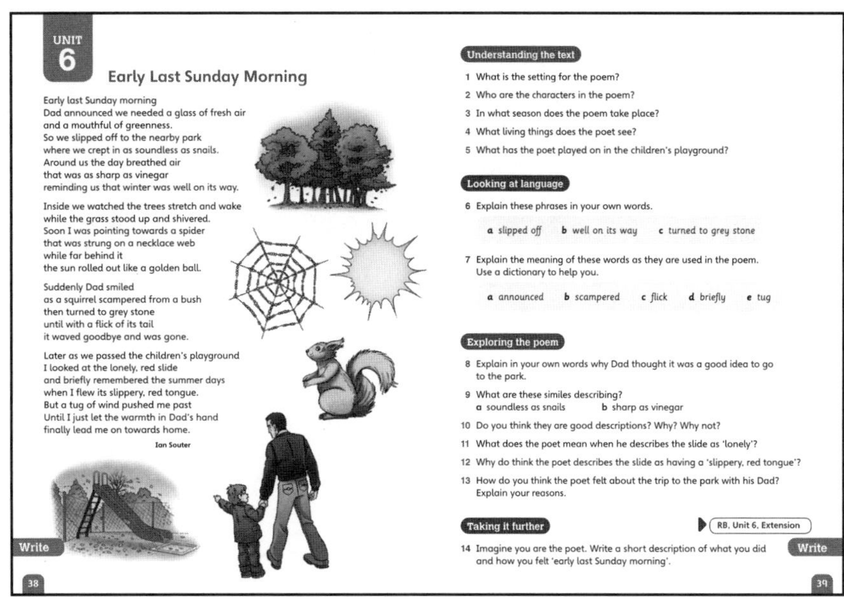

UNIT 6

Early Last Sunday Morning

Early last Sunday morning
Dad announced we needed a glass of fresh air
and a mouthful of greenness.
So we slipped off to the nearby park
where we crept in as soundless as snails.
Around us the day breathed air
that was as sharp as vinegar
reminding us that winter was well on its way.

Inside we watched the trees stretch and wake
while the grass stood up and shivered.
Soon I was pointing towards a spider
that was strung on a necklace web
while far behind it
the sun rolled out like a golden ball.

Suddenly Dad smiled
as a squirrel scampered from a bush
then turned to grey stone
until with a flick of its tail
it waved goodbye and was gone.

Later as we passed the children's playground
I looked at the lonely, red slide
and briefly remembered the summer days
when I flew its slippery, red tongue.
But a tug of wind pushed me past
Until I just let the warmth in Dad's hand
finally lead me on towards home.

Ian Souter

Write

38

Understanding the text

1 What is the setting for the poem?

2 Who are the characters in the poem?

3 In what season does the poem take place?

4 What living things does the poet see?

5 What has the poet played on in the children's playground?

Looking at language

6 Explain these phrases in your own words.

a *slipped off* **b** *well on its way* **c** *turned to grey stone*

7 Explain the meaning of these words as they are used in the poem. Use a dictionary to help you.

a *announced* **b** *scampered* **c** *flick* **d** *briefly* **e** *tug*

Exploring the poem

8 Explain in your own words why Dad thought it was a good idea to go to the park.

9 What are these similes describing?
a soundless as snails b sharp as vinegar

10 Do you think they are good descriptions? Why? Why not?

11 What does the poet mean when he describes the slide as 'lonely'?

12 Why do think the poet describes the slide as having a 'slippery, red tongue'?

13 How do you think the poet felt about the trip to the park with his Dad? Explain your reasons.

Taking it further

RB, Unit 6, Extension

14 Imagine you are the poet. Write a short description of what you did and how you felt 'early last Sunday morning'.

Write

39

PUPIL BOOK ANSWERS

1 The park.

2 The poet / his dad.

3 Late autumn – 'winter was well on its way'.

4 Squirrel / spider.

5 The slide.

6 **a** left with no fuss **b** almost here **c** stopped still / motionless

7 **a** said quite determinedly **b** moved quickly with small steps **c** a quick, sudden movement **d** for a moment **e** strong, short pull

8 They had been indoors for a long time and needed some fresh air.

9 **a** how they crept into the park **b** the coldness of the air

10 Individual answers.

11 No one is playing on it.

12 The shape and colour of the slide is like a tongue.

13 The poet is happy to be with his Dad / sad to see how empty the park is.

14 Individual answers.

RESOURCE SHEET SUPPORT ANSWERS

A

1 the park

2 the narrator and Dad

3 autumn

4 a spider and a squirrel

5 the slide

B

1 Dad **announced** we were going to the park.

2 We **crept** quietly into the park.

3 A squirrel **scampered** by.

4 The squirrel **flicked** his tail.

5 We **passed** the playground.

GOING DEEPER

- Children compare the three narrative poems. In what way are they similar and different? Which one do the children like the best? Why?

UNIT FOCUS: Stories From Around the World

Investigating …

- the genre of 'other cultures'
- straightforward stories from other cultures
- characters who are moved into another culture by force of circumstances

TEACH

- Ask children what they understand by the term 'game reserve'. Where would they expect to find one? What do they know about Africa?
- Explain to children they are going to read an extract from a story called *The White Giraffe*. It is set on a game reserve in Africa. The main character, Martine, used to live in England with her parents. They were killed in a fire and Martine has been sent to live with her grandmother, who runs a game reserve in Africa. The extract begins on Martine's first morning in her new home.
- Read the extract to the class; ask individual children to read it aloud in turn; or read in silence individually.

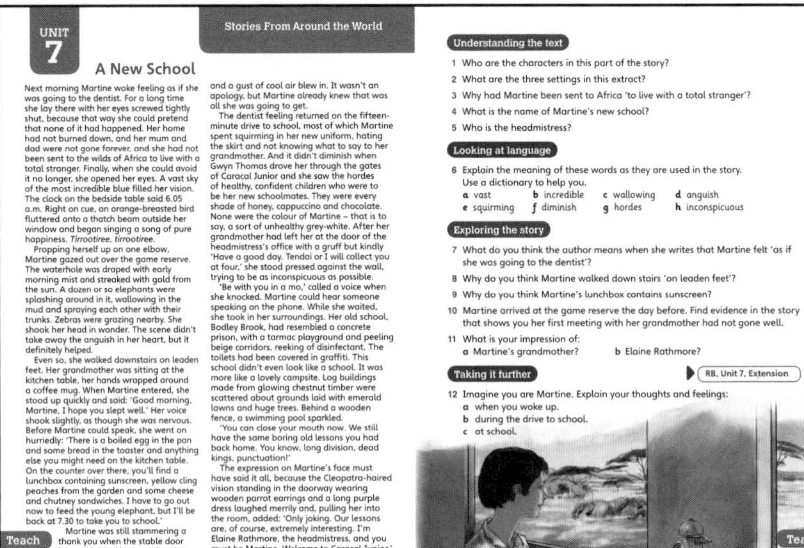

UNIT 7 Stories From Around the World

A New School

Next morning Martine woke feeling as if she was going to the dentist. For a long time she lay there with her eyes screwed tightly shut, because that way she could pretend that none of it had happened. Her home had not burned down, and her mum and dad were not gone forever, and she had not been sent to the wilds of Africa to live with a total stranger. Finally, when she could avoid it no longer, she opened her eyes. A vast sky of the most incredible blue filled her vision. The clock on the bedside table said 6.05 a.m. Right on cue, an orange-breasted bird fluttered onto a thatch beam outside her window and began singing a song of pure happiness. *Tirrootiree, tirrootiree.*

Propping herself up on one elbow, Martine gazed out over the game reserve. The waterhole was draped with early morning mist and streaked with gold from the sun. A dozen or so elephants were splashing around in it, wallowing in the mud and spraying each other with their trunks. Zebras were grazing nearby. She shook her head in wonder. The scene didn't take away the anguish in her heart, but it definitely helped.

Even so, she walked downstairs on leaden feet. Her grandmother was sitting at the kitchen table, her hands wrapped around a coffee mug. When Martine entered, she stood up quickly and said: 'Good morning, Martine, I hope you slept well.' Her voice shook slightly, as though she was nervous. Before Martine could speak, she went on hurriedly: 'There is a boiled egg in the pan and some bread in the toaster and anything else you might need on the kitchen table. On the counter over there, you'll find a lunchbox containing sunscreen, yellow cling peaches from the garden and some cheese and chutney sandwiches. I have to go out now to feed the young elephant, but I'll be back at 7.30 to take you to school.'

Martine was still stammering a thank you when the stable door banged behind her grandmother and a gust of cool air blew in. It wasn't an apology, but Martine already knew that was all she was going to get.

The dentist feeling returned on the fifteen-minute drive to school, most of which Martine spent squirming in her new uniform, hating the skirt and not knowing what to say to her grandmother. And it didn't diminish when Gwyn Thomas drove her through the gates of Caracal Junior and she saw the hordes of healthy, confident children who were to be her new schoolmates. They were every shade of honey, cappuccino and chocolate. None were the colour of Martine – that is to say, a sort of unhealthy grey-white. After her grandmother had left her at the door of the headmistress's office with a gruff but kindly 'Have a good day. Tendai or I will collect you at four,' she stood pressed against the wall, trying to be as inconspicuous as possible.

'Be with you in a mo,' called a voice when she knocked. Martine could hear someone speaking on the phone. While she waited, she took in her surroundings. Her old school, Bodley Brook, had resembled a concrete prison, with a tarmac playground and peeling beige corridors, reeking of disinfectant. The toilets had been covered in graffiti. This school didn't even look like a school. It was more like a lovely campsite. Log buildings made from glowing chestnut timber were scattered about grounds laid with emerald lawns and huge trees. Behind a wooden fence, a swimming pool sparkled.

'You can close your mouth now. We still have the same boring old lessons you had back home. You know, long division, dead kings, punctuation!'

The expression on Martine's face must have said it all, because the Cleopatra-haired vision standing in the doorway wearing wooden parrot earrings and a long purple dress laughed merrily and, pulling her into the room, added: 'Only joking. Our lessons are, of course, extremely interesting. I'm Elaine Rathmore, the headmistress, and you must be Martine. Welcome to Caracal Junior.'

The White Giraffe, Lauren St John

Understanding the text

1 Who are the characters in this part of the story?
2 What are the three settings in this extract?
3 Why had Martine been sent to Africa 'to live with a total stranger'?
4 What is the name of Martine's new school?
5 Who is the headmistress?

Looking at language

6 Explain the meaning of these words as they are used in the story. Use a dictionary to help you.
a vast b incredible c wallowing d anguish
e squirming f diminish g hordes h inconspicuous

Exploring the story

7 What do you think the author means when she writes that Martine felt 'as if she was going to the dentist'?
8 Why do you think Martine walked down stairs 'on leaden feet'?
9 Why do you think Martine's lunchbox contains sunscreen?
10 Martine arrived at the game reserve the day before. Find evidence in the story that shows you her first meeting with her grandmother had not gone well.
11 What is your impression of:
a Martine's grandmother? b Elaine Rathmore?

Taking it further RB, Unit 7, Extension

12 Imagine you are Martine. Explain your thoughts and feelings:
a when you woke up.
b during the drive to school.
c at school.

Teach 40 Teach 41

RESOURCES & ASSESSMENT BOOK

- **Support** (comprehension support): narrative sequence; (vocabulary support): identifying correct words to complete sentences.
- **Extension:** empathising.

PUPIL BOOK ANSWERS

1 Martine / her Grandmother / Elaine Rathmore.

2 The game reserve / the car journey / the school.

3 Her home had 'burned down' and 'her mum and dad were gone forever'.

4 Caracal Junior.

5 Elaine Rathmore.

6 **a** extremely large **b** unbelievable **c** rolling about **d** grief / emotional pain **e** twisting and turning in discomfort **f** grow less **g** a large number **h** unnoticeable

7 She had a sense of dread.

8 She wasn't looking forward to going downstairs so she walked slowly as if her feet were as heavy as lead.

9 The sun in Africa is very strong and she would need protection.

10 She wasn't looking forward to going downstairs / something had happened and she felt she was owed an apology / her grandmother's 'voice shook slightly, as though she was nervous'.

11 **a** Martine's grandmother: uneasy about the situation as Martine – 'Her voice shook slightly as though she was nervous' / practical and thoughtful – she has prepared Martine's lunch and provided sunscreen **b** Elaine Rathmore: has a sense of humour – 'long division, dead kings, punctuation' / very friendly and informal – 'Be with you in a mo'.

12 Individual answers.

RESOURCE SHEET SUPPORT ANSWERS

A

a She saw elephants at the waterhole. 2

b Martine walked downstairs. 3

c At school, Martine met Elaine Rathbone. 6

d Martine woke up at 6.05. 1

e They drove to school. 5

f Grandmother had prepared Martine's breakfast. 4

B

1 Martine was very sad and had **anguish** in her heart.

2 Martine saw loads of children. There were **hordes** of them!

3 The sky was an **incredible** blue colour.

4 Martine didn't want to be noticed. She tried to make herself **inconspicuous**.

5 Martine was **squirming** because her uniform was uncomfortable.

6 The elephants were at the waterhole, **wallowing** in the mud.

7 Martine felt just as scared on the way to school. The fear hadn't **diminished**.

GOING DEEPER

- How would children feel in Martine's situation?
- Discuss what differences there would be if the extract was told from the grandmother's point of view.

TALK

- Ask children to imagine that they had not seen their parents for such a long time that they could not remember them. How would they feel when they met them again? What would they say and do?
- Explain to children that they are going to read the beginning of a story called *Jeffie Lemmington and me*. (Jeffie Lemmington does not appear in this part of the story.) The narrator remembers when he was seven years old and saw snow for the first time.
- Read the extract to the class; ask individual children to read it aloud in turn; or read in silence individually.

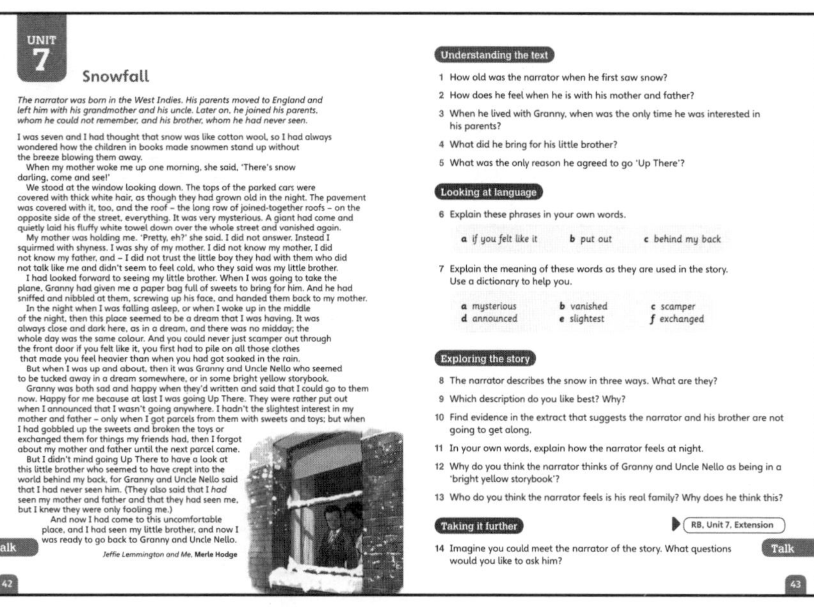

UNIT 7

Snowfall

The narrator was born in the West Indies. His parents moved to England and left him with his grandmother and his uncle. Later on, he joined his parents, whom he could not remember, and his brother, whom he had never seen.

I was seven and I had thought that snow was like cotton wool, so I had always wondered how the children in books made snowmen stand up without the breeze blowing them away.

When my mother woke me up one morning, she said, 'There's snow darling, come and see!'

We stood at the window looking down. The tops of the parked cars were covered with thick white hair, as though they had grown old in the night. The pavement was covered with it, too, and the roof – the long row of joined-together roofs – on the opposite side of the street, everything. It was very mysterious. A giant had come and quietly laid his fluffy white towel down over the whole street and vanished again.

My mother was holding me. 'Pretty, eh?' she said. I did not answer. Instead I squirmed with shyness. I was shy of my mother. I did not know my mother, I did not know my father, and – I did not trust the little boy they had with them who did not talk like me and didn't seem to feel cold, who they said was my little brother.

I had looked forward to seeing my little brother. When I was going to take the plane, Granny had given me a paper bag full of sweets to bring for him. And he had sniffed and nibbled at them, screwing up his face, and handed them back to my mother.

In the night when I was falling asleep, or when I woke up in the middle of the night, then this place seemed to be a dream that I was having. It was always close and dark here, as in a dream, and there was no midday; the whole day was the same colour. And you could never just scamper out through the front door if you felt like it, you first had to pile on all those clothes that made you feel heavier than when you had got soaked in the rain.

But when I was up and about, then it was Granny and Uncle Nello who seemed to be tucked away in a dream somewhere, or in some bright yellow storybook.

Granny was both sad and happy when they'd written and said that I could go to them now. Happy for me because at last I was going Up There. They were rather put out when I announced that I wasn't going anywhere. I hadn't the slightest interest in my mother and father – only when I got parcels from them with sweets and toys; but when I had gobbled up the sweets and broken the toys or exchanged them for things my friends had, then I forgot about my mother and father until the next parcel came.

But I didn't mind going Up There to have a look at this little brother who seemed to have crept into the world behind my back, for Granny and Uncle Nello said that I had never seen him. (They also said that I *had* seen my mother and father and that they had seen me, but I knew they were only fooling me.)

And now I had come to this uncomfortable place, and I had seen my little brother, and now I was ready to go back to Granny and Uncle Nello.

Jeffie Lemmington and Me, **Merle Hodge**

Talk

42

Understanding the text

1 How old was the narrator when he first saw snow?

2 How does he feel when he is with his mother and father?

3 When he lived with Granny, when was the only time he was interested in his parents?

4 What did he bring for his little brother?

5 What was the only reason he agreed to go 'Up There'?

Looking at language

6 Explain these phrases in your own words.

a *if you felt like it* **b** *put out* **c** *behind my back*

7 Explain the meaning of these words as they are used in the story. Use a dictionary to help you.

a *mysterious* **b** *vanished* **c** *scamper*
d *announced* **e** *slightest* **f** *exchanged*

Exploring the story

8 The narrator describes the snow in three ways. What are they?

9 Which description do you like best? Why?

10 Find evidence in the extract that suggests the narrator and his brother are not going to get along.

11 In your own words, explain how the narrator feels at night.

12 Why do you think the narrator thinks of Granny and Uncle Nello as being in a 'bright yellow storybook'?

13 Who do you think the narrator feels is his real family? Why does he think this?

Taking it further

RB, Unit 7, Extension

14 Imagine you could meet the narrator of the story. What questions would you like to ask him?

Talk

43

RESOURCES & ASSESSMENT BOOK

- **Support** (comprehension support): matching sentence beginnings and endings; (vocabulary support): choosing correct answers for clues.
- **Extension:** writing questions.

PUPIL BOOK ANSWERS

1. Seven years old.
2. Shy.
3. When he 'got parcels from them with sweets and toys'.
4. A bag of sweets.
5. To have a look at his little brother.
6. **a** if you wanted to do it **b** annoyed / not happy **c** without me knowing / in secret
7. **a** strange **b** disappeared **c** run about **d** stated strongly **e** least **f** swapped
8. Cotton wool, thick white hair, fluffy white towel.
9. Individual answers.
10. 'I did not trust the little boy they had with them who did not talk like me' / When the narrator gives him sweets 'he had sniffed and nibbled at them, screwing up his face, and handed them back to my mother'.
11. He was homesick – 'this place seemed like a dream'.
12. The narrator remembers the world he has come from as colourful and full of sunshine.
13. Granny and Uncle Nello – 'They also said I *had* seen my mother and father and that they had seen me, but I knew they were only fooling me' / 'now I was ready to go back to Granny and Uncle Nello'.
14. Individual answers.

RESOURCE SHEET SUPPORT ANSWERS

A

1. The narrator thought snow was like cotton wool.
2. Mother said that the snow was pretty.
3. He gave his brother a bag of sweets.
4. The narrator had to pile on clothes to go outside.
5. The narrator had no interest in his mother and father.
6. His mother and father sent him parcels.
7. He was ready to go back to Granny and Uncle Nello.

B

1. If something is strange, it is **mysterious**.
2. If you are not interested, you haven't the **slightest** interest.
3. If you swapped something, you have **exchanged** it.
4. To run about, is to **scamper**.
5. If something has disappeared, it has **vanished**.

GOING DEEPER

- Use groups' ideas for the 'Taking it further' activity as a basis for a class discussion.
- Discuss how the story would be different if told from the little brother's point of view.

WRITE

- Ask children what they know about Australia. Have any of them ever visited Australia? What kind of landscape would they find over most of the country?
- Explain to children they are going to read the beginning of a story called *Walkabout*, which is set in the Australian desert.
- Read the extract to the class; ask individual children to read it aloud in turn; or read in silence individually.

RESOURCES & ASSESSMENT BOOK

- **Support** (comprehension support): identifying True / False statements, correcting false statements; (vocabulary support): identifying adjectives.
- **Extension:** empathising, writing notes.

PUPIL BOOK ANSWERS

1. Peter / Mary.
2. The Australian desert.
3. Mary.
4. On his thigh.
5. Mopoke / dingo / flying foxes.
6. **a** disappear altogether **b** leave gradually **c** a long way off in distance and time
7. **a** a river valley **b** huge size **c** a feeling of being so worried you cannot relax **d** decreasing / growing smaller **e** disobedient **f** wander slowly
8. **a** Mary: caring and feels responsible for her brother – 'she felt for his hand, and held it, very tightly' / 'All right, Peter, I'm here' / 'Aren't you comfy?' / She tied the handkerchief round Peter's wound. **b** Peter: dependent on his sister and is afraid – 'He was trembling' / 'the trembling die gradually away' / 'When a boy is only eight a big sister of thirteen can be wonderfully comforting'
9. She wanted Peter to make it last as long as possible because it was their only food.
10. She was going to eat it later / save it for Peter.

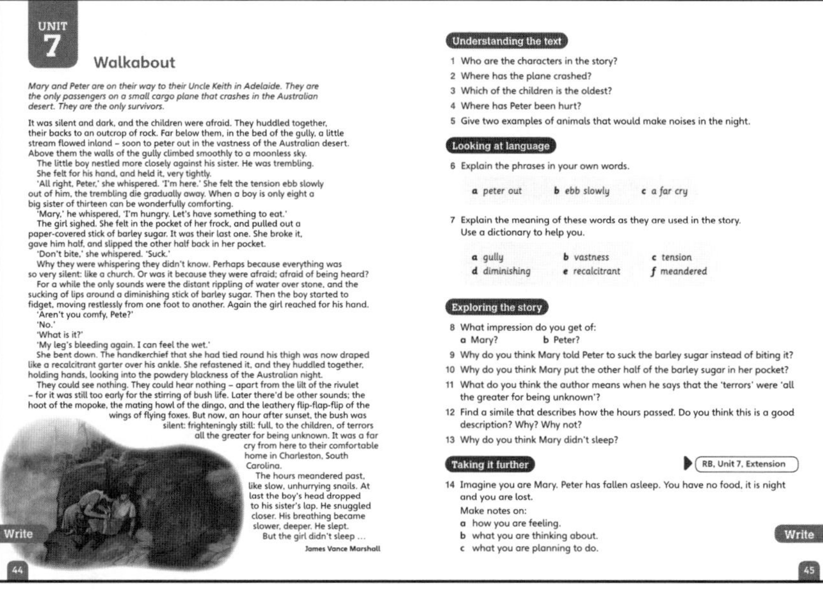

UNIT 7

Walkabout

Mary and Peter are on their way to their Uncle Keith in Adelaide. They are the only passengers on a small cargo plane that crashes in the Australian desert. They are the only survivors.

It was silent and dark, and the children were afraid. They huddled together, their backs to an outcrop of rock. Far below them, in the bed of the gully, a little stream flowed inland – soon to peter out in the vastness of the Australian desert. Above them the walls of the gully climbed smoothly to a moonless sky.

The little boy nestled more closely against his sister. He was trembling. She felt for his hand, and held it, very tightly.

'All right, Peter,' she whispered. 'I'm here.' She felt the tension ebb slowly out of him, the trembling die gradually away. When a boy is only eight a big sister of thirteen can be wonderfully comforting.

'Mary,' he whispered, 'I'm hungry. Let's have something to eat.'

The girl sighed. She felt in the pocket of her frock, and pulled out a paper-covered stick of barley sugar. It was their last one. She broke it, gave him half, and slipped the other half back in her pocket.

'Don't bite,' she whispered. 'Suck.'

Why they were whispering they didn't know. Perhaps because everything was so very silent: like a church. Or was it because they were afraid; afraid of being heard?

For a while the only sounds were the distant rippling of water over stone, and the sucking of lips around a diminishing stick of barley sugar. Then the boy started to fidget, moving restlessly from one foot to another. Again the girl reached for his hand.

'Aren't you comfy, Pete?'

'No.'

'What is it?'

'My leg's bleeding again. I can feel the wet.'

She bent down. The handkerchief that she had tied round his thigh was now draped like a recalcitrant garter over his ankle. She refastened it, and they huddled together, holding hands, looking into the powdery blackness of the Australian night.

They could see nothing. They could hear nothing – apart from the lilt of the rivulet – for it was still too early for the stirring of bush life. Later there'd be other sounds; the hoot of the mopoke, the mating howl of the dingo, and the leathery flip-flap-flip of the wings of flying foxes. But now, an hour after sunset, the bush was silent: frighteningly still: full, to the children, of terrors all the greater for being unknown. It was a far cry from here to their comfortable home in Charleston, South Carolina.

The hours meandered past, like slow, unhurrying snails. At last the boy's head dropped to his sister's lap. He snuggled closer. His breathing became slower, deeper. He slept.

But the girl didn't sleep …

James Vance Marshall

Write

44

Understanding the text

1 Who are the characters in the story?
2 Where has the plane crashed?
3 Which of the children is the oldest?
4 Where has Peter been hurt?
5 Give two examples of animals that would make noises in the night.

Looking at language

6 Explain the phrases in your own words.

a *peter out* **b** *ebb slowly* **c** *a far cry*

7 Explain the meaning of these words as they are used in the story. Use a dictionary to help you.

a *gully* **b** *vastness* **c** *tension*
d *diminishing* **e** *recalcitrant* **f** *meandered*

Exploring the story

8 What impression do you get of:
a Mary? b Peter?
9 Why do you think Mary told Peter to suck the barley sugar instead of biting it?
10 Why do you think Mary put the other half of the barley sugar in her pocket?
11 What do you think the author means when he says that the 'terrors' were 'all the greater for being unknown'?
12 Find a simile that describes how the hours passed. Do you think this is a good description? Why? Why not?
13 Why do you think Mary didn't sleep?

Taking it further RB, Unit 7, Extension

14 Imagine you are Mary. Peter has fallen asleep. You have no food, it is night and you are lost.
Make notes on:
a how you are feeling.
b what you are thinking about.
c what you are planning to do.

Write

45

11. If you don't know exactly what is frightening you, your imagination can make it far worse than it actually is.
12. 'like snow, unhurrying snails' – individual answers.
13. She stayed awake to watch over Peter.
14. Individual answers.

RESOURCE SHEET SUPPORT ANSWERS

A

1. FALSE
2. TRUE
3. FALSE
4. TRUE
5. TRUE
6. FALSE

B

1. The plane crashed in the desert.
2. Peter had been injured.
3. Peter fell asleep.

C

1. little stream
2. paper-covered stick of barley sugar
3. distant rippling of water
4. comfortable home

GOING DEEPER

- Use children's answers to the 'Taking it further' activity as a basis for a class discussion.
- Compare the situations in which the children find themselves in the three extracts. What are the similarities and differences?

UNIT FOCUS: Persuasive Language

Investigating …

- three texts linked by the theme of healthy living
- a newspaper article that appears convincing but, on closer inspection, has little foundation
- a letter commenting on the article and highlighting its shortcomings
- a more persuasive piece with expert sources and statistics

TEACH

- Discuss 'healthy eating' with children. What do they think of as healthy / unhealthy foods?
- Ask children why we should think carefully about what we eat.
- Draw children's attention to the fact that every day, in newspapers, magazines and on TV, there are articles on the latest ways to stay healthy and the best foods to eat. But which ones should we believe?
- Explain to children that they are going to read a newspaper article about healthy eating.
- Read the article to the class; ask individual children to read it aloud in turn; or read in silence individually.

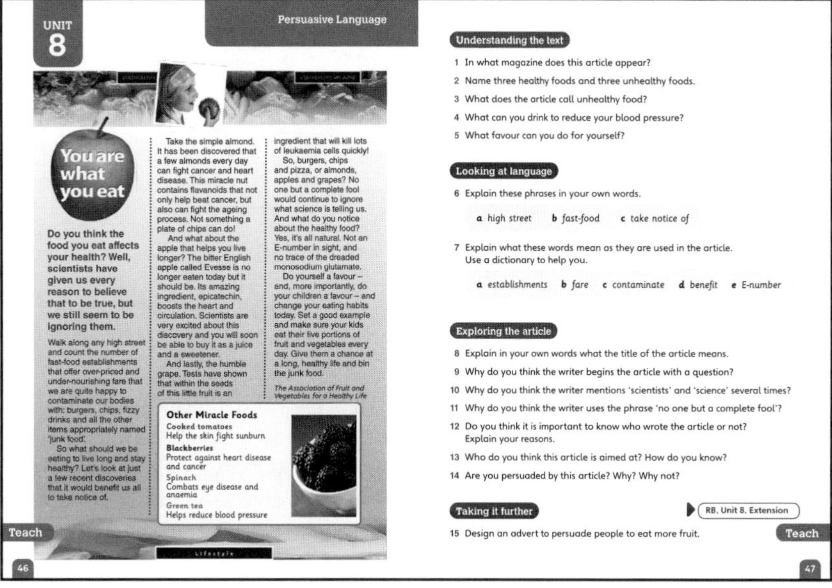

UNIT 8

Persuasive Language

You are what you eat

Do you think the food you eat affects your health? Well, scientists have given us every reason to believe that to be true, but we still seem to be ignoring them.

Walk along any high street and count the number of fast-food establishments that offer over-priced and under-nourishing fare that we are quite happy to contaminate our bodies with: burgers, chips, fizzy drinks and all the other items appropriately named 'junk food'.

So what should we be eating to live long and stay healthy? Let's look at just a few recent discoveries that it would benefit us all to take notice of.

Take the simple almond. It has been discovered that a few almonds every day can fight cancer and heart disease. This miracle nut contains flavanoids that not only help beat cancer, but also can fight the ageing process. Not something a plate of chips can do!

And what about the apple that helps you live longer? The bitter English apple called Evesse is no longer eaten today but it should be. Its amazing ingredient, epicatechin, boosts the heart and circulation. Scientists are very excited about this discovery and you will soon be able to buy it as a juice and a sweetener.

And lastly, the humble grape. Tests have shown that within the seeds of this little fruit is an ingredient that will kill lots of leukaemia cells quickly!

So, burgers, chips and pizza, or almonds, apples and grapes? No one but a complete fool would continue to ignore what science is telling us. And what do you notice about the healthy food? Yes, it's all natural. Not an E-number in sight, and no trace of the dreaded monosodium glutamate.

Do yourself a favour – and, more importantly, do your children a favour – and change your eating habits today. Set a good example and make sure your kids eat their five portions of fruit and vegetables every day. Give them a chance at a long, healthy life and bin the junk food.

The Association of Fruit and Vegetables for a Healthy Life

Other Miracle Foods

Cooked tomatoes
Help the skin fight sunburn

Blackberries
Protect against heart disease and cancer

Spinach
Combats eye disease and anaemia

Green tea
Helps reduce blood pressure

Lifestyle

Teach

46

Understanding the text

1 In what magazine does this article appear?
2 Name three healthy foods and three unhealthy foods.
3 What does the article call unhealthy food?
4 What can you drink to reduce your blood pressure?
5 What favour can you do for yourself?

Looking at language

6 Explain these phrases in your own words.

a high street *b* fast-food *c* take notice of

7 Explain what these words mean as they are used in the article. Use a dictionary to help you.

a establishments *b* fare *c* contaminate *d* benefit *e* E-number

Exploring the article

8 Explain in your own words what the title of the article means.
9 Why do you think the writer begins the article with a question?
10 Why do you think the writer mentions 'scientists' and 'science' several times?
11 Why do you think the writer uses the phrase 'no one but a complete fool'?
12 Do you think it is important to know who wrote the article or not? Explain your reasons.
13 Who do you think this article is aimed at? How do you know?
14 Are you persuaded by this article? Why? Why not?

Taking it further

RB, Unit 8, Extension

15 Design an advert to persuade people to eat more fruit.

Teach

47

RESOURCES & ASSESSMENT BOOK

- **Support** (comprehension support): matching sentence beginnings and endings; (vocabulary support): sorting jumbled words, choosing correct definitions.
- **Extension:** planning an advert.

PUPIL BOOK ANSWERS

1 *Stayhealthy* magazine.

2 Healthy foods – almonds / grapes / apples / tomatoes / blackberries / spinach / green tea / fruit / vegetables; unhealthy foods – burger / chips / fizzy drink / pizza.

3 Junk food.

4 Green tea.

5 'change your eating habits today'.

6 **a** main street in a town or city **b** food made and served very quickly that you can take away with you **c** listen to

7 **a** businesses **b** food **c** poison / pollutes **d** advantage **e** a number that represents a chemical added to food

8 The food we eat affects how healthy we are.

9 The writer is drawing in the reader who will need to read on to find the answer to the question.

10 To make the article appear serious, as if it is based on scientific fact.

11 It is a strong phrase that 'persuades' the reader to agree with the article / no one wants to think of themself as a 'complete idiot'.

12 Individual answers.

13 That the article is aimed at parents – 'Do yourself a favour – and more importantly, do your children a favour'.

14 Individual answers.

15 Individual answers.

RESOURCE SHEET SUPPORT ANSWERS

A

1 *Stayhealthy* is the name of the magazine.

2 Blackberries are a healthy food.

3 Chips are an unhealthy food.

4 Unhealthy food is called junk food.

5 Green tea can reduce blood pressure.

B

Healthy food	Unhealthy food
1 almond	**1** chips
2 apple	**2** pizza
3 grape	**3** burger

C

1 Fast food businesses are **establishments**.

2 If you eat unhealthy food, you are eating unhealthy **fare**.

3 Unhealthy food **contaminates** your body.

4 Advantages of healthy food are its **benefits**.

5 Chemicals added to food are shown as **E-numbers**.

GOING DEEPER

- Children may have found the article persuasive, but discuss what would have made it more persuasive. You will have to 'lead' them to understand that there is not much foundation to the article. It is vague about the 'tests' done by the 'scientists'; there is no statistical evidence; its persuasiveness comes from its use of language rather than rigorous research.

TALK

- Discuss why children think people write to newspapers and magazines. What do they write about?
- Ask children to recap on the article 'You Are What You Eat'.
- Read the letter to the class; ask individual children to read it aloud in turn; or read in silence individually.

RESOURCES & ASSESSMENT BOOK

- **Support** (comprehension support): identifying True / False statements, correcting false statements; (vocabulary support): matching words and definitions.
- **Extension:** making notes, planning a letter.

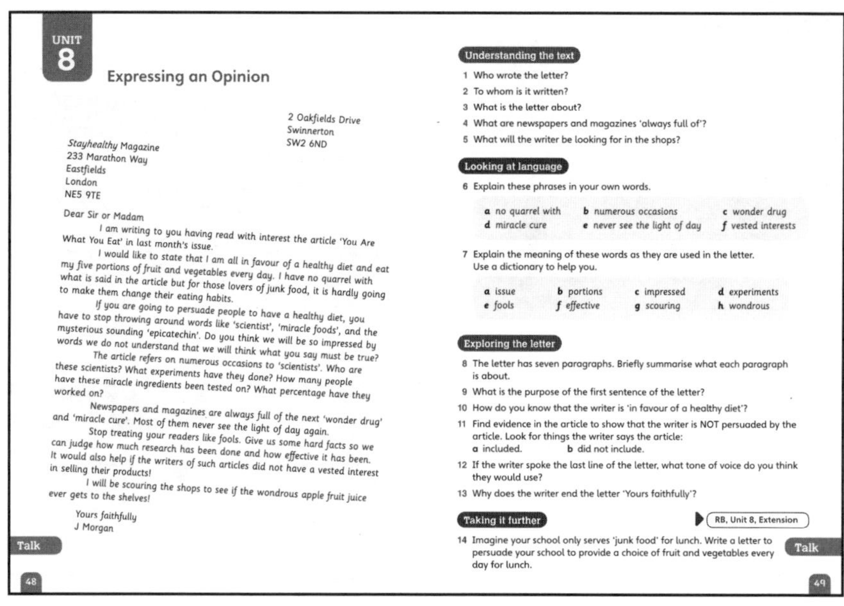

UNIT 8

Expressing an Opinion

2 Oakfields Drive
Swinnerton
SW2 6ND

Stayhealthy Magazine
233 Marathon Way
Eastfields
London
NE5 9TE

Dear Sir or Madam

I am writing to you having read with interest the article 'You Are What You Eat' in last month's issue.

I would like to state that I am all in favour of a healthy diet and eat my five portions of fruit and vegetables every day. I have no quarrel with what is said in the article but for those lovers of junk food, it is hardly going to make them change their eating habits.

If you are going to persuade people to have a healthy diet, you have to stop throwing around words like 'scientist', 'miracle foods', and the mysterious sounding 'epicatechin'. Do you think we will be so impressed by words we do not understand that we will think what you say must be true?

The article refers on numerous occasions to 'scientists'. Who are these scientists? What experiments have they done? How many people have these miracle ingredients been tested on? What percentage have they worked on?

Newspapers and magazines are always full of the next 'wonder drug' and 'miracle cure'. Most of them never see the light of day again.

Stop treating your readers like fools. Give us some hard facts so we can judge how much research has been done and how effective it has been. It would also help if the writers of such articles did not have a vested interest in selling their products!

I will be scouring the shops to see if the wondrous apple fruit juice ever gets to the shelves!

Yours faithfully
J Morgan

Talk

48

Understanding the text

1 Who wrote the letter?
2 To whom is it written?
3 What is the letter about?
4 What are newspapers and magazines 'always full of'?
5 What will the writer be looking for in the shops?

Looking at language

6 Explain these phrases in your own words.

a no quarrel with **b** numerous occasions **c** wonder drug **d** miracle cure **e** never see the light of day **f** vested interests

7 Explain the meaning of these words as they are used in the letter. Use a dictionary to help you.

a issue **b** portions **c** impressed **d** experiments **e** fools **f** effective **g** scouring **h** wondrous

Exploring the letter

8 The letter has seven paragraphs. Briefly summarise what each paragraph is about.
9 What is the purpose of the first sentence of the letter?
10 How do you know that the writer is 'in favour of a healthy diet'?
11 Find evidence in the article to show that the writer is NOT persuaded by the article. Look for things the writer says the article:
a included. b did not include.
12 If the writer spoke the last line of the letter, what tone of voice do you think they would use?
13 Why does the writer end the letter 'Yours faithfully'?

Taking it further RB, Unit 8, Extension

14 Imagine your school only serves 'junk food' for lunch. Write a letter to persuade your school to provide a choice of fruit and vegetables every day for lunch.

Talk

49

PUPIL BOOK ANSWERS

1. J Morgan.
2. *Stayhealthy* magazine.
3. The article 'You Are What You Eat'.
4. The next 'wonder drug' and 'miracle cure'.
5. 'wondrous apple fruit juice'.
6. **a** do not disagree with **b** many times **c** a medicine that can do marvellous things **d** something unexpected that can cure an illness **e** never happens / never seen **f** something happening that will be advantageous to you
7. **a** magazine **b** amounts **c** admire / influenced **d** scientific tests **e** silly people **f** how well it works **g** searching thoroughly **h** amazing
8. Paragraph 1: reason for writing Paragraph 2: writer's views in general Paragraph 3: what is wrong with the language of the article Paragraph 4: questions about scientists Paragraph 5: wonder drugs and miracle cures Paragraph 6: how to make the article more persuasive Paragraph 7: conclusion showing the writer is not convinced.
9. It is designed to ensure the reader knows immediately what is being written about.
10. 'I am all in favour of a healthy diet and I eat my five portions of fruit and vegetables every day'.
11. **a** Included: words like 'scientist', 'miracle foods' and 'epicatechin' / references to 'scientists'.

    b Not included: who the scientists are / what experiments the scientists have done / how many people the ingredients have been tested on / the percentage they have worked on / hard facts.
12. The tone would be mocking / sarcastic / disbelieving.
13. It is the correct ending of a letter where the writer does not know the person he / she is writing to.
14. Individual answers.

RESOURCE SHEET SUPPORT ANSWERS

A

1. TRUE
2. FALSE
3. TRUE
4. FALSE
5. TRUE
6. FALSE

B

1. He wrote to *Stayhealthy* magazine.
2. The writer is in favour of a healthy diet.
3. The writer will be 'scouring the shops' for the juice.

C

1. issue – magazine
2. portions – amounts
3. experiment – scientific test
4. effective – works well
5. scouring – searching thoroughly

GOING DEEPER

- Read and discuss the letters for the 'Taking it further' activity. Choose the best one by a class vote. Ask individuals who voted for the winning letter to give their reasons.

WRITE

- Discuss what children know about sunbeds. Why do people use them?
- Ask children if they think they are a good idea? Why? Why not?
- Discuss the terms 'dermatology' / 'dermatological'.
- Explain to children they are going to read a newspaper article with the headline 'Outlaw sunbeds plea as cases of skin cancer soar'.
- Read the article to the class; ask individual children to read it aloud in turn; or read in silence individually.

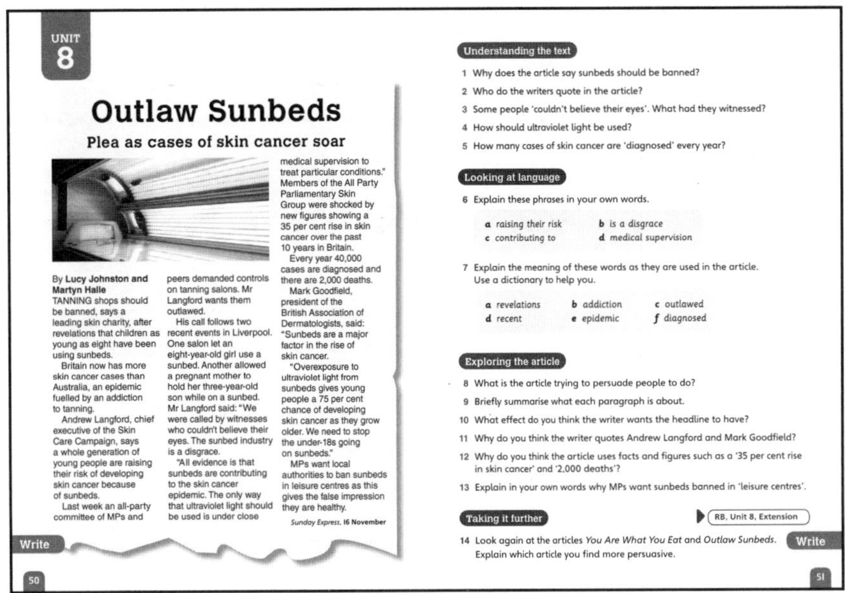

UNIT 8

Outlaw Sunbeds

Plea as cases of skin cancer soar

By **Lucy Johnston and Martyn Halle**

TANNING shops should be banned, says a leading skin charity, after revelations that children as young as eight have been using sunbeds.

Britain now has more skin cancer cases than Australia, an epidemic fuelled by an addiction to tanning.

Andrew Langford, chief executive of the Skin Care Campaign, says a whole generation of young people are raising their risk of developing skin cancer because of sunbeds.

Last week an all-party committee of MPs and peers demanded controls on tanning salons. Mr Langford wants them outlawed.

His call follows two recent events in Liverpool. One salon let an eight-year-old girl use a sunbed. Another allowed a pregnant mother to hold her three-year-old son while on a sunbed. Mr Langford said: "We were called by witnesses who couldn't believe their eyes. The sunbed industry is a disgrace.

"All evidence is that sunbeds are contributing to the skin cancer epidemic. The only way that ultraviolet light should be used is under close medical supervision to treat particular conditions."

Members of the All Party Parliamentary Skin Group were shocked by new figures showing a 35 per cent rise in skin cancer over the past 10 years in Britain.

Every year 40,000 cases are diagnosed and there are 2,000 deaths.

Mark Goodfield, president of the British Association of Dermatologists, said: "Sunbeds are a major factor in the rise of skin cancer.

"Overexposure to ultraviolet light from sunbeds gives young people a 75 per cent chance of developing skin cancer as they grow older. We need to stop the under-18s going on sunbeds."

MPs want local authorities to ban sunbeds in leisure centres as this gives the false impression they are healthy.

Sunday Express, 16 November

Write

50

Understanding the text

1 Why does the article say sunbeds should be banned?
2 Who do the writers quote in the article?
3 Some people 'couldn't believe their eyes'. What had they witnessed?
4 How should ultraviolet light be used?
5 How many cases of skin cancer are 'diagnosed' every year?

Looking at language

6 Explain these phrases in your own words.

a raising their risk *b* is a disgrace
c contributing to *d* medical supervision

7 Explain the meaning of these words as they are used in the article. Use a dictionary to help you.

a revelations *b* addiction *c* outlawed
d recent *e* epidemic *f* diagnosed

Exploring the article

8 What is the article trying to persuade people to do?
9 Briefly summarise what each paragraph is about.
10 What effect do you think the writer wants the headline to have?
11 Why do you think the writer quotes Andrew Langford and Mark Goodfield?
12 Why do you think the article uses facts and figures such as a '35 per cent rise in skin cancer' and '2,000 deaths'?
13 Explain in your own words why MPs want sunbeds banned in 'leisure centres'.

Taking it further

RB, Unit 8, Extension

14 Look again at the articles *You Are What You Eat* and *Outlaw Sunbeds*. Explain which article you find more persuasive.

Write

51

RESOURCES & ASSESSMENT BOOK

- **Support** (comprehension support): cloze activity on proper nouns; (vocabulary support): choosing correct definitions.
- **Extension:** identifying persuasive writing.

PUPIL BOOK ANSWERS

1. They cause skin cancer.
2. Andrew Langford and Mark Goodfield.
3. A pregnant mother holding a three year old child while on a sunbed.
4. 'under close medical supervision to treat particular conditions'.
5. 40,000.
6. **a** making it more likely **b** very bad **c** adding to **d** when a doctor or nurse is present
7. **a** surprising pieces of information **b** a strong need to have / do something **c** made illegal **d** happened in the near past **e** quickly spreading problem **f** discovered
8. Not to use sunbeds.
9. Paragraph 1: main reason why tanning shops should be banned Paragraph 2: skin cancer cases in Britain Paragraph 3: risk to young people Paragraph 4: MPs' views Paragraph 5: events in Liverpool Paragraph 6: how ultraviolet light should be used, rise in skin cancer Paragraph 7: number of skin cancer cases every year Paragraph 8: sunbeds and skin cancer Paragraph 9: stop under 18s going on sunbeds Paragraph 10: banning sunbeds in leisure centres.
10. The headline is attention-grabbing to draw the reader into reading the article / 'Skin cancer' and 'soar' are shocking.
11. They are experts and their opinion is based on evidence and should be listened to.
12. They add authority to the article and show how serious the problem is.
13. Individual answers.
14. Individual answers.

RESOURCE SHEET SUPPORT ANSWERS

A

1. One of the writers of the article is **Lucy Johnson** OR **Martyn Halle**.
2. The other writer is **Martyn Halle** OR **Lucy Johnson**.
3. **Andrew Langford** works for the Skin Care Campaign.
4. **Britain** has more cases of skin cancer than **Australia**.
5. **Mark Goodfield** works for the Association of Dermatologists.
6. An eight-year-old girl used a sunbed in **Liverpool**.

B

1. increase the danger
2. very bad
3. add to something
4. with a doctor or a nurse

GOING DEEPER

- Use children's answers to the 'Taking it further' activity as a basis for class discussion.
- Recap on what children have learned about persuasive writing.

UNIT FOCUS: Reading Older Novels

Investigating ...

- older literature dating from 1906, 1868 and 1911 respectively
- extracts concerning children in difficult situations and show explicitly, or implicitly, their relationships with adults

TEACH

- Discuss how children think the relationship between children and their parents has changed over the last 100 years. Are children more / less obedient? Are parents more / less strict?
- Explain to children they are going to read an extract from *The Railway Children*, a story that was written in 1906. The three children, Roberta, Peter and Phyllis, live happily until one day when their father is given bad news by a couple of men and leaves in a cab. Their mother doesn't explain why to the children.
- Read the extract to the class; ask individual children to read it aloud in turn; or read in silence individually.

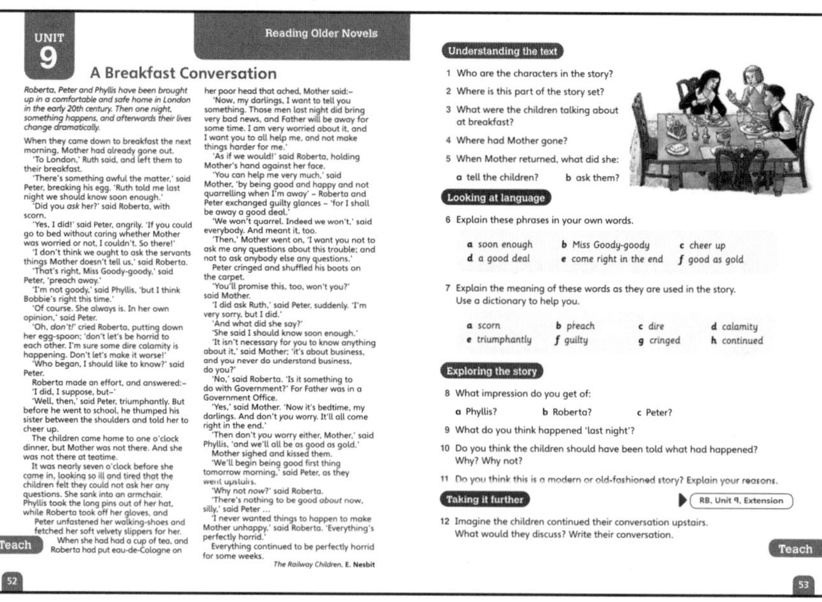

UNIT 9

Reading Older Novels

A Breakfast Conversation

Roberta, Peter and Phyllis have been brought up in a comfortable and safe home in London in the early 20th century. Then one night, something happens, and afterwards their lives change dramatically.

When they came down to breakfast the next morning, Mother had already gone out.

'To London,' Ruth said, and left them to their breakfast.

'There's something awful the matter,' said Peter, breaking his egg. 'Ruth told me last night we should know soon enough.'

'Did you *ask* her?' said Roberta, with scorn.

'Yes, I did!' said Peter, angrily. 'If you could go to bed without caring whether Mother was worried or not, I couldn't. So there!'

'I don't think we ought to ask the servants things Mother doesn't tell us,' said Roberta.

'That's right, Miss Goody-goody,' said Peter, 'preach away.'

'I'm not goody,' said Phyllis, 'but I think Bobbie's right this time.'

'Of course. She always is. In her own opinion,' said Peter.

'Oh, *don't!*' cried Roberta, putting down her egg-spoon; 'don't let's be horrid to each other. I'm sure some dire calamity is happening. Don't let's make it worse!'

'Who began, I should like to know?' said Peter.

Roberta made an effort, and answered:–

'I did, I suppose, but–'

'Well, then,' said Peter, triumphantly. But before he went to school, he thumped his sister between the shoulders and told her to cheer up.

The children came home to one o'clock dinner, but Mother was not there. And she was not there at teatime.

It was nearly seven o'clock before she came in, looking so ill and tired that the children felt they could not ask her any questions. She sank into an armchair. Phyllis took the long pins out of her hat, while Roberta took off her gloves, and Peter unfastened her walking-shoes and fetched her soft velvety slippers for her. When she had had a cup of tea, and Roberta had put eau-de-Cologne on her poor head that ached, Mother said:–

'Now, my darlings, I want to tell you something. Those men last night did bring very bad news, and Father will be away for some time. I am very worried about it, and I want you to all help me, and not make things harder for me.'

'As if we would!' said Roberta, holding Mother's hand against her face.

'You can help me very much,' said Mother, 'by being good and happy and not quarrelling when I'm away' – Roberta and Peter exchanged guilty glances – 'for I shall be away a good deal.'

'We won't quarrel. Indeed we won't,' said everybody. And meant it, too.

'Then,' Mother went on, 'I want you not to ask me any questions about this trouble; and not to ask anybody else any questions.'

Peter cringed and shuffled his boots on the carpet.

'You'll promise this, too, won't you?' said Mother.

'I did ask Ruth,' said Peter, suddenly. 'I'm very sorry, but I did.'

'And what did she say?'

'She said I should know soon enough.'

'It isn't necessary for you to know anything about it,' said Mother; 'it's about business, and you never do understand business, do you?'

'No,' said Roberta. 'Is it something to do with Government?' For Father was in a Government Office.

'Yes,' said Mother. 'Now it's bedtime, my darlings. And don't *you* worry. It'll all come right in the end.'

'Then don't *you* worry either, Mother,' said Phyllis, 'and we'll all be as good as gold.'

Mother sighed and kissed them.

'We'll begin being good first thing tomorrow morning,' said Peter, as they went upstairs.

'Why not *now*?' said Roberta.

'There's nothing to be good *about* now, silly,' said Peter ...

'I never wanted things to happen to make Mother unhappy,' said Roberta. 'Everything's perfectly horrid.'

Everything continued to be perfectly horrid for some weeks.

The Railway Children, **E. Nesbit**

Understanding the text

1 Who are the characters in the story?

2 Where is this part of the story set?

3 What were the children talking about at breakfast?

4 Where had Mother gone?

5 When Mother returned, what did she:

a tell the children? b ask them?

Looking at language

6 Explain these phrases in your own words.

a soon enough b Miss Goody-goody c cheer up
d a good deal e come right in the end f good as gold

7 Explain the meaning of these words as they are used in the story. Use a dictionary to help you.

a scorn b preach c dire d calamity
e triumphantly f guilty g cringed h continued

Exploring the story

8 What impression do you get of:

a Phyllis? b Roberta? c Peter?

9 What do you think happened 'last night'?

10 Do you think the children should have been told what had happened? Why? Why not?

11 Do you think this is a modern or old-fashioned story? Explain your reasons.

Taking it further RB, Unit 9, Extension

12 Imagine the children continued their conversation upstairs. What would they discuss? Write their conversation.

Teach

52 53

RESOURCES & ASSESSMENT BOOK

- **Support** (comprehension support): who did what?; (vocabulary support): choosing correct definitions.
- **Extension:** writing a conversation.

PUPIL BOOK ANSWERS

1. Ruth / Peter / Phyllis / Roberta / Mother.
2. In their home.
3. What happened the night before.
4. To London.
5. **a** 'Those men last night did bring very bad news, and Father will be away for some time.' **b** 'I want you to all help me, and not make things harder for me.' / 'I want you not to ask me any questions about this trouble; and not to ask anybody else any questions.'
6. **a** at the right time **b** someone who always does the right thing **c** be happier **d** a lot **e** will be all right **f** behave very well
7. **a** a way of saying something to show you do not approve **b** tell people how to behave **c** very serious **d** disaster **e** knowing you are right **f** ashamed **g** felt embarrassed **h** carried on
8. **a** Phyllis: least talkative but says what she thinks **b** Roberta: likes to do the right thing / a bit bossy / can admit when she is in the wrong / doesn't like to quarrel / 'is a bit goody-goody' [according to Peter] **c** Peter: headstrong / doesn't care about doing the right thing / feels bossed about by Roberta
9. Individual answers.
10. Individual answers.
11. Individual answers.
12. Individual answers.

RESOURCE SHEET SUPPORT ANSWERS

A

1. Peter
2. Roberta
3. Mother
4. Phyllis
5. Roberta
6. Peter

B

1. disapprove
2. serious
3. something bad
4. felt ashamed
5. felt embarrassed
6. carried on

GOING DEEPER

- Discuss what children think may have happened to Father. Why did the two men visit him? Why did they take him away? How do children think they would have reacted in that situation?

TALK

- Discuss the American Civil War with the children.
- It is unlikely that many children will have knowledge of this conflict but elicit / explain that a 'civil' war is when people of the same country fight one another. The North and the South of America fought over issues such as slavery.
- Explain to children they are going to read the beginning of *Little Women*, a story that was written in 1868.
- Read the extract to the class; ask individual children to read it aloud in turn; or read in silence individually.

UNIT 9

Christmas Presents

The story is set during the American Civil War in a small town in New England. Mr March is an army chaplain, and is at the front. The main characters are his four daughters and their mother.

'Christmas won't be Christmas without any presents,' grumbled Jo, lying on the rug.

'It's so dreadful to be poor!' sighed Meg, looking down at her old dress.

'I don't think it's fair for some girls to have lots of pretty things, and other girls nothing at all,' added little Amy with an injured sniff.

'We've got Father and Mother, and each other, anyhow,' said Beth contentedly, from her corner.

The four young faces on which the firelight shone brightened at the cheerful words, but darkened again as Jo said sadly:

'We haven't got Father, and shall not have him for a long time.' She didn't say 'perhaps never', but each silently added it, thinking of Father far away, where the fighting was.

Nobody spoke for a minute; then Meg said in an altered tone:

'You know the reason Mother proposed not having any presents this Christmas was because it's going to be a hard winter for everyone; and she thinks we ought not to spend money for pleasure, when our men are suffering so in the army. We can't do much, but we can make our little sacrifices, and ought to do it gladly. But I'm afraid I don't,' and Meg shook her head, as she thought regretfully of all the pretty things she wanted.

'But I don't think the little we should spend would do any good. We've each got a dollar, and the army wouldn't be much helped by our giving that. I agree not to expect anything from Mother or you, but I do want to buy Undine and Sintram for myself; I've wanted it so long,' said Jo, who was a bookworm.

'I planned to spend mine in new music,' said Beth, with a little sigh, which no one heard but the hearth-brush and the kettle-holder.

'I shall get a nice box of Faber's drawing pencils: I really need them,' said Amy, decidedly.

'Mother didn't say anything about our money, and she won't wish us to give up everything. Let's each buy what we want, and have a little fun; I'm sure we grub hard enough to earn it,' cried Jo, examining the heels of her boots in a gentlemanly manner.

'I know *I* do, teaching those dreadful children nearly all day, when I'm longing to enjoy myself at home,' began Meg in a complaining tone again.

'You don't have half such a hard time as I do,' said Jo. 'How would you like to be shut up for hours with a nervous, fussy old lady, who keeps you trotting, is never satisfied, and worries you till you're ready to fly out of the window or box her ears?'

'It's naughty to fret, but I do think washing dishes and keeping things tidy is the worst work in the world. It makes me cross; and my hands get so stiff, I can't practise … '

'I don't believe any of you suffer as I do,' cried Amy, 'for you don't have to go to school with impertinent girls, who plague you if you don't know your lessons, and laugh at your dresses, and label your father if he isn't rich, and insult you when your nose isn't nice.'

Little Women, **Louisa May Alcott**

Talk

54

Understanding the text

1 What are the names of the four daughters in the story?
2 Who:
  a liked drawing and went to school?
  b liked reading and looked after an old lady?
  c liked music and did housework?
  d liked pretty things and taught children?
3 Where was Father?
4 How much money did each of the girls have?

Looking at language

5 Explain the meaning of these words as they are used in the story. Use a dictionary to help you.

a contentedly *b proposed* *c sacrifices* *d regretfully*
e decidedly *f fret* *g impertinent* *h plague*

Exploring the story

6 Why do you think each of the girls silently added 'perhaps never' when they talked about their father?
7 How do you know the girls were unhappy about not having any presents?
8 Which of the four girls do you think 'suffers' the most? Explain your reasons.
9 What did the girls agree to do about presents this Christmas?
10 Is that what you would have done? Why? Why not?

Taking it further RB, Unit 9, Extension

11 Imagine Mother comes into the room at this point, and the girls explain to her what they have decided to do. How does Mother react? Role-play the scene.

Talk

55

RESOURCES & ASSESSMENT BOOK

- **Support** (comprehension support): who said what?; (vocabulary support): using adverbs in correct context.
- **Extension:** writing dialogue, role-playing.

PUPIL BOOK ANSWERS

1. Jo / Meg / Beth / Amy.
2. **a** Amy **b** Jo **c** Beth **d** Meg
3. 'far away, where the fighting was'.
4. A dollar.
5. **a** satisfied with life **b** suggested **c** things that are given up **d** sadly **e** firmly **f** worry / complain (this usage is now archaic) **g** rude **h** pester
6. Answers that suggest their father may die in the fighting.
7. Jo: 'Christmas won't be Christmas without any presents' / 'I don't think the little we should spend would do any good' / 'Let's each buy what we want and have a little fun'.

   Amy: 'I don't think it's fair that some girls have lots of pretty things, and other girls nothing at all'.

   Meg: doesn't make the sacrifice of not having presents 'gladly'.
8. Individual answers.
9. To buy what they wanted but not expect presents from Mother or one another.
10. Individual answers.
11. Individual answers.

RESOURCE SHEET SUPPORT ANSWERS

A

1. Jo
2. Jo
3. Meg
4. Amy
5. Beth
6. Beth

B

1. contentedly
2. regretfully
3. decidedly

GOING DEEPER

- Discuss the situation the children find themselves in, in the first and second extracts, in terms of similarities and differences. If time allows, let groups act out their scenes.

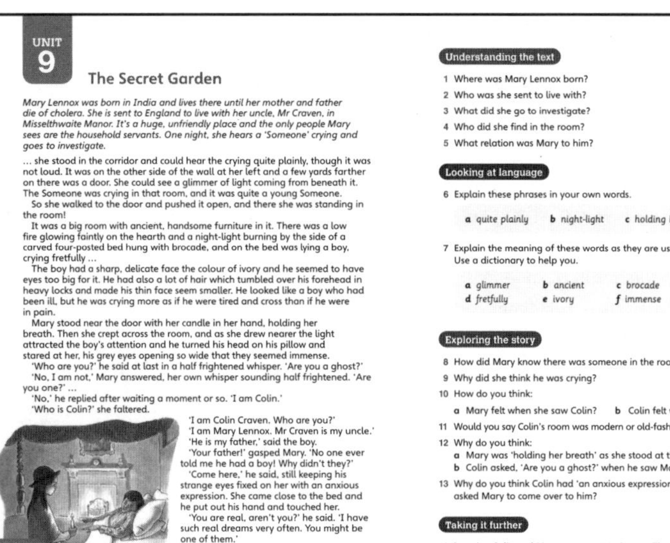

UNIT 9

The Secret Garden

Mary Lennox was born in India and lives there until her mother and father die of cholera. She is sent to England to live with her uncle, Mr Craven, in Misselthwaite Manor. It's a huge, unfriendly place and the only people Mary sees are the household servants. One night, she hears a 'Someone' crying and goes to investigate.

... she stood in the corridor and could hear the crying quite plainly, though it was not loud. It was on the other side of the wall at her left and a few yards farther on there was a door. She could see a glimmer of light coming from beneath it. The Someone was crying in that room, and it was quite a young Someone.

So she walked to the door and pushed it open, and there she was standing in the room!

It was a big room with ancient, handsome furniture in it. There was a low fire glowing faintly on the hearth and a night-light burning by the side of a carved four-posted bed hung with brocade, and on the bed was lying a boy, crying fretfully ...

The boy had a sharp, delicate face the colour of ivory and he seemed to have eyes too big for it. He had also a lot of hair which tumbled over his forehead in heavy locks and made his thin face seem smaller. He looked like a boy who had been ill, but he was crying more as if he were tired and cross than if he were in pain.

Mary stood near the door with her candle in her hand, holding her breath. Then she crept across the room, and as she drew nearer the light attracted the boy's attention and he turned his head on his pillow and stared at her, his grey eyes opening so wide that they seemed immense.

'Who are you?' he said at last in a half frightened whisper. 'Are you a ghost?'

'No, I am not,' Mary answered, her own whisper sounding half frightened. 'Are you one?' ...

'No,' he replied after waiting a moment or so. 'I am Colin.'

'Who is Colin?' she faltered.

'I am Colin Craven. Who are you?'

'I am Mary Lennox. Mr Craven is my uncle.'

'He is my father,' said the boy.

'Your father!' gasped Mary. 'No one ever told me he had a boy! Why didn't they?'

'Come here,' he said, still keeping his strange eyes fixed on her with an anxious expression. She came close to the bed and he put out his hand and touched her.

'You are real, aren't you?' he said. 'I have such real dreams very often. You might be one of them.'

Frances Hodgson Burnett

Write

56

Understanding the text

1 Where was Mary Lennox born?
2 Who was she sent to live with?
3 What did she go to investigate?
4 Who did she find in the room?
5 What relation was Mary to him?

Looking at language

6 Explain these phrases in your own words.

a *quite plainly* **b** *night-light* **c** *holding her breath*

7 Explain the meaning of these words as they are used in the story. Use a dictionary to help you.

a *glimmer* **b** *ancient* **c** *brocade*
d *fretfully* **e** *ivory* **f** *immense*

Exploring the story

8 How did Mary know there was someone in the room?
9 Why did she think he was crying?
10 How do you think:
a Mary felt when she saw Colin? **b** Colin felt when he saw Mary?
11 Would you say Colin's room was modern or old-fashioned? Explain your reasons.
12 Why do you think:
a Mary was 'holding her breath' as she stood at the door?
b Colin asked, 'Are you a ghost?' when he saw Mary?
13 Why do you think Colin had 'an anxious expression' on his face when he asked Mary to come over to him?

Taking it further

RB, Unit 9, Extension

14 Imagine Colin and Mary go to see Mr Craven. They ask him why he had not told them about each other. Write their conversation.

Write

57

WRITE

- Discuss with the children that the British ruled in India until 1947.
- It is unlikely that many children will have knowledge of this, but elicit / explain that when the British ruled India, many British people went out there to work and, consequently, many British children were born there.
- Explain to children that they are going to read an extract from *The Secret Garden*, a story that was written in 1911.
- Read the extract to the class; ask individual children to read it aloud in turn; or read in silence individually.

RESOURCES & ASSESSMENT BOOK

- **Support** (comprehension support): narrative sequence; (vocabulary support): answering questions with given vocabulary.
- **Extension:** writing dialogue.

PUPIL BOOK ANSWERS

1. India.
2. Her uncle, Mr Craven.
3. She heard someone crying in the night.
4. Colin Craven, Mr Craven's son.
5. Cousin.
6. **a** easily seen or heard **b** small light left burning through the night **c** not daring to breathe
7. **a** a soft, weak light **b** very old **c** rich fabric **d** with distress or irritation **e** pale yellow-white in colour **f** huge
8. She 'could see a glimmer of light' under the door and could hear crying.
9. 'he was crying more as if he were tired and cross than if he were in pain'.
10. **a** curious / a little frightened **b** startled / a little frightened / couldn't believe his eyes
11. The room was old fashioned – four-poster bed / brocade / fire.
12. **a** she did not want to be noticed / did not want to startle the boy **b** no one told him about Mary / he spent so much time alone he couldn't believe she was real
13. Because she may leave / may not be real.
14. Individual answers.

RESOURCE SHEET SUPPORT ANSWERS

A

1. She stood in the room. 4
2. The boy turned to look at her. 7
3. Mary opened the door. 3
4. Mary heard someone crying. 1
5. Colin asked her to come closer. 8
6. Mary stood in the corridor. 2
7. Mary saw a boy crying. 5
8. Mary crept across the room. 6

B

1. glimmer
2. crying
3. big
4. ancient
5. four-poster

GOING DEEPER

- Use children's answers to the 'Taking it further' activity as a basis for a class discussion.
- Ask children what they have learned about childhood over a hundred years ago. Would they rather be children now or then? Why?

UNIT FOCUS: The Roles of Heroes and Heroines

Investigating ...

- myths and legends from around the world
- heroes and heroines

TEACH

- Ask children what they understand by the terms 'myth' and 'legend'. What myths / legends do they know already? What do they know about King Arthur?
- Explain to the children that they are going to read a retelling of a King Arthur story. The king, Uther Pendragon, has died after a long illness. But who will now be king?
- This is a challenging text for this year group, and you may wish to read it and discuss questions as a class or in groups before asking children to tackle it on their own.

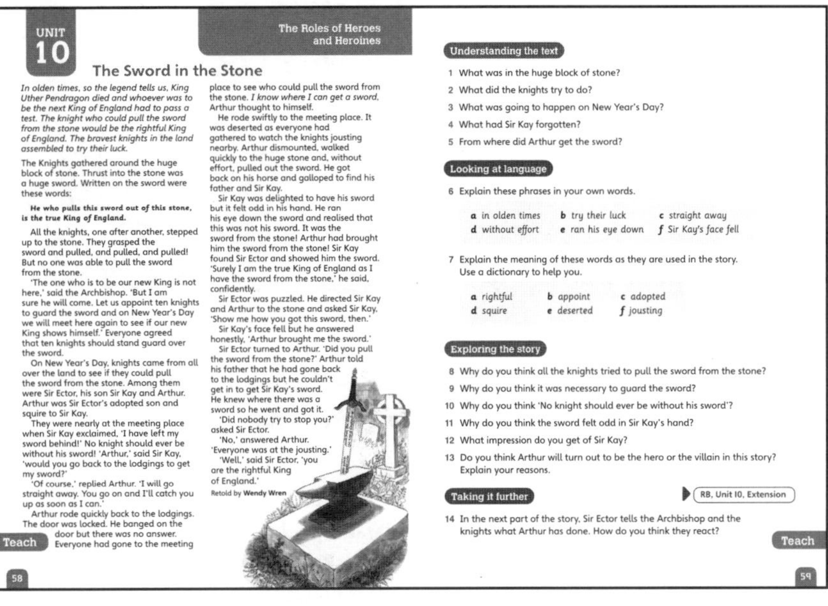

UNIT 10

The Roles of Heroes and Heroines

The Sword in the Stone

In olden times, so the legend tells us, King Uther Pendragon died and whoever was to be the next King of England had to pass a test. The knight who could pull the sword from the stone would be the rightful King of England. The bravest knights in the land assembled to try their luck.

The Knights gathered around the huge block of stone. Thrust into the stone was a huge sword. Written on the sword were these words:

He who pulls this sword out of this stone, is the true King of England.

All the knights, one after another, stepped up to the stone. They grasped the sword and pulled, and pulled, and pulled! But no one was able to pull the sword from the stone.

'The one who is to be our new King is not here,' said the Archbishop. 'But I am sure he will come. Let us appoint ten knights to guard the sword and on New Year's Day we will meet here again to see if our new King shows himself.' Everyone agreed that ten knights should stand guard over the sword.

On New Year's Day, knights came from all over the land to see if they could pull the sword from the stone. Among them were Sir Ector, his son Sir Kay and Arthur. Arthur was Sir Ector's adopted son and squire to Sir Kay.

They were nearly at the meeting place when Sir Kay exclaimed, 'I have left my sword behind!' No knight should ever be without his sword! 'Arthur,' said Sir Kay, 'would you go back to the lodgings to get my sword?'

'Of course,' replied Arthur. 'I will go straight away. You go on and I'll catch you up as soon as I can.'

Arthur rode quickly back to the lodgings. The door was locked. He banged on the door but there was no answer. Everyone had gone to the meeting place to see who could pull the sword from the stone. *I know where I can get a sword,* Arthur thought to himself.

He rode swiftly to the meeting place. It was deserted as everyone had gathered to watch the knights jousting nearby. Arthur dismounted, walked quickly to the huge stone and, without effort, pulled out the sword. He got back on his horse and galloped to find his father and Sir Kay.

Sir Kay was delighted to have his sword but it felt odd in his hand. He ran his eye down the sword and realised that this was not his sword. It was the sword from the stone! Arthur had brought him the sword from the stone! Sir Kay found Sir Ector and showed him the sword. 'Surely I am the true King of England as I have the sword from the stone,' he said, confidently.

Sir Ector was puzzled. He directed Sir Kay and Arthur to the stone and asked Sir Kay, 'Show me how you got this sword, then.'

Sir Kay's face fell but he answered honestly, 'Arthur brought me the sword.'

Sir Ector turned to Arthur. 'Did you pull the sword from the stone?' Arthur told his father that he had gone back to the lodgings but he couldn't get in to get Sir Kay's sword. He knew where there was a sword so he went and got it.

'Did nobody try to stop you?' asked Sir Ector.

'No,' answered Arthur. 'Everyone was at the jousting.'

'Well,' said Sir Ector, 'you are the rightful King of England.'

Retold by **Wendy Wren**

Teach

58

Understanding the text

1 What was in the huge block of stone?
2 What did the knights try to do?
3 What was going to happen on New Year's Day?
4 What had Sir Kay forgotten?
5 From where did Arthur get the sword?

Looking at language

6 Explain these phrases in your own words.

a *in olden times* **b** *try their luck* **c** *straight away*
d *without effort* **e** *ran his eye down* **f** *Sir Kay's face fell*

7 Explain the meaning of these words as they are used in the story. Use a dictionary to help you.

a *rightful* **b** *appoint* **c** *adopted*
d *squire* **e** *deserted* **f** *jousting*

Exploring the story

8 Why do you think all the knights tried to pull the sword from the stone?
9 Why do you think it was necessary to guard the sword?
10 Why do you think 'No knight should ever be without his sword'?
11 Why do you think the sword felt odd in Sir Kay's hand?
12 What impression do you get of Sir Kay?
13 Do you think Arthur will turn out to be the hero or the villain in this story? Explain your reasons.

Taking it further RB, Unit 10, Extension

14 In the next part of the story, Sir Ector tells the Archbishop and the knights what Arthur has done. How do you think they react?

Teach

59

RESOURCES & ASSESSMENT BOOK

- **Support** (comprehension support): identifying wrong words in sentences, correcting sentences; (vocabulary support): matching words and definitions.
- **Extension:** making notes, writing dialogue.

PUPIL BOOK ANSWERS

1. A sword.
2. Pull the sword from the stone.
3. The knights were going to try to pull the sword from the stone to see if the new King was there.
4. His sword.
5. The huge block of stone.
6. **a** long, long ago **b** have a go **c** immediately **d** easily **e** looked at it **f** Sir Kay looked disappointed
7. **a** true **b** choose someone to do a particular job **c** legally made part of a family that you were not born into **d** a young man who worked for a knight **e** no one there **f** fighting on horseback
8. Each knight wanted to be king.
9. Someone may try to steal it.
10. A knight had to be ready to fight at all times and would need a sword to defend himself.
11. It was not his sword – a knight would know the feel and weight of his own sword.
12. He was ambitious [wanted to be king] / not entirely honest [implied he pulled the sword from the stone].
13. Individual answers.
14. Individual answers.

RESOURCE SHEET SUPPORT ANSWERS

A

1. small / huge
2. Seven / ten
3. Eve / Day
4. son / father
5. Arthur / Kay
6. Kay / Arthur
7. Ector / Arthur
8. Kay / Arthur

B

1. rightful – true
2. appoint – choose someone to do a particular job
3. adopted – legally make part of a family
4. squire – young man who worked for a knight
5. deserted – no one there
6. jousting – fighting on horseback

GOING DEEPER

- Discuss the idea of 'heroes' and 'villains'. What characteristics does each character type have? Does Arthur have the characteristics of a hero?

TALK

- Discuss *The Jungle Book* with the children. Many will have seen the Disney version. Did they like the film?
- What can they remember about:
  - the story?
  - the characters?
- Explain to children that they are going to read an extract from *The Jungle Book* where Mowgli is captured by the monkeys.
- Read the extract to the class; ask individual children to read it aloud in turn; or read in silence individually.

RESOURCES & ASSESSMENT BOOK

- **Support** (comprehension support): identifying paragraph content; (vocabulary support): choosing correct definitions.
- **Extension:** making notes, writing a plan based on text extract.

PUPIL BOOK ANSWERS

1. Black panther.
2. The monkeys.
3. Surrounded by the monkeys.
4. Into the summer-house.
5. Kaa.
6. **a** flat area outside a house **b** hitting **c** fighting **d** semi-circular roof **e** hurry **f** upper parts of the leg
7. Biting / scratching / tearing / pulling.
8. 'the cloud hid the moon'.
9. He felt relieved / hopeful / fearful that Bagheera would get hurt.
10. He 'had lived with a wolf pack in the jungle since he was a baby' so would have been trained by the wolves.
11. Once he was in the water 'the monkeys could not follow'.
12. The first strike scattered the monkeys and they were so afraid of the python, they didn't wait for him to strike twice.
13. Individual answers.
14. Individual answers.

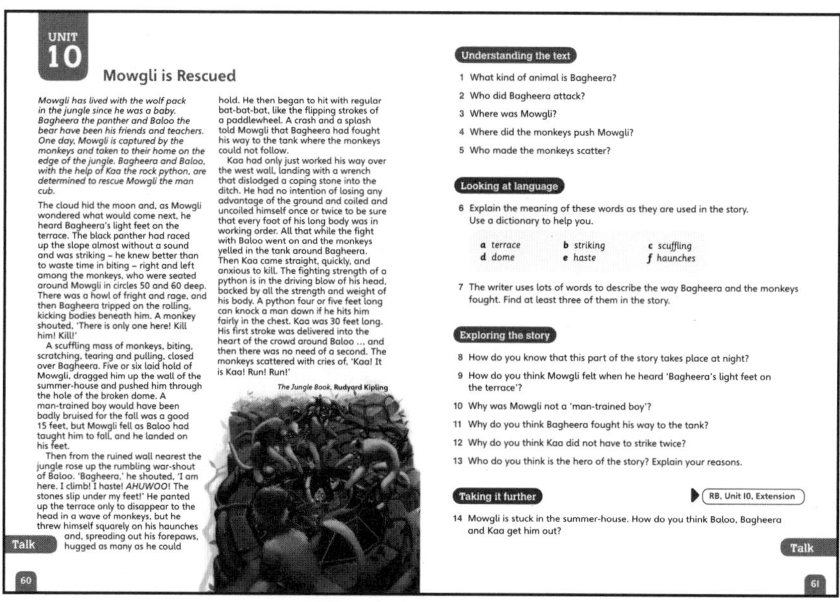

UNIT 10

Mowgli is Rescued

Mowgli has lived with the wolf pack in the jungle since he was a baby. Bagheera the panther and Baloo the bear have been his friends and teachers. One day, Mowgli is captured by the monkeys and taken to their home on the edge of the jungle. Bagheera and Baloo, with the help of Kaa the rock python, are determined to rescue Mowgli the man cub.

The cloud hid the moon and, as Mowgli wondered what would come next, he heard Bagheera's light feet on the terrace. The black panther had raced up the slope almost without a sound and was striking – he knew better than to waste time in biting – right and left among the monkeys, who were seated around Mowgli in circles 50 and 60 deep. There was a howl of fright and rage, and then Bagheera tripped on the rolling, kicking bodies beneath him. A monkey shouted, 'There is only one here! Kill him! Kill!'

A scuffling mass of monkeys, biting, scratching, tearing and pulling, closed over Bagheera. Five or six laid hold of Mowgli, dragged him up the wall of the summer-house and pushed him through the hole of the broken dome. A man-trained boy would have been badly bruised for the fall was a good 15 feet, but Mowgli fell as Baloo had taught him to fall, and he landed on his feet.

Then from the ruined wall nearest the jungle rose up the rumbling war-shout of Baloo. 'Bagheera,' he shouted, 'I am here. I climb! I haste! *AHUWOO*! The stones slip under my feet!' He panted up the terrace only to disappear to the head in a wave of monkeys, but he threw himself squarely on his haunches and, spreading out his forepaws, hugged as many as he could hold. He then began to hit with regular bat-bat-bat, like the flipping strokes of a paddlewheel. A crash and a splash told Mowgli that Bagheera had fought his way to the tank where the monkeys could not follow.

Kaa had only just worked his way over the west wall, landing with a wrench that dislodged a coping stone into the ditch. He had no intention of losing any advantage of the ground and coiled and uncoiled himself once or twice to be sure that every foot of his long body was in working order. All that while the fight with Baloo went on and the monkeys yelled in the tank around Bagheera. Then Kaa came straight, quickly, and anxious to kill. The fighting strength of a python is in the driving blow of his head, backed by all the strength and weight of his body. A python four or five feet long can knock a man down if he hits him fairly in the chest. Kaa was 30 feet long. His first stroke was delivered into the heart of the crowd around Baloo ... and then there was no need of a second. The monkeys scattered with cries of, 'Kaa! It is Kaa! Run! Run!'

The Jungle Book, **Rudyard Kipling**

Talk

60

Understanding the text

1 What kind of animal is Bagheera?
2 Who did Bagheera attack?
3 Where was Mowgli?
4 Where did the monkeys push Mowgli?
5 Who made the monkeys scatter?

Looking at language

6 Explain the meaning of these words as they are used in the story. Use a dictionary to help you.

a terrace *b striking* *c scuffling*
d dome *e haste* *f haunches*

7 The writer uses lots of words to describe the way Bagheera and the monkeys fought. Find at least three of them in the story.

Exploring the story

8 How do you know that this part of the story takes place at night?
9 How do you think Mowgli felt when he heard 'Bagheera's light feet on the terrace'?
10 Why was Mowgli not a 'man-trained boy'?
11 Why do you think Bagheera fought his way to the tank?
12 Why do you think Kaa did not have to strike twice?
13 Who do you think is the hero of the story? Explain your reasons.

Taking it further RB, Unit 10, Extension

14 Mowgli is stuck in the summer-house. How do you think Baloo, Bagheera and Kaa get him out?

Talk

61

RESOURCE SHEET SUPPORT ANSWERS

A

Paragraph 1: Bagheera fights the monkeys. **Paragraph 2:** Mowgli is put in the summer-house. **Paragraph 3:** Baloo arrives and fights his way to the tank. **Paragraph 4:** Kaa arrives and scatters the monkeys.

B

1. hurry
2. hit them
3. fight
4. semi-circular
5. upper part of a leg

GOING DEEPER

- Discuss with the children what they have learned about 'heroes' and 'villains' so far e.g. their characteristics / actions and the situations they find themselves in.

WRITE

- Ask children if they know stories of heroines who saved people at the risk of their own life, e.g. Grace Darling.
- Do they think it is easy or difficult to risk your own life to help others? Encourage them to explain their reasons.
- Explain to children that they are going to read a legend called 'The Storm' in which the spirit of a young girl helps people in trouble at sea.
- This is a challenging text for this year group, and you may wish to read it and discuss questions as a class or in groups before asking children to tackle it on their own.

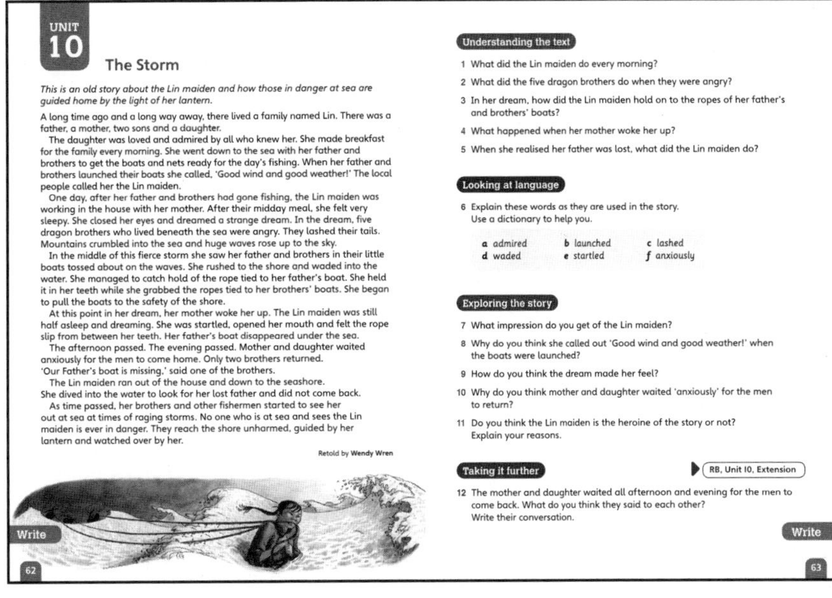

UNIT 10

The Storm

This is an old story about the Lin maiden and how those in danger at sea are guided home by the light of her lantern.

A long time ago and a long way away, there lived a family named Lin. There was a father, a mother, two sons and a daughter.

The daughter was loved and admired by all who knew her. She made breakfast for the family every morning. She went down to the sea with her father and brothers to get the boats and nets ready for the day's fishing. When her father and brothers launched their boats she called, 'Good wind and good weather!' The local people called her the Lin maiden.

One day, after her father and brothers had gone fishing, the Lin maiden was working in the house with her mother. After their midday meal, she felt very sleepy. She closed her eyes and dreamed a strange dream. In the dream, five dragon brothers who lived beneath the sea were angry. They lashed their tails. Mountains crumbled into the sea and huge waves rose up to the sky.

In the middle of this fierce storm she saw her father and brothers in their little boats tossed about on the waves. She rushed to the shore and waded into the water. She managed to catch hold of the rope tied to her father's boat. She held it in her teeth while she grabbed the ropes tied to her brothers' boats. She began to pull the boats to the safety of the shore.

At this point in her dream, her mother woke her up. The Lin maiden was still half asleep and dreaming. She was startled, opened her mouth and felt the rope slip from between her teeth. Her father's boat disappeared under the sea.

The afternoon passed. The evening passed. Mother and daughter waited anxiously for the men to come home. Only two brothers returned.

'Our Father's boat is missing,' said one of the brothers.

The Lin maiden ran out of the house and down to the seashore.

She dived into the water to look for her lost father and did not come back.

As time passed, her brothers and other fishermen started to see her out at sea at times of raging storms. No one who is at sea and sees the Lin maiden is ever in danger. They reach the shore unharmed, guided by her lantern and watched over by her.

Retold by **Wendy Wren**

Write

62

Understanding the text

1 What did the Lin maiden do every morning?

2 What did the five dragon brothers do when they were angry?

3 In her dream, how did the Lin maiden hold on to the ropes of her father's and brothers' boats?

4 What happened when her mother woke her up?

5 When she realised her father was lost, what did the Lin maiden do?

Looking at language

6 Explain these words as they are used in the story. Use a dictionary to help you.

a admired **b** launched **c** lashed
d waded **e** startled **f** anxiously

Exploring the story

7 What impression do you get of the Lin maiden?

8 Why do you think she called out 'Good wind and good weather!' when the boats were launched?

9 How do you think the dream made her feel?

10 Why do you think mother and daughter waited 'anxiously' for the men to return?

11 Do you think the Lin maiden is the heroine of the story or not? Explain your reasons.

Taking it further RB, Unit 10, Extension

12 The mother and daughter waited all afternoon and evening for the men to come back. What do you think they said to each other? Write their conversation.

Write

63

RESOURCES & ASSESSMENT BOOK

- **Support** (comprehension support): multiple choice; (vocabulary support): cloze activity for vocabulary reinforcement.
- **Extension:** writing thoughts and dialogue.

PUPIL BOOK ANSWERS

1. She made breakfast for the family / helped her father and brothers get their boats and nets ready.
2. They lashed their tails.
3. She held the rope attached to her father's boats 'in her teeth' and the ropes attached to her brothers' boats in her hands.
4. She opened her mouth and in her dream 'felt the rope slip from between her teeth'.
5. She 'ran out of the house and down to the seashore' / 'dived into the water to look for her lost father and did not come back'.
6. **a** respected / thought well of **b** got the boats into the water **c** flung about with great force **d** walked into **e** surprised **f** worriedly
7. Hard working – makes breakfast / helps with the boats / works in the house; very caring – grief stricken when father was lost at sea; impulsive / brave – dived into the water.
8. She was wishing her father and brothers would have a good day's fishing / wishing the wind and the weather would be kind to them and they would return safely.
9. Worried / frightened.
10. Waiting was an 'anxious' time as there was always the real possibility that the men would not come back.
11. Individual answers.
12. Individual answers.

RESOURCE SHEET SUPPORT ANSWERS

A

1. breakfast
2. fishermen
3. the Lin maiden
4. three ropes
5. a lantern

B

The Lin Maiden was **admired** by all who knew her. She called 'Good wind and good weather' when her father and brothers **launched** their boats. She dreamed of five dragons that **lashed** their tails. In her dream, she **waded** into the water. When her mother woke her up she was **startled**. She and her mother waited **anxiously** for the men to return.

GOING DEEPER

- Discuss the three 'heroes' in this unit. In what ways are they similar? In what ways are they different?

Book 6 Scope and Sequence

Unit	Unit Focus	Texts	Oxford Level	Oxford Reading Criterion Scale	Genre / text type	Resources & Assessment Book Support	Resources & Assessment Book Extension
1	Looking at Biographies	Emmeline Pankhurst	19	standard 7, criteria 3, 4, 5, 8, 10, 19	non-fiction: biography	multiple choice; underlining correct definitions	presenting information in a chart; undertaking research
		Neil Armstrong	18			presenting information in a chart; underlining correct definitions	undertaking research and presenting it in a chart; writing a biography
		Louis Braille	17			cloze activity; matching words and definitions; reading Braille	writing in Braille
2	Building Tension	*Frankenstein*, adapted by Patrick Nobes from the novel by Mary Shelley	18	standard 7, criteria 4, 6, 10, 13, 15, 21	fiction	matching beginnings and endings of sentences; matching words and definitions; finding adjectives	thinking and writing about what happens next
		Theseus and the Minotaur, retold by Wendy Wren	18			cloze activity; matching words and definitions	retelling a story from a character's point of view
		Jurassic Park, adapted by Gail Herman from the novel by Michael Crichton	15			multiple choice; finding synonyms	retelling a story from a character's point of view
3	The Rules of Argument	Text Messaging – Good or Bad?	17	standard 7, criteria 3, 4, 7, 10, 18	non-fiction: persuasive texts	identifying advantages and disadvantages; underlining correct definitions	presenting information in a chart
		Animal Testing	18			cloze activity; underlining correct definitions	writing persuasive text
		UFOs Do Not Exist!	17			identifying true and false statements; correcting statements; matching words and definitions	writing persuasive text
4	Exploring Issues in Poetry	'The Loner', Julie Holder	15	standard 7, criteria 4, 10, 11, 12, 15, 21	poetry	matching verbs to characters; cloze activity	learning and reciting a poem by heart
		'Bullied', Patricia Leighton	15			multiple choice; cloze activity	thinking about characters' motives; writing using personal experience and opinion
		'The New Boy', John Walsh	15			identifying what happened; finding rhyming words; underlining correct definitions	thinking about characters' motives; writing using personal experience and opinion
5	Understanding Formal Writing	The Tower of London	19	standard 7, criteria 3, 4, 5, 8, 10, 19	non-fiction: formal writing	presenting information in a chart; finding measurements; matching words to definitions	summarising information; presenting information in a chart
		A Guide to the Tower of London	18			matching answers to questions; underlining the odd one out; cloze activity	writing a plan
		Animals in the Tower	18			matching paragraphs to their summaries; identifying animals; finding and writing names in alphabetical order	comparing the three extracts in this unit

6	Themes and Techniques	*Why the Whales Came*, Michael Morpurgo	18	standard 7, criteria 4, 10, 12, 15, 17, 20, 21	fiction	identifying the wrong words in a sentence; underlining correct definitions	predicting what happens next and writing an end to the story
		'Lost at Sea' from *The Ghost of Grania O'Malley*, Michael Morpurgo	17			putting narrative sequence in order; writing out contractions; matching words to definitions	predicting what happens next and writing the next section of the story
		'Alone in the Ocean' from *Kensuke's Kingdom*, Michael Morpurgo	17			identifying true and false statements; correcting sentences; matching definitions to words	comparing the three extracts in the unit
7	Viewpoints in Journalistic Writing	The Beast of Bodmin Moor	18	standard 7, criteria 3, 4, 5, 7, 9, 10, 14, 18, 19	non-fiction: journalistic writing	writing questions for answers; cloze activity; finding adjectives	writing using facts and your own opinions
		Islands of Fire	18			presenting information in a chart; matching beginnings and endings of sentences; underlining correct definitions	planning an article
		The Northern Lights Fantastic	18			cloze activity; identifying adjectives; matching words to definitions	planning and writing questions
8	Exploring Atmosphere and Tension	'Marley's Ghost' from *A Christmas Carol*, Charles Dickens	20	standard 7, criteria 4, 6, 10, 12, 13, 15, 16, 17, 21	fiction	multiple choice; identifying the odd ones out; matching words to definitions	rewriting a playscript in modern English
		'Hamlet, Prince of Denmark' from *The Enchanted Island*, Ian Serraillier	19			identifying true statements; correcting statements; matching words to definitions	turning a narrative into a playscript and preparing it for performance
		'The Ghostly Girl' from *Dream Ghost*, Sydney J Bounds	18			cloze activity; categorising narrative details	comparing the three texts in this unit
9	Looking at Personification	'The Brook', Alfred Lord Tennyson	20	standard 7, criteria 4, 7, 9, 10, 12, 14, 15, 21	poetry	multiple choice; categorising words	learning and reciting a poem by heart
		'The River's Story', Brian Patten	18			multiple choice; cloze activity; matching words to definitions	designing a poster and writing the copy
		'Coral Reef', Clare Bevan	19			finding correct adjectives; underlining correct definitions	comparing the three poems in this unit
10	Tales from Personal Experience	'*Endurance's* Last Voyage' from *South*, Sir Ernest Shackleton	20	standard 7, criteria 4, 5, 7, 10, 14, 15, 17, 19, 21	non-fiction: personal recounts	identifying true and false statements; correcting sentences; matching words to definitions	writing about how language helps express feelings and situations
		20 HRS, 40 MIN … Our Flight in the Friendship, Amelia Earhart	20			cloze activity; who did what; multiple choice	using facts and opinions to write about your views
		Touching the Void, Joe Simpson	19			multiple choice; cloze activity	writing about thoughts and feelings from someone else's point of view

UNIT FOCUS: Looking at Biographies

Investigating …

- the common features of biographical writing
- autobiographical writing
- comparisons in autobiographical writing

TEACH

- Ask children what they understand by the term 'biography'. Why do they think people read biographies?
- Ask children what biographies they have read. They may say that they haven't read any, but articles in magazines that deal with part of a person's life can be deemed biographical.
- Investigate the idea of voting with children. What experience have they had of voting?
- Explain that not everyone has always had the right to vote, and it wasn't until 1928 that women could vote. This biographical sketch is about Emmeline Pankhurst, who made it her life's work to get votes for women.
- Read the text to the class; ask individual children to read it aloud in turn; or read in silence individually.

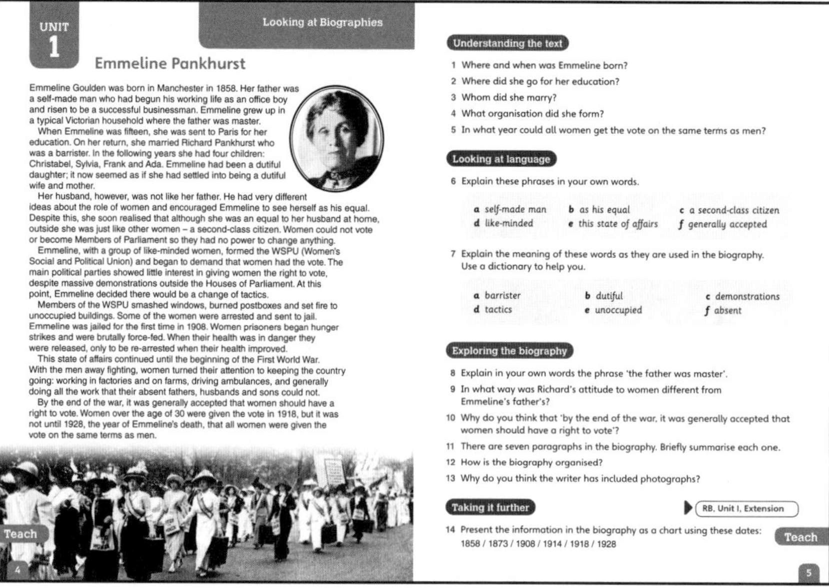
UNIT 1 Looking at Biographies

Emmeline Pankhurst

Emmeline Goulden was born in Manchester in 1858. Her father was a self-made man who had begun his working life as an office boy and risen to be a successful businessman. Emmeline grew up in a typical Victorian household where the father was master.

When Emmeline was fifteen, she was sent to Paris for her education. On her return, she married Richard Pankhurst who was a barrister. In the following years she had four children: Christabel, Sylvia, Frank and Ada. Emmeline had been a dutiful daughter; it now seemed as if she had settled into being a dutiful wife and mother.

Her husband, however, was not like her father. He had very different ideas about the role of women and encouraged Emmeline to see herself as his equal. Despite this, she soon realised that although she was an equal to her husband at home, outside she was just like other women – a second-class citizen. Women could not vote or become Members of Parliament so they had no power to change anything.

Emmeline, with a group of like-minded women, formed the WSPU (Women's Social and Political Union) and began to demand that women had the vote. The main political parties showed little interest in giving women the right to vote, despite massive demonstrations outside the Houses of Parliament. At this point, Emmeline decided there would be a change of tactics.

Members of the WSPU smashed windows, burned postboxes and set fire to unoccupied buildings. Some of the women were arrested and sent to jail. Emmeline was jailed for the first time in 1908. Women prisoners began hunger strikes and were brutally force-fed. When their health was in danger they were released, only to be re-arrested when their health improved.

This state of affairs continued until the beginning of the First World War. With the men away fighting, women turned their attention to keeping the country going: working in factories and on farms, driving ambulances, and generally doing all the work that their absent fathers, husbands and sons could not.

By the end of the war, it was generally accepted that women should have a right to vote. Women over the age of 30 were given the vote in 1918, but it was not until 1928, the year of Emmeline's death, that all women were given the vote on the same terms as men.

Teach 4

Understanding the text

1 Where and when was Emmeline born?
2 Where did she go for her education?
3 Whom did she marry?
4 What organisation did she form?
5 In what year could all women get the vote on the same terms as men?

Looking at language

6 Explain these phrases in your own words.

a *self-made man* **b** *as his equal* **c** *a second-class citizen*
d *like-minded* **e** *this state of affairs* **f** *generally accepted*

7 Explain the meaning of these words as they are used in the biography. Use a dictionary to help you.

a *barrister* **b** *dutiful* **c** *demonstrations*
d *tactics* **e** *unoccupied* **f** *absent*

Exploring the biography

8 Explain in your own words the phrase 'the father was master'.
9 In what way was Richard's attitude to women different from Emmeline's father's?
10 Why do you think that 'by the end of the war, it was generally accepted that women should have a right to vote'?
11 There are seven paragraphs in the biography. Briefly summarise each one.
12 How is the biography organised?
13 Why do you think the writer has included photographs?

Taking it further RB, Unit 1, Extension

14 Present the information in the biography as a chart using these dates: 1858 / 1873 / 1908 / 1914 / 1918 / 1928

Teach 5

RESOURCES & ASSESSMENT BOOK

- **Focus** (comprehension support): answering questions based on extract; (vocabulary support): choosing the correct definition.
- **Extension:** creating a chart, finding additional information.

PUPIL BOOK ANSWERS

1. Manchester, 1858.
2. Paris.
3. Richard Pankhurst.
4. WSPU [Women's Social and Political Union].
5. 1928.
6. **a** someone who becomes a success through their own efforts **b** to be treated exactly the same **c** someone who does not have the same rights as other people **d** in agreement **e** this situation **f** most people in agreement
7. **a** a lawyer who argues someone's case before a judge **b** obedient **c** protests against something **d** methods / plans for achieving something **e** not used or lived in **f** not there
8. Emmeline's father was the 'boss' in the house whom all the family members obeyed.
9. Richard thought women were equal to men. Emmeline's father thought women were inferior to men.
10. 'With the men away, women turned their attention to keeping the country going'. Women had proved they were essential members of society and were, therefore, entitled to the same rights as men.
11. Paragraph 1: early years.
Paragraph 2: education / marriage / children.
Paragraph 3: her husband's attitude to women / society's attitude to women.
Paragraph 4: WSUP formed.
Paragraph 5: change of tactics.
Paragraph 6: women during the First World War.
Paragraph 7: women get the vote.
12. Chronologically.
13. Photographs give the reader more information and bring the text 'to life'.
14. 1858: Emmeline born
1873: Emmeline sent to Paris
1908: Emmeline jailed for the first time
1914: Start of First World War
1918: End of First World War
1928: Women given the vote on the same terms as men.

RESOURCE SHEET SUPPORT ANSWERS

A

1. 1858
2. Paris
3. a barrister
4. vote or be an MP
5. Emmeline

B

1. through his own efforts
2. well
3. differently to men
4. the same as one another
5. most people agreed

GOING DEEPER

- Discuss the change of tactics. Do children think Emmeline was right to use violence? Why? Why not?
- Ask children what impression they get of Emmeline. Ask them what question they would ask her if they met her.

TALK

- Ask children what they know about space travel.
- Ask them what they know about the moon landing. Have they seen any films / documentaries or read any books on the moon landing?
- Explain to children that after the Second World War, the Americans and the Russians began a 'space race'. For most of the time the Russians were winning the race: they put the first living creature into space in 1957 – Laika, a dog; the first man into space in 1961 – Yuri Gagarin; the first woman into space in 1963 – Valentina Tereshkova. Both countries were working towards landing an astronaut on the moon, and the Americans got there first. This is a biographical sketch of the first human being to walk on the moon.
- Read the text to the class; ask individual children to read it aloud in turn; or read in silence individually.

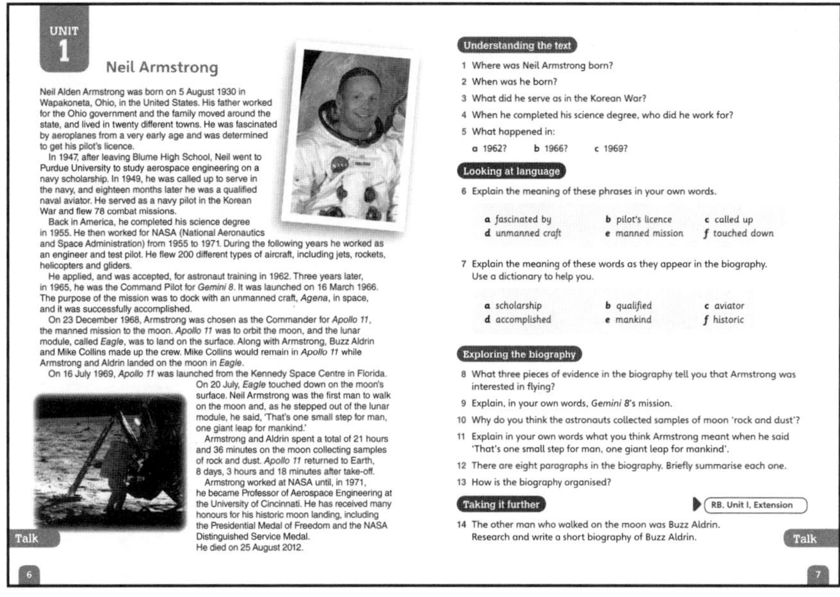

UNIT 1

Neil Armstrong

Neil Alden Armstrong was born on 5 August 1930 in Wapakoneta, Ohio, in the United States. His father worked for the Ohio government and the family moved around the state, and lived in twenty different towns. He was fascinated by aeroplanes from a very early age and was determined to get his pilot's licence.

In 1947, after leaving Blume High School, Neil went to Purdue University to study aerospace engineering on a navy scholarship. In 1949, he was called up to serve in the navy, and eighteen months later he was a qualified naval aviator. He served as a navy pilot in the Korean War and flew 78 combat missions.

Back in America, he completed his science degree in 1955. He then worked for NASA (National Aeronautics and Space Administration) from 1955 to 1971. During the following years he worked as an engineer and test pilot. He flew 200 different types of aircraft, including jets, rockets, helicopters and gliders.

He applied, and was accepted, for astronaut training in 1962. Three years later, in 1965, he was the Command Pilot for *Gemini 8*. It was launched on 16 March 1966. The purpose of the mission was to dock with an unmanned craft, *Agena*, in space, and it was successfully accomplished.

On 23 December 1968, Armstrong was chosen as the Commander for *Apollo 11*, the manned mission to the moon. *Apollo 11* was to orbit the moon, and the lunar module, called *Eagle*, was to land on the surface. Along with Armstrong, Buzz Aldrin and Mike Collins made up the crew. Mike Collins would remain in *Apollo 11* while Armstrong and Aldrin landed on the moon in *Eagle*.

On 16 July 1969, *Apollo 11* was launched from the Kennedy Space Centre in Florida. On 20 July, *Eagle* touched down on the moon's surface. Neil Armstrong was the first man to walk on the moon and, as he stepped out of the lunar module, he said, 'That's one small step for man, one giant leap for mankind.'

Armstrong and Aldrin spent a total of 21 hours and 36 minutes on the moon collecting samples of rock and dust. *Apollo 11* returned to Earth, 8 days, 3 hours and 18 minutes after take-off.

Armstrong worked at NASA until, in 1971, he became Professor of Aerospace Engineering at the University of Cincinnati. He has received many honours for his historic moon landing, including the Presidential Medal of Freedom and the NASA Distinguished Service Medal.
He died on 25 August 2012.

Talk

6

Understanding the text

1 Where was Neil Armstrong born?
2 When was he born?
3 What did he serve as in the Korean War?
4 When he completed his science degree, who did he work for?
5 What happened in:
a 1962? b 1966? c 1969?

Looking at language

6 Explain the meaning of these phrases in your own words.
a fascinated by *b pilot's licence* *c called up* *d unmanned craft* *e manned mission* *f touched down*

7 Explain the meaning of these words as they appear in the biography. Use a dictionary to help you.
a scholarship *b qualified* *c aviator* *d accomplished* *e mankind* *f historic*

Exploring the biography

8 What three pieces of evidence in the biography tell you that Armstrong was interested in flying?
9 Explain, in your own words, *Gemini 8*'s mission.
10 Why do you think the astronauts collected samples of moon 'rock and dust'?
11 Explain in your own words what you think Armstrong meant when he said 'That's one small step for man, one giant leap for mankind'.
12 There are eight paragraphs in the biography. Briefly summarise each one.
13 How is the biography organised?

Taking it further RB, Unit 1, Extension

14 The other man who walked on the moon was Buzz Aldrin. Research and write a short biography of Buzz Aldrin.

Talk

7

RESOURCES & ASSESSMENT BOOK

- **Focus** (comprehension support): completing a chart; (vocabulary support): choosing the correct definition.
- **Extension:** researching, creating a chart, writing a short biography.

PUPIL BOOK ANSWERS

1. Wapakoneta, Ohio, USA.
2. 5 August, 1930.
3. A naval pilot.
4. NASA [National Aeronautics and Space Administration].
5. **a** accepted for astronaut training **b** Command pilot on *Gemini 8* **c** walked on the moon
6. **a** really interested in **b** qualification enabling him to fly **c** ordered to join one of the armed forces **d** spacecraft with no people on board **e** journey in space involving humans **f** landed
7. **a** university fees paid for [by the navy] **b** studied and passed the necessary exams **c** aircraft pilot **d** completed **e** all the people in the world **f** famous or important in history
8. 'he was fascinated by aeroplanes' / 'was determined to get his pilot's licence' / studied 'aerospace engineering' at university.
9. *Gemini 8* had to join with *Agena* in space.
10. Scientists would want to study them to find out more about the moon.
11. A small step to get from the spacecraft to the surface of the moon, but to actually stand on the moon was a 'giant' step in terms of achievement.
12. Paragraph 1: early years.
Paragraph 2: education and navy service.
Paragraph 3: education and work for NASA.
Paragraph 4: astronaut training and first mission.
Paragraph 5: Commander of *Apollo 11*
Paragraph 6: moon landing.
Paragraph 7: on the moon and return to Earth.
Paragraph 8: after the moon landing.
13. Chronologically.
14. Individual answers.

RESOURCE SHEET SUPPORT ANSWERS

A

Date	What happened?
1930	born in Wapakoneta, Ohio, USA, 5 August
1947	left Blume High School
1955	completed science degree
1955–1971	worked for NASA
1962	accepted for astronaut training
1965	Command Pilot for *Gemini 8*
1966	launch of *Gemini 8*
1968	chosen as Commander for *Apollo 11*
1969	first man to step on to the moon's surface
1971	became Professor of Aerospace Engineering, University of Cincinnati

B

1. really interested
2. a manned mission
3. complete it

GOING DEEPER

- Ask children what impression they get of Neil Armstrong. If they could meet him, what would they ask him?

WRITE

- Discuss what children understand about 'braille'. If possible, have a Braille book available for children look at and feel.
- Explain to children that the books written in Braille are widely used by blind and partially sighted people so that they can read. The Braille alphabet was the invention of one man who was determined to overcome blindness.
- Read the text to the class; ask individual children to read it aloud in turn; or read in silence individually.

RESOURCES & ASSESSMENT BOOK

- **Focus** (comprehension support): completing the sentence; (vocabulary support): matching words to definitions.
- **Extension:** writing in Braille.

PUPIL BOOK ANSWERS

1. Coupray, near Paris.
2. 1809.
3. Injured himself and became blind in both eyes.
4. Royal Institute for Blind Youth in Paris.
5. Published his first Braille book.
6. **a** didn't work well **b** was made up of **c** less difficult / easier **d** not really appreciated by people **e** in use worldwide
7. **a** strong leather bands to control a horse **b** full of bacteria **c** large / heavy / difficult to handle **d** signs or marks that stand for something else
8. You would have to rely on your memory / couldn't go back and reread something / couldn't use notes to revise.
9. – Raised dots and dashes stood for letters.

   – By feeling the raised dots and dashes the reader could work out what the message said.
10. Very slow / dashes took up a lot of space / little could be written on the page.
11. – Clever: 'a very bright pupil'.

    – Imaginative: 'he was sure there must be a way to make reading with his fingers quicker and easier'.

    – Determined: 'spent a great deal of time trying to improve the night writing'.
12. Paragraph 1: early years.

    Paragraph 2: his injury.

    Paragraph 3: local schooling.

    Paragraph 4: Royal Institute for Blind Youth.

    Paragraph 5: Charles Barbier and night writing.

    Paragraph 6: improving night writing.

    Paragraph 7: the solution.

    Paragraph 8: the Braille system.
13. Chronologically.
14. Individual answers.

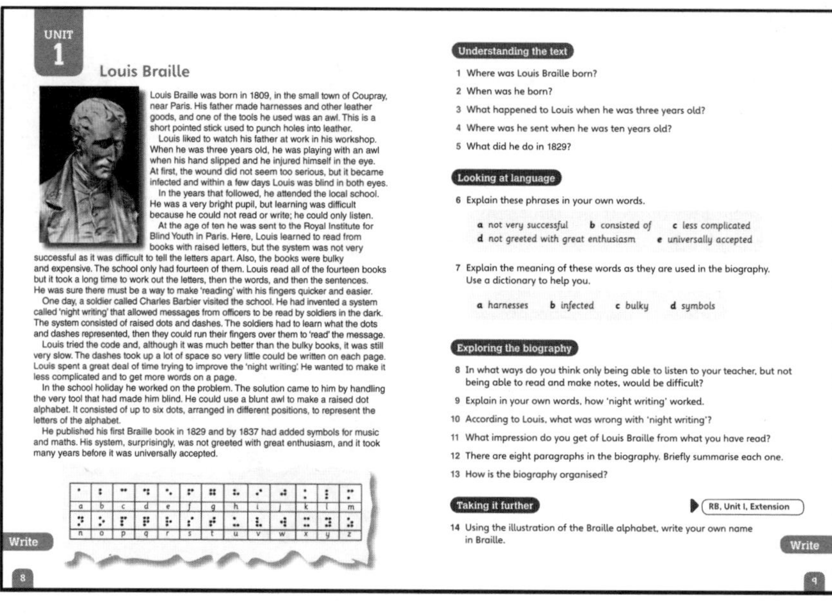

UNIT 1

Louis Braille

Louis Braille was born in 1809, in the small town of Coupray, near Paris. His father made harnesses and other leather goods, and one of the tools he used was an awl. This is a short pointed stick used to punch holes into leather.

Louis liked to watch his father at work in his workshop. When he was three years old, he was playing with an awl when his hand slipped and he injured himself in the eye. At first, the wound did not seem too serious, but it became infected and within a few days Louis was blind in both eyes.

In the years that followed, he attended the local school. He was a very bright pupil, but learning was difficult because he could not read or write; he could only listen.

At the age of ten he was sent to the Royal Institute for Blind Youth in Paris. Here, Louis learned to read from books with raised letters, but the system was not very successful as it was difficult to tell the letters apart. Also, the books were bulky and expensive. The school only had fourteen of them. Louis read all of the fourteen books but it took a long time to work out the letters, then the words, and then the sentences. He was sure there must be a way to make 'reading' with his fingers quicker and easier.

One day, a soldier called Charles Barbier visited the school. He had invented a system called 'night writing' that allowed messages from officers to be read by soldiers in the dark. The system consisted of raised dots and dashes. The soldiers had to learn what the dots and dashes represented, then they could run their fingers over them to 'read' the message.

Louis tried the code and, although it was much better than the bulky books, it was still very slow. The dashes took up a lot of space so very little could be written on each page. Louis spent a great deal of time trying to improve the 'night writing'. He wanted to make it less complicated and to get more words on a page.

In the school holiday he worked on the problem. The solution came to him by handling the very tool that had made him blind. He could use a blunt awl to make a raised dot alphabet. It consisted of up to six dots, arranged in different positions, to represent the letters of the alphabet.

He published his first Braille book in 1829 and by 1837 had added symbols for music and maths. His system, surprisingly, was not greeted with great enthusiasm, and it took many years before it was universally accepted.

a b c d e f g h i j k l m

n o p q r s t u v w x y z

Write

8

Understanding the text

1 Where was Louis Braille born?

2 When was he born?

3 What happened to Louis when he was three years old?

4 Where was he sent when he was ten years old?

5 What did he do in 1829?

Looking at language

6 Explain these phrases in your own words.

a *not very successful* **b** *consisted of* **c** *less complicated* **d** *not greeted with great enthusiasm* **e** *universally accepted*

7 Explain the meaning of these words as they are used in the biography. Use a dictionary to help you.

a *harnesses* **b** *infected* **c** *bulky* **d** *symbols*

Exploring the biography

8 In what ways do you think only being able to listen to your teacher, but not being able to read and make notes, would be difficult?

9 Explain in your own words, how 'night writing' worked.

10 According to Louis, what was wrong with 'night writing'?

11 What impression do you get of Louis Braille from what you have read?

12 There are eight paragraphs in the biography. Briefly summarise each one.

13 How is the biography organised?

Taking it further RB, Unit I, Extension

14 Using the illustration of the Braille alphabet, write your own name in Braille.

Write

9

RESOURCE SHEET SUPPORT ANSWERS

A

1. 1809
2. Coupray
3. eye
4. infected
5. blind
6. night
7. 1829
8. maths

B

1. strong leather bands
2. full of bacteria
3. large / heavy
4. signs or marks that stand for something else

C

HELLO

GOING DEEPER

- If children could meet Louis Braille, what would they ask him?
- Discuss the similarities in the characters of the three people they have read about and the common features of a biographical text.

UNIT FOCUS: Building Tension

Investigating ...

- the enduring appeal of 'monsters' in fiction
- fantasy and science fiction writing

TEACH

- Ask children to give examples of books / films that have monsters. Why do they think they are popular?
- Have children heard of Frankenstein? What do they know about him?
- Explain to children that they are going to read an extract from an adaptation of *Frankenstein*, a novel published in 1818.
- Explain the story so far: Victor Frankenstein grew up in Switzerland with his parents and their adopted daughter, Elizabeth. Victor went to university to study science and became interested in creating human life. The extract begins when Victor has made his creature and tries to bring it to life.
- Read the extract to the class; ask individual children to read it aloud in turn; or read in silence individually.

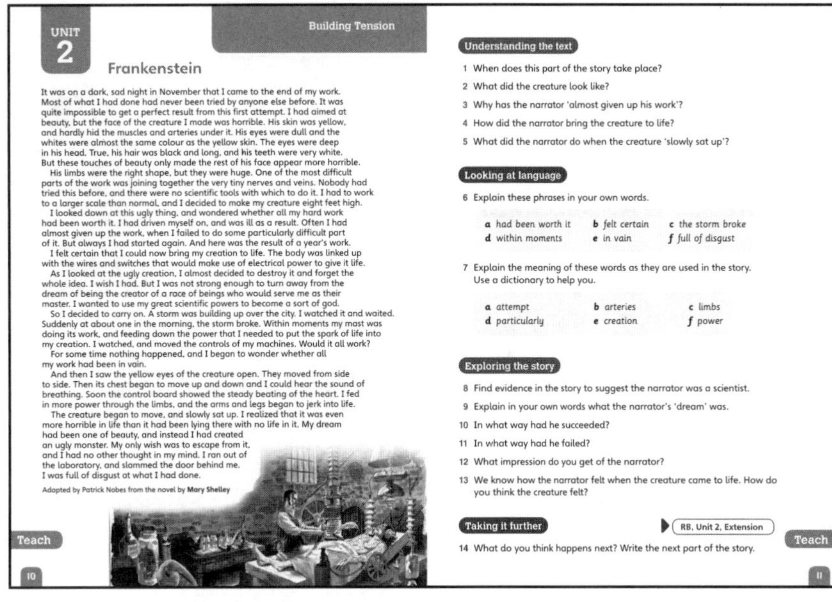

UNIT 2 Building Tension

Frankenstein

It was on a dark, sad night in November that I came to the end of my work. Most of what I had done had never been tried by anyone else before. It was quite impossible to get a perfect result from this first attempt. I had aimed at beauty, but the face of the creature I made was horrible. His skin was yellow, and hardly hid the muscles and arteries under it. His eyes were dull and the whites were almost the same colour as the yellow skin. The eyes were deep in his head. True, his hair was black and long, and his teeth were very white. But these touches of beauty only made the rest of his face appear more horrible.

His limbs were the right shape, but they were huge. One of the most difficult parts of the work was joining together the very tiny nerves and veins. Nobody had tried this before, and there were no scientific tools with which to do it. I had to work to a larger scale than normal, and I decided to make my creature eight feet high.

I looked down at this ugly thing, and wondered whether all my hard work had been worth it. I had driven myself on, and was ill as a result. Often I had almost given up the work, when I failed to do some particularly difficult part of it. But always I had started again. And here was the result of a year's work.

I felt certain that I could now bring my creation to life. The body was linked up with the wires and switches that would make use of electrical power to give it life.

As I looked at the ugly creation, I almost decided to destroy it and forget the whole idea. I wish I had. But I was not strong enough to turn away from the dream of being the creator of a race of beings who would serve me as their master. I wanted to use my great scientific powers to become a sort of god.

So I decided to carry on. A storm was building up over the city. I watched it and waited. Suddenly at about one in the morning, the storm broke. Within moments my mast was doing its work, and feeding down the power that I needed to put the spark of life into my creation. I watched, and moved the controls of my machines. Would it all work?

For some time nothing happened, and I began to wonder whether all my work had been in vain.

And then I saw the yellow eyes of the creature open. They moved from side to side. Then its chest began to move up and down and I could hear the sound of breathing. Soon the control board showed the steady beating of the heart. I fed in more power through the limbs, and the arms and legs began to jerk into life.

The creature began to move, and slowly sat up. I realized that it was even more horrible in life than it had been lying there with no life in it. My dream had been one of beauty, and instead I had created an ugly monster. My only wish was to escape from it, and I had no other thought in my mind. I ran out of the laboratory, and slammed the door behind me. I was full of disgust at what I had done.

Adapted by Patrick Nobes from the novel by **Mary Shelley**

Teach 10

Understanding the text

1 When does this part of the story take place?

2 What did the creature look like?

3 Why has the narrator 'almost given up his work'?

4 How did the narrator bring the creature to life?

5 What did the narrator do when the creature 'slowly sat up'?

Looking at language

6 Explain these phrases in your own words.

a had been worth it b felt certain c the storm broke
d within moments e in vain f full of disgust

7 Explain the meaning of these words as they are used in the story. Use a dictionary to help you.

a attempt b arteries c limbs
d particularly e creation f power

Exploring the story

8 Find evidence in the story to suggest the narrator was a scientist.

9 Explain in your own words what the narrator's 'dream' was.

10 In what way had he succeeded?

11 In what way had he failed?

12 What impression do you get of the narrator?

13 We know how the narrator felt when the creature came to life. How do you think the creature felt?

Taking it further RB, Unit 2, Extension

14 What do you think happens next? Write the next part of the story.

Teach 11

RESOURCES & ASSESSMENT BOOK

- **Focus** (comprehension support): making sentences; (vocabulary support): matching words to definitions, using adjectives.
- **Extension:** writing the next part of the story.

PUPIL BOOK ANSWERS

1 'on a dark, sad night in November'.

2 'the face ... was horrible' / 'skin was yellow' /'eyes were dull' / 'eyes were deep in his head' / 'hair was black and long' / 'teeth very white'.

3 Made himself ill / he felt like giving up / discouraged when he failed to do some difficult part of it.

4 With 'electrical power'.

5 'ran out of the laboratory'.

6 **a** had been worth doing **b** was sure **c** the storm began **d** almost immediately **e** with no success **f** full of revulsion / hatred for what he had done

7 **a** try **b** tubes that carry blood around the body **c** arms and legs **d** especially **e** something made **f** electricity

8 'scientific tools' / 'laboratory'.

9 He wanted to be powerful and make creatures that obeyed him.

10 Made the creature and brought it to life.

11 He had not created something 'beautiful' but something 'horrible'.

12 Determined /ambitious / crazy.

13 Confused / frightened.

14 Individual answers.

RESOURCE SHEET SUPPORT ANSWERS

A

1 horrible

2 black and long

3 of my hard work

4 to bring it to life

5 building up over the city

6 of the creature open

7 began to jerk into life

8 at what I had done

B

1 try

2 tubes

3 arms and legs

4 especially

5 something made

6 electricity

C

1 yellow skin

2 dull eyes

3 long / black hair

4 white teeth

5 huge limbs

6 tiny nerves

GOING DEEPER

- Discuss whether children think Frankenstein was right or wrong to create his monster. Do they think the story will end happily or sadly? Why?

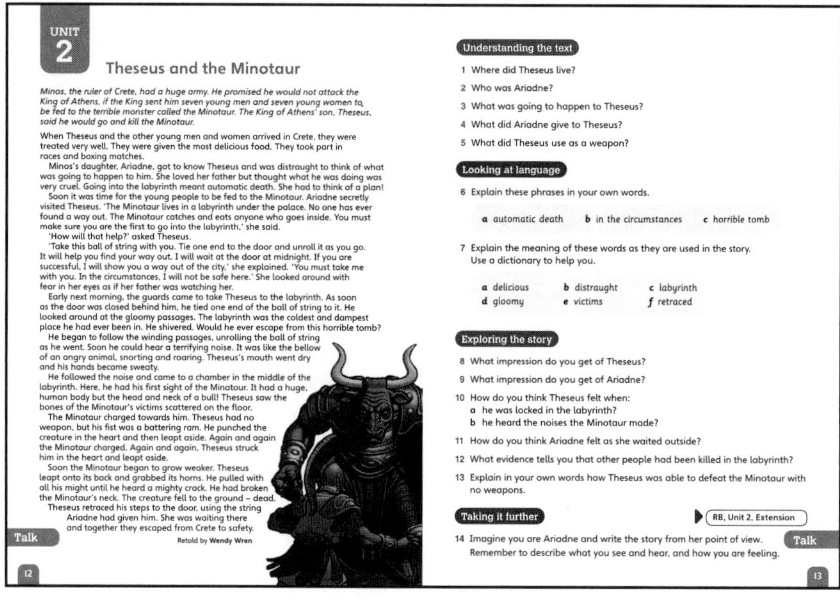

UNIT 2

Theseus and the Minotaur

Minos, the ruler of Crete, had a huge army. He promised he would not attack the King of Athens, if the King sent him seven young men and seven young women to be fed to the terrible monster called the Minotaur. The King of Athens' son, Theseus, said he would go and kill the Minotaur.

When Theseus and the other young men and women arrived in Crete, they were treated very well. They were given the most delicious food. They took part in races and boxing matches.

Minos's daughter, Ariadne, got to know Theseus and was distraught to think of what was going to happen to him. She loved her father but thought what he was doing was very cruel. Going into the labyrinth meant automatic death. She had to think of a plan!

Soon it was time for the young people to be fed to the Minotaur. Ariadne secretly visited Theseus. 'The Minotaur lives in a labyrinth under the palace. No one has ever found a way out. The Minotaur catches and eats anyone who goes inside. You must make sure you are the first to go into the labyrinth,' she said.

'How will that help?' asked Theseus.

'Take this ball of string with you. Tie one end to the door and unroll it as you go. It will help you find your way out. I will wait at the door at midnight. If you are successful, I will show you a way out of the city,' she explained. 'You must take me with you. In the circumstances, I will not be safe here.' She looked around with fear in her eyes as if her father was watching her.

Early next morning, the guards came to take Theseus to the labyrinth. As soon as the door was closed behind him, he tied one end of the ball of string to it. He looked around at the gloomy passages. The labyrinth was the coldest and dampest place he had ever been in. He shivered. Would he ever escape from this horrible tomb?

He began to follow the winding passages, unrolling the ball of string as he went. Soon he could hear a terrifying noise. It was like the bellow of an angry animal, snorting and roaring. Theseus's mouth went dry and his hands became sweaty.

He followed the noise and came to a chamber in the middle of the labyrinth. Here, he had his first sight of the Minatour. It had a huge, human body but the head and neck of a bull! Theseus saw the bones of the Minotaur's victims scattered on the floor.

The Minotaur charged towards him. Theseus had no weapon, but his fist was a battering ram. He punched the creature in the heart and then leapt aside. Again and again the Minotaur charged. Again and again, Theseus struck him in the heart and leapt aside.

Soon the Minotaur began to grow weaker. Theseus leapt onto its back and grabbed its horns. He pulled with all his might until he heard a mighty crack. He had broken the Minotaur's neck. The creature fell to the ground – dead.

Theseus retraced his steps to the door, using the string Ariadne had given him. She was waiting there and together they escaped from Crete to safety.

Retold by **Wendy Wren**

Talk

12

Understanding the text

1 Where did Theseus live?

2 Who was Ariadne?

3 What was going to happen to Theseus?

4 What did Ariadne give to Theseus?

5 What did Theseus use as a weapon?

Looking at language

6 Explain these phrases in your own words.

a automatic death *b* in the circumstances *c* horrible tomb

7 Explain the meaning of these words as they are used in the story. Use a dictionary to help you.

a delicious *b* distraught *c* labyrinth
d gloomy *e* victims *f* retraced

Exploring the story

8 What impression do you get of Theseus?

9 What impression do you get of Ariadne?

10 How do you think Theseus felt when:
a he was locked in the labyrinth?
b he heard the noises the Minotaur made?

11 How do you think Ariadne felt as she waited outside?

12 What evidence tells you that other people had been killed in the labyrinth?

13 Explain in your own words how Theseus was able to defeat the Minotaur with no weapons.

Taking it further

RB, Unit 2, Extension

14 Imagine you are Ariadne and write the story from her point of view. Remember to describe what you see and hear, and how you are feeling.

Talk

13

TALK

- Recap on what children understand by the term 'legend'.
- What legends do they know?
- Why do they think that legends, written so long ago, are still popular today?
- Explain to children that they are going to read the legend of *Theseus and the Minotaur.*
- Read the extract to the class; ask individual children to read it aloud in turn; or read in silence individually.

RESOURCES & ASSESSMENT BOOK

- **Focus** (comprehension support): completing sentences; (vocabulary support): matching words to correct definitions.
- **Extension:** making notes from a character's point of view.

PUPIL BOOK ANSWERS

1. Athens.
2. Daughter of the ruler of Crete / Minos's daughter.
3. Going to be fed to the Minotaur.
4. A ball of string.
5. His fist.
6. **a** certain death / there was no escape **b** in this situation **c** awful place to die
7. **a** tasty / good to eat **b** very upset **c** maze **d** dark **e** people who the Minotaur had killed **f** went back
8. Brave: he tells his father he will go and kill the Minotaur; sensible: he takes advice from Ariadne; strong: he defeats the Minotaur with just his hands.
9. Kind-hearted: she was upset when she knew what was to happen to Theseus; quick-witted: she came up with the plan that would save Theseus; realistic: she knew she could not stay after helping Theseus.
10. **a** pessimistic: 'Would he ever escape from this horrible tomb?' / determined to succeed: 'He tied one end of the ball of string' [to the door] **b** frightened: 'Theseus's mouth went dry and his hands began to sweat.'
11. Individual answers.
12. 'Theseus saw the bones of the Minotaur's victims scattered on the floor.'
13. Theseus punched the Minotaur in the heart again and again until he grew weaker / Theseus leapt onto the Minotaur's back and pulled on its horns to break its neck.
14. Individual answers.

RESOURCE SHEET SUPPORT ANSWERS

A

1. Theseus lived in **Athens**.
2. Ariadne lived in **Crete**.
3. The Minotaur lived in a **labyrinth** under the **palace**.
4. Ariadne gave Theseus a **ball of string**.
5. As Theseus walked down the passage, he heard a **terrifying noise**.
6. The Minotaur had a **human** body but the **head** and **neck** of a bull.
7. Theseus used his **fist** as a weapon.
8. He killed the Minotaur by **breaking** its neck.

B

1. tasty
2. very upset
3. maze
4. dark
5. people killed by the Minotaur
6. went back

GOING DEEPER

- Discuss with children the difference between Frankenstein's monster and the Minotaur. In what ways are they similar? In what ways are they different?

WRITE

- Discuss what children understand by the term 'Jurassic'.
- Elicit / explain that this is the name given to a time when dinosaurs roamed the earth.
- Ask children if they have seen the film *Jurassic Park*. If so, what did they think of it?
- Explain to the children that they are going to read an extract from an adaptation of a book called *Jurassic Park*, on which the film was based.
- Read the extract to the class; ask individual children to read it aloud in turn; or read in silence individually.

RESOURCES & ASSESSMENT BOOK

- **Focus** (comprehension support): choosing the correct answer; (vocabulary support): finding the correct words in the extract.
- **Extension:** writing notes from character's point of view.

PUPIL BOOK ANSWERS

1. 'recreated the world of dinosaurs on a remote island'.
2. Touring the island in 'electric cars'.
3. Power to the electric fence was not working.
4. 'bolted out of the car'/ 'raced towards a small building' / 'ran inside'.
5. 'It can't see us if we don't move'.
6. **a** shuddering / shaking **b** small backward and forward movements **c** ran quickly / escaped **d** looking at **e** a bright light to show where something is **f** hit with the head
7. Answers that suggest the reader is made aware of the noise and movement but the dinosaur does not appear. The tension is built up as we are waiting to find out what is making the 'quaking' sounds' and causing 'the vibrations'.
8. Worried about his own safety / selfishly leaves the others in the car / stupid to think a 'small building' will protect him from the dinosaur.
9. Knows not to move because the T-rex has poor eyesight.

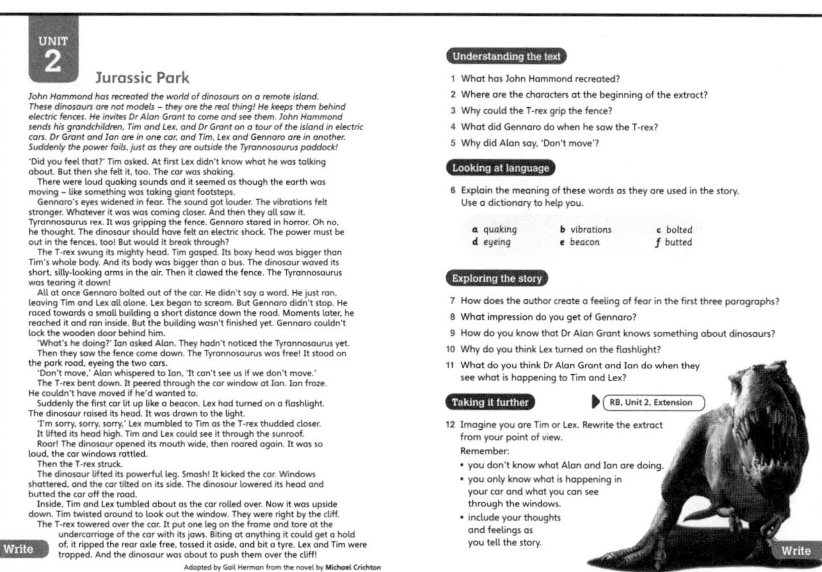

UNIT 2

Jurassic Park

John Hammond has recreated the world of dinosaurs on a remote island. These dinosaurs are not models – they are the real thing! He keeps them behind electric fences. He invites Dr Alan Grant to come and see them. John Hammond sends his grandchildren, Tim and Lex, and Dr Grant on a tour of the island in electric cars. Dr Grant and Ian are in one car, and Tim, Lex and Gennaro are in another. Suddenly the power fails, just as they are outside the Tyrannosaurus paddock!

'Did you feel that?' Tim asked. At first Lex didn't know what he was talking about. But then she felt it, too. The car was shaking.

There were loud quaking sounds and it seemed as though the earth was moving – like something was taking giant footsteps.

Gennaro's eyes widened in fear. The sound got louder. The vibrations felt stronger. Whatever it was was coming closer. And then they all saw it. Tyrannosaurus rex. It was gripping the fence. Gennaro stared in horror. Oh no, he thought. The dinosaur should have felt an electric shock. The power must be out in the fences, too! But would it break through?

The T-rex swung its mighty head. Tim gasped. Its boxy head was bigger than Tim's whole body. And its body was bigger than a bus. The dinosaur waved its short, silly-looking arms in the air. Then it clawed the fence. The Tyrannosaurus was tearing it down!

All at once Gennaro bolted out of the car. He didn't say a word. He just ran, leaving Tim and Lex all alone. Lex began to scream. But Gennaro didn't stop. He raced towards a small building a short distance down the road. Moments later, he reached it and ran inside. But the building wasn't finished yet. Gennaro couldn't lock the wooden door behind him.

'What's he doing?' Ian asked Alan. They hadn't noticed the Tyrannosaurus yet.

Then they saw the fence come down. The Tyrannosaurus was free! It stood on the park road, eyeing the two cars.

'Don't move,' Alan whispered to Ian, 'It can't see us if we don't move.'

The T-rex bent down. It peered through the car window at Ian. Ian froze. He couldn't have moved if he'd wanted to.

Suddenly the first car lit up like a beacon. Lex had turned on a flashlight. The dinosaur raised its head. It was drawn to the light.

'I'm sorry, sorry, sorry,' Lex mumbled to Tim as the T-rex thudded closer.

It lifted its head high. Tim and Lex could see it through the sunroof.

Roar! The dinosaur opened its mouth wide, then roared again. It was so loud, the car windows rattled.

Then the T-rex struck.

The dinosaur lifted its powerful leg. Smash! It kicked the car. Windows shattered, and the car tilted on its side. The dinosaur lowered its head and butted the car off the road.

Inside, Tim and Lex tumbled about as the car rolled over. Now it was upside down. Tim twisted around to look out the window. They were right by the cliff.

The T-rex towered over the car. It put one leg on the frame and tore at the undercarriage of the car with its jaws. Biting at anything it could get a hold of, it ripped the rear axle free, tossed it aside, and bit a tyre. Lex and Tim were trapped. And the dinosaur was about to push them over the cliff!

Adapted by Gail Herman from the novel by **Michael Crichton**

Write

14

Understanding the text

1 What has John Hammond recreated?
2 Where are the characters at the beginning of the extract?
3 Why could the T-rex grip the fence?
4 What did Gennaro do when he saw the T-rex?
5 Why did Alan say, 'Don't move'?

Looking at language

6 Explain the meaning of these words as they are used in the story. Use a dictionary to help you.

a *quaking* **b** *vibrations* **c** *bolted*
d *eyeing* **e** *beacon* **f** *butted*

Exploring the story

7 How does the author create a feeling of fear in the first three paragraphs?
8 What impression do you get of Gennaro?
9 How do you know that Dr Alan Grant knows something about dinosaurs?
10 Why do you think Lex turned on the flashlight?
11 What do you think Dr Alan Grant and Ian do when they see what is happening to Tim and Lex?

Taking it further

RB, Unit 2, Extension

12 Imagine you are Tim or Lex. Rewrite the extract from your point of view.
Remember:
- you don't know what Alan and Ian are doing.
- you only know what is happening in your car and what you can see through the windows.
- include your thoughts and feelings as you tell the story.

Write

15

10. Frightened in the dark and wanted to see what was going on / thought the light may scare off the dinosaur.
11. Individual answers.
12. Individual answers.

RESOURCE SHEET SUPPORT ANSWERS

A

1. a
2. c
3. b
4. c
5. b

B

1. quaking
2. vibrations
3. bolted
4. eyeing
5. beacon
6. butted

GOING DEEPER

- Discuss the three monsters that the children have read about. Do they think they are all frightening? Which of these stories would they like to read?

UNIT FOCUS: The Rules of Argument

Investigating …

- balanced and one-sided arguments
- their own arguments for a debate

TEACH

- Ask children what they understand by the terms 'balanced argument' and 'pros and cons'.
- Elicit understanding or explain the terms indicating that a balanced argument considers all the points of view, in other words, both pros and cons.
- Explain that children are going to read an article called 'Text Messaging – Good or Bad?', which is an example of a balanced article.
- Read the article to the class; ask individual children to read it aloud in turn; or read in silence individually.

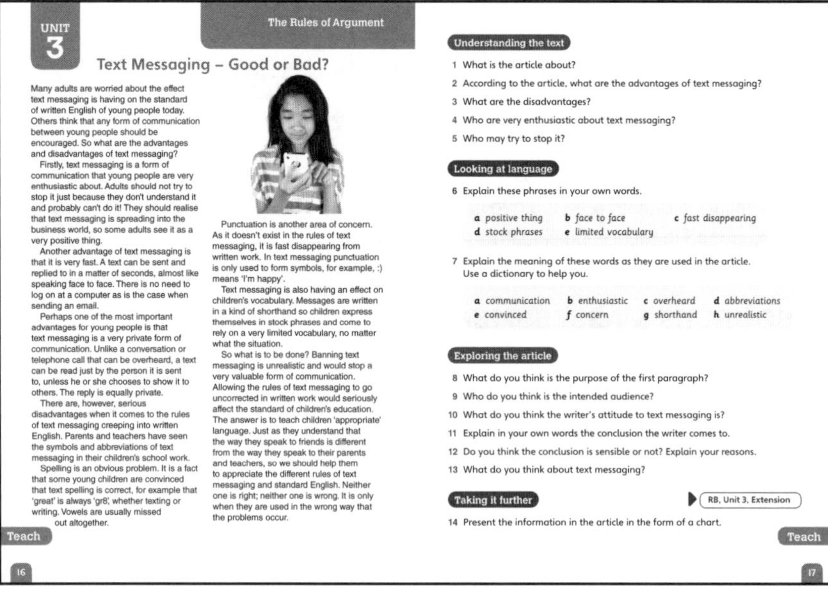

UNIT 3 The Rules of Argument

Text Messaging – Good or Bad?

Many adults are worried about the effect text messaging is having on the standard of written English of young people today. Others think that any form of communication between young people should be encouraged. So what are the advantages and disadvantages of text messaging?

Firstly, text messaging is a form of communication that young people are very enthusiastic about. Adults should not try to stop it just because they don't understand it and probably can't do it! They should realise that text messaging is spreading into the business world, so some adults see it as a very positive thing.

Another advantage of text messaging is that it is very fast. A text can be sent and replied to in a matter of seconds, almost like speaking face to face. There is no need to log on at a computer as is the case when sending an email.

Perhaps one of the most important advantages for young people is that text messaging is a very private form of communication. Unlike a conversation or telephone call that can be overheard, a text can be read just by the person it is sent to, unless he or she chooses to show it to others. The reply is equally private.

There are, however, serious disadvantages when it comes to the rules of text messaging creeping into written English. Parents and teachers have seen the symbols and abbreviations of text messaging in their children's school work.

Spelling is an obvious problem. It is a fact that some young children are convinced that text spelling is correct, for example that 'great' is always 'gr8', whether texting or writing. Vowels are usually missed out altogether.

Punctuation is another area of concern. As it doesn't exist in the rules of text messaging, it is fast disappearing from written work. In text messaging punctuation is only used to form symbols, for example, :) means 'I'm happy'.

Text messaging is also having an effect on children's vocabulary. Messages are written in a kind of shorthand so children express themselves in stock phrases and come to rely on a very limited vocabulary, no matter what the situation.

So what is to be done? Banning text messaging is unrealistic and would stop a very valuable form of communication. Allowing the rules of text messaging to go uncorrected in written work would seriously affect the standard of children's education. The answer is to teach children 'appropriate' language. Just as they understand that the way they speak to friends is different from the way they speak to their parents and teachers, so we should help them to appreciate the different rules of text messaging and standard English. Neither one is right; neither one is wrong. It is only when they are used in the wrong way that the problems occur.

Teach

16

Understanding the text

1 What is the article about?

2 According to the article, what are the advantages of text messaging?

3 What are the disadvantages?

4 Who are very enthusiastic about text messaging?

5 Who may try to stop it?

Looking at language

6 Explain these phrases in your own words.

a *positive thing* **b** *face to face* **c** *fast disappearing*
d *stock phrases* **e** *limited vocabulary*

7 Explain the meaning of these words as they are used in the article. Use a dictionary to help you.

a communication **b** enthusiastic **c** overheard **d** abbreviations
e convinced **f** concern **g** shorthand **h** unrealistic

Exploring the article

8 What do you think is the purpose of the first paragraph?

9 Who do you think is the intended audience?

10 What do you think the writer's attitude to text messaging is?

11 Explain in your own words the conclusion the writer comes to.

12 Do you think the conclusion is sensible or not? Explain your reasons.

13 What do you think about text messaging?

Taking it further RB, Unit 3, Extension

14 Present the information in the article in the form of a chart.

Teach

17

RESOURCES & ASSESSMENT BOOK

- **Focus** (comprehension support): exploring advantages and disadvantages; (vocabulary support): choosing the correct definition.
- **Extension:** presenting information in a chart.

PUPIL BOOK ANSWERS

1. Text messaging.
2. Fast / private.
3. Rules creeping into written English / affecting spelling, punctuation / limited vocabulary.
4. Young people.
5. Adults.
6. **a** something good and helpful **b** as if standing next to each other **c** quickly going **d** a phrase used so often it has very little meaning **e** knowing few words
7. **a** the process of exchanging information through talking or writing **b** very keen **c** to hear a conversation you are not involved in **d** shortened forms **e** really think **f** worry **g** not in full **h** not possible
8. To introduce the reader to what the article is about.
9. Adults.
10. Can see both points of view.
11. Writer thinks the advantages should be recognised and the disadvantages dealt with by teaching appropriate language.
12. Individual answers.
13. Individual answers.
14. Individual answers.

RESOURCE SHEET SUPPORT ANSWERS

A

1. ADVANTAGE
2. DISADVANTAGE
3. DISADVANTAGE
4. ADVANTAGE
5. DISADVANTAGE
6. ADVANTAGE

B

1. a
2. b
3. a
4. b
5. b
6. a

GOING DEEPER

- Discuss the article with the children in terms of how fair they think the writer is. Can they think of any more advantages or disadvantages of text messages?

TALK

- Ask children what they understand by the term 'animal testing'. Do they think it is wrong or right? Why?
- Take a vote on who is for and who is against animal testing before reading the article.
- Explain to the children that they are going to read an article called 'Animal Testing', where the writer is putting forward arguments in support of using animals in scientific experiments.
- Read the article to the class; ask individual children to read it aloud in turn; or read in silence individually.

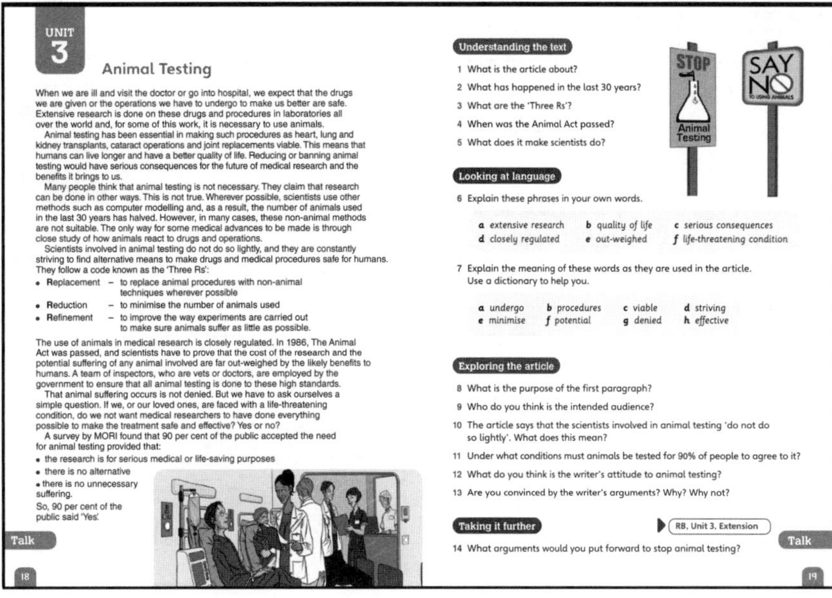

UNIT 3

Animal Testing

When we are ill and visit the doctor or go into hospital, we expect that the drugs we are given or the operations we have to undergo to make us better are safe. Extensive research is done on these drugs and procedures in laboratories all over the world and, for some of this work, it is necessary to use animals.

Animal testing has been essential in making such procedures as heart, lung and kidney transplants, cataract operations and joint replacements viable. This means that humans can live longer and have a better quality of life. Reducing or banning animal testing would have serious consequences for the future of medical research and the benefits it brings to us.

Many people think that animal testing is not necessary. They claim that research can be done in other ways. This is not true. Wherever possible, scientists use other methods such as computer modelling and, as a result, the number of animals used in the last 30 years has halved. However, in many cases, these non-animal methods are not suitable. The only way for some medical advances to be made is through close study of how animals react to drugs and operations.

Scientists involved in animal testing do not do so lightly, and they are constantly striving to find alternative means to make drugs and medical procedures safe for humans. They follow a code known as the 'Three Rs':

- Replacement – to replace animal procedures with non-animal techniques wherever possible
- Reduction – to minimise the number of animals used
- Refinement – to improve the way experiments are carried out to make sure animals suffer as little as possible.

The use of animals in medical research is closely regulated. In 1986, The Animal Act was passed, and scientists have to prove that the cost of the research and the potential suffering of any animal involved are far out-weighed by the likely benefits to humans. A team of inspectors, who are vets or doctors, are employed by the government to ensure that all animal testing is done to these high standards.

That animal suffering occurs is not denied. But we have to ask ourselves a simple question. If we, or our loved ones, are faced with a life-threatening condition, do we not want medical researchers to have done everything possible to make the treatment safe and effective? Yes or no?

A survey by MORI found that 90 per cent of the public accepted the need for animal testing provided that:

- the research is for serious medical or life-saving purposes
- there is no alternative
- there is no unnecessary suffering.

So, 90 per cent of the public said 'Yes'.

Talk

18

Understanding the text

1 What is the article about?
2 What has happened in the last 30 years?
3 What are the 'Three Rs'?
4 When was the Animal Act passed?
5 What does it make scientists do?

Looking at language

6 Explain these phrases in your own words.

a extensive research *b* quality of life *c* serious consequences *d* closely regulated *e* out-weighed *f* life-threatening condition

7 Explain the meaning of these words as they are used in the article. Use a dictionary to help you.

a undergo *b* procedures *c* viable *d* striving *e* minimise *f* potential *g* denied *h* effective

Exploring the article

8 What is the purpose of the first paragraph?
9 Who do you think is the intended audience?
10 The article says that the scientists involved in animal testing 'do not do so lightly'. What does this mean?
11 Under what conditions must animals be tested for 90% of people to agree to it?
12 What do you think is the writer's attitude to animal testing?
13 Are you convinced by the writer's arguments? Why? Why not?

Taking it further RB, Unit 3, Extension

14 What arguments would you put forward to stop animal testing?

Talk

19

RESOURCES & ASSESSMENT BOOK

- **Focus** (comprehension support): completing words in sentences; (vocabulary support): choosing the correct answers.
- **Extension:** writing a paragraph on given stimulus.

PUPIL BOOK ANSWERS

1. Animal testing / using animals in scientific experiments.
2. the number of animals used has been halved.
3. Replacement / Reduction / Refinement.
4. 1986.
5. Scientists 'have to prove that the cost of research and the potential suffering of any animal involved are far out-weighed by the likely benefits to humans'.
6. **a** looking into the situation very thoroughly **b** how pleasant or otherwise life is **c** dangerous results **d** happens under strict rules that have to be obeyed **e** when one thing is more important than another **f** an illness that could end in death
7. **a** have / experience **b** medical treatments **c** possible / able to be done **d** trying really hard **e** reduce / make as small as possible **f** likely [in the future] **g** say is untrue **h** working well / producing the intended result
8. To introduce the reader to what the article is about and to show which side the writer is on.
9. People who are against animal testing.
10. They do it very seriously.
11. Research is for serious medical purposes / there is no other way of doing it / there is no unnecessary suffering.
12. Writer supports animal testing to make drugs and medicines as safe as possible for humans.
13. Individual answers.
14. Individual answers.

RESOURCE SHEET SUPPORT ANSWERS

A

1. Animal testing has helped in heart, lung and kidney transplants.
2. Scientist need to study closely how animals react to drugs and operations.
3. Scientists follow a code that involves Replacement, Reduction, and Refinement.
4. The team of inspectors is made up of vets and doctors.
5. Animal testing is supported by 90% of people if: **a** the research is for life saving purposes; **b** there is no alternative; **c** there is no unnecessary suffering.

B

1. a
2. b
3. b
4. a
5. b

GOING DEEPER

- Use children's opinions about whether they are convinced or not of the writers' arguments together with the 'Taking it further' activity as the basis for class discussion. Take another vote on animal testing. Has the article made a difference? Explore why children's opinions may have changed.
- Compare 'Text Messaging – Good or Bad?' with 'Animal Testing' and discuss the similarities and differences.

WRITE

- Discuss what children understand by the term 'UFO'.
- Take a class vote to see how many children believe in UFOs.
- Explain that they are going to read an article called 'UFOs Do Not Exist!' by a writer who does not believe in them.
- Read the article to the class; ask individual children to read it aloud in turn; or read in silence individually.

RESOURCES & ASSESSMENT BOOK

- **Focus** (comprehension support): exploring: True / False statements, correcting false statements; (vocabulary support): matching words with correct definitions.
- **Extension:** writing a paragraph on given stimulus.

PUPIL BOOK ANSWERS

1. The existence or not of UFOs.
2. 'at night'.
3. 'in lonely rural areas'.
4. 1950s.
5. The UFOs' purpose in coming here.
6. **a** what they are called is not necessarily what they are **b** actual 'things' left behind that prove what they say **c** people are able to live there **d** came up with another theory **e** better at technology than us
7. **a** taken away against your will **b** countryside **c** not known **d** beings who supposedly come from Venus **e** people who are very keen on something **f** groups of stars and planets
8. To introduce what the article is about.
9. People who believe in UFOs to try to dissuade them.
10. Individual answers (a light show led to reports of UFOs).
11. That these people are lying or mistaken.
12. Individual answers (he doesn't believe in UFOs and thinks other people shouldn't either).
13. No – he thinks it is ridiculous.
14. Individual answers.
15. Individual answers.

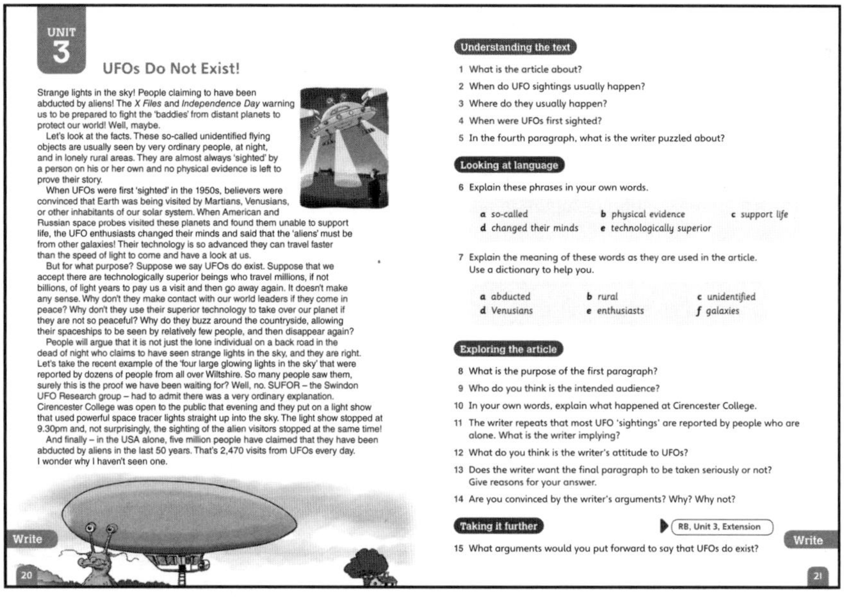

UNIT 3

UFOs Do Not Exist!

Strange lights in the sky! People claiming to have been abducted by aliens! The *X Files* and *Independence Day* warning us to be prepared to fight the 'baddies' from distant planets to protect our world! Well, maybe.

Let's look at the facts. These so-called unidentified flying objects are usually seen by very ordinary people, at night, and in lonely rural areas. They are almost always 'sighted' by a person on his or her own and no physical evidence is left to prove their story.

When UFOs were first 'sighted' in the 1950s, believers were convinced that Earth was being visited by Martians, Venusians, or other inhabitants of our solar system. When American and Russian space probes visited these planets and found them unable to support life, the UFO enthusiasts changed their minds and said that the 'aliens' must be from other galaxies! Their technology is so advanced they can travel faster than the speed of light to come and have a look at us.

But for what purpose? Suppose we say UFOs do exist. Suppose that we accept there are technologically superior beings who travel millions, if not billions, of light years to pay us a visit and then go away again. It doesn't make any sense. Why don't they make contact with our world leaders if they come in peace? Why don't they use their superior technology to take over our planet if they are not so peaceful? Why do they buzz around the countryside, allowing their spaceships to be seen by relatively few people, and then disappear again?

People will argue that it is not just the lone individual on a back road in the dead of night who claims to have seen strange lights in the sky, and they are right. Let's take the recent example of the 'four large glowing lights in the sky' that were reported by dozens of people from all over Wiltshire. So many people saw them, surely this is the proof we have been waiting for? Well, no. SUFOR – the Swindon UFO Research group – had to admit there was a very ordinary explanation. Cirencester College was open to the public that evening and they put on a light show that used powerful space tracer lights straight up into the sky. The light show stopped at 9.30pm and, not surprisingly, the sighting of the alien visitors stopped at the same time!

And finally – in the USA alone, five million people have claimed that they have been abducted by aliens in the last 50 years. That's 2,470 visits from UFOs every day. I wonder why I haven't seen one.

Write

20

Understanding the text

1 What is the article about?
2 When do UFO sightings usually happen?
3 Where do they usually happen?
4 When were UFOs first sighted?
5 In the fourth paragraph, what is the writer puzzled about?

Looking at language

6 Explain these phrases in your own words.
a so-called **b** physical evidence **c** support life
d changed their minds **e** technologically superior

7 Explain the meaning of these words as they are used in the article. Use a dictionary to help you.
a abducted **b** rural **c** unidentified
d Venusians **e** enthusiasts **f** galaxies

Exploring the article

8 What is the purpose of the first paragraph?
9 Who do you think is the intended audience?
10 In your own words, explain what happened at Cirencester College.
11 The writer repeats that most UFO 'sightings' are reported by people who are alone. What is the writer implying?
12 What do you think is the writer's attitude to UFOs?
13 Does the writer want the final paragraph to be taken seriously or not? Give reasons for your answer.
14 Are you convinced by the writer's arguments? Why? Why not?

Taking it further RB, Unit 3, Extension

15 What arguments would you put forward to say that UFOs do exist?

Write

21

RESOURCE SHEET SUPPORT ANSWERS

A

1. FALSE
2. TRUE
3. FALSE
4. TRUE
5. TRUE
6. FALSE

B

1. UFOs are usually seen by people on their own.
2. Space probes found that Mars and Venus were unable to support life.
3. Five million people in the USA claimed to have been abducted by aliens.

C

1. taken away against your will
2. countryside
3. not known
4. people who are keen on something
5. groups of stars and planets

GOING DEEPER

- Use children's opinions about whether they are convinced or not of the writer's arguments together with the 'Taking it further' activity as a basis for a class discussion. Take another class vote on UFOs. Have children's opinions changed? Explore why.
- Ask children which of the arguments they have read are balanced and which are one-sided. Conclude the unit by setting up a series of mini debates. Children work in pairs to propose or oppose a statement. Children can come up with suggestions and then be allocated a topic. Suggestions for suitable topics include: 'Children under 15 should not be allowed mobile phones'; 'Everyone should be a vegetarian'; 'Computers make people lazy'.

UNIT FOCUS: Exploring Issues in Poetry

Investigating ...

- poems that raise issues
- the connecting theme of 'school life' and issues that children will have witnessed or have experience of

TEACH

- Discuss 'friendship' with children.
- Ask children what makes us friends with some people and not others.
- Explore why children think we like to be part of a group.
- Explain that they are going to read a poem called 'The Loner', told from the point of view of a child who is part of a group but watches a child who is on their own.
- Read the poem to the class; ask individual children to read it aloud in turn; or read in silence individually.

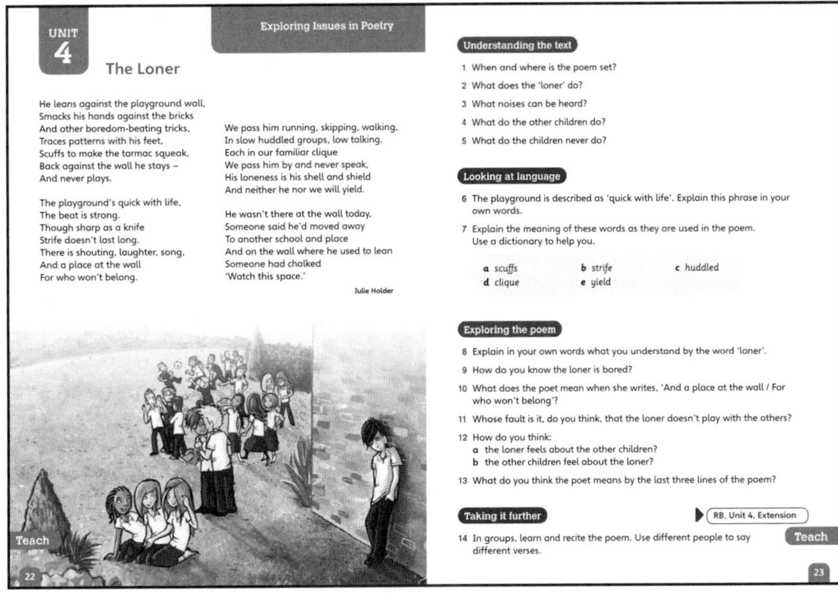

UNIT 4

Exploring Issues in Poetry

The Loner

He leans against the playground wall,
Smacks his hands against the bricks
And other boredom-beating tricks,
Traces patterns with his feet,
Scuffs to make the tarmac squeak,
Back against the wall he stays –
And never plays.

The playground's quick with life,
The beat is strong.
Though sharp as a knife
Strife doesn't last long.
There is shouting, laughter, song,
And a place at the wall
For who won't belong.

We pass him running, skipping, walking,
In slow huddled groups, low talking.
Each in our familiar clique
We pass him by and never speak,
His loneness is his shell and shield
And neither he nor we will yield.

He wasn't there at the wall today,
Someone said he'd moved away
To another school and place
And on the wall where he used to lean
Someone had chalked
'Watch this space.'

Julie Holder

Teach

22

Understanding the text

1 When and where is the poem set?
2 What does the 'loner' do?
3 What noises can be heard?
4 What do the other children do?
5 What do the children never do?

Looking at language

6 The playground is described as 'quick with life'. Explain this phrase in your own words.
7 Explain the meaning of these words as they are used in the poem. Use a dictionary to help you.
   a scuffs   b strife   c huddled
   d clique   e yield

Exploring the poem

8 Explain in your own words what you understand by the word 'loner'.
9 How do you know the loner is bored?
10 What does the poet mean when she writes, 'And a place at the wall / For who won't belong'?
11 Whose fault is it, do you think, that the loner doesn't play with the others?
12 How do you think:
   a the loner feels about the other children?
   b the other children feel about the loner?
13 What do you think the poet means by the last three lines of the poem?

Taking it further — RB, Unit 4, Extension

14 In groups, learn and recite the poem. Use different people to say different verses.

Teach

23

RESOURCES & ASSESSMENT BOOK

- **Focus** (comprehension support): choosing the correct words to complete sentences; (vocabulary support): ordering verbs.
- **Extension:** learning and reciting a poem.

PUPIL BOOK ANSWERS

1. In the playground either before morning school or at playtime.
2. 'leans against the playground wall' / 'smacks his hands against the bricks' / 'traces patterns with his feet'.
3. 'shouting, laughter, song'.
4. 'running, skipping, walking', 'slow huddled groups, low talking', 'pass him by'.
5. 'never speak' to the loner.
6. There is a lot of activity and energy in the playground.
7. **a** marks / scrapes shoe **b** arguments / disagreements **c** standing close together **d** small, exclusive group **e** give in
8. Someone who wants to be alone, or is alone because no one wants to know them.
9. He does things that are 'boredom-beating'.
10. The boy refuses to join in.
11. It could be the boy's fault as he 'won't' join in, although he could be shy. It could be that the other children haven't tried to make friends with him.
12. **a** he may not care about them / may be envious because he would like to be one of them or play with them **b** they don't care about him / they may feel sorry for him
13. Individual answers.
14. Individual answers.

RESOURCE SHEET SUPPORT ANSWERS

A

the loner: to lean / to scuff / to smack / to trace / to stay
the other children: to skip / to sing / to laugh / to talk / to pass / to shout / to chalk / to huddle / to run

B

1. If you **scuff** your shoes, you make marks on them.
2. The black material playgrounds are often made from is **tarmac**.
3. **Strife** is when people argue and disagree.
4. If you **huddle**, you stand close together.
5. A **clique** is a small group of people who usually go around together.
6. If you **yield**, you give in.

GOING DEEPER

- Discuss what children think of the poem. How do they feel about the loner? If they had been one of the other children, what would they have done?

TALK

- Ask children if that have been a victim of, or have witnessed, bullying.
- Explore why they think people bully other people and what they think of bullies.
- Explain that they are going to read a poem called 'Bullied', written from the viewpoint of someone being bullied.
- Read the poem to the class; ask individual children to read it aloud in turn; or read in silence individually.

RESOURCES & ASSESSMENT BOOK

- **Focus** (comprehension support): choosing the correct answer; (vocabulary support): choosing the correct words to finish sentences.
- **Extension:** writing paragraphs / advice on given stimulus.

PUPIL BOOK ANSWERS

1. 'loners' / 'quiet ones' / 'different ones'.
2. 'the in-betweens'.
3. 'Keep my eyes skinned' / 'find a crowd to vanish into' / 'not to look at the floor' / 'to try and walk tall' / 'to talk in my head'.
4. 'just don't give in' / 'Don't let them win'.
5. **a** be on the look out **b** head up, shoulders back, looking like you have nothing to be afraid of **c** register / make sense / finally realise.
6. **a** tracking device **b** lacking in confidence **c** taunting **d** causing you trouble **e** never stopping **f** people who do not fit in
7. That bullies are really cowards who need to show off and pick on others so people will think they are tough.
8. 'a relentless horde / of nagging, pecking birds' – a good comparison as a group of birds with beaks and flapping wings is very intimidating.
9. Looking at the floor is a sign of weakness that the bullies are 'tuned into'.
10. This is the first step to combating the bullies / if someone feels it is their fault they are being bullied, it will keep happening.
11. Individual answers.

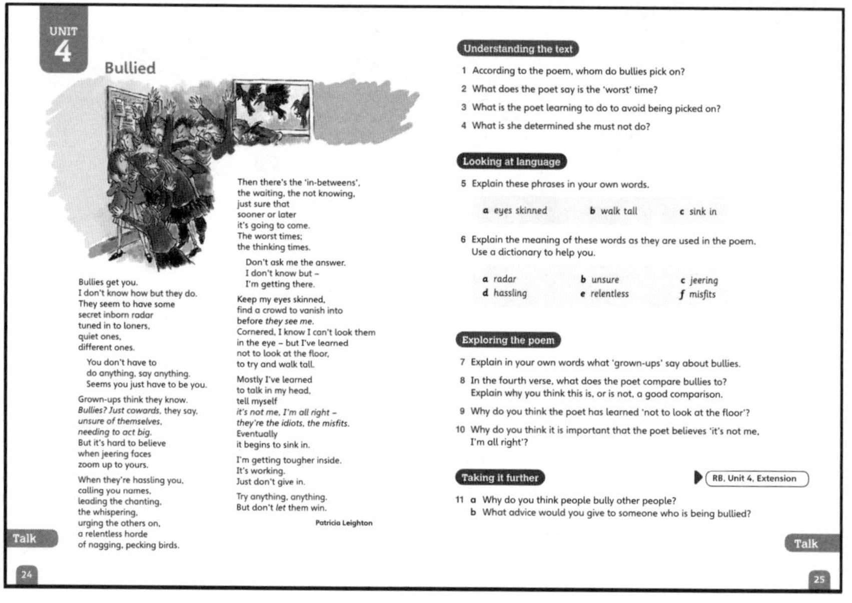

UNIT 4

Bullied

Bullies get you.
I don't know how but they do.
They seem to have some
secret inborn radar
tuned in to loners,
quiet ones,
different ones.

You don't have to
do anything, say anything.
Seems you just have to be you.

Grown-ups think they know.
Bullies? Just cowards, they say,
unsure of themselves,
needing to act big.
But it's hard to believe
when jeering faces
zoom up to yours.

When they're hassling you,
calling you names,
leading the chanting,
the whispering,
urging the others on,
a relentless horde
of nagging, pecking birds.

Then there's the 'in-betweens',
the waiting, the not knowing,
just sure that
sooner or later
it's going to come.
The worst times;
the thinking times.

Don't ask me the answer.
I don't know but –
I'm getting there.

Keep my eyes skinned,
find a crowd to vanish into
before *they see me.*
Cornered, I know I can't look them
in the eye – but I've learned
not to look at the floor,
to try and walk tall.

Mostly I've learned
to talk in my head,
tell myself
it's not me, I'm all right –
they're the idiots, the misfits.
Eventually
it begins to sink in.

I'm getting tougher inside.
It's working.
Just don't give in.

Try anything, anything.
But don't *let* them win.

Patricia Leighton

Talk

24

Understanding the text

1 According to the poem, whom do bullies pick on?
2 What does the poet say is the 'worst' time?
3 What is the poet learning to do to avoid being picked on?
4 What is she determined she must not do?

Looking at language

5 Explain these phrases in your own words.
a *eyes skinned* **b** *walk tall* **c** *sink in*

6 Explain the meaning of these words as they are used in the poem. Use a dictionary to help you.
a *radar* **b** *unsure* **c** *jeering*
d *hassling* **e** *relentless* **f** *misfits*

Exploring the poem

7 Explain in your own words what 'grown-ups' say about bullies.
8 In the fourth verse, what does the poet compare bullies to? Explain why you think this is, or is not, a good comparison.
9 Why do you think the poet has learned 'not to look at the floor'?
10 Why do you think it is important that the poet believes 'it's not me, I'm all right'?

Taking it further

RB, Unit 4, Extension

11 **a** Why do you think people bully other people?
b What advice would you give to someone who is being bullied?

Talk

25

RESOURCE SHEET SUPPORT ANSWERS

A

1. b
2. b
3. a
4. c

B

1. If you are lacking in confidence, you are **unsure** of yourself.
2. If people are taunting you, they are **jeering** at you.
3. People cause you trouble if they **hassle** you.
4. If something is relentless, it never **stops**.
5. Misfits are people who do not **fit in**.

GOING DEEPER

- Use the group's answers to the 'Taking it further' activity as a basis for a class discussion.

WRITE

- Ask children if they have come from another class / school and been the new boy or girl. If so, how did it make them feel?
- Explore how it must feel to be the new boy or girl. If none of the children have been in this position, ask them to imagine how it would feel.
- Explain that they are going to read a poem called 'The New Boy', which is told from the point of view of a boy who has started a new school where everyone else knows one another.
- Read the poem to the class; ask individual children to read it aloud in turn; or read in silence individually.

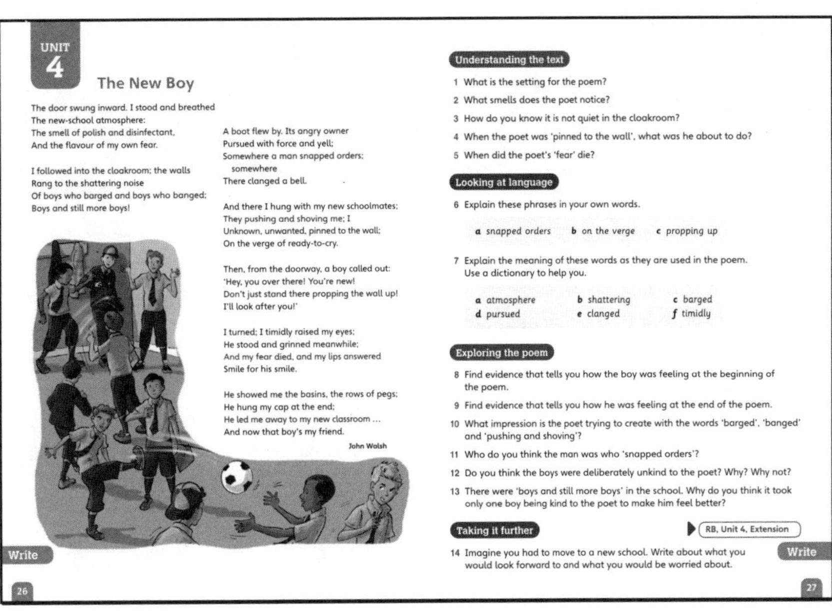

UNIT 4

The New Boy

The door swung inward. I stood and breathed
The new-school atmosphere:
The smell of polish and disinfectant,
And the flavour of my own fear.

I followed into the cloakroom; the walls
Rang to the shattering noise
Of boys who barged and boys who banged;
Boys and still more boys!

A boot flew by. Its angry owner
Pursued with force and yell;
Somewhere a man snapped orders;
  somewhere
There clanged a bell.

And there I hung with my new schoolmates;
They pushing and shoving me; I
Unknown, unwanted, pinned to the wall;
On the verge of ready-to-cry.

Then, from the doorway, a boy called out:
'Hey, you over there! You're new!
Don't just stand there propping the wall up!
I'll look after you!'

I turned; I timidly raised my eyes;
He stood and grinned meanwhile;
And my fear died, and my lips answered
Smile for his smile.

He showed me the basins, the rows of pegs;
He hung my cap at the end;
He led me away to my new classroom …
And now that boy's my friend.

John Walsh

Write

26

Understanding the text

1 What is the setting for the poem?
2 What smells does the poet notice?
3 How do you know it is not quiet in the cloakroom?
4 When the poet was 'pinned to the wall', what was he about to do?
5 When did the poet's 'fear' die?

Looking at language

6 Explain these phrases in your own words.
  a snapped orders b on the verge c propping up
7 Explain the meaning of these words as they are used in the poem. Use a dictionary to help you.
  a atmosphere b shattering c barged
  d pursued e clanged f timidly

Exploring the poem

8 Find evidence that tells you how the boy was feeling at the beginning of the poem.
9 Find evidence that tells you how he was feeling at the end of the poem.
10 What impression is the poet trying to create with the words 'barged', 'banged' and 'pushing and shoving'?
11 Who do you think the man was who 'snapped orders'?
12 Do you think the boys were deliberately unkind to the poet? Why? Why not?
13 There were 'boys and still more boys' in the school. Why do you think it took only one boy being kind to the poet to make him feel better?

Taking it further RB, Unit 4, Extension

14 Imagine you had to move to a new school. Write about what you would look forward to and what you would be worried about. Write

27

RESOURCES & ASSESSMENT BOOK

- **Focus** (comprehension support): answering questions, finding rhyming words; (vocabulary support): choosing the correct definitions.
- **Extension:** writing ideas based on given stimulus.

PUPIL BOOK ANSWERS

1. The poet's new school.
2. 'polish and disinfectant'.
3. 'rang to the shattering noise'.
4. Cry.
5. Another boy 'grinned' at him.
6. **a** a command curtly **b** about to **c** keeping something from falling over
7. **a** a mood / feeling of a place **b** ear-splitting / very noisy **c** moved quickly and carelessly **d** chased **e** loud, metallic sound **f** fearfully / shyly
8. Scared: 'my own fear' / 'unknown, unwanted' / 'on the verge of ready-to-cry'.
9. Happier: 'my fear died' / 'answered smile for his smile' / 'that boy's my friend'.
10. The impression of noise, frantic activity and confusion that the poet finds himself in.
11. A teacher.
12. The boys were not deliberately being unkind – just behaving as normal and hadn't really noticed him.
13. He only needed one person to notice and help him, to make him feel better.
14. Individual answers.

RESOURCE SHEET SUPPORT ANSWERS

A

1. the poet
2. the walls
3. the boys
4. the man
5. the bell
6. a boy

B

1. atmosphere / fear
2. noise / boys
3. yell / bell
4. I / cry
5. new / you
6. meanwhile / smile
7. end / friend

C

1. a
2. b
3. b
4. a

GOING DEEPER

- Discuss the issues raised by the three poems. Ask children which of the three poems they liked best and why. Conclude the unit by asking groups to dramatise a scene based on one of the poems and present it to the class. For example:
  - 'The Loner': one of the children could go up to the boy and try to get him to join in;
  - 'Bullied': the poet could stand up to the bullies;
  - 'The New Boy': a conversation between the new boy and the boy who befriends him.

UNIT FOCUS: Understanding Formal Writing

Investigating …

- formal writing through three extracts about the Tower of London

TEACH

- Ask children what they know about the Tower of London. Have they ever visited the Tower?
- Explore why children think the Tower is so popular.
- Explain to the children that they are going to read an introduction to the Tower of London where a brief history is given.
- Read the introduction to the class; ask individual children to read it aloud in turn; or read in silence individually.

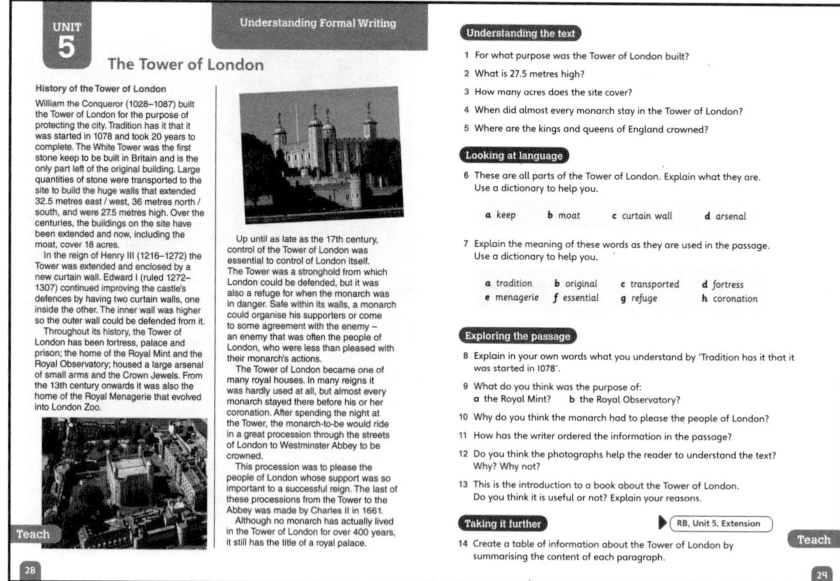

UNIT 5 Understanding Formal Writing

The Tower of London

History of the Tower of London

William the Conqueror (1028–1087) built the Tower of London for the purpose of protecting the city. Tradition has it that it was started in 1078 and took 20 years to complete. The White Tower was the first stone keep to be built in Britain and is the only part left of the original building. Large quantities of stone were transported to the site to build the huge walls that extended 32.5 metres east / west, 36 metres north / south, and were 27.5 metres high. Over the centuries, the buildings on the site have been extended and now, including the moat, cover 18 acres.

In the reign of Henry III (1216–1272) the Tower was extended and enclosed by a new curtain wall. Edward I (ruled 1272–1307) continued improving the castle's defences by having two curtain walls, one inside the other. The inner wall was higher so the outer wall could be defended from it.

Throughout its history, the Tower of London has been fortress, palace and prison; the home of the Royal Mint and the Royal Observatory; housed a large arsenal of small arms and the Crown Jewels. From the 13th century onwards it was also the home of the Royal Menagerie that evolved into London Zoo.

Up until as late as the 17th century, control of the Tower of London was essential to control of London itself. The Tower was a stronghold from which London could be defended, but it was also a refuge for when the monarch was in danger. Safe within its walls, a monarch could organise his supporters or come to some agreement with the enemy – an enemy that was often the people of London, who were less than pleased with their monarch's actions.

The Tower of London became one of many royal houses. In many reigns it was hardly used at all, but almost every monarch stayed there before his or her coronation. After spending the night at the Tower, the monarch-to-be would ride in a great procession through the streets of London to Westminster Abbey to be crowned.

This procession was to please the people of London whose support was so important to a successful reign. The last of these processions from the Tower to the Abbey was made by Charles II in 1661.

Although no monarch has actually lived in the Tower of London for over 400 years, it still has the title of a royal palace.

Understanding the text

1 For what purpose was the Tower of London built?
2 What is 27.5 metres high?
3 How many acres does the site cover?
4 When did almost every monarch stay in the Tower of London?
5 Where are the kings and queens of England crowned?

Looking at language

6 These are all parts of the Tower of London. Explain what they are. Use a dictionary to help you.
a keep b moat c curtain wall d arsenal

7 Explain the meaning of these words as they are used in the passage. Use a dictionary to help you.
a tradition b original c transported d fortress
e menagerie f essential g refuge h coronation

Exploring the passage

8 Explain in your own words what you understand by 'Tradition has it that it was started in 1078'.
9 What do you think was the purpose of:
a the Royal Mint? b the Royal Observatory?
10 Why do you think the monarch had to please the people of London?
11 How has the writer ordered the information in the passage?
12 Do you think the photographs help the reader to understand the text? Why? Why not?
13 This is the introduction to a book about the Tower of London. Do you think it is useful or not? Explain your reasons.

Taking it further RB, Unit 5, Extension

14 Create a table of information about the Tower of London by summarising the content of each paragraph.

Teach 28 Teach 29

RESOURCES & ASSESSMENT BOOK

- **Focus** (comprehension support): completing a chart, answering questions; (vocabulary support): matching words with correct definition.
- **Extension:** creating a table of information.

PUPIL BOOK ANSWERS

1. 'protecting the city'.
2. The walls.
3. 18.
4. 'before his or her coronation'.
5. Westminster Abbey.
6. **a** large tower inside the walls **b** deep ditch around a castle **c** a wall connecting two towers **d** store of weapons
7. **a** what has always been said **b** first **c** carried **d** military stronghold **e** large collection of wild animals **f** absolutely necessary **g** place of safety **i** crowning of a king or queen
8. While it is thought that the Tower was started in 1078, there is no actual proof.
9. **a** to make coins [money] **b** for scientific study, especially astronomy
10. 'an enemy that was often the people of London' / the monarch needed to keep the people on his or her side so they did not turn against him or her.
11. Chronologically from the Tower being built through to the present day.
12. Photographs help as they show what the text is about.
13. Individual answers.
14. Individual answers.

RESOURCE SHEET SUPPORT ANSWERS

A

Date	What happened
1078	building of the Tower of London began
1098	the Tower of London completed
1216–1272	reign of King Henry III
1272–1307	reign of Edward I
1661	Charles II went from the Tower to Westminster Abbey for his coronation.

B

1. length of walls east to west
2. length of walls north to south
3. height of walls

C

1. large tower inside the walls
2. deep ditch around the castle
3. a wall connecting two towers
4. store of weapons

GOING DEEPER

- Tackle the concept of 'formal writing'. Pick out words and phrases and 'translate' them into informal language and ask the children to comment, for example: *monarch – the bloke in charge; prison – nick.* Ask children why it is appropriate to use Standard English in a guidebook.

TALK

- Ask children why they think it is called a 'guide'.
- As well as the history, what else do children think they will find in a guide to the Tower of London?
- Explain to children that they are going to read an extract from the guide to the Tower of London, giving information about the places in the Tower that should not be missed.
- Read the extract to the class; ask individual children to read it aloud in turn; or read in silence individually.

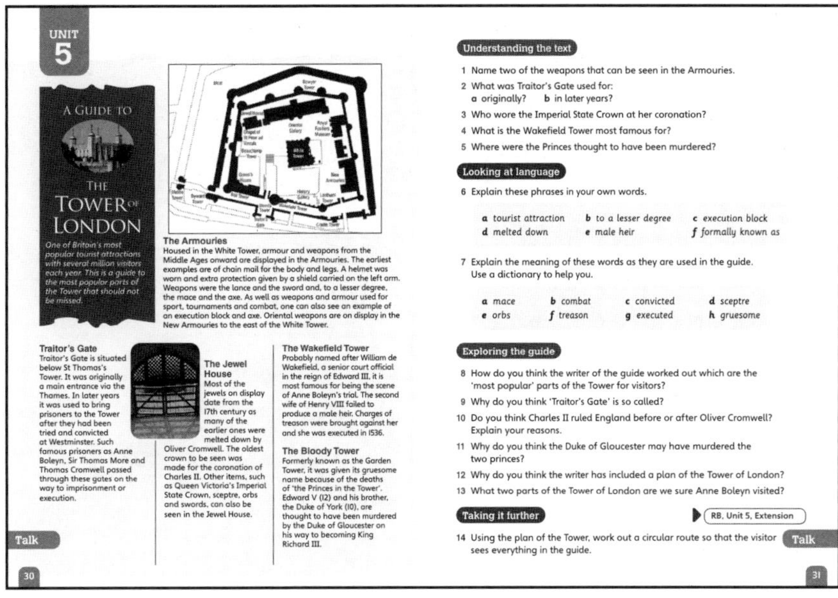

UNIT 5

A GUIDE TO THE TOWER OF LONDON

One of Britain's most popular tourist attractions with several million visitors each year. This is a guide to the most popular parts of the Tower that should not be missed.

The Armouries
Housed in the White Tower, armour and weapons from the Middle Ages onward are displayed in the Armouries. The earliest examples are of chain mail for the body and legs. A helmet was worn and extra protection given by a shield carried on the left arm. Weapons were the lance and the sword and, to a lesser degree, the mace and the axe. As well as weapons and armour used for sport, tournaments and combat, one can also see an example of an execution block and axe. Oriental weapons are on display in the New Armouries to the east of the White Tower.

Traitor's Gate
Traitor's Gate is situated below St Thomas's Tower. It was originally a main entrance via the Thames. In later years it was used to bring prisoners to the Tower after they had been tried and convicted at Westminster. Such famous prisoners as Anne Boleyn, Sir Thomas More and Thomas Cromwell passed through these gates on the way to imprisonment or execution.

The Jewel House
Most of the jewels on display date from the 17th century as many of the earlier ones were melted down by Oliver Cromwell. The oldest crown to be seen was made for the coronation of Charles II. Other items, such as Queen Victoria's Imperial State Crown, sceptre, orbs and swords, can also be seen in the Jewel House.

The Wakefield Tower
Probably named after William de Wakefield, a senior court official in the reign of Edward III, it is most famous for being the scene of Anne Boleyn's trial. The second wife of Henry VIII failed to produce a male heir. Charges of treason were brought against her and she was executed in 1536.

The Bloody Tower
Formerly known as the Garden Tower, it was given its gruesome name because of the deaths of 'the Princes in the Tower'. Edward V (12) and his brother, the Duke of York (10), are thought to have been murdered by the Duke of Gloucester on his way to becoming King Richard III.

Talk

30

Understanding the text

1 Name two of the weapons that can be seen in the Armouries.
2 What was Traitor's Gate used for:
a originally? b in later years?
3 Who wore the Imperial State Crown at her coronation?
4 What is the Wakefield Tower most famous for?
5 Where were the Princes thought to have been murdered?

Looking at language

6 Explain these phrases in your own words.
a tourist attraction b to a lesser degree c execution block
d melted down e male heir f formally known as

7 Explain the meaning of these words as they are used in the guide. Use a dictionary to help you.
a mace b combat c convicted d sceptre
e orbs f treason g executed h gruesome

Exploring the guide

8 How do you think the writer of the guide worked out which are the 'most popular' parts of the Tower for visitors?
9 Why do you think 'Traitor's Gate' is so called?
10 Do you think Charles II ruled England before or after Oliver Cromwell? Explain your reasons.
11 Why do you think the Duke of Gloucester may have murdered the two princes?
12 Why do you think the writer has included a plan of the Tower of London?
13 What two parts of the Tower of London are we sure Anne Boleyn visited?

Taking it further RB, Unit 5, Extension

14 Using the plan of the Tower, work out a circular route so that the visitor sees everything in the guide.

Talk

31

RESOURCES & ASSESSMENT BOOK

- **Focus** (comprehension support): answering questions; (vocabulary support): choosing the odd word, completing paragraph with correct words.
- **Extension:** planning a route.

PUPIL BOOK ANSWERS

1 Lance / sword / mace / axe.

2 **a** as a main entrance to the Tower **b** to bring prisoners to the Tower

3 Queen Victoria.

4 Scene of Anne Boleyn's trial.

5 The Bloody Tower (formerly known as the Garden Tower).

6 **a** something that people on holiday want to see **b** not so much **c** block of wood on which people were beheaded **d** apply heat to make metal liquid **e** a son **f** once called

7 **a** heavy club **b** fighting **c** found guilty **d** decorated rod **e** globe shaped ornaments **f** crimes against the monarch **g** put to death **h** horrible / disgusting

8 Researched visitor numbers / spoke to people who worked at the Tower.

9 Because prisoners convicted of being traitors entered the Tower through this gate.

10 Charles II ruled after Oliver Cromwell – Cromwell had melted down many of the jewels but visitors can still see Charles II's coronation crown.

11 The Princes were the next in line to the throne / the Duke of Gloucester wanted them out of the way so he could be King.

12 To show visitors where the places are and how to get to them.

13 Traitor's Gate and The Wakefield Tower.

14 Individual answers.

RESOURCE SHEET SUPPORT ANSWERS

A

1 **a** The Armouries **b** The Jewel House

2 **a** Traitor's Gate **b** The Bloody Tower

3 **a** The Wakefield Tower **b** The Bloody Tower

B

1 orb

2 lance

3 sir

C

When prisoners were **suspected** of treason, they were **tried** and **convicted** at Westminster. Both Anne Boleyn and Sir Thomas More **passed** through Traitor's Gate into the Tower. Both were **executed**.

GOING DEEPER

- Use children's answers to the 'Taking it further' activity as the basis for a class discussion.
- Revisit the extract using the same technique as for the first extract in the unit, that is, by selecting words and phrases to translate into informal language, for example: *imprisonment – being banged up; execution – getting the chop*, etc.

WRITE

- Discuss zoos with children.
- Do they think animals should be kept in zoos? Why? Why not?
- What 'exotic' creatures have they seen? Where?
- Explain they are going to read an article called 'Animals in the Tower'.
- Read the article to the class; ask individual children to read it aloud in turn; or read in silence individually.

RESOURCES & ASSESSMENT BOOK

- **Focus** (comprehension support): matching paragraphs and content; (vocabulary support): finishing names of animals, alphabetical ordering.
- **Extension:** making notes, answering questions on opinion.

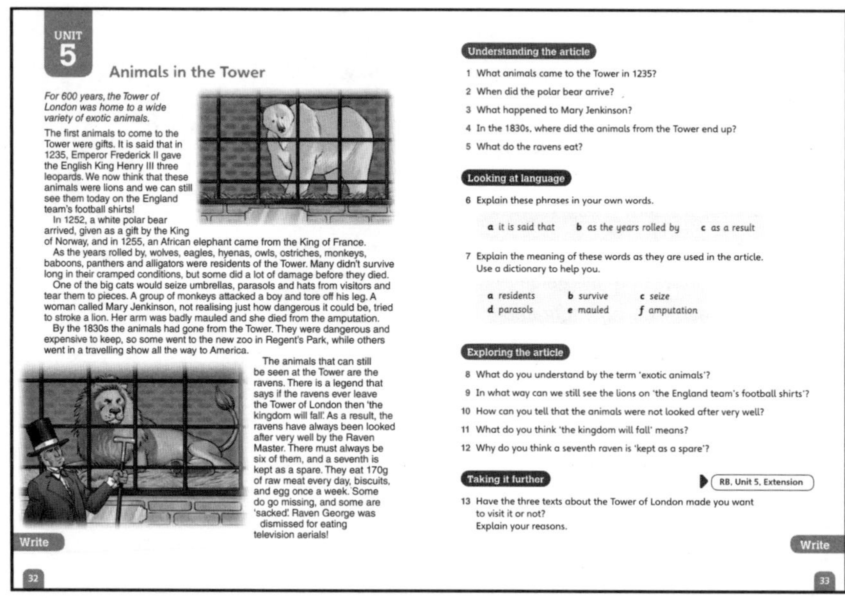

UNIT 5

Animals in the Tower

For 600 years, the Tower of London was home to a wide variety of exotic animals.

The first animals to come to the Tower were gifts. It is said that in 1235, Emperor Frederick II gave the English King Henry III three leopards. We now think that these animals were lions and we can still see them today on the England team's football shirts!

In 1252, a white polar bear arrived, given as a gift by the King of Norway, and in 1255, an African elephant came from the King of France.

As the years rolled by, wolves, eagles, hyenas, owls, ostriches, monkeys, baboons, panthers and alligators were residents of the Tower. Many didn't survive long in their cramped conditions, but some did a lot of damage before they died.

One of the big cats would seize umbrellas, parasols and hats from visitors and tear them to pieces. A group of monkeys attacked a boy and tore off his leg. A woman called Mary Jenkinson, not realising just how dangerous it could be, tried to stroke a lion. Her arm was badly mauled and she died from the amputation.

By the 1830s the animals had gone from the Tower. They were dangerous and expensive to keep, so some went to the new zoo in Regent's Park, while others went in a travelling show all the way to America.

The animals that can still be seen at the Tower are the ravens. There is a legend that says if the ravens ever leave the Tower of London then 'the kingdom will fall'. As a result, the ravens have always been looked after very well by the Raven Master. There must always be six of them, and a seventh is kept as a spare. They eat 170g of raw meat every day, biscuits, and egg once a week. Some do go missing, and some are 'sacked'. Raven George was dismissed for eating television aerials!

Write

32

Understanding the article

1 What animals came to the Tower in 1235?
2 When did the polar bear arrive?
3 What happened to Mary Jenkinson?
4 In the 1830s, where did the animals from the Tower end up?
5 What do the ravens eat?

Looking at language

6 Explain these phrases in your own words.
a it is said that **b** as the years rolled by **c** as a result

7 Explain the meaning of these words as they are used in the article. Use a dictionary to help you.
a residents **b** survive **c** seize
d parasols **e** mauled **f** amputation

Exploring the article

8 What do you understand by the term 'exotic animals'?
9 In what way can we still see the lions on 'the England team's football shirts'?
10 How can you tell that the animals were not looked after very well?
11 What do you think 'the kingdom will fall' means?
12 Why do you think a seventh raven is 'kept as a spare'?

Taking it further

RB, Unit 5, Extension

13 Have the three texts about the Tower of London made you want to visit it or not? Explain your reasons.

Write

33

PUPIL BOOK ANSWERS

1. Three leopards – now thought to be lions.
2. 1252.
3. She tried to stroke a lion, had her arm mauled and died.
4. Regent's Park Zoo / travelling show in America.
5. 170g raw meat daily / biscuits / eggs.
6. **a** information passed down orally **b** as time passed **c** because of this
7. **a** animals that lived in the Tower **b** stay alive **c** grab **d** sunshades **e** attacked with claws and teeth **f** removal of a limb
8. Animals that were unusual / strange / never seen before / came from far away.
9. The three lions became a symbol of 'England' and their picture is on the football shirt.
10. 'Many didn't survive long in their cramped conditions'.
11. England will be in danger and may even be conquered.
12. Something may happen to one of the other ravens e.g. die / sacked / go missing.
13. Individual answers.

RESOURCE SHEET SUPPORT ANSWERS

A

1. first animals in the Tower
2. polar bear / elephant
3. other animals arrive
4. damage done by animals
5. animals leave the Tower
6. ravens

B

1. lion
2. polar bear
3. elephant
4. wolf
5. eagle
6. hyena
7. owl
8. monkey
9. baboon
10. panther
11. ostrich
12. alligator

C

1. alligator
2. baboon
3. eagle
4. elephant
5. hyena
6. lion
7. monkey
8. ostrich
9. owl
10. panther
11. polar bear
12. wolf

GOING DEEPER

- Discuss why children think people like to visit old buildings. What old buildings have they visited?

UNIT FOCUS: Themes and Techniques

Investigating …

- the work of the author Michael Morpurgo
- identifying common themes of the sea and child characters

TEACH

- Discuss the children's favourite authors.
- Discuss Michael Morpurgo with the children, and any of his books they have read, for example, *Private Peaceful* and *Kensuke's Kingdom.*
- Explain to the children that they are going to read an extract from *Why the Whales Came.*
- Explain the story so far: Gracie and Daniel are friends and live in the Scilly Isles. When the men go off to war, times are hard. Gracie's mother works hard but is always short of money. Gracie and Daniel decide to go fishing, hoping to catch enough fish for her mother to sell – and that's when they get into difficulties.
- Read the extract to the class; ask individual children to read it aloud in turn; or read in silence individually.

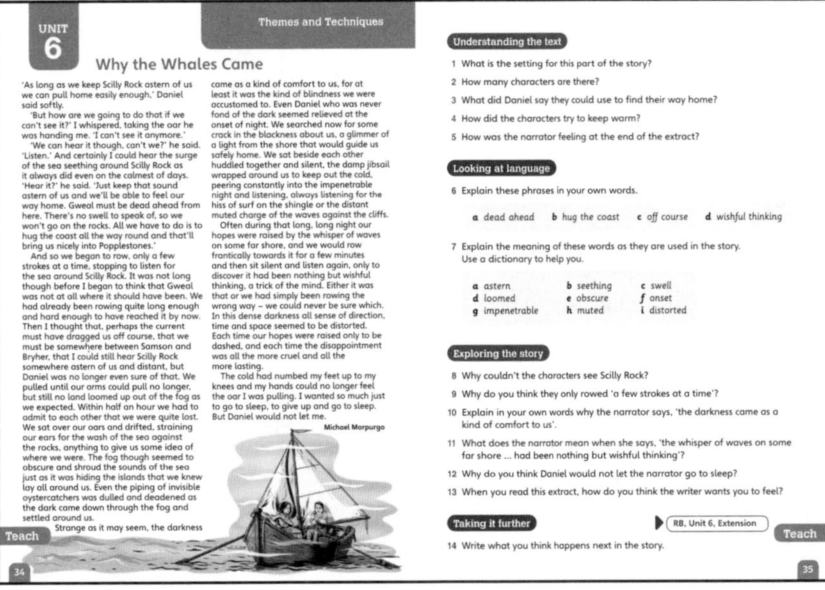

UNIT 6

Themes and Techniques

Why the Whales Came

'As long as we keep Scilly Rock astern of us we can pull home easily enough,' Daniel said softly.

'But how are we going to do that if we can't see it?' I whispered, taking the oar he was handing me. 'I can't see it anymore.'

'We can hear it though, can't we?' he said. 'Listen.' And certainly I could hear the surge of the sea seething around Scilly Rock as it always did even on the calmest of days. 'Hear it?' he said. 'Just keep that sound astern of us and we'll be able to feel our way home. Gweal must be dead ahead from here. There's no swell to speak of, so we won't go on the rocks. All we have to do is to hug the coast all the way round and that'll bring us nicely into Popplestones.'

And so we began to row, only a few strokes at a time, stopping to listen for the sea around Scilly Rock. It was not long though before I began to think that Gweal was not at all where it should have been. We had already been rowing quite long enough and hard enough to have reached it by now. Then I thought that, perhaps the current must have dragged us off course, that we must be somewhere between Samson and Bryher, that I could still hear Scilly Rock somewhere astern of us and distant, but Daniel was no longer even sure of that. We pulled until our arms could pull no longer, but still no land loomed up out of the fog as we expected. Within half an hour we had to admit to each other that we were quite lost. We sat over our oars and drifted, straining our ears for the wash of the sea against the rocks, anything to give us some idea of where we were. The fog though seemed to obscure and shroud the sounds of the sea just as it was hiding the islands that we knew lay all around us. Even the piping of invisible oystercatchers was dulled and deadened as the dark came down through the fog and settled around us.

Strange as it may seem, the darkness came as a kind of comfort to us, for at least it was the kind of blindness we were accustomed to. Even Daniel who was never fond of the dark seemed relieved at the onset of night. We searched now for some crack in the blackness about us, a glimmer of a light from the shore that would guide us safely home. We sat beside each other huddled together and silent, the damp jibsail wrapped around us to keep out the cold, peering constantly into the impenetrable night and listening, always listening for the hiss of surf on the shingle or the distant muted charge of the waves against the cliffs.

Often during that long, long night our hopes were raised by the whisper of waves on some far shore, and we would row frantically towards it for a few minutes and then sit silent and listen again, only to discover it had been nothing but wishful thinking, a trick of the mind. Either it was that or we had simply been rowing the wrong way – we could never be sure which. In this dense darkness all sense of direction, time and space seemed to be distorted. Each time our hopes were raised only to be dashed, and each time the disappointment was all the more cruel and all the more lasting.

The cold had numbed my feet up to my knees and my hands could no longer feel the oar I was pulling. I wanted so much just to go to sleep, to give up and go to sleep. But Daniel would not let me.

Michael Morpurgo

Teach 34

Understanding the text

1 What is the setting for this part of the story?

2 How many characters are there?

3 What did Daniel say they could use to find their way home?

4 How did the characters try to keep warm?

5 How was the narrator feeling at the end of the extract?

Looking at language

6 Explain these phrases in your own words.

a *dead ahead* **b** *hug the coast* **c** *off course* **d** *wishful thinking*

7 Explain the meaning of these words as they are used in the story. Use a dictionary to help you.

a astern **b** seething **c** swell
d loomed **e** obscure **f** onset
g impenetrable **h** muted **i** distorted

Exploring the story

8 Why couldn't the characters see Scilly Rock?

9 Why do you think they only rowed 'a few strokes at a time'?

10 Explain in your own words why the narrator says, 'the darkness came as a kind of comfort to us'.

11 What does the narrator mean when she says, 'the whisper of waves on some far shore ... had been nothing but wishful thinking'?

12 Why do you think Daniel would not let the narrator go to sleep?

13 When you read this extract, how do you think the writer wants you to feel?

Taking it further RB, Unit 6, Extension

14 Write what you think happens next in the story.

Teach 35

RESOURCES & ASSESSMENT BOOK

- **Focus** (comprehension support): choosing the incorrect word; (vocabulary support): choosing the correct definition.
- **Extension:** making notes, writing the end of the story.

PUPIL BOOK ANSWERS

1. A boat at sea.
2. Two: Daniel and the narrator.
3. their hearing / 'the surge of sea seething around Scilly Rock'
4. they 'huddled together' / 'damp jibsail wrapped around us'.
5. 'The cold had numbed my feet up to the knees and my hands could no longer feel the oar I was pulling. I wanted so much just to go to sleep, to give up.'
6. **a** straight in front **b** to row as near to the coastline as possible **c** not going where you want to **d** believe what is probably not true
7. **a** to the back of the boat **b** bubbling in an agitated manner **c** heaving of the sea with waves that do not break **d** appeared **e** hide / conceal **f** beginning **g** cannot be seen through / into **h** muffled **i** changed
8. Because of the fog.
9. Rowing made a noise that meant they could not hear the waves around Scilly Rock / they stopped regularly to listen to see if they were still going in the right direction.
10. They were used to not being able to see in the darkness / the darker it became, there was the more chance of seeing a light from the land.
11. They wanted to hear the waves on the shore so badly that they made themselves believe they could.
12. It is dangerous to go to sleep when you are really cold.
13. Individual answers.
14. Individual answers.

RESOURCE SHEET SUPPORT ANSWERS

A

1. keep away / hug
2. away from / towards
3. an hour / half an hour
4. talkative / silent
5. Daniel / The narrator

B

1. b
2. a
3. a
4. b
5. a
6. b

GOING DEEPER

- If the children know the story, ask them if they can relate what happens. If they don't know the story, can they predict what may happen?

TALK

- Recap on the main features of the previous extract: characters live on an island / sail boats / get into difficulty.
- Explain to children that they are going to read an extract from *The Ghost of Grania O'Malley* where, again, the sea plays an important part.
- Read the extract to the class; ask individual children to read it aloud in turn; or read in silence individually.

RESOURCES & ASSESSMENT BOOK

- **Focus** (comprehension support): numbering sentences; (vocabulary support): writing contractions, matching correct words to definitions.
- **Extension:** answering questions on given extracts, writing ideas.

PUPIL BOOK ANSWERS

1. The rocks and the sea.
2. He caught a fish and was reeling it in.
3. 'Jessie reached out for him.'
4. 'The sea smothered her.'
5. 'We've got to keep floating.'
6. **a** stiffened his legs [to take the weight of the fish] **b** a split second **c** saw briefly **d** don't give up **e** nothing done would make it any better
7. **a** very quickly / with great energy **b** without thinking **c** swinging wildly about **d** lost feeling in **e** hid **f** a feeble, frightened sound
8. She was frightened that she would drown / wanted to save herself.
9. She did not know what was happening / she was panicking.
10. He did not really believe what he was saying / he was trying to calm Jessie so he could hold on to her.
11. 'The shore was already a long way off' / 'they were being carried away from it' / 'she could see the bank of mist rolling over the sea towards them' / 'the mist would swallow them and then no one would ever see them'.
12. **a** shocked / fearful **b** feeling he had to do something **c** very scared / desperate
13. Individual answers.

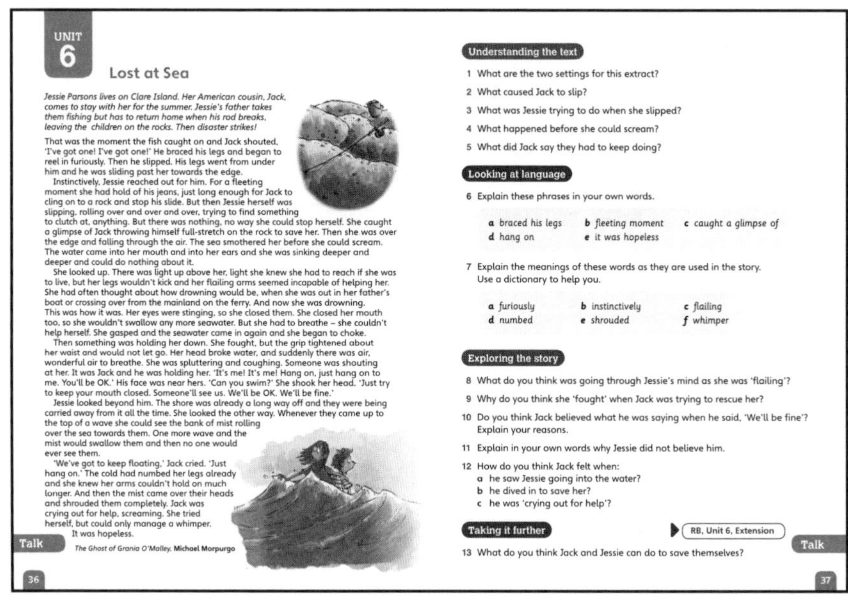

UNIT 6

Lost at Sea

Jessie Parsons lives on Clare Island. Her American cousin, Jack, comes to stay with her for the summer. Jessie's father takes them fishing but has to return home when his rod breaks, leaving the children on the rocks. Then disaster strikes!

That was the moment the fish caught on and Jack shouted, 'I've got one! I've got one!' He braced his legs and began to reel in furiously. Then he slipped. His legs went from under him and he was sliding past her towards the edge.

Instinctively, Jessie reached out for him. For a fleeting moment she had hold of his jeans, just long enough for Jack to cling on to a rock and stop his slide. But then Jessie herself was slipping, rolling over and over and over, trying to find something to clutch at, anything. But there was nothing, no way she could stop herself. She caught a glimpse of Jack throwing himself full-stretch on the rock to save her. Then she was over the edge and falling through the air. The sea smothered her before she could scream. The water came into her mouth and into her ears and she was sinking deeper and deeper and could do nothing about it.

She looked up. There was light up above her, light she knew she had to reach if she was to live, but her legs wouldn't kick and her flailing arms seemed incapable of helping her. She had often thought about how drowning would be, when she was out in her father's boat or crossing over from the mainland on the ferry. And now she was drowning. This was how it was. Her eyes were stinging, so she closed them. She closed her mouth too, so she wouldn't swallow any more seawater. But she had to breathe – she couldn't help herself. She gasped and the seawater came in again and she began to choke.

Then something was holding her down. She fought, but the grip tightened about her waist and would not let go. Her head broke water, and suddenly there was air, wonderful air to breathe. She was spluttering and coughing. Someone was shouting at her. It was Jack and he was holding her. 'It's me! It's me! Hang on, just hang on to me. You'll be OK.' His face was near hers. 'Can you swim?' She shook her head. 'Just try to keep your mouth closed. Someone'll see us. We'll be OK. We'll be fine.'

Jessie looked beyond him. The shore was already a long way off and they were being carried away from it all the time. She looked the other way. Whenever they came up to the top of a wave she could see the bank of mist rolling over the sea towards them. One more wave and the mist would swallow them and then no one would ever see them.

'We've got to keep floating,' Jack cried. 'Just hang on.' The cold had numbed her legs already and she knew her arms couldn't hold on much longer. And then the mist came over their heads and shrouded them completely. Jack was crying out for help, screaming. She tried herself, but could only manage a whimper.

It was hopeless.

The Ghost of Grania O'Malley, **Michael Morpurgo**

Talk

36

Understanding the text

1 What are the two settings for this extract?
2 What caused Jack to slip?
3 What was Jessie trying to do when she slipped?
4 What happened before she could scream?
5 What did Jack say they had to keep doing?

Looking at language

6 Explain these phrases in your own words.

a *braced his legs* **b** *fleeting moment* **c** *caught a glimpse of*
d *hang on* **e** *it was hopeless*

7 Explain the meanings of these words as they are used in the story. Use a dictionary to help you.

a *furiously* **b** *instinctively* **c** *flailing*
d *numbed* **e** *shrouded* **f** *whimper*

Exploring the story

8 What do you think was going through Jessie's mind as she was 'flailing'?
9 Why do you think she 'fought' when Jack was trying to rescue her?
10 Do you think Jack believed what he was saying when he said, 'We'll be fine'? Explain your reasons.
11 Explain in your own words why Jessie did not believe him.
12 How do you think Jack felt when:
a he saw Jessie going into the water?
b he dived in to save her?
c he was 'crying out for help'?

Taking it further

RB, Unit 6, Extension

13 What do you think Jack and Jessie can do to save themselves?

Talk

37

RESOURCE SHEET SUPPORT ANSWERS

A

1. 3
2. 7
3. 2
4. 8
5. 1
6. 5
7. 4
8. 6

B

1. I've: I have
2. it's: it is
3. you'll: you will
4. we'll: we shall
5. we've: we have
6. couldn't: could not

C

1. furiously: very quickly / energetically
2. instinctively: without thinking
3. flailing: swinging wildly about
4. shrouded: hidden
5. numbed: lost feeling in

GOING DEEPER

- Use children's answers for the 'Taking it further' activity as the basis for a class discussion.
- What are the similarities and differences between the two extracts?

WRITE

- Ask children how they would feel about going around the world in a boat.
- Ask children what places they would like to visit.
- Explore what they would miss about not living on land.
- Explain to the children that they are going to read an extract from *Kensuke's Kingdom*, a third Michael Morpurgo story.
- Read the extract to the class; ask individual children to read it aloud in turn; or read in silence individually.

RESOURCES & ASSESSMENT BOOK

- **Focus** (comprehension support): exploring True / False statements, correcting false statements; (vocabulary support): matching correct words to definitions.
- **Extension:** writing ideas based on opinion.

PUPIL BOOK ANSWERS

1. The *Peggy Sue* / the ocean.
2. 'someone was singing out there in the darkness'.
3. She would not come when she was called / she would not move when Michael dragged her by the collar.
4. No safety harness / no lifejacket.
5. 'I thought then of sharks cruising the black water beneath me'. / 'I would drown slowly'.
6. **a** lost your job **b** make her obey **c** wasn't going to happen
7. **a** made a grab for **b** very dear to / liked it a lot **c** not willing **d** changed direction suddenly **e** moving slowly and easily
8. By leaving it, the boat would drift in any direction the sea pushed it.
9. It could be the only thing he had to play with / reminded him of home.
10. **a** a safety harness **b** a safety harness / lifejacket
11. Terrified – 'the terrors came fast, one upon another'.
12. Individual answers.
13. Individual answers.

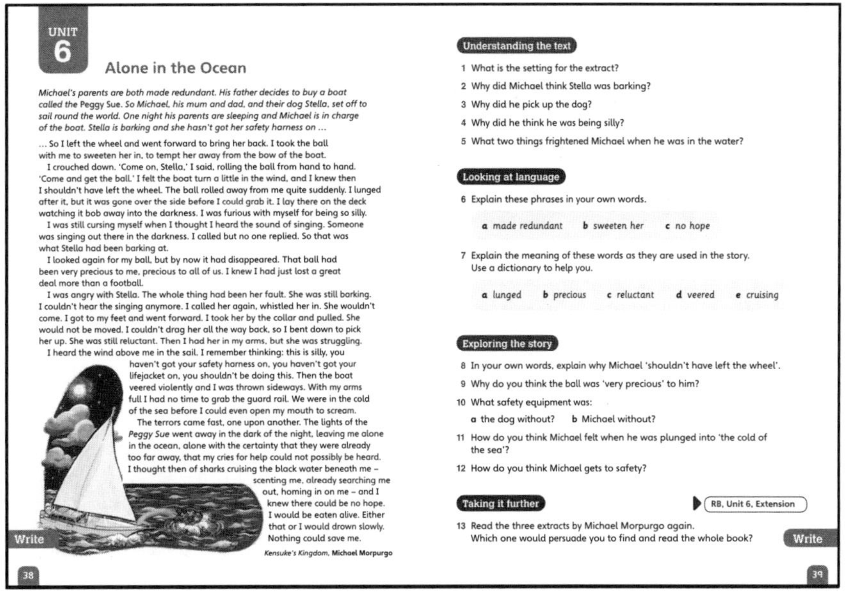

UNIT 6

Alone in the Ocean

Michael's parents are both made redundant. His father decides to buy a boat called the Peggy Sue. *So Michael, his mum and dad, and their dog Stella, set off to sail round the world. One night his parents are sleeping and Michael is in charge of the boat. Stella is barking and she hasn't got her safety harness on …*

… So I left the wheel and went forward to bring her back. I took the ball with me to sweeten her in, to tempt her away from the bow of the boat.

I crouched down. 'Come on, Stella,' I said, rolling the ball from hand to hand. 'Come and get the ball.' I felt the boat turn a little in the wind, and I knew then I shouldn't have left the wheel. The ball rolled away from me quite suddenly. I lunged after it, but it was gone over the side before I could grab it. I lay there on the deck watching it bob away into the darkness. I was furious with myself for being so silly.

I was still cursing myself when I thought I heard the sound of singing. Someone was singing out there in the darkness. I called but no one replied. So that was what Stella had been barking at.

I looked again for my ball, but by now it had disappeared. That ball had been very precious to me, precious to all of us. I knew I had just lost a great deal more than a football.

I was angry with Stella. The whole thing had been her fault. She was still barking. I couldn't hear the singing anymore. I called her again, whistled her in. She wouldn't come. I got to my feet and went forward. I took her by the collar and pulled. She would not be moved. I couldn't drag her all the way back, so I bent down to pick her up. She was still reluctant. Then I had her in my arms, but she was struggling.

I heard the wind above me in the sail. I remember thinking: this is silly, you haven't got your safety harness on, you haven't got your lifejacket on, you shouldn't be doing this. Then the boat veered violently and I was thrown sideways. With my arms full I had no time to grab the guard rail. We were in the cold of the sea before I could even open my mouth to scream.

The terrors came fast, one upon another. The lights of the *Peggy Sue* went away in the dark of the night, leaving me alone in the ocean, alone with the certainty that they were already too far away, that my cries for help could not possibly be heard. I thought then of sharks cruising the black water beneath me – scenting me, already searching me out, homing in on me – and I knew there could be no hope. I would be eaten alive. Either that or I would drown slowly. Nothing could save me.

Kensuke's Kingdom, **Michael Morpurgo**

Write

38

Understanding the text

1 What is the setting for the extract?

2 Why did Michael think Stella was barking?

3 Why did he pick up the dog?

4 Why did he think he was being silly?

5 What two things frightened Michael when he was in the water?

Looking at language

6 Explain these phrases in your own words.

a made redundant *b sweeten her* *c no hope*

7 Explain the meaning of these words as they are used in the story. Use a dictionary to help you.

a lunged *b precious* *c reluctant* *d veered* *e cruising*

Exploring the story

8 In your own words, explain why Michael 'shouldn't have left the wheel'.

9 Why do you think the ball was 'very precious' to him?

10 What safety equipment was:

a the dog without? b Michael without?

11 How do you think Michael felt when he was plunged into 'the cold of the sea'?

12 How do you think Michael gets to safety?

Taking it further

RB, Unit 6, Extension

13 Read the three extracts by Michael Morpurgo again. Which one would persuade you to find and read the whole book?

Write

39

RESOURCE SHEET SUPPORT ANSWERS

A

1. FALSE
2. TRUE
3. FALSE
4. TRUE
5. FALSE
6. TRUE

B

1. Stella was a dog.
2. Michael pulled Stella by the collar.
3. Michael was not wearing a life jacket.

C

1. lunged – made a grab for
2. veered – changed direction suddenly
3. cruising – moving slowly and easily

GOING DEEPER

- Discuss the three extracts. In what ways are they similar? In what ways are they different? What do children think Michael Morpurgo knows a lot about and is interested in?

UNIT FOCUS: Viewpoints in Journalistic Writing

Investigating …

- journalistic news reports
- key features of this text type

TEACH

- Have children heard of the 'beast' that people claim to have seen on Bodmin Moor?
- Have children seen any creatures at night where they live? e.g. urban foxes / badgers.
- Is it always easy to identify what they are?
- Explain to the children that they are going to read an article called 'The Beast of Bodmin Moor' centring on some mysterious sightings of an unidentified creature.
- Read the article to the class; ask individual children to read it aloud in turn; or read in silence individually.

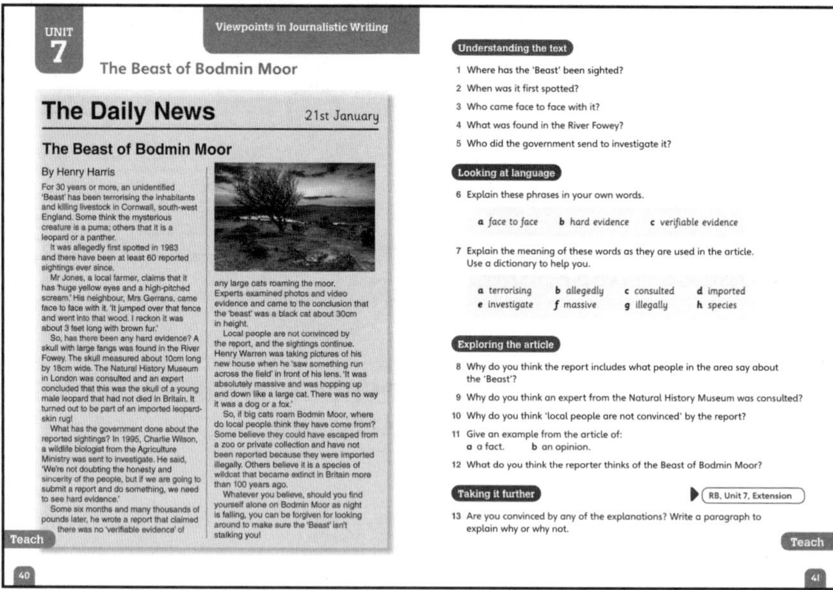

UNIT 7 Viewpoints in Journalistic Writing

The Beast of Bodmin Moor

The Daily News 21st January

The Beast of Bodmin Moor

By Henry Harris

For 30 years or more, an unidentified 'Beast' has been terrorising the inhabitants and killing livestock in Cornwall, south-west England. Some think the mysterious creature is a puma; others that it is a leopard or a panther.

It was allegedly first spotted in 1983 and there have been at least 60 reported sightings ever since.

Mr Jones, a local farmer, claims that it has 'huge yellow eyes and a high-pitched scream.' His neighbour, Mrs Gerrans, came face to face with it. 'It jumped over that fence and went into that wood. I reckon it was about 3 feet long with brown fur.'

So, has there been any hard evidence? A skull with large fangs was found in the River Fowey. The skull measured about 10cm long by 18cm wide. The Natural History Museum in London was consulted and an expert concluded that this was the skull of a young male leopard that had not died in Britain. It turned out to be part of an imported leopard-skin rug!

What has the government done about the reported sightings? In 1995, Charlie Wilson, a wildlife biologist from the Agriculture Ministry was sent to investigate. He said, 'We're not doubting the honesty and sincerity of the people, but if we are going to submit a report and do something, we need to see hard evidence.'

Some six months and many thousands of pounds later, he wrote a report that claimed there was no 'verifiable evidence' of any large cats roaming the moor. Experts examined photos and video evidence and came to the conclusion that the 'beast' was a black cat about 30cm in height.

Local people are not convinced by the report, and the sightings continue. Henry Warren was taking pictures of his new house when he 'saw something run across the field' in front of his lens. 'It was absolutely massive and was hopping up and down like a large cat. There was no way it was a dog or a fox.'

So, if big cats roam Bodmin Moor, where do local people think they have come from? Some believe they could have escaped from a zoo or private collection and have not been reported because they were imported illegally. Others believe it is a species of wildcat that became extinct in Britain more than 100 years ago.

Whatever you believe, should you find yourself alone on Bodmin Moor as night is falling, you can be forgiven for looking around to make sure the 'Beast' isn't stalking you!

Teach

40

Understanding the text

1 Where has the 'Beast' been sighted?

2 When was it first spotted?

3 Who came face to face with it?

4 What was found in the River Fowey?

5 Who did the government send to investigate it?

Looking at language

6 Explain these phrases in your own words.

a *face to face* **b** *hard evidence* **c** *verifiable evidence*

7 Explain the meaning of these words as they are used in the article. Use a dictionary to help you.

a *terrorising* **b** *allegedly* **c** *consulted* **d** *imported*
e *investigate* **f** *massive* **g** *illegally* **h** *species*

Exploring the article

8 Why do you think the report includes what people in the area say about the 'Beast'?

9 Why do you think an expert from the Natural History Museum was consulted?

10 Why do you think 'local people are not convinced' by the report?

11 Give an example from the article of:
a a fact. b an opinion.

12 What do you think the reporter thinks of the Beast of Bodmin Moor?

Taking it further RB, Unit 7, Extension

13 Are you convinced by any of the explanations? Write a paragraph to explain why or why not.

Teach

41

RESOURCES & ASSESSMENT BOOK

- **Focus** (comprehension support): writing questions for given answers (vocabulary support): completing sentences, choosing adjectives.
- **Extension:** writing paragraphs based on opinion.

PUPIL BOOK ANSWERS

1 Cornwall, south-west England.

2 1983.

3 Mrs Gerrans.

4 'a skull with large fangs'.

5 Charlie Wilson.

6 **a** in the presence of / directly in front of **b** proof **c** evidence that can be checked or proved

7 **a** frightening with violent actions **b** supposedly **c** asked for opinion **d** brought from another country **e** look into **f** huge **g** against the law **h** animal group

8 These were eyewitness accounts and readers would be interested in what they have seen.

9 An expert would have knowledge and be able to identify the skull properly.

10 They are convinced of what they have seen / the sightings continue.

11 **a** e.g. a skull was found / Charlie Wilson was sent to investigate **b** e.g. some people think it is a puma / leopard / panther

12 Individual answers.

13 Individual answers.

RESOURCE SHEET SUPPORT ANSWERS

A

1 For how long has the 'Beast of Bodmin' been terrorizing the inhabitants and killing livestock in Cornwall?

2 When was the 'Beast' first spotted?

3 What is the name of the local farmer who describes the 'Beast'?

4 Which animal's skull was found in the River Fowey?

5 Who reportedly saw the 'Beast' while he was taking pictures of his new house?

B

1 An expert was consulted about the skull.

2 The leopard-skin rug had been imported.

3 Charlie Wilson was sent to investigate.

4 Henry Warren said what he saw was massive.

5 No hard evidence has yet been found.

C

1 mysterious creature

2 local farmer

3 large fangs

4 private collection

GOING DEEPER

- Investigate the features of the report with the children e.g. headline, organisation, fact and opinion, illustration etc.

TALK

- Discuss volcanoes with the children. What famous volcanoes do they know about?
- Explain to the children that they are going to read an article called 'Islands of Fire' about the startling effects of volcanic eruptions.
- Read the article to the class; ask individual children to read it aloud in turn; or read in silence individually.

RESOURCES & ASSESSMENT BOOK

- **Focus** (comprehension support): completing a chart; (vocabulary support): matching beginning/ending of sentences, choosing the correct definition.
- **Extension:** planning an article.

PUPIL BOOK ANSWERS

1. Volcanoes.
2. Tongatapu – 16–19 March, 2009 / Krakatoa – 20 May–27 August, 1883 / Krakatoa – 29 December, 1927.
3. **a** each was caused by a volcanic eruption **b** Tongatapu – an island was created / Krakatoa – most of the island was submerged
4. 'observe the eruption' / ' measure the island'.
5. 'the volcanic eruption that rained down ash and produced lava flows that reached up to 700 degrees C' / 'ensuing tsunamis'.
6. **a** used to measure the strength of an earthquake **b** danger that is immediate **c** a few months **d** stopped erupting **e** completely cleared **f** the best guess based on evidence
7. **a** thrown up violently **b** worn away **c** almost **d** under water **e** huge waves caused by underwater earthquakes **f** following
8. Photographs / maps.
9. Individual answers e.g. Tongatapu lies in the Pacific Ocean.
10. The reader will want to know exact facts / shows the writer has done the research needed to write an informative article.
11. It would have been impossible to count the number of dead as there were so many.

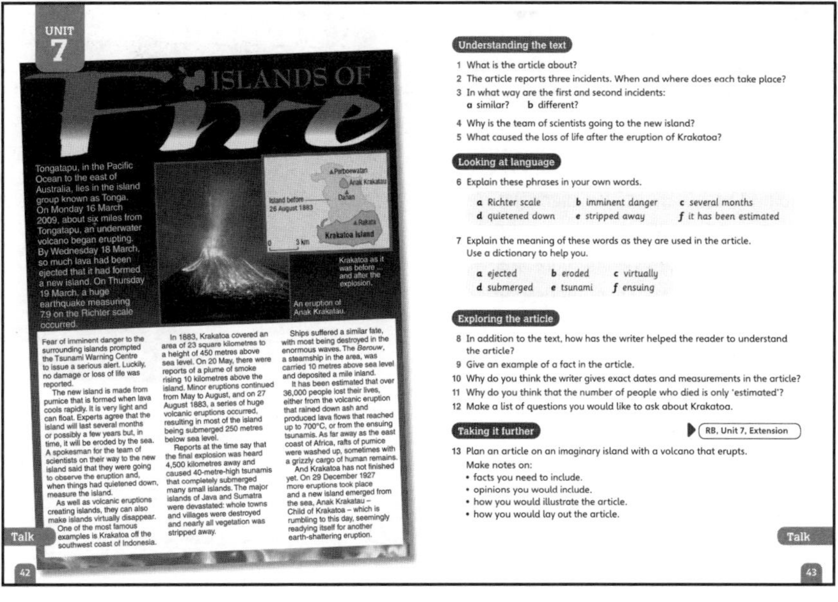
UNIT 7

ISLANDS OF Fire

Tongatapu, in the Pacific Ocean to the east of Australia, lies in the island group known as Tonga. On Monday 16 March 2009, about six miles from Tongatapu, an underwater volcano began erupting. By Wednesday 18 March, so much lava had been ejected that it had formed a new island. On Thursday 19 March, a huge earthquake measuring 7.9 on the Richter scale occurred.

Krakatoa as it was before ... and after the explosion.

An eruption of Anak Krakatau.

Fear of imminent danger to the surrounding islands prompted the Tsunami Warning Centre to issue a serious alert. Luckily, no damage or loss of life was reported.

The new island is made from pumice that is formed when lava cools rapidly. It is very light and can float. Experts agree that the island will last several months or possibly a few years but, in time, it will be eroded by the sea. A spokesman for the team of scientists on their way to the new island said that they were going to observe the eruption and, when things had quietened down, measure the island.

As well as volcanic eruptions creating islands, they can also make islands virtually disappear. One of the most famous examples is Krakatoa off the southwest coast of Indonesia.

In 1883, Krakatoa covered an area of 23 square kilometres to a height of 450 metres above sea level. On 20 May, there were reports of a plume of smoke rising 10 kilometres above the island. Minor eruptions continued from May to August, and on 27 August 1883, a series of huge volcanic eruptions occurred, resulting in most of the island being submerged 250 metres below sea level.

Reports at the time say that the final explosion was heard 4,500 kilometres away and caused 40-metre-high tsunamis that completely submerged many small islands. The major islands of Java and Sumatra were devastated: whole towns and villages were destroyed and nearly all vegetation was stripped away.

Ships suffered a similar fate, with most being destroyed in the enormous waves. The *Berouw*, a steamship in the area, was carried 10 metres above sea level and deposited a mile inland.

It has been estimated that over 36,000 people lost their lives, either from the volcanic eruption that rained down ash and produced lava flows that reached up to 700°C, or from the ensuing tsunamis. As far away as the east coast of Africa, rafts of pumice were washed up, sometimes with a grizzly cargo of human remains.

And Krakatoa has not finished yet. On 29 December 1927 more eruptions took place and a new island emerged from the sea, Anak Krakatau – Child of Krakatoa – which is rumbling to this day, seemingly readying itself for another earth-shattering eruption.

Talk

42

Understanding the text

1 What is the article about?
2 The article reports three incidents. When and where does each take place?
3 In what way are the first and second incidents:
a similar? b different?
4 Why is the team of scientists going to the new island?
5 What caused the loss of life after the eruption of Krakatoa?

Looking at language

6 Explain these phrases in your own words.
a Richter scale b imminent danger c several months
d quietened down e stripped away f it has been estimated
7 Explain the meaning of these words as they are used in the article. Use a dictionary to help you.
a ejected b eroded c virtually
d submerged e tsunami f ensuing

Exploring the article

8 In addition to the text, how has the writer helped the reader to understand the article?
9 Give an example of a fact in the article.
10 Why do you think the writer gives exact dates and measurements in the article?
11 Why do you think that the number of people who died is only 'estimated'?
12 Make a list of questions you would like to ask about Krakatoa.

Taking it further RB, Unit 7, Extension

13 Plan an article on an imaginary island with a volcano that erupts.
Make notes on:
- facts you need to include.
- opinions you would include.
- how you would illustrate the article.
- how you would lay out the article.

Talk

43

12. Individual answers.
13. Individual answers.

RESOURCE SHEET SUPPORT ANSWERS

A

Incident	Where?	When?
Tongatapu	in the island group of Tonga / west of Australia / Pacific Ocean	16 – 19 March, 2009
Krakatoa	south-west coast of Indonesia	20 May to 27 August, 1883
Anak Krakatau	south-west coast of Indonesia	29 December, 1927

B

1. that a new island was formed
2. issued a serious alert
3. and can float
4. went to measure the island
5. was heard 4.500 miles away

C

1. thrown up
2. worn away
3. under water
4. follow on

GOING DEEPER

- Use the children's list of questions about Krakatoa as the basis for a class discussion. Let groups read one another's articles and comment critically on them. Point out where journalistic features have been used to good effect.

WRITE

- Ask children what they understand by the term 'Northern Lights'. Have any children seen them?
- Explain to the children that they are going to read an article called 'The Northern Lights Fantastic', where the reporter interviews a photographer who has spent many years photographing the Northern Lights.
- Read the article to the class; ask individual children to read it aloud in turn; or read in silence individually.

RESOURCES & ASSESSMENT BOOK

- **Focus** (comprehension support): completing sentences, answering questions; (vocabulary support): matching words with correct definitions.
- **Extension:** making notes and writing questions.

PUPIL BOOK ANSWERS

1 Penny Stretton.

2 Mountains of Yukon / Brooks Range / Hudson Bay.

3 Aurora Borealis.

4 10 years.

5 'at night ... in winter'.

6 **a** surprising **b** suggesting they have the power to **c** be brighter than **d** cover **e** mysterious **f** able to be seen

7 It is darker earlier in winter / a cloudless sky [as on a frosty night] will make them easier to see.

8 Dedicated / almost obsessive / a very good photographer.

9 It is very difficult to get good photographs of them.

10 Individual answers.

11 Individual answers.

12 Individual answers.

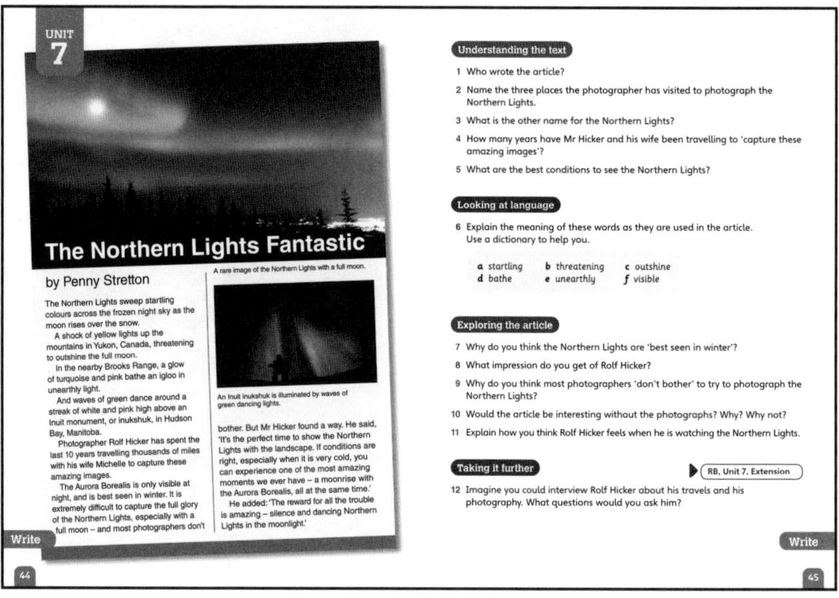

UNIT 7

The Northern Lights Fantastic

by Penny Stretton

The Northern Lights sweep startling colours across the frozen night sky as the moon rises over the snow.

A shock of yellow lights up the mountains in Yukon, Canada, threatening to outshine the full moon.

In the nearby Brooks Range, a glow of turquoise and pink bathe an igloo in unearthly light.

And waves of green dance around a streak of white and pink high above an Inuit monument, or inukshuk, in Hudson Bay, Manitoba.

Photographer Rolf Hicker has spent the last 10 years travelling thousands of miles with his wife Michelle to capture these amazing images.

The Aurora Borealis is only visible at night, and is best seen in winter. It is extremely difficult to capture the full glory of the Northern Lights, especially with a full moon – and most photographers don't bother. But Mr Hicker found a way. He said, 'It's the perfect time to show the Northern Lights with the landscape. If conditions are right, especially when it is very cold, you can experience one of the most amazing moments we ever have – a moonrise with the Aurora Borealis, all at the same time.'

He added: 'The reward for all the trouble is amazing – silence and dancing Northern Lights in the moonlight.'

A rare image of the Northern Lights with a full moon.

An Inuit inukshuk is illuminated by waves of green dancing lights.

Write 44

Understanding the text

1 Who wrote the article?

2 Name the three places the photographer has visited to photograph the Northern Lights.

3 What is the other name for the Northern Lights?

4 How many years have Mr Hicker and his wife been travelling to 'capture these amazing images'?

5 What are the best conditions to see the Northern Lights?

Looking at language

6 Explain the meaning of these words as they are used in the article. Use a dictionary to help you.

a startling **b** threatening **c** outshine
d bathe **e** unearthly **f** visible

Exploring the article

7 Why do you think the Northern Lights are 'best seen in winter'?

8 What impression do you get of Rolf Hicker?

9 Why do you think most photographers 'don't bother' to try to photograph the Northern Lights?

10 Would the article be interesting without the photographs? Why? Why not?

11 Explain how you think Rolf Hicker feels when he is watching the Northern Lights.

Taking it further RB, Unit 7. Extension

12 Imagine you could interview Rolf Hicker about his travels and his photography. What questions would you ask him?

Write 45

RESOURCE SHEET SUPPORT ANSWERS

A

1 Penny Stretton

2 Canada

3 Brooks Range

4 Manitoba

5 Michelle

6 Aurora Borealis

B

1 yellow

2 turquoise and pink

3 green

4 white and pink

C

1 surprising

2 be brighter than

3 cover

4 mysterious

GOING DEEPER

- Use children's answers to the 'Taking it further' activity as the basis for a class discussion.
- Review with the children what they understand by 'journalistic writing'.

UNIT FOCUS: Exploring Atmosphere and Tension

Investigating ...

- ghost stories
- the common feature of a 'visitation' in the night
- general features of the ghost story

TEACH

- Explore what ghost stories children have read or seen on television or on DVD.
- Ask children if they like ghost stories. Why? Why not?
- Explain to children that they are going to read an extract from *A Christmas Carol*. The story so far: Ebenezer Scrooge and Jacob Marley were business partners. All they cared about was making money – they were not bothered that no one liked them. At the beginning of the story, Jacob Marley has died. Scrooge continues in his mean, grasping ways until he is visited by the ghost of his dead partner.
- This is a challenging text for this year group, and you may wish to read it and discuss questions as a class or in groups before asking children to tackle it on their own.

RESOURCES & ASSESSMENT BOOK

- **Focus** (comprehension support): choosing the correct ending, choosing the odd one out; (vocabulary support): choosing the correct meaning.
- **Extension:** rewriting extract in modern English.

PUPIL BOOK ANSWERS

1 Jacob Marley.

2 Scrooge.

3 Any two of: cash-boxes / keys / padlocks / ledgers / deeds / heavy purses.

4 Three.

5 The first spirit.

6 **a** business account books **b** ghost / spirit **c** not able to believe **d** sarcastic / biting **e** faint **f** ghost / spirit **g** patience in difficult situations **h** avoid

7 **a** Scrooge does not believe in the ghost. **b** He does believe in the ghost.

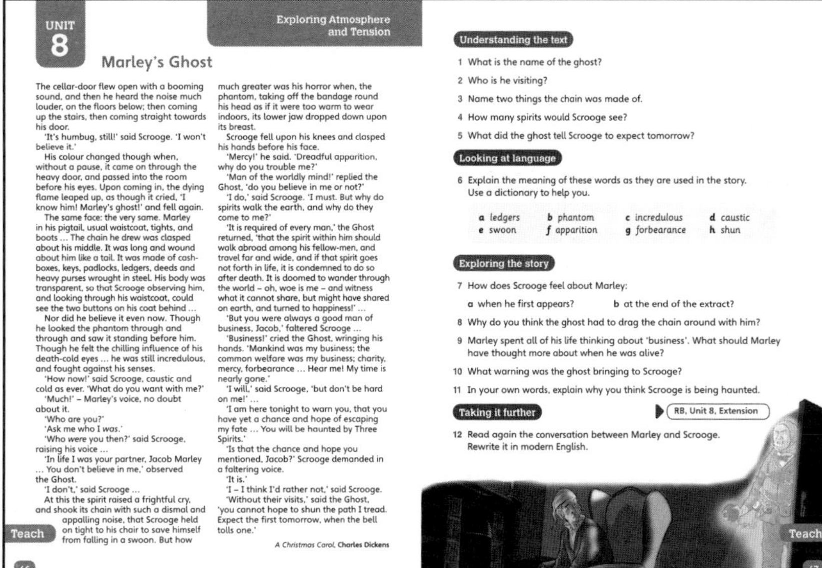

UNIT 8

Exploring Atmosphere and Tension

Marley's Ghost

The cellar-door flew open with a booming sound, and then he heard the noise much louder, on the floors below; then coming up the stairs, then coming straight towards his door.

'It's humbug, still!' said Scrooge. 'I won't believe it.'

His colour changed though when, without a pause, it came on through the heavy door, and passed into the room before his eyes. Upon coming in, the dying flame leaped up, as though it cried, 'I know him! Marley's ghost!' and fell again.

The same face: the very same. Marley in his pigtail, usual waistcoat, tights, and boots ... The chain he drew was clasped about his middle. It was long and wound about him like a tail. It was made of cash-boxes, keys, padlocks, ledgers, deeds and heavy purses wrought in steel. His body was transparent, so that Scrooge observing him, and looking through his waistcoat, could see the two buttons on his coat behind ...

Nor did he believe it even now. Though he looked the phantom through and through and saw it standing before him. Though he felt the chilling influence of his death-cold eyes ... he was still incredulous, and fought against his senses.

'How now!' said Scrooge, caustic and cold as ever. 'What do you want with me?'

'Much!' – Marley's voice, no doubt about it.

'Who are you?'

'Ask me who I *was*.'

'Who *were* you then?' said Scrooge, raising his voice ...

'In life I was your partner, Jacob Marley ... You don't believe in me,' observed the Ghost.

'I don't,' said Scrooge ...

At this the spirit raised a frightful cry, and shook its chain with such a dismal and appalling noise, that Scrooge held on tight to his chair to save himself from falling in a swoon. But how much greater was his horror when, the phantom, taking off the bandage round his head as if it were too warm to wear indoors, its lower jaw dropped down upon its breast.

Scrooge fell upon his knees and clasped his hands before his face.

'Mercy!' he said. 'Dreadful apparition, why do you trouble me?'

'Man of the worldly mind!' replied the Ghost, 'do you believe in me or not?'

'I do,' said Scrooge. 'I must. But why do spirits walk the earth, and why do they come to me?'

'It is required of every man,' the Ghost returned, 'that the spirit within him should walk abroad among his fellow-men, and travel far and wide, and if that spirit goes not forth in life, it is condemned to do so after death. It is doomed to wander through the world – oh, woe is me – and witness what it cannot share, but might have shared on earth, and turned to happiness!' ...

'But you were always a good man of business, Jacob,' faltered Scrooge ...

'Business!' cried the Ghost, wringing his hands. 'Mankind was my business; the common welfare was my business; charity, mercy, forbearance ... Hear me! My time is nearly gone.'

'I will,' said Scrooge, 'but don't be hard on me!' ...

'I am here tonight to warn you, that you have yet a chance and hope of escaping my fate ... You will be haunted by Three Spirits.'

'Is that the chance and hope you mentioned, Jacob?' Scrooge demanded in a faltering voice.

'It is.'

'I – I think I'd rather not,' said Scrooge.

'Without their visits,' said the Ghost, 'you cannot hope to shun the path I tread. Expect the first tomorrow, when the bell tolls one.'

A Christmas Carol, **Charles Dickens**

Teach

46

Understanding the text

1 What is the name of the ghost?

2 Who is he visiting?

3 Name two things the chain was made of.

4 How many spirits would Scrooge see?

5 What did the ghost tell Scrooge to expect tomorrow?

Looking at language

6 Explain the meaning of these words as they are used in the story. Use a dictionary to help you.

a ledgers **b** phantom **c** incredulous **d** caustic
e swoon **f** apparition **g** forbearance **h** shun

Exploring the story

7 How does Scrooge feel about Marley:

a when he first appears? **b** at the end of the extract?

8 Why do you think the ghost had to drag the chain around with him?

9 Marley spent all of his life thinking about 'business'. What should Marley have thought more about when he was alive?

10 What warning was the ghost bringing to Scrooge?

11 In your own words, explain why you think Scrooge is being haunted.

Taking it further

RB, Unit 8, Extension

12 Read again the conversation between Marley and Scrooge. Rewrite it in modern English.

Teach

47

8 The chain is a punishment; it is made of all the things he most cared about in life.

9 He should have cared more for other human beings.

10 He had to think about more than business while he was alive – he had to start caring about other people.

11 Individual answers.

12 Individual answers.

RESOURCE SHEET SUPPORT ANSWERS

A

1 b

2 a

3 a

4 b

5 a

B

1 flame

2 bandage

3 clasped hands

4 transparent body

C

1 account books

2 ghost

3 unfriendly

4 faint

5 doesn't believe it

6 ghost

7 patience

8 avoid

GOING DEEPER

- If children know the story, ask them to relate what happens. If they don't know the story, ask them to predict what may happen.

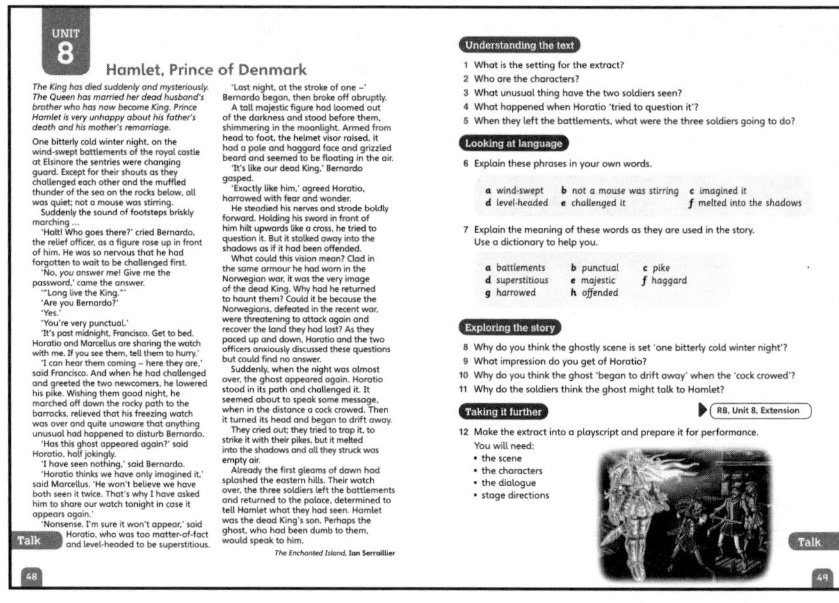

UNIT 8

Hamlet, Prince of Denmark

The King has died suddenly and mysteriously. The Queen has married her dead husband's brother who has now become King. Prince Hamlet is very unhappy about his father's death and his mother's remarriage.

One bitterly cold winter night, on the wind-swept battlements of the royal castle at Elsinore the sentries were changing guard. Except for their shouts as they challenged each other and the muffled thunder of the sea on the rocks below, all was quiet; not a mouse was stirring.

Suddenly the sound of footsteps briskly marching ...

'Halt! Who goes there?' cried Bernardo, the relief officer, as a figure rose up in front of him. He was so nervous that he had forgotten to wait to be challenged first.

'No, *you* answer *me*! Give me the password,' came the answer.

'"Long live the King."'

'Are you Bernardo?'

'Yes.'

'You're very punctual.'

'It's past midnight, Francisco. Get to bed. Horatio and Marcellus are sharing the watch with me. If you see them, tell them to hurry.'

'I can hear them coming – here they are,' said Francisco. And when he had challenged and greeted the two newcomers, he lowered his pike. Wishing them good night, he marched off down the rocky path to the barracks, relieved that his freezing watch was over and quite unaware that anything unusual had happened to disturb Bernardo.

'Has this ghost appeared again?' said Horatio, half jokingly.

'I have seen nothing,' said Bernardo.

'Horatio thinks we have only imagined it,' said Marcellus. 'He won't believe we have both seen it twice. That's why I have asked him to share our watch tonight in case it appears again.'

'Nonsense. I'm sure it won't appear,' said Horatio, who was too matter-of-fact and level-headed to be superstitious.

'Last night, at the stroke of one –' Bernardo began, then broke off abruptly.

A tall majestic figure had loomed out of the darkness and stood before them, shimmering in the moonlight. Armed from head to foot, the helmet visor raised, it had a pale and haggard face and grizzled beard and seemed to be floating in the air.

'It's like our dead King,' Bernardo gasped.

'Exactly like him,' agreed Horatio, harrowed with fear and wonder.

He steadied his nerves and strode boldly forward. Holding his sword in front of him hilt upwards like a cross, he tried to question it. But it stalked away into the shadows as if it had been offended.

What could this vision mean? Clad in the same armour he had worn in the Norwegian war, it was the very image of the dead King. Why had he returned to haunt them? Could it be because the Norwegians, defeated in the recent war, were threatening to attack again and recover the land they had lost? As they paced up and down, Horatio and the two officers anxiously discussed these questions but could find no answer.

Suddenly, when the night was almost over, the ghost appeared again. Horatio stood in its path and challenged it. It seemed about to speak some message, when in the distance a cock crowed. Then it turned its head and began to drift away.

They cried out; they tried to trap it, to strike it with their pikes, but it melted into the shadows and all they struck was empty air.

Already the first gleams of dawn had splashed the eastern hills. Their watch over, the three soldiers left the battlements and returned to the palace, determined to tell Hamlet what they had seen. Hamlet was the dead King's son. Perhaps the ghost, who had been dumb to them, would speak to him.

The Enchanted Island, **Ian Serraillier**

Talk

48

Understanding the text

1 What is the setting for the extract?
2 Who are the characters?
3 What unusual thing have the two soldiers seen?
4 What happened when Horatio 'tried to question it'?
5 When they left the battlements, what were the three soldiers going to do?

Looking at language

6 Explain these phrases in your own words.

a wind-swept **b** not a mouse was stirring **c** imagined it
d level-headed **e** challenged it **f** melted into the shadows

7 Explain the meaning of these words as they are used in the story. Use a dictionary to help you.

a battlements **b** punctual **c** pike
d superstitious **e** majestic **f** haggard
g harrowed **h** offended

Exploring the story

8 Why do you think the ghostly scene is set 'one bitterly cold winter night'?
9 What impression do you get of Horatio?
10 Why do you think the ghost 'began to drift away' when the 'cock crowed'?
11 Why do the soldiers think the ghost might talk to Hamlet?

Taking it further

RB, Unit 8, Extension

12 Make the extract into a playscript and prepare it for performance.
You will need:
- the scene
- the characters
- the dialogue
- stage directions

Talk

49

TALK

- Ask children to recap on why Marley haunted Scrooge (to warn him about his ways), and ask children if they can think of any other reasons why a ghost may haunt someone.
- Explain to children that they are going to read an extract from *Hamlet*. It was originally a play by Shakespeare but here it has been written as a story.
- Read the extract to the class; ask individual children to read it aloud in turn; or read in silence individually.

RESOURCES & ASSESSMENT BOOK

- **Focus** (comprehension support): choosing true statements, correcting false statements; (vocabulary support): matching words to correct definitions.
- **Extension:** creating playscript from extract, performing playscript.

PUPIL BOOK ANSWERS

1. 'One bitterly cold winter night on the wind-swept battlements of the royal castle of Elsinore'.
2. Bernardo / Francisco / Horatio / Marcellus / the ghost.
3. A ghost.
4. 'it stalked away into the shadows as if it had been offended'.
5. Tell Hamlet what they had seen.
6. **a** wind blowing across it **b** everything was still **c** seeing things **d** sensible **e** demanded that it explain **f** disappeared
7. **a** wall on top of a castle **b** on time **c** a pole with a steel pointed end **d** believing in magic / supernatural **e** magnificent / noble **f** thin and care-worn **g** greatly distressed / upset **h** insulted
8. It adds to the atmosphere of mystery and fear the writer wants to create / much more frightening than a bright summer's day.
9. – Not superstitious: 'matter-of-fact and level-headed'.

   – Brave: 'He steadied his nerves and strode boldly forward' / 'stood in its path and challenged it'.
10. Ghosts traditionally appear at night and have to return to where they come from when daylight comes.
11. It looks like the dead King and Hamlet is his son.
12. Individual answers.

RESOURCE SHEET SUPPORT ANSWERS

A

1. TRUE
2. FALSE
3. TRUE
4. FALSE
5. FALSE
6. TRUE

B

1. Bernardo was taking Francisco's place on the battlements.
2. The ghost looked like the dead King.

C

1. wall on top of a castle
2. on time
3. a pole with a steel pointed end
4. believing in magic
5. magnificent
6. thin and care-worn
7. upset
8. insulted

GOING DEEPER

- Discuss what children think Hamlet will do when he hears about the ghost. Explain that Hamlet does meet the ghost on the battlements. What do they think the ghost will say to Hamlet?

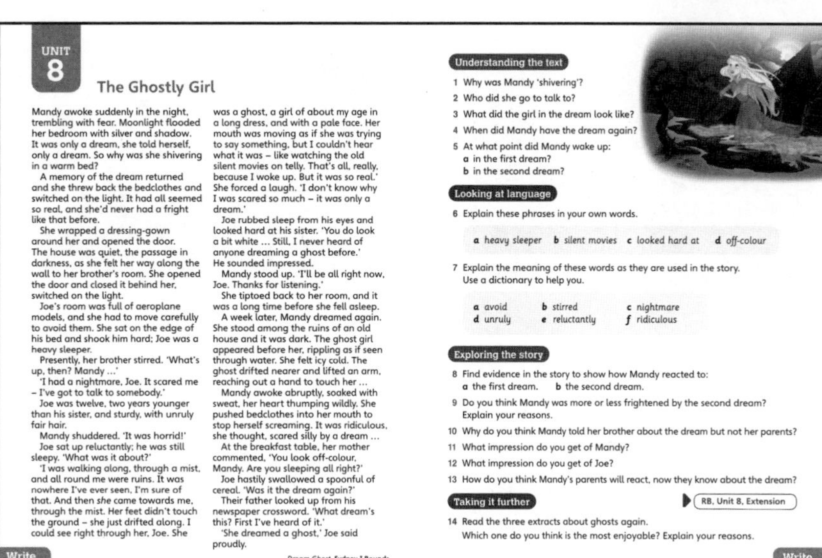

UNIT 8

The Ghostly Girl

Mandy awoke suddenly in the night, trembling with fear. Moonlight flooded her bedroom with silver and shadow. It was only a dream, she told herself, only a dream. So why was she shivering in a warm bed?

A memory of the dream returned and she threw back the bedclothes and switched on the light. It had all seemed so real, and she'd never had a fright like that before.

She wrapped a dressing-gown around her and opened the door. The house was quiet, the passage in darkness, as she felt her way along the wall to her brother's room. She opened the door and closed it behind her, switched on the light.

Joe's room was full of aeroplane models, and she had to move carefully to avoid them. She sat on the edge of his bed and shook him hard; Joe was a heavy sleeper.

Presently, her brother stirred. 'What's up, then? Mandy …'

'I had a nightmare, Joe. It scared me – I've got to talk to somebody.'

Joe was twelve, two years younger than his sister, and sturdy, with unruly fair hair.

Mandy shuddered. 'It was horrid!'

Joe sat up reluctantly; he was still sleepy. 'What was it about?'

'I was walking along, through a mist, and all round me were ruins. It was nowhere I've ever seen, I'm sure of that. And then *she* came towards me, through the mist. Her feet didn't touch the ground – she just drifted along. I could see right through her, Joe. She was a ghost, a girl of about my age in a long dress, and with a pale face. Her mouth was moving as if she was trying to say something, but I couldn't hear what it was – like watching the old silent movies on telly. That's all, really, because I woke up. But it was so real.' She forced a laugh. 'I don't know why I was scared so much – it was only a dream.'

Joe rubbed sleep from his eyes and looked hard at his sister. 'You do look a bit white … Still, I never heard of anyone dreaming a ghost before.' He sounded impressed.

Mandy stood up. 'I'll be all right now, Joe. Thanks for listening.'

She tiptoed back to her room, and it was a long time before she fell asleep.

A week later, Mandy dreamed again. She stood among the ruins of an old house and it was dark. The ghost girl appeared before her, rippling as if seen through water. She felt icy cold. The ghost drifted nearer and lifted an arm, reaching out a hand to touch her …

Mandy awoke abruptly, soaked with sweat, her heart thumping wildly. She pushed bedclothes into her mouth to stop herself screaming. It was ridiculous, she thought, scared silly by a dream …

At the breakfast table, her mother commented, 'You look off-colour, Mandy. Are you sleeping all right?'

Joe hastily swallowed a spoonful of cereal. 'Was it the dream again?'

Their father looked up from his newspaper crossword. 'What dream's this? First I've heard of it.'

'She dreamed a ghost,' Joe said proudly.

Dream Ghost, **Sydney J Bounds**

Understanding the text

1 Why was Mandy 'shivering'?
2 Who did she go to talk to?
3 What did the girl in the dream look like?
4 When did Mandy have the dream again?
5 At what point did Mandy wake up:
a in the first dream?
b in the second dream?

Looking at language

6 Explain these phrases in your own words.

a *heavy sleeper* **b** *silent movies* **c** *looked hard at* **d** *off-colour*

7 Explain the meaning of these words as they are used in the story. Use a dictionary to help you.

a *avoid* **b** *stirred* **c** *nightmare*
d *unruly* **e** *reluctantly* **f** *ridiculous*

Exploring the story

8 Find evidence in the story to show how Mandy reacted to:
a the first dream. b the second dream.
9 Do you think Mandy was more or less frightened by the second dream? Explain your reasons.
10 Why do you think Mandy told her brother about the dream but not her parents?
11 What impression do you get of Mandy?
12 What impression do you get of Joe?
13 How do you think Mandy's parents will react, now they know about the dream?

Taking it further RB, Unit 8, Extension

14 Read the three extracts about ghosts again. Which one do you think is the most enjoyable? Explain your reasons.

Write 50 Write 51

WRITE

- Discuss the idea of recurring dreams. Have the children ever had them?
- Explore why children think people have recurring dreams.
- Explain to children that they are going to read an extract from a story called *Dream Ghost*.
- Read the extract to the class; ask individual children to read it aloud in turn; or read in silence individually.

RESOURCES & ASSESSMENT BOOK

- **Focus** (comprehension support): completing each sentence; (vocabulary support): ordering details.
- **Extension:** writing ideas based on opinion.

PUPIL BOOK ANSWERS

1. She had had a nightmare.
2. Her brother, Joe.
3. 'a girl of about my age in a long dress, and with a pale face'.
4. A week later.
5. **a** when the ghost was speaking but Mandy couldn't hear **b** when 'the ghost drifted nearer and lifted an arm, reaching out to touch her'
6. **a** takes a lot to wake him up **b** early films that had no sound **c** stared closely **d** unwell
7. **a** keep away from **b** began to wake up **c** bad dream **d** hard to control **e** unwillingly **f** stupid
8. **a** 'trembling with fear' / 'shivering' / needed company – 'I've got to talk to somebody' / 'shuddered' **b** 'awoke abruptly' / 'soaked with sweat' / 'heart thumping wildly' / 'bedclothes into her mouth to stop herself from screaming'
9. More frightened – her reaction was stronger.
10. Her brother would be a more sympathetic listener / she thought her parents would think she was being silly.
11. – Is sensitive to be affected by the dream – 'It was horrid'.
    – Tries to be sensible and not over-dramatic – 'She forced a laugh' / 'I don't know why I was scared so much – it was only a dream'.
12. He is a good listener and sympathetic / he does not get cross with Mandy when she wakes him up.
13. Individual answers.
14. Individual answers.

RESOURCE SHEET SUPPORT ANSWERS

A

1. Mandy was shivering because she had had a nightmare.
2. Mandy went to talk to her brother.
3. The girl in the dream was wearing a long dress.
4. Mandy had the dream again a week later.
5. Mandy woke up when the girl tried to touch her.

B

First dream	Second dream
mist	reaching out a hand
long dress	dark
pale face	icy cold
couldn't hear her	lifted an arm
ruins	ruins

GOING DEEPER

- Use the answers to the 'Taking it further' activity as the basis of a class discussion. Discuss the three extracts. In what ways are they similar? In what ways are they different?

UNIT FOCUS: Looking at Personification

Investigating …

- personification
- elements of the natural world
- words used to describe the natural world

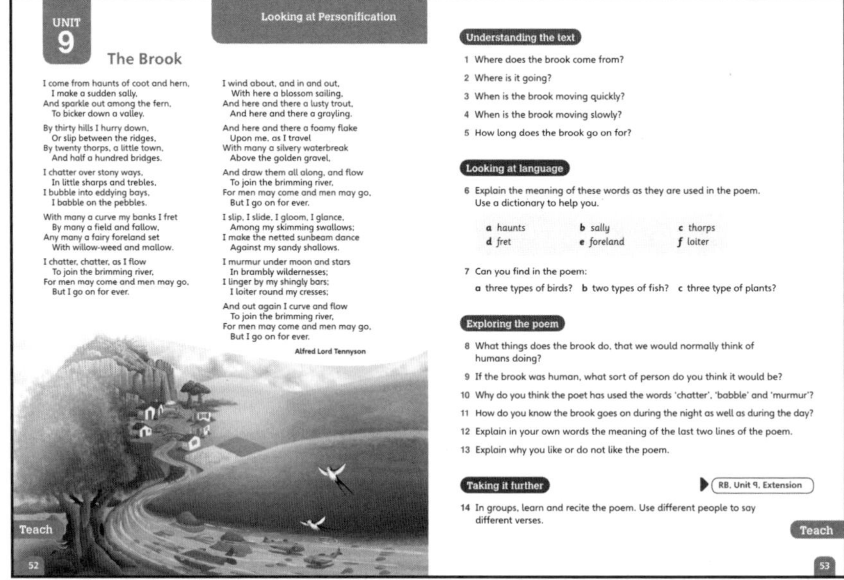

UNIT 9

Looking at Personification

The Brook

I come from haunts of coot and hern,
I make a sudden sally,
And sparkle out among the fern,
To bicker down a valley.

By thirty hills I hurry down,
Or slip between the ridges,
By twenty thorps, a little town,
And half a hundred bridges.

I chatter over stony ways,
In little sharps and trebles,
I bubble into eddying bays,
I babble on the pebbles.

With many a curve my banks I fret
By many a field and fallow,
Any many a fairy foreland set
With willow-weed and mallow.

I chatter, chatter, as I flow
To join the brimming river,
For men may come and men may go,
But I go on for ever.

I wind about, and in and out,
With here a blossom sailing,
And here and there a lusty trout,
And here and there a grayling.

And here and there a foamy flake
Upon me, as I travel
With many a silvery waterbreak
Above the golden gravel,

And draw them all along, and flow
To join the brimming river,
For men may come and men may go,
But I go on for ever.

I slip, I slide, I gloom, I glance,
Among my skimming swallows;
I make the netted sunbeam dance
Against my sandy shallows.

I murmur under moon and stars
In brambly wildernesses;
I linger by my shingly bars;
I loiter round my cresses;

And out again I curve and flow
To join the brimming river,
For men may come and men may go,
But I go on for ever.

Alfred Lord Tennyson

Teach 52

Understanding the text

1 Where does the brook come from?
2 Where is it going?
3 When is the brook moving quickly?
4 When is the brook moving slowly?
5 How long does the brook go on for?

Looking at language

6 Explain the meaning of these words as they are used in the poem. Use a dictionary to help you.

a *haunts* **b** *sally* **c** *thorps*
d *fret* **e** *foreland* **f** *loiter*

7 Can you find in the poem:

a three types of birds? **b** two types of fish? **c** three type of plants?

Exploring the poem

8 What things does the brook do, that we would normally think of humans doing?
9 If the brook was human, what sort of person do you think it would be?
10 Why do you think the poet has used the words 'chatter', 'babble' and 'murmur'?
11 How do you know the brook goes on during the night as well as during the day?
12 Explain in your own words the meaning of the last two lines of the poem.
13 Explain why you like or do not like the poem.

Taking it further RB, Unit 9, Extension

14 In groups, learn and recite the poem. Use different people to say different verses.

Teach 53

TEACH

- Ask children what they understand by the term 'personification'.
- Ask why they think writers give non-living things human characteristics in their work.
- Give and ask for examples such as 'the sun smiled', 'the sea raged'.
- Explain to children that they are going to read a poem called 'The Brook', where the brook itself tells its life story. It was written in the 19th century.
- This is a challenging text for this year group, and you may wish to read it and discuss questions as a class or in groups before asking children to tackle it on their own.

RESOURCES & ASSESSMENT BOOK

- **Focus** (comprehension support): choosing the correct answer; (vocabulary support): ordering words.
- **Extension:** learning and reciting a poem.

PUPIL BOOK ANSWERS

1 'haunts of coot and hern' [the place where these birds live and feed].

2 'to join the brimming river'.

3 'by thirty hills' / 'over stony ways' / 'into eddying bays'.

4 'under moon and stars' / 'in brambly wildernesses'.

5 'ever'.

6 **a** places where people or animals are usually found **b** a quick burst of activity **c** old-fashioned name for villages **d** wear away **e** a piece of land **f** hang about / linger

7 **a** coot / hern / swallow **b** trout / grayling **c** willow-weed / mallow / brambles

8 Talk / think / decide on what it does and where it goes.

9 Cheerful / energetic / determined.

10 They are onomatopoeic words that sound like the noise they make.

11 'I murmur under moon and stars'.

12 Individual answers (humans will live and die while the brook goes on).

13 Individual answers.

14 Individual answers.

RESOURCE SHEET SUPPORT ANSWERS

A

1 a

2 c

3 b

4 c

5 a

B

fish	birds	plants
trout	coot	willow-weed
grayling	hern	mallow
	swallows	brambles

GOING DEEPER

- Use the children's answers to the final 'Exploring the poem' question as the basis for a class discussion. What do children think the poem would have lost or gained if it had just been a description of a brook by the poet?

TALK

- Explain to children that the brook in the first poem gives the impression of being clean, flowing and fresh. Do they think all rivers are like this?
- Ask children if they live near any rivers. What are they like?
- Explain to children that they are going to read a poem called 'The River's Story'. For some time this river is just like the brook in the first poem, but things go badly wrong.
- Read the poem to the class; ask individual children to read it aloud in turn; or read in silence individually.

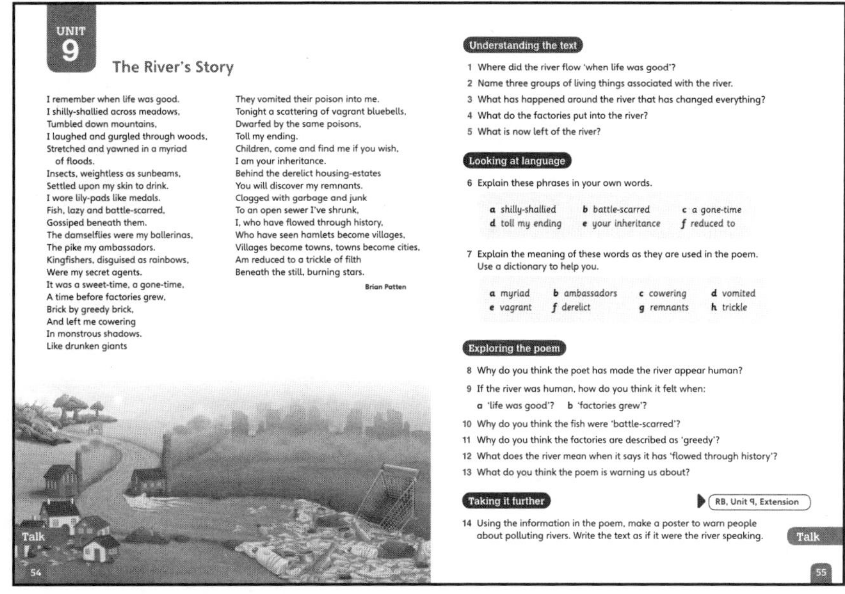
UNIT 9

The River's Story

I remember when life was good.
I shilly-shallied across meadows,
Tumbled down mountains,
I laughed and gurgled through woods,
Stretched and yawned in a myriad
of floods.
Insects, weightless as sunbeams,
Settled upon my skin to drink.
I wore lily-pads like medals.
Fish, lazy and battle-scarred,
Gossiped beneath them.
The damselflies were my ballerinas,
The pike my ambassadors.
Kingfishers, disguised as rainbows,
Were my secret agents.
It was a sweet-time, a gone-time,
A time before factories grew,
Brick by greedy brick,
And left me cowering
In monstrous shadows.
Like drunken giants
They vomited their poison into me.
Tonight a scattering of vagrant bluebells,
Dwarfed by the same poisons,
Toll my ending.
Children, come and find me if you wish,
I am your inheritance.
Behind the derelict housing-estates
You will discover my remnants.
Clogged with garbage and junk
To an open sewer I've shrunk,
I, who have flowed through history,
Who have seen hamlets become villages,
Villages become towns, towns become cities,
Am reduced to a trickle of filth
Beneath the still, burning stars.

Brian Patten

Understanding the text

1 Where did the river flow 'when life was good'?
2 Name three groups of living things associated with the river.
3 What has happened around the river that has changed everything?
4 What do the factories put into the river?
5 What is now left of the river?

Looking at language

6 Explain these phrases in your own words.
a shilly-shallied b battle-scarred c a gone-time
d toll my ending e your inheritance f reduced to

7 Explain the meaning of these words as they are used in the poem. Use a dictionary to help you.
a myriad b ambassadors c cowering d vomited
e vagrant f derelict g remnants h trickle

Exploring the poem

8 Why do you think the poet has made the river appear human?
9 If the river was human, how do you think it felt when:
a 'life was good'? b 'factories grew'?
10 Why do you think the fish were 'battle-scarred'?
11 Why do you think the factories are described as 'greedy'?
12 What does the river mean when it says it has 'flowed through history'?
13 What do you think the poem is warning us about?

Taking it further

RB, Unit 9, Extension

14 Using the information in the poem, make a poster to warn people about polluting rivers. Write the text as if it were the river speaking.

Talk

Talk

54 55

RESOURCES & ASSESSMENT BOOK

- **Focus** (comprehension support): choosing the correct answer, completing sentences; (vocabulary support): matching words to correct definitions.
- **Extension:** making a poster.

PUPIL BOOK ANSWERS

1. 'across meadows' / 'down mountains' / 'through woods'.
2. Any three from: plants / insects / fish / birds.
3. 'factories grew'.
4. 'poison'.
5. 'a trickle of filth'.
6. **a** went unhurriedly **b** carrying marks that come from injuries **c** a time that is past **d** mark my death [like a bell at a funeral] **e** thing that is passed down **d** shrunk down to
7. **a** a great number **b** representatives **c** crouching / shrinking back **d** poured forth / was sick **e** only there now and then **f** abandoned / ruined **g** remains **h** a small amount
8. It makes what has happened to the river more terrible / if readers think of the river as they would another human being, it makes them realise how badly humans have treated the river.
9. **a** happy / contented **b** fearful / miserable / full of despair
10. They have been in fights or are scarred by fishermen's hooks.
11. They destroy everything around them almost as if they eat everything up.
12. It has been there for a long, long time.
13. To take care of our natural resources / the planet.
14. Individual answers.

RESOURCE SHEET SUPPORT ANSWERS

A

1. a
2. c
3. b
4. c
5. a

B

1. A pike is a fish.
2. A kingfisher is a bird.
3. A damselfly is an insect.

C

1. ambassadors: representatives
2. vomited: was sick
3. derelict: abandoned / ruined

GOING DEEPER

- Discuss the children's posters and encourage constructive criticism.
- In what ways are the brook in the first poem and the river similar, and in what ways are they different?

WRITE

- Discuss what children understand by the term 'coral reef'. Where can coral reefs be found? What would you have to do to see a coral reef?
- Explain to children that they are going to read a poem called 'Coral Reef', where the reef itself describes what it looks like.
- Read the poem to the class; ask individual children to read it aloud in turn; or read in silence individually.

RESOURCES & ASSESSMENT BOOK

- **Focus** (comprehension support): choosing the correct adjectives from text; (vocabulary support): choosing the correct definition.
- **Extension:** writing ideas based on opinion.

PUPIL BOOK ANSWERS

1. Any three from: 'city' / 'garden' / 'forest' / 'palace' / 'maze' / 'sculpture'.
2. 'a hiding place'.
3. 'endlessly growing'.
4. 'brittle'.
5. To look after the coral reef or to destroy it.
6. **a** underwater **b** lost **c** prowling **d** ancient **e** priceless **f** precious
7. **a** full of life **b** made of bones **c** hiding **d** bright / shining **e** fragile / easily broken **f** something you inherit from an older generation
8. It is made up of the skeletons of numerous sea creatures.
9. Large, fierce fish.
10. They are such amazing shapes it seems difficult to believe they are real.
11. That it will disappear if we do not protect it.
12. Individual answers.
13. Individual answers.
14. Individual answers.

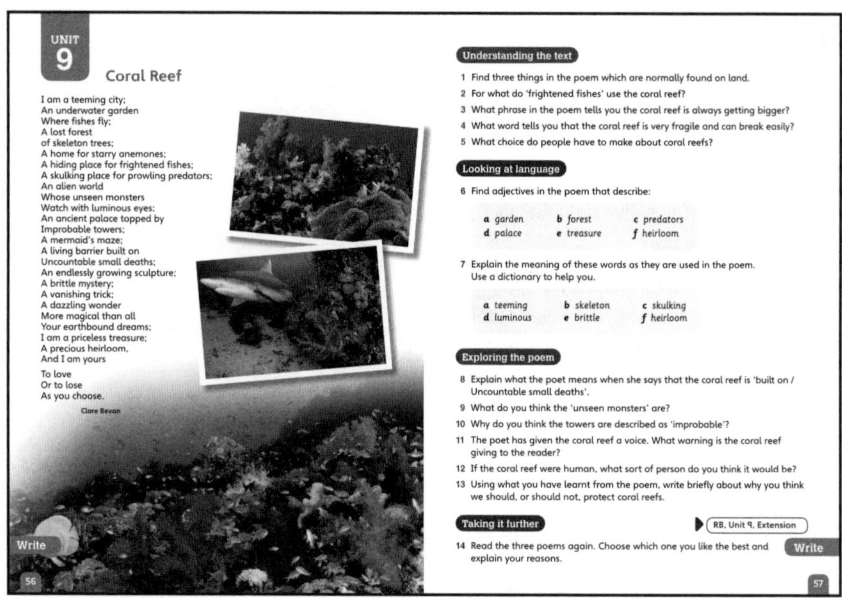

UNIT 9

Coral Reef

I am a teeming city;
An underwater garden
Where fishes fly;
A lost forest
of skeleton trees;
A home for starry anemones;
A hiding place for frightened fishes;
A skulking place for prowling predators;
An alien world
Whose unseen monsters
Watch with luminous eyes:
An ancient palace topped by
Improbable towers;
A mermaid's maze;
A living barrier built on
Uncountable small deaths;
An endlessly growing sculpture;
A brittle mystery;
A vanishing trick;
A dazzling wonder
More magical than all
Your earthbound dreams;
I am a priceless treasure;
A precious heirloom,
And I am yours

To love
Or to lose
As you choose.

Clare Bevan

Write

56

Understanding the text

1 Find three things in the poem which are normally found on land.
2 For what do 'frightened fishes' use the coral reef?
3 What phrase in the poem tells you the coral reef is always getting bigger?
4 What word tells you that the coral reef is very fragile and can break easily?
5 What choice do people have to make about coral reefs?

Looking at language

6 Find adjectives in the poem that describe:

a garden *b* forest *c* predators
d palace *e* treasure *f* heirloom

7 Explain the meaning of these words as they are used in the poem. Use a dictionary to help you.

a teeming *b* skeleton *c* skulking
d luminous *e* brittle *f* heirloom

Exploring the poem

8 Explain what the poet means when she says that the coral reef is 'built on / Uncountable small deaths'.
9 What do you think the 'unseen monsters' are?
10 Why do you think the towers are described as 'improbable'?
11 The poet has given the coral reef a voice. What warning is the coral reef giving to the reader?
12 If the coral reef were human, what sort of person do you think it would be?
13 Using what you have learnt from the poem, write briefly about why you think we should, or should not, protect coral reefs.

Taking it further

RB, Unit 9, Extension

14 Read the three poems again. Choose which one you like the best and explain your reasons.

Write

57

RESOURCE SHEET SUPPORT ANSWERS

A

1. a teeming city
2. an underwater garden
3. a lost forest
4. a hiding / skulking place
5. a living barrier
6. a dazzling wonder
7. a priceless treasure
8. a precious heirloom

B

1. a
2. b
3. b
4. b
5. a

GOING DEEPER

- Use children's answers to the 'Taking it further' activity as the basis for a class discussion. Ask children which of the three poems they like the best. Why?

UNIT FOCUS: Tales from Personal Experience

Investigating …

- autobiographical extracts
- common features of autobiographical writing, for example, first person account, past tense, facts, opinion and feelings

TEACH

- Ask children what they understand by the term 'autobiography'.
- Explore why they think people like to read autobiographies.
- Ask children what autobiographies they've read. Children may at first say they haven't read any, but articles in magazines that are first person accounts about a particular aspect of someone's life can be deemed autobiographical writing.
- Explain to children that they are going to read an extract from Sir Ernest Shackleton's autobiography *South* and discuss what they know about the South Pole.
- Give children background information: Shackleton was a British explorer. He was born in 1874 and died in 1922. He accompanied Scott on his expedition to the South Pole in 1901–04, and his own expedition of 1908–09, nearly made it there. He tried again in 1914 on the ship *Endurance*, and it is from this expedition that the extract is taken.
- This is a challenging text for this year group, and you may wish to read it and discuss questions as a class or in groups before asking children to tackle it on their own.

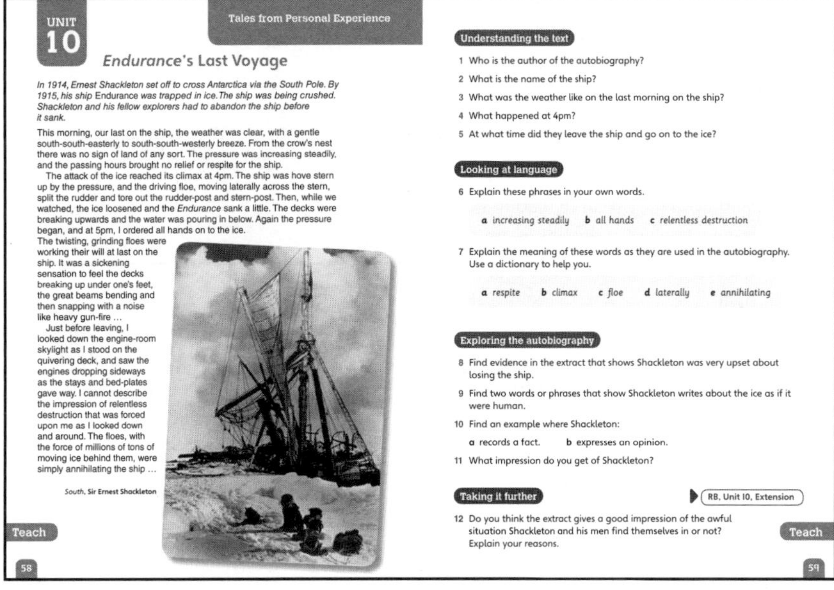

UNIT 10

Tales from Personal Experience

Endurance's Last Voyage

In 1914, Ernest Shackleton set off to cross Antarctica via the South Pole. By 1915, his ship Endurance *was trapped in ice. The ship was being crushed. Shackleton and his fellow explorers had to abandon the ship before it sank.*

This morning, our last on the ship, the weather was clear, with a gentle south-south-easterly to south-south-westerly breeze. From the crow's nest there was no sign of land of any sort. The pressure was increasing steadily, and the passing hours brought no relief or respite for the ship.

The attack of the ice reached its climax at 4pm. The ship was hove stern up by the pressure, and the driving floe, moving laterally across the stern, split the rudder and tore out the rudder-post and stern-post. Then, while we watched, the ice loosened and the *Endurance* sank a little. The decks were breaking upwards and the water was pouring in below. Again the pressure began, and at 5pm, I ordered all hands on to the ice. The twisting, grinding floes were working their will at last on the ship. It was a sickening sensation to feel the decks breaking up under one's feet, the great beams bending and then snapping with a noise like heavy gun-fire …

Just before leaving, I looked down the engine-room skylight as I stood on the quivering deck, and saw the engines dropping sideways as the stays and bed-plates gave way. I cannot describe the impression of relentless destruction that was forced upon me as I looked down and around. The floes, with the force of millions of tons of moving ice behind them, were simply annihilating the ship …

South, Sir Ernest Shackleton

Teach

58

Understanding the text

1 Who is the author of the autobiography?

2 What is the name of the ship?

3 What was the weather like on the last morning on the ship?

4 What happened at 4pm?

5 At what time did they leave the ship and go on to the ice?

Looking at language

6 Explain these phrases in your own words.

a *increasing steadily* **b** *all hands* **c** *relentless destruction*

7 Explain the meaning of these words as they are used in the autobiography. Use a dictionary to help you.

a *respite* **b** *climax* **c** *floe* **d** *laterally* **e** *annihilating*

Exploring the autobiography

8 Find evidence in the extract that shows Shackleton was very upset about losing the ship.

9 Find two words or phrases that show Shackleton writes about the ice as if it were human.

10 Find an example where Shackleton:

a records a fact. **b** expresses an opinion.

11 What impression do you get of Shackleton?

Taking it further

RB, Unit 10, Extension

12 Do you think the extract gives a good impression of the awful situation Shackleton and his men find themselves in or not? Explain your reasons.

Teach

59

RESOURCES & ASSESSMENT BOOK

- **Focus** (comprehension support): exploring True / False statements, correcting false statements; (vocabulary support): matching words with the correct definition.
- **Extension:** making notes, writing explanations.

PUPIL BOOK ANSWERS

1 Sir Ernest Shackleton.

2 *Endurance.*

3 'clear', with a gentle breeze.

4 'The attack of the ice reached its climax'.

5 5pm.

6 **a** growing stronger moment by moment **b** everyone on the ship **c** destroying without stopping

7 **a** breather / rest **b** height **c** sheet of floating ice **d** from side to side **e** totally destroying

8 He takes one last look 'before leaving' / 'I cannot describe the impression of relentless destruction that was forced upon me'.

9 Any two of: 'attack' / 'were working their will' / 'the floes ... were simply annihilating the ship'.

10 **a** e.g. 'at 5pm, I ordered all hands on to the ice' **b** e.g. 'It was a sickening sensation ...'

11 Courageous / practical / cared about his crew / deeply affected by the lost of the ship.

12 Individual answers.

RESOURCE SHEET SUPPORT ANSWERS

A

1 FALSE

2 TRUE

3 TRUE

4 FALSE

5 FALSE

6 TRUE

B

1 The last morning on the ship was clear.

2 The decks were breaking up under their feet.

3 They left the ship at 5pm.

C

1 breather / stopping

2 height

3 sheet of floating ice

4 from side to side

5 totally destroying

GOING DEEPER

- Ask children to imagine they were one of the sailors on the *Endurance* and they now face a 364-mile walk across the ice to find shelter: How would they be feeling? What would their attitude be towards Shackleton?

TALK

- Explain to children that they are going to read an extract from an autobiography called *20 HRS, 40 MIN ... Our Flight in the* Friendship by Amelia Earhart, the first woman to fly across the Atlantic.
- Give children background information: Amelia Earhart was born in America in 1897. She was the first woman to fly accompanied across the Atlantic Ocean and to fly solo across it (1932). Her plane was lost over the Pacific Ocean on an attempted flight around the world in 1937.
- This is a challenging text for this year group, and you may wish to read it and discuss questions as a class or in groups before asking children to tackle it on their own.

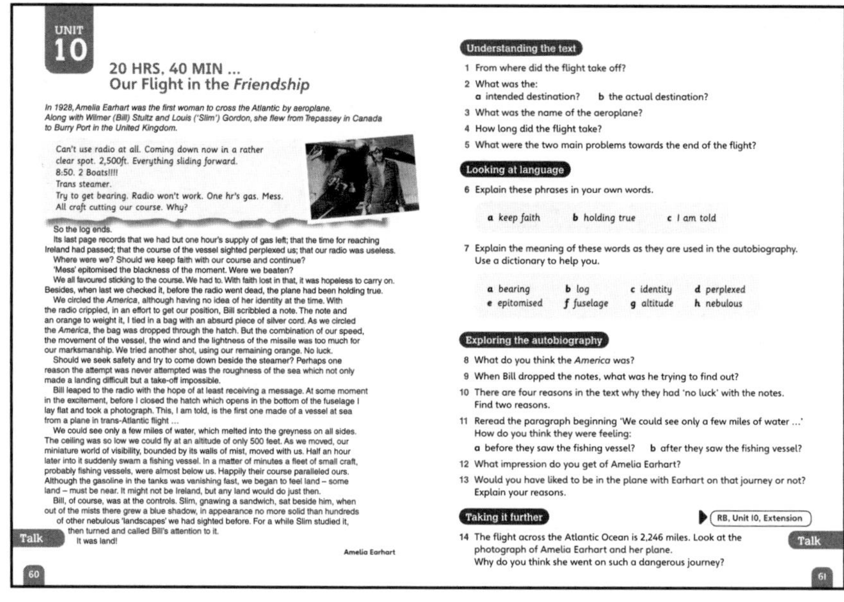

UNIT 10

20 HRS, 40 MIN ...
Our Flight in the *Friendship*

In 1928, Amelia Earhart was the first woman to cross the Atlantic by aeroplane. Along with Wilmer (Bill) Stultz and Louis ('Slim') Gordon, she flew from Trepassey in Canada to Burry Port in the United Kingdom.

Can't use radio at all. Coming down now in a rather clear spot. 2,500ft. Everything sliding forward.
8:50. 2 Boats!!!!
Trans steamer.
Try to get bearing. Radio won't work. One hr's gas. Mess.
All craft cutting our course. Why?

So the log ends.

Its last page records that we had but one hour's supply of gas left; that the time for reaching Ireland had passed; that the course of the vessel sighted perplexed us; that our radio was useless.

Where were we? Should we keep faith with our course and continue?

'Mess' epitomised the blackness of the moment. Were we beaten?

We all favoured sticking to the course. We had to. With faith lost in that, it was hopeless to carry on. Besides, when last we checked it, before the radio went dead, the plane had been holding true.

We circled the *America*, although having no idea of her identity at the time. With the radio crippled, in an effort to get our position, Bill scribbled a note. The note and an orange to weight it, I tied in a bag with an absurd piece of silver cord. As we circled the *America*, the bag was dropped through the hatch. But the combination of our speed, the movement of the vessel, the wind and the lightness of the missile was too much for our marksmanship. We tried another shot, using our remaining orange. No luck.

Should we seek safety and try to come down beside the steamer? Perhaps one reason the attempt was never attempted was the roughness of the sea which not only made a landing difficult but a take-off impossible.

Bill leaped to the radio with the hope of at least receiving a message. At some moment in the excitement, before I closed the hatch which opens in the bottom of the fuselage I lay flat and took a photograph. This, I am told, is the first one made of a vessel at sea from a plane in trans-Atlantic flight ...

We could see only a few miles of water, which melted into the greyness on all sides. The ceiling was so low we could fly at an altitude of only 500 feet. As we moved, our miniature world of visibility, bounded by its walls of mist, moved with us. Half an hour later into it suddenly swam a fishing vessel. In a matter of minutes a fleet of small craft, probably fishing vessels, were almost below us. Happily their course paralleled ours. Although the gasoline in the tanks was vanishing fast, we began to feel land – some land – must be near. It might not be Ireland, but any land would do just then.

Bill, of course, was at the controls. Slim, gnawing a sandwich, sat beside him, when out of the mists there grew a blue shadow, in appearance no more solid than hundreds of other nebulous 'landscapes' we had sighted before. For a while Slim studied it, then turned and called Bill's attention to it.

It was land!

Amelia Earhart

Talk

60

Understanding the text

1 From where did the flight take off?
2 What was the:
a intended destination? b the actual destination?
3 What was the name of the aeroplane?
4 How long did the flight take?
5 What were the two main problems towards the end of the flight?

Looking at language

6 Explain these phrases in your own words.
a *keep faith* b *holding true* c *I am told*

7 Explain the meaning of these words as they are used in the autobiography. Use a dictionary to help you.
a *bearing* b *log* c *identity* d *perplexed*
e *epitomised* f *fuselage* g *altitude* h *nebulous*

Exploring the autobiography

8 What do you think the *America* was?
9 When Bill dropped the notes, what was he trying to find out?
10 There are four reasons in the text why they had 'no luck' with the notes. Find two reasons.
11 Reread the paragraph beginning 'We could see only a few miles of water ...' How do you think they were feeling:
a before they saw the fishing vessel? b after they saw the fishing vessel?
12 What impression do you get of Amelia Earhart?
13 Would you have liked to be in the plane with Earhart on that journey or not? Explain your reasons.

Taking it further

RB, Unit 10, Extension

14 The flight across the Atlantic Ocean is 2,246 miles. Look at the photograph of Amelia Earhart and her plane.
Why do you think she went on such a dangerous journey?

Talk

61

RESOURCES & ASSESSMENT BOOK

- **Focus** (comprehension support): completing sentences from text, answering questions; (vocabulary support): choosing answers based on definitions.
- **Extension:** writing an explanatory paragraph.

PUPIL BOOK ANSWERS

1. Trepassey, Canada.
2. **a** Ireland **b** Burry Port
3. *Friendship.*
4. 20 hours 40 minutes.
5. 'we had but one hour's supply of gas left' / 'our radio was useless'.
6. **a** stick to **b** on the right course **c** don't personally know
7. **a** position **b** written record of the flight **c** what it was **d** puzzled **e** the perfect word for **f** body of the aeroplane **g** height **h** cloud-like
8. A type of ship.
9. Where they were i.e. how close to land.
10. Any two of: 'our speed' [going too fast], 'the movement of the vessel' [the ship wasn't still], 'the wind' [carrying the bag off course], 'the lightness of the missile, [it wasn't heavy enough to drop straight down] meant they had no luck with the notes.
11. **a** quite desperate – couldn't see through cloud / no radio contact / running out of fuel **b** relieved – near land
12. Courageous / adventurous / loved flying / foolhardy.
13. Individual answers.
14. Individual answers.

RESOURCE SHEET SUPPORT ANSWERS

A

1. We had one hour's supply of gas left.
2. We all favoured sticking to our course.
3. We used an orange to weigh down the note.
4. We could only fly at an altitude of 500ft.

B

1. Bill
2. Amelia
3. Slim

C

1. a
2. a
3. b

GOING DEEPER

- Use children's answers to the 'Taking it further' activity as the basis for class discussion.

WRITE

- Discuss what children think about mountain climbing. Can they see the appeal?
- Explore what sort of people the children think go mountain climbing.
- Ask children if they would like to do it. Why / Why not?
- Explain to children that they are going to read an extract from an autobiography called *Touching the Void*, an incredible story of courage and survival.
- Read the extract to the class; ask individual children to read it aloud in turn; or read in silence individually.

RESOURCES & ASSESSMENT BOOK

- **Focus** (comprehension support): choosing the correct ending; (vocabulary support): choosing the correct verb to complete sentences.
- **Extension:** making notes, writing from a character's point of view.

PUPIL BOOK ANSWERS

1 Joe Simpson / Simon Yates.

2 Siula Grande.

3 6,344 metres.

4 East Face.

5 'a death sentence'.

6 **a** unnaturally out of shape **b** sickness **c** flooded

7 **a** became rigid / immovable / unable to bend **b** threw violently **c** pulled roughly **d** loosely / not pulled tight **e** burst **f** force

8 Simon is at the other end of the rope and, when Joe falls, he will find it almost impossible to hang on and will probably fall too.

9 That he was probably going to die.

10 He would not accept that he had injured his leg / he wanted to prove that his leg was alright.

11 Courageous / didn't give up but tried to help himself / unselfish as he thought of Simon's situation / foolhardy.

12 Individual answers.

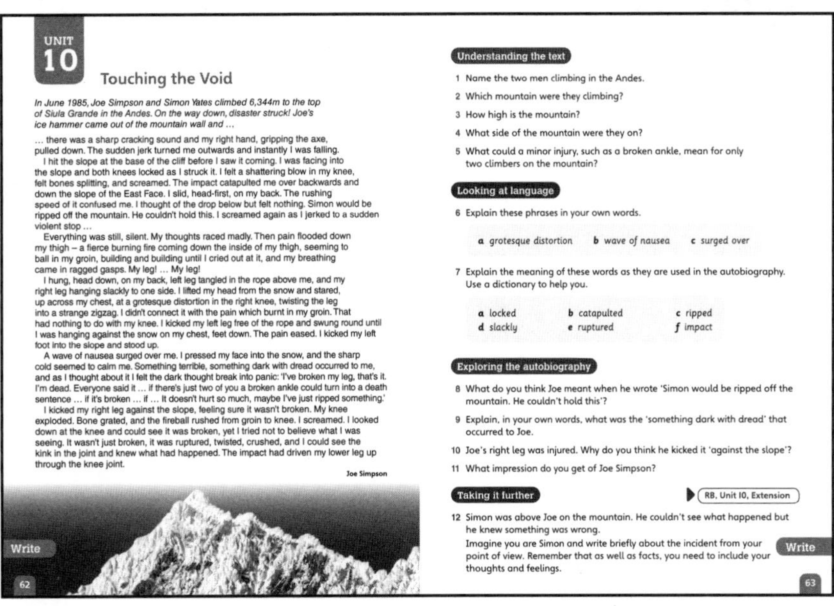

UNIT 10

Touching the Void

In June 1985, Joe Simpson and Simon Yates climbed 6,344m to the top of Siula Grande in the Andes. On the way down, disaster struck! Joe's ice hammer came out of the mountain wall and …

… there was a sharp cracking sound and my right hand, gripping the axe, pulled down. The sudden jerk turned me outwards and instantly I was falling.

I hit the slope at the base of the cliff before I saw it coming. I was facing into the slope and both knees locked as I struck it. I felt a shattering blow in my knee, felt bones splitting, and screamed. The impact catapulted me over backwards and down the slope of the East Face. I slid, head-first, on my back. The rushing speed of it confused me. I thought of the drop below but felt nothing. Simon would be ripped off the mountain. He couldn't hold this. I screamed again as I jerked to a sudden violent stop …

Everything was still, silent. My thoughts raced madly. Then pain flooded down my thigh – a fierce burning fire coming down the inside of my thigh, seeming to ball in my groin, building and building until I cried out at it, and my breathing came in ragged gasps. My leg! … My leg!

I hung, head down, on my back, left leg tangled in the rope above me, and my right leg hanging slackly to one side. I lifted my head from the snow and stared, up across my chest, at a grotesque distortion in the right knee, twisting the leg into a strange zigzag. I didn't connect it with the pain which burnt in my groin. That had nothing to do with my knee. I kicked my left leg free of the rope and swung round until I was hanging against the snow on my chest, feet down. The pain eased. I kicked my left foot into the slope and stood up.

A wave of nausea surged over me. I pressed my face into the snow, and the sharp cold seemed to calm me. Something terrible, something dark with dread occurred to me, and as I thought about it I felt the dark thought break into panic: 'I've broken my leg, that's it. I'm dead. Everyone said it … if there's just two of you a broken ankle could turn into a death sentence … if it's broken … if … It doesn't hurt so much, maybe I've just ripped something.'

I kicked my right leg against the slope, feeling sure it wasn't broken. My knee exploded. Bone grated, and the fireball rushed from groin to knee. I screamed. I looked down at the knee and could see it was broken, yet I tried not to believe what I was seeing. It wasn't just broken, it was ruptured, twisted, crushed, and I could see the kink in the joint and knew what had happened. The impact had driven my lower leg up through the knee joint.

Joe Simpson

Write

62

Understanding the text

1 Name the two men climbing in the Andes.

2 Which mountain were they climbing?

3 How high is the mountain?

4 What side of the mountain were they on?

5 What could a minor injury, such as a broken ankle, mean for only two climbers on the mountain?

Looking at language

6 Explain these phrases in your own words.

a *grotesque distortion* **b** *wave of nausea* **c** *surged over*

7 Explain the meaning of these words as they are used in the autobiography. Use a dictionary to help you.

a *locked* **b** *catapulted* **c** *ripped*
d *slackly* **e** *ruptured* **f** *impact*

Exploring the autobiography

8 What do you think Joe meant when he wrote 'Simon would be ripped off the mountain. He couldn't hold this'?

9 Explain, in your own words, what was the 'something dark with dread' that occurred to Joe.

10 Joe's right leg was injured. Why do you think he kicked it 'against the slope'?

11 What impression do you get of Joe Simpson?

Taking it further RB, Unit 10, Extension

12 Simon was above Joe on the mountain. He couldn't see what happened but he knew something was wrong.
Imagine you are Simon and write briefly about the incident from your point of view. Remember that as well as facts, you need to include your thoughts and feelings.

Write

63

RESOURCE SHEET SUPPORT ANSWERS

A

1 c

2 b

3 a

4 c

5 a

B

When Joe hit the slope, both his knees **locked**. He was **catapulted** backwards. Everything happened so quickly, he was **confused**. He realised that Simon would be **ripped** off the mountain. As he screamed, Joe **jerked** violently to a stop. He was in great pain. He had **ruptured** his knee.

GOING DEEPER

- Use children's answers to the 'Taking it further' activity as the basis for a class discussion.
- How do the children know that Joe did not die on the mountain?
- Recap on what children have learnt about autobiographical writing (first person accounts, past tense, facts, feelings).

Year 4 Example Test Paper Answers

CONTENT DOMAINS

1a	1b	1c	1d	1e	1f	1g	1h
Give / explain the meaning of words in context.	*Retrieve and record information / identify key details from fiction and non-fiction.*	*Summarize main ideas from more than one paragraph.*	*Make inferences from the text / explain and justify inferences with evidence from the text*	*Predict what might happen from details stated and implied.*	*Identify / explain how information / narrative content is related and contributes to meaning as a whole.*	*Identify / explain how meaning is enhanced through choice of words and phrases*	*Make comparisons within the text.*

Paper 1

Jake's Shadow

Qu	Domain	Answers	Mark	Comment
1	1b	a tell Mum b scratch the baby c cooking d on the doormat	2	Award **one** mark for two correct answers. Award **two** marks for four correct answers.
2	1d	The shadow was: 1 *spiky-haired* 2 *Jake-shaped*	2	
3	1a	didn't believe Jake	1	
4	1c	Answers that suggest: 1 Jake's shadow didn't just **copy** what Jake did – it moved independently. 2 It could still be seen when the sun went in.	2	
5	1d	Answers that suggest when Mum wanted to see the shadow *messing around*, the shadow was on *its best behaviour / just a shadow* and didn't do anything.	1	
6	1d	Answers based on evidence at the beginning of the extract. The shadow *poked out its tongue, waggled its ears* and *picked its nose.*	2	Award **one** mark for two details. Award **two** marks for all three details.
7	1g	Answers that suggest Mum was feeling cross / losing her patience with Jake.	1	
8	1a	*distractedly*	1	
9	1d	Any two of: • Mum is anxious that the cat doesn't hurt Polly even though it has been around for years. • She listened to Jake but not for long: *Jake saw she wasn't listening any more…Already she had gone back to fussing with Polly in her buggy…* • When Dad does listen to Jake he thinks maybe Jake is acting up because of the new baby getting lots of attention: *All these strange ideas… it's not the baby, is it? Is Polly getting to you a bit?*	2	
10	1d	Answers that suggest: • he was cross with Dad because he wasn't taking him seriously • he was cross with both his parents because neither of them would take him seriously	2	Award **one** mark if the answer concerns only Dad. Give **two** marks if the pupil has realized that this is a build up of feeling because of the reaction of his Mum, then his Dad.

11	1c	1 Jake's shadow was messing around. 2 Jake decided to tell his Mum. 3 Mum was in the garden with Polly. 4 His Mum wanted to see Jake's shadow messing around. 5 The shadow behaved itself. 6 Jake went to tell Dad. 7 Dad was too busy cooking to listen to him.	1	
12	1a	signaled for	1	
13	1e	Answers that suggest that Jake and his shadow will probably: • have some sort of adventure • get into trouble Evidence: in the story so far: • the shadow has not behaved itself; • the shadow does not do as Jake tells it; • the shadow beckons Jake to follow him so the shadow is obviously up to something.	2	Award **two** marks for an acceptable point supported by text based evidence.

Shadow puppets

14	1a	something to do	1	
15	1b	*one of the easiest shadow shapes to make*	1	
16	1d	Answers that suggest this makes the movement of the wings.	1	
17	1b	a a dog b a bird	1	
18	1c	You need one hand to make the bird shadow. [F] You put your palms together when you make a dog shadow. [T] You stick a straw to the back of your shadow puppet. [T] You make the stage out of a wooden box. [F]	1	
19	1d	Answers that suggest: a the paper needs to be stiff so the puppets will stand up; b the paper has to be thick so the light won't shine through it.	2	
20	1b	1 *whole plays* 2 *your favourite stories.*	1	
21	1a	life-like	1	
22	1d	Answers that suggest the darker it is in the room, the better the puppet show will be. It will be easier to see.	1	
23	1a	*audience*	1	
24	1b	crouching down behind the table	2	Award only **one** mark for *behind the table.*
25	1e	Individual answers	2	Award marks for specific details of story and characters.
		TOTAL	**35**	

Paper 2

Oliver and the Seawigs

Qu	Domain	Answers	Mark	Comment
1	1a	a the beginning of rivers b mountains that have not been climbed c new journeys d twisting lanes e islands not on a map	2	Award **one** mark for two correct answers. Award **two** marks for five correct answers.
2	1b	Any three of: • live in his house for more than two weeks at a time • make friends • feel at home anywhere • go to school • have a proper bedroom • have all his things around him	2	Award **one** mark for two details. Award **two** marks for three details.
3	1b	1 time 2 money	1	
4	1a	covering in patches	1	
5	1b	shaggy, steep-sided islands	1	
6	1a	Acceptable points for *sheer*: complete / total Acceptable points for amazement: wonder / surprise	2	Award **one** mark for an interpretation of **either** *sheer* or *amazement.* Award **two** marks for an interpretation of both *sheer* and *amazement.*
7	1d	Answers that suggest the rooms are *dimly familiar* because the reader has been told that *The house he was coming home to was one he'd only seen on holidays; brief two-week breaks before fresh expeditions.*	1	
8	1c	• unlocked the house • carried boxes and bags and suitcases inside • took off dustsheets • ran upstairs • bounced on the bed • opened the window • brought his suitcase upstairs • set out his favourite things • arranged his books • hung up his clothes	1	
9	1d	Answers that suggest Oliver's parents could still live in the house while exploring the islands: *at least they can explore these islands from home.*	1	
10	1d	Answers that suggest they were fine with leaving Oliver at home alone while they went off to explore the islands.	1	
11	1b	1 the islands 2 his parents	2	
12	1e	Answers that suggest he went to find his parents. Evidence: • his explorer background; • his parents had vanished; • the dingy was within reach.	3	Award **one** mark for a reasonable suggestion as to what Oliver did. Award **three** marks if the suggestion is supported by evidence.

Facing Danger

13	1b	Explorers like the challenge of visiting dangerous parts of the world and enjoy testing their survival skills against them.	2	Award **one** mark for one detail. Award **two** marks for both details.
14	1d	Answers should include reference to the number of 'firsts' he has achieved and the number of expeditions he has lead.	2	
15	1a	distant	1	

16	1b	Russian Norgay fallen through the ice sailor and explorer	1	
17	1b	a Matthew Henson b David Hempleman-Adams	1	
18	1b	a over 30 b 48 times	2	
19	1c	1909: discovery of Geographic North Pole 1953: first people to reach top of Mount Everest 1963: first woman in space 1982: first team to go around the Earth 1993: first unsupported walk across Antarctica	1	
20	1g	Answers that suggest the weather made the journey even more difficult. They had to 'fight' the weather.	1	
21	1d	Answers that suggest: a protection against the freezing temperatures; b to keep their body temperature up.	2	
22	1c	metal freezes [F] eyeball liquid freezes [T] sweat freezes [T] hot drinks freeze [F]	1	
23	1b	Any two of: • goosebumps • blue lips • hands and feet go numb • muscles seize up • confusion sets in • heart beats faster • body's organs begin to fail	1	
24	1a	done something no one else has done	1	
25	1a	Answers that suggest you do not think clearly and begin to lose your grasp of reality.	1	
		TOTAL	**35**	

Revision Book Answers

CONTENT DOMAINS

1a	1b	1c	1d	1e	1f	1g	1h
Give / explain the meaning of words in context.	*Retrieve and record information / identify key details from fiction and non-fiction.*	*Summarize main ideas from more than one paragraph.*	*Make inferences from the text / explain and justify inferences with evidence from the text*	*Predict what might happen from details stated and implied.*	*Identify / explain how information / narrative content is related and contributes to meaning as a whole.*	*Identify / explain how meaning is enhanced through choice of words and phrases*	*Make comparisons within the text.*

Paper 1

Horses in Fact and Fiction

Qu	Domain	Answers	Mark	Comment
1	1b	1 work / 2 sport / 3 war / 4 companions	1	Accept answers in any order.
2	1a	*when he was most well known*	1	
3	1b	Red Rum: won the Grand National three times Shergar: won Epsom Derby by the biggest margin in the race's history	2	Accept explanations in children's own words.
4	1a	brave search.	1	
5	1g	Acceptable synonyms for constant: faithful dependable unchanging Acceptable synonyms for companion: friend ally comrade e.g. It shows that Silver was always with the Lone Ranger as a friend and ally.	2	Award **two** marks for answers that interpret both constant and companion.
6	1d	Accept answers that suggest Dick Turpin was pursued by the forces of the law as he was a criminal.	1	
7	1g	a a simile b very quickly / swiftly / at a fast speed	1 1	
8	1b	*in mortal danger*	1	
9	1d	rode into battle / pulled ambulance / pulled artillery wagon	2	Accept any two of the three listed.
10	1a	Appeared to be doing something that they were not actually doing.	1	
11	1d	Answers that suggest the Greeks pretended to sail away so as to trick the Trojans into thinking they had left and had accepted defeat.	1	
12	1d	Answers that suggest: • they wanted to make sure there was no one about. • the Trojans would be sleeping. • under cover of darkness they could open the gates.	2	Give **two** marks for a full answer, not just 'none would see them'.
13	1c	1 Pegasus 2 the wooden horse	1	

14	1d	Joey is the most famous horse of the 20th century. opinion The Lone Ranger's horse was called Silver. fact Dick Turpin was alive in the 18th century fact The Greeks were braver than the Trojans. opinion	1	Award **one** mark for all four correct.
15	1d	The Greeks built the horse. The Trojans did not suspect a trick and took the horse inside the city.	2	Award **one** mark for 'The Greeks built the horse'. Award **two** marks if children compare the trickery of the Greeks with the stupidity of the Trojans.
16	1b	The Lone Ranger Silver Dick Turpin Black Bess Bellerophon Pegasus Walter Swinburn Shergar	1	

Black Beauty

17	1b	a to do business in the town. b late in the afternoon. c windy. d across the bridge.	2	Award **one** mark for two correct answers. Award **two** marks for four correct answers.
18	1b	*Along the skirts of a wood*	1	
19	1a	stronger	1	
20	1d	When his hooves touched the bridge, he felt sure there was something wrong.	1	
21	1b	1 stopped still 2 trembled	1 1	
22	1a	Ran out of the house / 'Hoy, hoy, hoy, halloo, stop!' he cried / tossing a torch about like one mad	2	
23	1c	The tree blocks the way. true Black Beauty turns around when the tree falls. false The bridge has broken in the middle. true There is water over the middle of the bridge. true	1	
24	1a	a simile	1	
25	1d	• There was water over the middle of the bridge. • It was very nearly dark.	1 1	
26	1f	Two details from: • *'Thank God!' said my master* • *'You Beauty!' said John* • *took the bridle and gently turned me round*	2	
27	1g	• When the tree comes down, John jumped out and was in a moment at my head. • When Black Beauty won't go over the bridge, John gets out instead of whipping him. • John is gentle when he handles Black Beauty – gently turned me round.	2	Award only **one** mark for *behind the table.*
28	1e	Answers that suggest: • Black Beauty and the men would have fallen into the river and probably been hurt.	1	Award marks for specific details of story and characters.

Horses

29	1b	eyes	1	
30	1a	Acceptable points for explosion: sudden burst, outburst, noisy movement Acceptable points for power: strength, energy, activity	2	Award **one** mark for an interpretation of explosion OR power. Award **two** marks for responses that interpret both explosion AND power.
31	1a	• *Gigantically gentle with children* • *feel friendly to the touch* • *take sugar quietly*	1	Award **one** mark for any two details from the list.
32	1b	a Any two from: • *the rain fall mistily* • *the clouds move* • *the distance escaping from them* b Any two from: • *up hills* • *across fields*	1	
33	1a	hard / dangerous	1	
34	1d	Answers that suggest the horses are not free to roam. They see the distant scene but are not free to go there.	2	
35	1c	Answers that suggest: • patient: *Horses stand still on the skyline / Waiting for something to happen* • joyous / full of life: *Horses gallop sometimes…* • friendly: *Gigantically gentle with children…*	2	Award **one** mark for two moods. Award **two** marks for three.
		TOTAL	**50**	

Paper 2

The Rise of the Maya

Qu	Domain	Answers	Mark	Comment
1	1a	control	1	
2	1b	*The search for better farmland…*	1	
3	1b	Any two of: maize / beans / chilli peppers / chocolate	1	
4	1a	*enriched*	1	
5	1d	Answers that suggest the fields were only fertile for a few years then more area of jungle had to be cleared.	1	
6	1b	cacao tree.	1	
7	1d	The Olmec built large towns. [F] The Olmec died out because of food shortages. [O] The Olmec died out because of warfare. [O] The Olmec influenced the Maya. [F]	1	
8	1b	800BCE moved to lowlands 100BCE lived in large cities 3000BCE first settlements 300BCE built first temples and pyramids	1	

9	1c	Any three from: • 300BCE- built first temples and pyramids • statue of Mayan Maize god • 100BCE – built giant temples • *The structures of Mayan cities were closely linked to … religion.* • *Ceremonial buildings were adorned with figures from Mayan religion, such as a giant bird god.*	3	Award **one** mark for each piece of evidence cited.
10	1b	The Maya were farmers. [T] The Maya were the first civilization in Central America. [F] The Maya always lived in simple villages. [F] The Maya built pyramids to represent the mountains. [T]	1	
11	1b	Any two of: • well-developed writing system • calendar • achievements in art • achievements in science	2	
12	1b	radiocarbon dating	1	
13	1d	*fierce rivals*	1	
14	1g	General interpretation = the period in their history when they were at the peak of their wealth and success	2	
15	1d	Answers that suggest the clues are: • battles between cities • cities just a few miles apart • success depended on military strength	3	Award **one** mark for answers that only give 'fighting' as the clue. Award **two** marks for 'fighting' and 'distance' of enemy. Award **three** marks for fighting / distance and military strength.

Fearless Bushmen

16	1b	• themselves • giraffe • wildebeest	2	Award **one** mark for one / two examples. Award **two** marks for all three examples.
17	1b	a *food* b *sport*	2	
18	1a	*Being true to their word*	1	
19	1a	words they live their life by	1	
20	1d	• they don't hunt for sport • they don't kill if an animal invades their village i.e. the mamba has as much right to be there as they have so they don't attack and kill it, they just move on.	2	
21	1d	• three generations live together • younger generations feed older generations • younger generations hunt for / gather food	3	Award **one** mark for one reason. Award **two** marks for two reasons. Award **three** marks for all three reasons.
22	1a	Acceptable points for fearless: • brave / courageous Acceptable points for peaceful: • not warlike / not looking for a fight	2	Award **one** mark for an interpretation of fearless OR peaceful. Award **two** marks for responses that interpret both fearless AND peaceful.
23	1c	admires and respects them	1	

The Lost: The Dark Ground

24	1a	violent	1	
25	1d	to get dry	1	
26	1a	*massive*	1	
27	1b	*yelled as loudly as he could*	1	
28	1d	Answers that suggest: • He was very shocked and scared to realize that he was on his own and could easily die – he couldn't think about anything else while he was *taking it in.*	2	Award **one** mark for an answer that simply states he is scared. Award **two** marks for a fuller explanation.
29	1b	Any three of: • food • clothes • shelter • warmth • water • a way to keep safe	2	Award **one** mark for two examples. Award **two** marks for three examples.
30	1g	Answers that suggest Robert was feeling like he could think properly for the first time since the crash, because *he had slept and eaten.*	2	Award **one** mark for answers that state Robert was able to think. Award **two** marks for the reasons why.
31	1a	tough	1	
32	1b	The sound he made was quickly absorbed by the forest and turned to silence.	1	
33	1c	Robert had been in a train. [F] He had been travelling with his mum and dad. [T] He could see the wrecked fuselage. [F] He could hear voices in the distance. [F]	1	
34	1e	Answers that suggest EITHER: No because he has made as much noise as he could and didn't get any answers / very unlikely to survive a plane crash. OR: Yes because if he has survived, other passengers from the plane might have been able to as well.	2	Award **two** marks for a full answer supporting either point of view.
		TOTAL	**50**	

Paper 3

The Stray's Tail

Qu	Domain	Answers	Mark	Comment
1	1b	a a branch b shade c possible enemies d a cat e yellow	1	
2	1d	Any two of: • [sun] *glaring down* • [sun] *parch the last drop of moisture from the leaves* • *slight shade* • *air felt like a newly opened oven*	2	
3	1a	covered in patches	1	

4	1d	1 *people who did not seem to like lizards* 2 *people who liked lizards and who fed them*	2	
5	1d	Answers that use the evidence that Leli was *relieved* it was the ground lizard rather than *some other creature that might mistake him for food.*	1	
6	1a	dismissed	1	
7	1c	Lizards eat flies. [T] Lizards eat cats. [F] Lizards cannot climb walls. [F] Lizards don't build houses. [T]	1	
8	1a	Answers that suggest: a *do some activity that will use up energy and make you feel hungry* b *was looking at with something in mind / wanted and planned to do something* c *gave in to what he wanted to do / had to do it*	3	
9	1a	*He felt frightened.*	1	
10	1d	The sun was very hot, and showed no signs of stopping.	2	Award **one** mark for very hot. Award two marks for hot and not stopping.
11	1b	nervous / scared	1	
12	1d	Answers that suggest he was so scared he couldn't move for minutes.	1	
13	1h	Answers that suggest the following change: • before: seems nervous but determined. He becomes even more frightened and determined when he sees the cat. • on the window sill: almost beginning to have doubts about what he has done. He sees *the dry grass and the bushes he called home* and *he almost wished he was there right now, safe among his own kind.* But then becomes curious / excited / brave again.	2	
14	1c	Leli was on a branch. He was looking at the house. At midday the next day, Leli went towards the house. He heard a scurrying noise. He saw a ground lizard. He stopped by the bottom of the wall. He saw a skinny ginger cat. He began to climb. The cat stretched its paw to get him. Leli froze from fear. He got to the window sill.	1	
15	1e	Individual answers supported by evidence e.g. Leli encountered 'people' (evidence: the older lizards told him about meeting people in the house).	2	Award **one** mark for a reasonable suggestion as to what happened next. Award **two** marks if the suggestion is supported by evidence.

Snake

16	1b	The grass moves as the snake moves through it.	1	
17	1g	*twists / leaps / slithers*	3	
18	1a	smooth and beautiful	1	
19	1d	Answers that suggest: • he is tall • it is the snake that is describing the poet so he seems huge.	2	Award **one** mark for answers that state the poet is tall. Award **two** marks for answers that take the viewpoint into consideration.

20	1d	the snake's skin	1	
21	1a	passing on information	1	
22	1c	Answers that suggest we normally think of people being afraid of snakes. The poem turns this idea on its head and suggests that the snake is frightened of the man.	2	

The World of Reptiles

23	1b	1 *cold blooded* 2 *scales* 3 *lay eggs*	3	
24	1b	a don't have eyelids b don't sweat c detach their tails	1	
25	1a	very angry	1	
26	1c	• black mamba 4.5m • green anaconda 8.8m • green iguana 2m • Komodo dragon 3m • smallest lizard species 2cms • crocodile 4.6m • alligator 3.46m	2	Award **one** mark for five correct answers. Award **two** marks for all correct answers.
27	1b	southern and eastern Africa	1	
28	1a	slow	1	
29	1b	1 *seek prey* 2 *avoid predators*	2	
30	1d	*favouring swamps, marshes and slow-moving streams*	1	Award **no** marks unless all examples of water habitat are mentioned.
31	1b	a V shaped head C b found only in USA and China A c more aggressive C d 3.46m long A e freshwater A	2	Award **one** mark for three correct answers. Award **two** marks for all correct answers.
32	1a	Acceptable points for large: big / huge Acceptable points for docile: gentle / non-aggressive	2	Award **one** mark for an interpretation of large OR docile. Award **two** marks for responses that interpret both large AND docile.
33	1b	1 poison 2 squeezing	1 1	
34	1d	Either of the following: • *A typical Komodo dragon can eat 80% of its own body weight in one meal!* • *It lives on almost everything – deer, water buffalo and even humans*!	1	
35	1d	Answers that suggest a reptile has scales made of keratin, and humans have nails and hair made of keratin.	1	
		TOTAL	**53**	